Lecture Notes in Computer Science   7130

Commenced Publication in 1973
Founding and Former Series Editors:
Gerhard Goos, Juris Hartmanis, and Jan van Leeuwen

T0175341

Javier Lopez   Roberto Setola
Stephen D. Wolthusen (Eds.)

Critical Infrastructure Protection

Information Infrastructure Models,
Analysis, and Defense

 Springer

Volume Editors

Javier Lopez
University of Malaga
Computer Science Department
29071 Malaga, Spain
E-mail: jlm@lcc.uma.es

Roberto Setola
University CAMPUS Bio- Medico di Roma
Complex Systems and Security Lab
Via Alavro del Portillo, 21
00128 Roma, Italy
E-mail: r.setola@unicampus.it

Stephen D. Wolthusen
University of London
Information Security Group
Department of Mathematics
Egham, Surrey TW20 0EX, UK
and
Gjøvik University College
Norwegian Information Security Laboratory
Faculty of Computer Science
2802 Gjøvik, Norway
E-mail: stephen.wolthusen@rhul.ac.uk

ISSN 0302-9743   e-ISSN 1611-3349
ISBN 978-3-642-28919-4   ISBN 978-3-642-28920-0 (eBook)
DOI 10.1007/978-3-642-28920-0
Springer Heidelberg Dordrecht London New York

Library of Congress Control Number: 2012933456
CR Subject Classification (1998): D.4.6, K.6.5, E.3, C.2, H.4, H.3, I.6, J.1

LNCS Sublibrary: SL 4 – Security and Cryptology

Typesetting: Camera-ready by author, data conversion by Scientific Publishing Services, Chennai, India

Printed on acid-free paper

Springer is part of Springer Science+Business Media (www.springer.com)

Preface

Information and communication technology (ICT) systems form an integral part of critical infrastructure globally, whether in their own right or as a supporting or controlling mechanism for other sectors. Although there are large bodies of work on the safety and reliability of the underlying systems and components and on many security aspects affecting the critical infrastructure's ICT elements, there are a significant number of issues that are unique and both deserve and demand to be considered in their own right.

Although not the main focus of the present volume, it begins with an understanding of the effects and impacts of failures in the critical infrastructure including any cascading effects that may also occur in different locations or at later points in time, but also must take into account the conflict between more conventional security considerations and the often overriding imperative to ensure availability that imply a much greater reliance on a system's resilience to failure and compromise than is typically given consideration, e.g., in the development of cryptographic security mechanisms.

Moreover, the properties of critical information infrastructures make it inevitable that the inter-relationships with the physical infrastructure be considered, which can arise in many different forms from the need to satisfy hard real-time constraints to having to understand the way that a physical system state influences ICT components and vice versa.

Beyond such largely academic and technical considerations, however, the field also has a necessarily strong link to economic and policy considerations, which directly and indirectly influence any approach to the safety, security, and resilience of the critical (information) infrastructure. Recent developments have shown the need to regularly assess the validity of many explicit and tacit assumptions, including whether attacks on critical infrastructure by non-state (e.g., terrorist) or state actors ("cyber warfare") represent a genuine threat.

The present volume cannot begin to cover all of these issues in a satisfactory manner. However, in combining elementary concepts and models with policy-related issues and placing an emphasis on the timely area of control systems, the book aims to highlight some of the key issues facing the research community. The sector studies included provide further insights into selected issues encountered both in infrastructure sectors that have been studied extensively such as the electric grid, but also ones that have not seen similar attention despite their obvious significance, namely, the financial services sector, but also the oil and gas elements of the energy and the transportation sector with their reliance on ICT systems to ensure levels of efficiency and safety that would otherwise not be possible to achieve.

We hope that this book can serve as a timely introduction to the state of the art in critical infrastructure protection, particularly for the information infrastructure, and as such may aid both researchers to gain an overview of a field that is still largely dominated by conference publications and a disparate body of literature, but also lecturers wishing to prepare postgraduate-level courses in this rapidly moving and multifaceted field.

October 2011

Javier Lopez
Roberto Setola
Stephen D. Wolthusen

List of Contributors

Andreas Aas
Norwegian University of Science and Technology, Norway
E-mail: aasand@jbv.no

Cristina Alcaraz
Computer Science Department, University of Malaga, Spain
E-mail: alcaraz@lcc.uma.es

Ettore Bompard
Department of Electrical Engineering, Politecnico di Torino, Italy
E-mail: ettore.bompard@polito.it

Fernando Carvajal
INDRA, Spain
E-mail: jfcarvajal@indra.es

Paolo Cuccia
Department of Dispatching and Grid Operation, Terna S.p.A, Italy
E-mail: paolo.cuccia@terna.it

Jordi Cucurull
Department of Computer and Information Science,
Linköping University, Sweden
E-mail: g-jorcu@ida.liu.se

Myriam Dunn Cavelty
Center for Security Studies, ETH Zurich, Switzerland
E-mail: dunn@sipo.gess.ethz.ch

Gerardo Fernandez
Computer Science Department, University of Malaga, Spain
E-mail: gerardo@lcc.uma.es

Igor Nai Fovino
Institute for the Protection and Security of the Citizen, Joint Research Center,
European Commission
E-mail: igor.nai@jrc.ec.europa.eu

Andrea Glorioso
European Commission DG Information Society and Media, Unit A3 - Internet,
Network and Information Security
E-mail: Andrea.Glorioso@ec.europa.eu

Daniel Germanus
Computer Science Department, Technische Universität Darmstadt, Germany
E-mail: germanus@cs.tu-darmstadt.de

Rajni Goel
Department of Information Systems and Decision Sciences,
Howard University, USA
E-mail: rgoel@howard.edu

Stuart Goldman
USA
E-mail: familygoldman@gmail.com

Bernhard Hämmerli
Department of Computer Science, Norwegian Information Security Laboratory,
Gjøvik University Collage, Norway
E-mail: bmhaemmerli@acris.ch; E-mail: Bernhard.Hammerli@hig.no

Mark Hartong
Federal Railroad Administration, U.S. Department of Transportation, USA
E-mail: mark.hartong@dot.gov

Stig O. Johnsen
Norwegian University of Science and Technology, Norway
E-mail: Stig.O.Johnsen@gmail.com

Abdelmajid Khelil
Computer Science Department, Technische Universität Darmstadt, Germany
E-mail: khelil@cs.tu-darmstadt.de

Javier Lopez
Computer Science Department, University of Malaga, Spain
E-mail: jlm@lcc.uma.es

Eric Luiijf
Netherlands Organisation for Applied Scientific Research - TNO,
The Netherlands
E-mail: eric.luiijf@tno.nl

Marcelo Masera
Institute for Energy, Joint Research Center, European Commission
E-mail: marcelo.masera@jrc.it

Simin Nadjm-Tehrani
Department of Computer and Information Science, Linköping University,
Sweden
E-mail: simin@ida.liu.se

Ying Qian
Shanghai University, Shanghai
E-mail: iris_qian@hotmail.com

Massimiliano Raciti
Department of Computer and Information Science,
Linköping University, Sweden
E-mail: masra@ida.liu.se

Julian L. Rrushi
Faculty of Computer Science, University of New Brunswick, Canada
E-mail: jrrushi@unb.ca

Andrea Servida
European Commission DG Information Society and Media, Unit A3 - Internet,
Network and Information Security
E-mail: Andrea.Servida@ec.europa.eu

Roberto Setola
Faculty of Engineering, Universitá Campus Bio-Medico di Roma, Italy
E-mail: r.setola@unicampus.it

Neeraj Suri
Computer Science Department, Technische Universität Darmstadt, Germany
E-mail: suri@cs.tu-darmstadt.de

Manuel Suter
Center for Security Studies, ETH Zurich, Switzerland
E-mail: suter@sipo.gess.ethz.ch

Nils Kalstad Svendsen
Norwegian Information Security Laboratory, Faculty of Computer Science,
Gjøvik University College, Norway
E-mail: nils.svendsen@hig.no

Huseyin Uzunalioglu
Alcatel-Lucent, USA
E-mail: huseyin.uzunalioglu@alcatel-lucent.com

Dumida Wijesekra
Department of Computer Science, George Mason University, USA
E-mail: dwijesek@gmu.edu

Stephen D. Wolthusen
Norwegian Information Security Laboratory, Faculty of Computer Science,
Gjøvik University College, Norway
E-mail: stephen.wolthusen@hig.no and
Information Security Group, Department of Mathematics, Royal Holloway,
University of London, UK
E-mail: stephen.wolthusen@hig.no

Part I
Introduction to Critical Information Infrastructure Protection

The chapters in this part provide an overview of the concepts and terminology used throughout this volume and also serve as a high-level outlook on current developments in critical information infrastructure research. As these are inevitably interlinked, the following chapters also provide a perspectives on the larger critical infrastructure area, its interactions with the policy domain, and the risks and vulnerabilities that the critical information infrastructure is exposed to.

Part II
Models and Defensive Mechanisms

In this part, the current state of research on modeling critical infrastructures is elaborated with an emphasis on information infrastructures and the associated problems of early warning and attack detection mechanisms; the latter are critical as the critical information infrastructure is typically required to operate continuously and may not easily be shut down or degraded for defensive or recovery purposes. An example of the type of models involving physical as well as ICT elements is provided in the second chapter of this part, while further aspects of this problem area will be discussed in the following Parts III and IV as well.

Part III
Control Systems and Protocols

A key part of the critical information infrastructure is in fact not immediately visible as it is embedded in automation and control systems, which are the focus of Part III. Following an introduction to the problems of supervisory control and data acquisition (SCADA) and distributed control (DCS) systems, research on vulnerability of control systems with particular emphasis on areas where differences to standard network and information systems arise is discussed followed by a review of the security threats and possible countermeasures resulting from ongoing developments away from proprietary protocols and towards open standards, along with the increased risks of inadvertent and inadvisable interconnections.

Part IV
Infrastructure Sector Studies

The final part of this volume is devoted to a selection of sector studies. These deal with two sub-sectors of the energy sector, namely the electric grid with an emphasis on the conventional, large-scale grid and its robust operation, and also the oil, gas, and petrochemical industries. In addition, a chapter on telecommunications highlights some of the concerns raised by convergent next-generation telecommunications infrastructures that have been or are being deployed by many advanced telecommunications carriers. The chapter on the financial services industry focuses largely on the back-end infrastructure of banks and institutions in the sector, but also highlights some of the problems facing the sector from new technology being deployed before a review of the transportation sector with an emphasis on a case study for the rail transportation sector.

Table of Contents

Overview of Critical Information Infrastructure Protection

Javier Lopez[1], Roberto Setola[2], and Stephen D. Wolthusen[3]

[1] Computer Science Department, E.T.S. Ingenieria Informatica, Campus de Teatinos,
University of Malaga, Malaga, Spain
jlm@lcc.uma.es
[2] Faculty of Engineering, Universitá Campus Bio-Medico di Roma, Rome, Italy
r.setola@unicampus.it
[3] Department of Mathematics, Royal Holloway, University of London, Egham,
United Kingdom and Norwegian Information Security Laboratory,
Gjøvik University College, Gjøvik, Norway
stephen.wolthusen@rhul.ac.uk

Abstract. The present volume aims to provide an overview of the current understanding of the so-called *Critical Infrastructure* (CI), and particularly the *Critical
Information Infrastructure* (CII), which not only forms one of the constituent
sectors of the overall CI, but also is unique in providing an element of interconnection between sectors as well as often also intra-sectoral control mechanisms.

One problem faced by research on C(I)I is the extreme range of scales at which
security problems may arise. This is true for the time dimension where policy-
level decisions such as the deployment of physical infrastructure like roads and
high-tension transmission lines have impacts measured in decades whilst industrial control systems must provide guaranteed and secure real-time responses in
the millisecond range. It is, moreover, also the case for the physical extent of infrastructures where single physical facilities such as vaccine plants may be a vital
element of national or supra-national infrastructures, but where the trans-national
electrical power or natural gas transmission networks span entire continents.

The book hence surveys not only key high-level concepts and selected technical research areas with an emphasis on control systems as a highly active research
area, but also seeks to include policy aspects as well as a discussion on models
for validation and verification. This is rounded off by several studies of specific
issues and challenges faced by individual CI sectors including the telecommunications, electricity, transportation, and financial services sectors.

1 Introduction

Modern societies depend on the continuous and reliable availability of a number of
services and are at risk of severe economic impacts or loss of life and limb if such
products and services are disrupted or unavailable in a larger region for a significant
length of time. These services are those provided by the so called *critical infrastructures*
(CI). These infrastructures are not merely crucial in their own right but also exhibit
interdependencies which in some cases result in tight coupling between components.

J. Lopez et al. (Eds.): Critical Information Infrastructure Protection, LNCS 7130, pp. 1–14, 2012.

Risks related to critical infrastructures arise from a number of quarters, beginning with simple wear and tear of individual components leading to failures, natural disasters, but also including sabotage and acts of terrorism or war. In many cases individual incidents are "normal" and expected and can be dealt with accordingly in the course of regular operations for many such critical infrastructures. As an example, part of any electric power grid will, regardless of whether referring to the transmission or generation side, be inoperational for maintenance or because of malfunctions and other unforeseen events at any given point in time. In such cases long-standing experience as well as sector-specific practices and regulatory oversight ensure that sufficient redundancy exists to meet the service quality and reliability requirements unless exceptional circumstances arise. This limitation arises simply from the fact that any safety margin will, by necessity, be finite and one cannot anticipate any and all contingencies that may either be wholly unanticipated or have a very low probability of occurrence. As is discussed throughout thus book, however, research on the protection of critical infrastructures is not concerned primarily with such well-understood approaches to reliability theory and fault tolerance but rather with areas that are less well understood by these communities.

One such area is the need to consider cases in which faults and malfunctions are induced deliberately and hence cannot be described as easily by statistical means and ultimately as probability density functions. For such deliberate attacks and sabotage, it is therefore necessary to study different mechanisms for the design and analysis of infrastructure components which allow the efficient enhancement of their robustness and, moreover, the early detection and mitigation of such actions. The second area of research that is underpinning much of the work also documented in the present book is a need to understand interconnections between elements of the critical infrastructure that can lead to larger-scale and often unanticipated failures, particularly where interdependencies mean that infrastructures are mutually dependent on each other and can hence both propagate failures from one sector to another but also make recovery from such events difficult as assumptions on the availability of other sectors' services may not be valid.

The critical infrastructure is commonly considered to be divided into sectors, and while the precise composition varies in granularity and scope between analyses [6,3,8], the energy and particularly the information and communication (ICT) sector are typically singled out owing to their immediate impact on other infrastructure elements. This is particularly the case for the ICT sector which had to be considered in the same time a critical infrastructure by itself, but also an increasingly fundamental component to the operation of any other critical infrastructure for almost all other sectors from financial services to transportation. To stress the peculiar nature of ICT, it was coined the term *Critical Information Infrastructure* (CII), that has been identified as an area of particular concern.

Following pioneering efforts of the PCCCI in the U.S., considerable attention has been devoted to enhancing the robustness of the ICT infrastructures. This was driven in part by a recognition that this area has the potential to be the focus of an attack by asymmetrical adversaries without a need for geographical proximity, but also because it is still not well-understood where the limitations of attacks on the ICT infrastructures are relative to other threats. Moreover, unlike for attacks on physical entities, it is not necessarily possible to determine the origin of an attack reliably, making attribution one of the most difficult problems with any such attacks. As a result, however, the well-understood mechanisms and theories underlying reactions to and deterrence of malicious activity are not immediately applicable. This has led to ongoing efforts worldwide to increase protective measures, generally referred to as Critical Information Infrastructure Protection (CIIP). Howver, despite the identification of the need to have CII protection strategies, no clear consensus has emerged yet as to its exact scope and distinction from general computer, network, and information security and research in these fields on one hand and policy-related activities on the other. At the same time it is also increasingly clear from a number of incidents that targeted attacks on critical infrastructure have moved from the subject of largely academic inquiry [2,4,1] to a focal area of defence and intelligence establishments worldwide [5,7]. Moreover, although deliberate, coordinated attacks clearly are the more challenging problem, even relatively simple faults and human error must be better understood as unlike for physical events, there exists very little historical data or constraints imposed by underlying physical properties for the ICT sector that are relevant in other domains in constructing risk and vulnerability assessments.

This book hence aims to address this issue by providing a faceted view of core results and ongoing research in the area centered around the ICT domain, but also touching upon other sectors that are affected by the specific issues surrounding the ICT sector. The focus of the book will therefore be on aspects unique to critical information infrastructures and infrastructure sectors immediately affected by CII. Moreover, it will also emphasise issues arising from different aspects of interconnection specific to the critical information infrastructure and cover not just the immediate operational concerns but also the prevention, detection, and mitigation of threats and attacks through a number of approaches ranging from policies and procedures to early warning and detection mechanisms.

Given this remit, the contributions to this book cover not only the scientific and technical aspects of CII protection and security; instead, they are deliberately structured in such a way as to commence with a review of the policy level and the understanding of individual sectors and their interconnections as well as current understanding on existing and evolving threats and vulnerabilities. Given the ubiquitous nature of ICT systems, a comprehensive review of the impact on CII would require a much more extensive format. By focusing on an area which is both the subject of intensive scrutiny by the CII research community and with the potential for a disproportionate impact owing to the direct coupling between information and physical systems in the form of selected aspects of control systems security, the book seeks to highlight key problems that are not wholly addressed by general information security research.

1.1   Active Research Areas

Although research on critical infrastructures and particularly critical information infrastructures as identified in this book have been the subject of investigation for well over a decade at the time of writing, it is nevertheless still defining its precise boundaries. This is in part owing to developments in the infrastructure itself, often involving novel and unanticipated use of information and communication technology, but also to the identification of novel or re-assessment of existing hazards and threats. A further characteristic of C(I)IP research is that it is drawing on a number of disciplines to aid in understanding and enhancing the robustness, resilience, and security of critical infrastructure components and particularly interconnected components. Whilst this research is typically not inter-disciplinary in nature, it has been the case that similar questions particularly in the modelling and simulation domain have been approached by using significantly different techniques ranging from employing graph theory to autonomous agents approches and statistical physics. This creates difficulties not only in assessing work based on differing sets of assumptions, but also because of the very different methods used in such investigations, and consequently the difficultis to identify the "C(I)IP community" and the relevant sources of information.

Any collection must cope with such a multiplicity of perspectives, although in this case it is clearly inevitable that the range is necessarily broader than would be the case otherwise.

Except for cases where both data and results are qualitative in nature and hence unlikely to allow the derivation of actionable conclusions, most research in the C(I)IP domain is faced with the problem that its results can be either misused if obtained by unauthorised entities or that the very data on which it may be based is also sensitive in its own right as it may identify vulnerabilities or ways in which threats can be realised.

This problem also arises in case of other research, particularly in the information security domain where a vulnerability may be widespread and difficult to mitigate. Here, systematic vulnerabilities such as protocol weaknesses may require extended time periods for changes to affected systems or mitigation efforts during which the release of information on the vulnerability can still cause widespread damage.

For critical infrastructures, particularly where physical and cyber systems are interconnected, the potential for adverse effects may be substantially larger and involve larger-scale economic disruptions or loss of life and limb. This often imposes also an ethical onus on researchers in addition to legal requirements, and it is imperative that any such work is undertaken in full awareness of its potential ramifications.

2 Overview

The following section provides a brief overview of the structure and contents of the book. As the volume is intended to serve the dual purpose of a collection of active research whilst being suitable for use as a graduate-level text, it has been divided into four parts:

2.1 Part I: Introduction

The first part of the book consists of three chapters in addition to the present one and is intended primarily to set the scene and contextualise the problems and research discussed in the remaining three parts. This is necessary in no small part owing to the cross-connections between the technical and policy domains, but — as is made evident throughout the book — also illustrates that even within these two large domains, significant differences exist in terminology and usage, resulting in inevitable mis-communication at the necessary points of interaction. Such interaction is of course inevitable given the interconnections and interdependencies found throughout the critical information infrastructure and the further elements of the critical infrastructure that is coming to rely on the CII.

The chapter by Dunn Cavelty and Suter therefore begins by providing a policy-oriented delineation of the CIIP area. This not only requires the identification of what constitutes the immediate as well as indirect critical aspects forming both the CII and supporting roles as outlined above, but is also becoming increasingly connected to the area of cyber security and defence — itself a term that is very much evolving — as concepts and demonstrated activities from the realm of information warfare are becoming realised and also have an immediate impact on civilian infrastructure, forcing a re-assessment of risk and security assessments at the policy level that was not considered necessary whilst these threats were merely hypothetical in nature. These authors hence provide a systematic overview of protection goals that reach from the strategic level at the national and in some cases supra-national levels to general CII and ultimately also sector-specific goals and requirements, although particularly in the CII the relevant sectors are frequently not easily bounded by geographical or political entities. These different levels are illustrated with relevant national strategies and also reflect external constraints such as the association of CI and CII with different governmental departments since such organisational aspects can lead to significant differences in approaches even where all other aspects of the problem space are largely comparable. However, as noted by the authors, the development of relevant strategies is still very much an on-going activity and has not seen the level of co-ordination and reconciliation that would be considered desirable. A significant contribution of the chapter is therefore a review of the strategy development process itself and the different approaches chosen by countries that have already undertaken such development processes along with a discussion of insights gained from nations where such strategies have not only been discussed but also where at least some insight has been gained from their operationalisation. One such implementation aspect highlighted by Dunn Cavelty and Suter is the use of Public-Private information sharing arrangements; such co-ordination efforts are in place in several countries as the CII is typically held privately, necessitating means for translating and communicating protection strategies from the policy to the — private — operational level.

Following this tour d'horizon of the policy landscape driven mainly by national strategies, the chapter by Glorioso and Servida offers a more focused European perspective. As highlighted above, there is a strong influence on how an approach is framed based on the remit and constraints posed by the policy level, and this is clearly also the case for a European Union perspective that does not have the national security aspect within its mandate. The authors nevertheless highlight the European role in this domain beginning with recent efforts at co-ordinating prevention and preparedness measures for attacks on the CI, which is closely aligned to this boundary. Highlighting the various interlocking bodies and instruments that are not limited to the European Commission, this provides the background for the further study of the ICT sector and particularly the Communication on Critical Information Infrastructure Protection of 2009 that has come into force as an instrument in addition to the more conventional regulatory powers that the Commission has been able to exert directly or indirectly in the sectors related to the CII. This is traced along the lines of the five-pillar strategy of the European Commission in the remainder of the chapter. As in the preceding contribution by Dunn Cavelty and Suter, the lack of alignment between infrastructure ownership and the entities potentially suffering from their becoming unavailable is discussed, but with an emphasis on governance and monitoring structures. Such structures can, where more technical capabilities are affected, be co-ordinated provided that a common baseline and information exchange mechanisms are achieved. However, as Glorioso and Servida point out, there exist genuine differences in policy priorities that render higher levels of co-ordination problematic.

The final chapter in the introductory part of the book by Luiijf takes a more systematic approach to the threats and risks that the preceding chapters employed in a more intuitive manner. Although it is inevitable that the precise semantics of some of the terms and concepts required in the CI(I) domain are the subject of ongoing discussions that can even be influenced by the context in which terms are used, the taxonomy provided by Luiijf represents an useful point of departure. The main focus of the chapter is on providing a review of the threats considered relevant to the CII environment under an all-hazards perspective. This approach also considers threats to the CII environment rather than merely the CII itself, and so must take natural events ranging from phaenomena such as solar flares to even insects causing damage to physical equipment into account as well as externalities that involve human actions. The latter, however, need not even be deliberate and can be the result of accidents or actions that have indirect, unforeseen effects, which makes such threats very difficult to bound properly. In outlining a selection of threats specific to the ICT domain, the chapter also highlights a similar problem for identifying bounds; as is demonstrated for the case of control systems in Part III, this area also encompasses ICT systems that combine intricate functional requirements with what so far must be considered only limited resilience to deliberate threats. Characterising the threat actors is a further major contribution of the chapter by Luiijf, which also seeks to characterise the different unique roles that the CII has as not only the immediate target of attacks, but also indirect effects when the CII is used either as the means to achieve a threat agent's objective or even as a weapon in its own right. As Luiijf points out, however, many threats emerging in novel application areas of ICT such as electric mobility and the ICT systems embedded in Smart Grid environments will likely only be identified as having been encountered before in similar form after the fact; at the same time, however, the very flexibility and ability to create novel applications by combining ICT components in unforeseen ways make a comprehensive assessment of risks an extremely challenging task.

2.2   Part II: Models and Defensive Mechanisms

As with any other element of the Critical Infrastructures, protecting the Critical Information Infrastructure particularly against deliberate attacks cannot rely on reactive defence mechanisms and be limited in the ability to extrapolate current and future threats from historical data even for accidents and natural disasters since the information infrastructure's rate of change is likely to invalidate such conclusions rapidly. A major element of research on critical infrastructures and also the CII has therefore focused on model-building and, to a lesser extent, their validation. Such models are crucial in identifying not only in high-level interactions that are not obvious in their strength or potentially even existence, but can also be employed in exploratory settings. This can occur either systematically, exploring parts of the parameter space, or in the form of targeted exercises and scenarios that allow a more fine-grained investigation not only of the behaviour of the Critical Information Infrastructure, but also the entities interacting with it.

The chapter by Svendsen and Wolthusen provides a high-level survey of some of the most significant and influential strands of research on modelling and simulation of critical infrastructures. Such models typically include or are focused on the CII, but may also extend further and incorporate other sectors that have an impact on the CII. Moreover, similar to the hierarchy of strategic considerations found by Dunn Cavelty and Suter, modelling techniques span a very broad range of abstraction levels ranging from qualitative models describing national or even supranational entities on a sector-by-sector basis for the purpose of qualitative analyses of resilience or macro-economic effects to highly quantitative models of smaller-scale effects. The chapter therefore seeks to provide at least reference models sampled from this broad spectrum. These include, at the qualitative level, economic models such as Input-Output models but also models of interacting entities such as those based on System Dynamics. Although limited in their predictive ability, such models are valuable as aids to understanding dependencies and interactions, particularly for more complex models that cannot be understood easily without the support of simulation environments. Characterising or even predicting the behaviour of threat agents as well as neutral or friendly entities interacting in the CI(I) domain is, however, a highly desirable objective that has recently gained attention and is modelled using game-theoretical and related behavioural techniques in ongoing research that can aid in areas such as defensive resource allocation. A major part of the chapter is, however, devoted to the large body of research on graph-based models of critical infrastructures at different levels, which in turn can range from techniques found in statistical physics to highly accurate domain-specific models. The graph or other combinatorial representation, however, is often crucial in such models to gain an understanding of relations and structural properties that go significantly beyond artifacts and phaenomena arising from particular parameter choices.

The following chapter of this part, by Raciti, Cucurull and Nadjm-Tehrani, focus its attention on Water Management Systems as water quality has recently received considerable attention from the security research community. Authors argue that real-time monitoring of water quality requires analysis of sensor data gathered at distributed locations, as well as subsequent generation of alarms when quality indicators indicate anomalies. In these infrastructures, event detection systems should produce accurate alarms, with low latency and few false positives. In this sense, this chapter shows how an existing learning based anomaly detection technique is applied to the detection of contamination events in water distribution systems. The initial hypothesis of authors is that the clustering algorithm ADWICE that has earlier been successfully applied to n-dimensional data spaces in IP networks, can also be deployed for real-time anomaly detection in water management systems. The chapter describes the evaluation of the anomaly detection software when integrated in a SCADA system that manages water sensors and provides data for analysis within the Water Security initiative of the U.S. Environmental Protection Agency (EPA). Also, this chapter elaborates on the analysis of the performance of the approach for two stations using performance metrics such as detection rate, false positives, detection latency, and sensitivity to the contamination level of the attacks. The first results, in terms of detection rate and false positive rate, have shown some contaminants are easier to detected than others. Additionally, authors discuss on the reliability of the analysis when data sets are not perfect, that is, where data values may be missing or less accurate as indicated by sensor alerts.

2.3   Part III: Control Systems and Protocols

The necessity of considering the security and robustness of control systems was well-recognised by researchers at the time the present volume was conceived; it has since regrettably become a far more public concern that is unlikely to fade from sight. In part this is attributable to the prevalence of legacy systems dating back to insulated environments with limited capabilities, which is likely to become less of a concern over time as facilities are modernised or retired altogether. However, several other concerns such as the need to operate under hard real-time constraints or the overriding importance often placed on availability and reliability over security are likely to pose challenges for enhancing the robustness of control systems to different types of disruptions, which do also include deliberate attacks. Moreover, some concerns are less likely to arise in information systems otherwise, namely the need to trade off security and the confidence of having adequate controllability over a facility and its products against the risk of loss of function such as production outputs or even damage to equipment and endangering the environment or placing lives at risk. In such cases decisions must be made rapidly, often based on incomplete and unreliable information, which is unlikely to be possible in a fully automated manner. This aspect of protecting the critical information infrastructure hence inevitably also touches the boundaries of other areas including human-computer interaction and incident management rather than being able to restrict inquiries to the design of robust and secure systems since threats such as physical subversion, vulnerabilities, or malicious insider activities are likely to invalidate underlying assumptions.

The chapter by Alcaraz, Fernandez and Carvajal hence focuses on providing basic guidelines for a suitable secure management of current SCADA systems, which converge on the use and dependence on new ICT systems for automation and control from anywhere and anytime. These types of advances and the use of new technologies bring new security issues and a large number of potential risks due to threats, vulnerabilities and failures associated to them. As authors point out, it is necessary to take into account some security aspects that allow the system to protect itself against any possible anomalous event/situation. To this end, some aspects related to network architecture, interdependences and consequences are analysed in-depth throughout the chapter in order to identify problems and their security solutions. Most of these solutions are narrowly related to secure management by means of standards, security policies, official recommendations, best practices and technical specifications to ensure interoperability between SCADA components, systems and entities. Detection and prevention aspects, and incident response topics are also discussed, identifying tools, systems and methodologies to apply in these types of critical systems. Moreover, an adaptive alarm management system based on reputation is presented in order to show how a SCADA system could intelligently assign alarms to the best operators in the field, and thereby ensuring an efficiently speed up the response. Solutions and approaches are equally analysed for a Smart Grid context whose main control is located in a SCADA system.

Also in the scope of SCADA, a chapter on protocol vulnerabilities by Rrushi follows. As the author points out, most of network traffic in process control networks is generated by industrial communication protocols, what causes that a large number of attack techniques that apply to process control systems can be conducted over industrial communication protocols. The author provides with a technical discussion of possible vulnerabilities in industrial communication protocols, with specific reference to ModBus and the IEC 61850 protocols, considered as representatives of the protocols currently deployed in digitally controlled physical infrastructures such as power plants and electrical substations. In this sense, Modbus has been selected as representative of bit-oriented protocols in terms of design while IEC 61850 has been selected because it adopts the emerging paradigm of object-oriented process control communications. It is important to note that Rrushi elaborates on how the vulnerabilities are exploited. In detail, the chapter discusses vulnerabilities regarding weak or missing authentication and integrity checks of industrial protocol traffic along with some of the computer network attacks that exploit those vulnerabilities. Then, memory corruption vulnerabilities as applied to implementations of industrial communication protocols are also discussed. Besides, the chapter also includes a description of various techniques that leverage a computer network attack to cause physical damage via disruption of physical processes and equipment.

This part of the book finishes with a chapter authored by Khelil, Germanus and Suri that focuses on the protection of SCADA communication channels. Generally speaking, in this chapter the existing approaches for SCADA communication protection are comprehensively surveyed and categorized, and also upcoming research technologies on enhancing the protection of SCADA communication are presented. More precisely, the paper describes the communication assets of SCADA systems and their requirements on protection, and also outline the key threats, vulnerabilities and security weaknesses of SCADA systems that may present a danger for their proper operation. Then, existing techniques for the protection of SCADA communication channels are discussed. Interestingly, authors classify them into three main categories: techniques for resilience to network perturbations, cryptographic protection of SCADA communication, and trustworthy interconnection of SCADA systems. Further, authors focus on middleware techniques as they are have general applicability and also conform with the clear IP trend in SCADA components, and analyse two middleware add-on protection techniques, the INSPIRE P2P-based middleware and the GridStat middleware. As shown by authors, both techniques aim at augmenting the trustworthiness of deployed SCADA systems, primarily utilizing the approach of controllable data replication.

2.4 Part IV: Infrastructure Sector Studies

The book concludes with five sector studies, which aim to highlight the different but nevertheless crucial impact that the information systems aspect brings to securing the critical infrastructure. There is a notable imbalance in the availability of published information on different sectors, with the vast majority of material covering the telecommunications area and the interactions of this sector particularly with the energy sector, specifically the electricity sector. Other sectors may be equally dependent on information and communication systems, but this is far less visible. Confidentiality requirements are a major hindrance in any efforts seeking to ultimately publish outcomes, and in some areas even highlighting concerns appears to be problematic. In other environments, however, it is still necessary to exercise careful judgement in analysing security, reliability, and robustness characteristics of sectors and sector elements as some of the problems identified may well turn out to be difficult or time-consuming to rectify. This relative paucity of available information for some sectors is also problematic for the creation and ultimately also the verification and validation of models discussed in Part II, but is unlikely to be possible to rectify in the medium term.

The aforementioned electricity sub-sector of the energy domain is covered in the chapter by Bompard, Cuccia, Masera, and Nai Fovino, who provide a high-level survey of modern power systems with an emphasis on parts of the electric grid that are normally considered constituent elements of the critical infrastructure. These include the national and supra-national elements drawing on the European case as an example and range to the distribution grid, which only in rare instances would be concerned with the impact of end users. The chapter focuses on the current grid architecture concentrated around a relatively limited number of large-scale generation sites and similarly limited transmission capabilities. This necessitates the continuous monitoring of the grid state to ensure that operating parameters remain in an acceptable range both for a given area (e.g. national grid) and any adjacent or otherwise affected areas as these may differ. An intrinsic challenge in the electric grid is the need to maintain a equilibrium within a relatively narrow parameter space under real-time constraints despite considerable fluctuations in generating and transmission capacity as well as demand. Elaborate models exist for state and demand estimation as well as planning, but despite this situations may arise where it is not possible or cost-effective to compensate. Bompard et al. hence also discuss the protective measures available to grid operators before discussing the specific security risks and problems in the sector beginning with an overview of the communication and control systems employed in the electricity sector at different levels from control centres to individual SCADA components and concluding with an analysis of possible countermeasures. As the sector is likely to change in response to the need to reduce its carbon intensity and efficiency, a number of new challenges will arise; however, the current highly reliable infrastructure in place is likely to remain the backbone for the foreseeable future, and hence its security and robustness must be assured despite further efforts in securing the more modern smart grid of the future and its interplay with the conventional grid.

The chapter by Johnsen, Aas, and Qian studies a different aspect of the energy sector that is less concerned with real-time effects, but one where the impact of failure is potentially very severe to the ability to function, the environment, and loss of life and limb, namely the oil and gas sector. Although the risk of contamination as well as fires and explosions is inherent in the sector, the need to exploit resources that are increasingly difficult to reach and often stretch the limits of available technology or indeed require the development of novel techniques for exploration and exploitation altogether may well have increased the potential for accidents. Moreover, both the more sophisticated techniques themselves and the increasingly hostile environments such as off-shore or Arctic environments force reliance on automation and control systems that cannot, similar to the electric grid, be replaced or even bridged by manual intervention owing to the precision and complexity of the operations required. However, despite efforts to centralise some of these operations and an increasing reliance on highly specialised entities collaborating in all phases of the exploration, extraction, and transportation of hydrocarbons, the sector retains its emphasis on safety rather than security. The chapter by Johnsen hence reviews both the regulatory framework in which the industry must operate and the technical — mainly SCADA — systems used in the sector. Particular emphasis is placed on the ability to prevent and respond to accidents and incidents as well as methods for systematically identifying risks and hazards arising also from the deployment of ICT and SCADA systems in the security domain.

The core ICT sector of telecommunications is studied in the chapter by Goldman and Uzunalioglu; while the sector has been scrutinised extensively for a long time, this chapter focuses on the effects caused by the convergence of conventional telephony and packet-switched networks that have been the subject of major investment efforts by telecommunications carriers in recent years to bring about so-called Next Generation Networks (NGN). The incentive for carriers of having to maintain a single and highly flexible infrastructure rather than two separate systems is very much self-evident, as is the desire to provide differentiated services to clients that also can be the subject of different service provision as well as cost models. However, both the convergence towards NGN itself and the more complex policy-driven service provisioning architecture clearly present risks from faults and particular ones originating in malicious agency, with new threats arising from the desire to integrate services across what has conventionally been a strictly layered architecture with only limited exceptions provided such as call prioritisation for emergencies and certain government services. Goldman and Uzunalioglu hence review threats arising at both the transport and service layers and highlight effects of layering in their contribution. However, as in the case of other infrastructure sectors discussed throughout the present volume, there is also a need to interact and remain interoperable with legacy systems, which can limit the ability to provide services such as stronger security features (e.g. authentication and access control) that would be straightforward in more homogeneous environments.

The chapter by Hämmerli provides insights into a sector that has — albeit to different extents depending on the sub-sector — become extremely reliant on the use of information and communication technology, namely financial services. Although reliant on information in a wider sense, the ability to reliably perform transactions and safely retain or access information is at the key of the sector and must be maintained beyond any reasonable doubt as the loss of trust in the sector's ability to provide its core services has the potential to cause cascading effects far beyond any immediately affected institution or service provider affected. The chapter by Hämmerli focuses on conventional infrastructure for financial services, namely the payment and clearing services used both between financial service institutions internationally and also towards clients, also discussing the underlying legal and regulatory framework. This is crucial to consider as the sector is covered by a dense network of regulations and agreements as well as technical standards. The chapter also provides an overview of the interconnected technical infrastructure for providing the transactional services and the increasing interconnection with additional components such as advanced payment systems and supporting infrastructures such as identification and authentication mechanisms, briefly also highlighting the effects one can observe indirectly arising from so-called over-the-counter (OTC) trading, which can not only have significant influence on prices for equities and derivatives, but may also affect secondary parameters such as the volumes of transactions required for infrastructure services to handle. These developments highlight a number of dependencies even within the sector that must be understood and managed carefully, which is made all the more difficult by the speed of developments on one hand and the fact that some of the developments are not wholly captured by the previously mentioned legal and regulatory framework, but are largely taking place invisibly to public or even academic scrutiny.

The final chapter of the present volume by Hartong, Goel, and Wiejesekera, on the contrary, covers aspects of a sector whose adoption of information and telecommunication technology is somewhat more cautious and even halting, namely the transportation sector. Some of the sub-sectors are inherently international in nature, mainly aviation and seaborne shipments, requiring international standardisation and agreements that serve to limit the rate of adoption for new ICT services. Other sectors such as road or rail transportation have far fewer restrictions, but providing extensive road and rail networks with e.g. telematics services imposes a significant capital burden. Unlike the previously covered sectors, the time-scales relevant in the sub-sectors are much larger, but even so hard real-time constraints must be observed. As Hartong, Goel, and Wiejesekera highlight, significant elements of the transportation infrastructure are inherently inter-modal, whether transitioning from seaborne transport to road and rail, between different road transportation modes, or in some cases even to pipeline networks; these all rely on the availability and interconnection of ICT systems to ensure that resource planning, freight bills, and related information is exchanged in a timely and correct manner. The chapter highlights some of the ICT-related components found in the transportation infrastructure itself, including satellite navigation and telecommunication mechanisms that are used extensively before discussing the concrete case of a safety mechanism used in rail transportation and the susceptibility of this mechanism to deliberate attack.

3   Editor Information

3.1   Javier Lopez

Prof. Javier Lopez is Full Professor in the Computer Science Department at the University of Malaga, and Head of the Network, Information and Computer Security (NICS) Laboratory. His research activities are mainly focused on network security and critical information infrastructures protection, leading a number of national and international research projects in those areas, including projects in FP5, FP6 and FP7 European Framework Programmes. He is the Co-Editor in Chief of International Journal of Information Security (IJIS) and Chair of the ERCIM Working Group on Security and Trust Management. Besides, he is member of the Editorial Board of, amongst others, the journals Computers & Security, International Journal of Critical Infrastructures Protection,

Wireless Communications and Mobile Computing, Computer Communications, Journal of Network and Computer Applications, and International Journal of Communication Systems. Prof. Lopez is the Spanish representative in the IFIP Technical Committee 11 on Security and Protection in Information Systems.

3.2 Roberto Setola

R. Setola is the head of the Complex System & Security Lab of the University CAMPUS Bio-Medico di Roma (Italy) and the General Secretary of the AIIC (Italian Association of Critical Infrastructures' Experts). From 1999 to 2004 he served at the Italian Prime Minister's Office and he managed the Italian Government Working Group on Critical Information Infrastructure Protection. He has been member of the G8 High-Tech Crime Subgroup and of the G8 Senior CIIP Expert (2003-2005) and Point of Contact for the Italian Government in the G8 "International CIIP Directory" (2003-2008). He received his M.Sc. in Electronic Engineering and Ph.D. in Control Theory from the Universitá di Napoli, Italy. He is author of three books and more than 100 peer-reviewed publications about modelling and simulation of complex systems, CIP/CIIP and the security of critical infrastructures.

3.3 Stephen D. Wolthusen

Prof. S. D. Wolthusen is Reader in Mathematics with the Information Security Group in the Department of Mathematics at Royal Holloway, University of London, UK and holds a concurrent appointment as Full Professor of Information Security with the Norwegian Information Security Laboratory at the Department of Computer Science at Gjøvik University College, Norway and holds several appointments as guest and visiting professor. He is author and editor of several books as well as more than 90 peer-reviewed research publications as well as past Editor in Chief of the journal Computers & Security and has served on several national and international advisory bodies in the area of critical infrastructure protection and the modelling of infrastructures.

References

1. Albert, R., Albert, I., Nakarado, G.L.: Structural Vulnerability of the North American Power Grid. Physical Review E – Statistical, Nonlinear, and Soft Matter Physics 69(2), 025103 (2004), doi:10.1103/PhysRevE.69.025103
2. Albert, R., Jeong, H., Barabási, A.L.: Error and Attack Tolerance of Complex Networks. Nature 406, 378–382 (2000), doi:10.1038/35019019
3. Brömmelhörster, J., Fabry, S., Wirtz, N. (eds.): Internationale Aktivitäten zum Schutz Kritischer Infrastrukturen. Bundesamt für Sicherheit in der Informationstechnik, Bonn, Germany (2004)
4. Cohen, R., Erez, K., ben Avraham, D., Havlin, S.: Breakdown of the Internet under Intentional Attack. Physical Review Letters 86(16), 3682–3685 (2001), doi:10.1103/PhysRevLett.86.3682
5. Falliere, N., Murchu, L., Chien, E.: Stuxnet Dossier. Symantec Security Response (2011)

6. Marsh, R.T. (ed.): Critical Infrastructures: Protecting America's Infrastructures. United States Government Printing Office, Washington D.C., USA (1997); Report of the President's Commission on Critical Infrastructure Protection
7. United States Department of Defense: Department of Defense Strategy for Operating in Cyberspace. U.S. Government Printing Office (2011)
8. Wenger, A., Mauer, V., Dunn, M. (eds.): International CIIP Handbook 2008/2009. Center for Security Studies, ETH Zurich, Zurich, Switzerland (2008)

The Art of CIIP Strategy: Tacking Stock of Content and Processes

Myriam Dunn Cavelty and Manuel Suter

Center for Security Studies, ETH Zurich, 8092 Zurich, Switzerland
{dunn,suter}@sipo.gess.ethz.ch

Abstract. This chapter analyses and compares CI(I)P and cybersecurity strategies to discover key issues, developments, and trends and to make recommendations about strategy making in the field of CIIP. To this end, it will first define CIP, CIIP and cybersecurity. It will then show what kind of protection goals – statements about a desired state of security of a particular object/asset that is seen in need of protection from one or a variety of threats – are defined and what kind of countermeasures are foreseen. Third, it will move from the content to the process and will make recommendations about how an optimal strategy process in the field of CIIP should look like.

Keywords: cybersecurity policy, public-private partnerships, threat perception, protection goals, strategy process.

1   Introduction

> "[Critical infrastructures] are the foundations of our prosperity, enablers of our defense, and the vanguard of our future. They empower every element of our society. There is no more urgent priority than assuring the security, continuity, and availability of our critical infrastructures."
>
> (President's Commission on Critical Infrastructure Protection, 1997: vii)

The above statement, made over a decade ago, still rings true. Critical infrastructures (CI) are systems or assets so vital to a country that any extended incapacity or destruction of such systems would have a debilitating impact on security, the economy, national public health or safety, or any combination of the above. As a consequence, critical infrastructure protection (CIP) is currently seen as an essential part of national security in numerous countries around the world.

Not everything about CIP is new: under the heading of vital system security, protection concepts for strategically important infrastructures and objects have been part of national defense planning for decades, though they played a relatively minor role during the Cold War as compared to other concerns such as deterrence[1]. Today, however, CIP refers to a broader concept with a distinctly different flavor. First of all,

J. Lopez et al. (Eds.): Critical Information Infrastructure Protection, LNCS 7130, pp. 15–38, 2012.

it is no longer restricted to concrete defense against immediate dangers, but increasingly refers to preventive security measures as well. Second, contemporary modern societies have become significantly more vulnerable, and the spectrum of possible causes of disruptions and crises has become broader and more diffuse. Third, CIP is a security practice that reflects the fact that the security challenges to the state from 'inside' and 'outside' have become blurred in the new threat environment to the point where they have become the same. National security – traditionally dealing with extraordinary threats and countermeasures from the outside – is now also concerned with attempts to create resilience and redundancy in national infrastructure through cyber-security measures and other means. This means that measures that are generally regarded as being within the purview of information security may now also be included among measures to ensure national security. In this new logic of security, two formerly different notions of security are merging, as technical security and safety and national security become one.[2]

Ever since the landmark report of the President's Commission on Critical Infrastructure Protection of 1997 called "Critical Foundations, Protecting America's Infrastructures"[3], countries around the world have focused on ways how to identify and protect their critical assets against a variety of threats. As a result, a broad range of political and administrative initiatives and efforts are underway in the US, in Europe, and in other parts of the world.[4] While over the years, substantial differences between these governmental protection policies have become apparent, there also commonalities in the form of key challenges that almost all governments are confronted with.

This chapter aims to take stock of these efforts and said challenges. It will identify the key issues, developments, and trends by comparing a set of recent policy papers, especially strategies, in the domain. These governmental policies are at various stages of implementation – some are enforced, while others are just a set of suggestions – and come in various shapes and forms, ranging from a regulatory policy focus concerned with the smooth and routine operation of infrastructures and questions such as privacy or standards, to the inclusion of CIP into more general counter-terrorism efforts. While the chapter aims to discuss only aspects unique to critical information infrastructures (CII) and infrastructure sectors immediately affected by CII in sync with the aims of this book, it is not always so clear where to draw the line between CIP and CIIP in practice. Therefore, some groundwork in terms of definitions and concepts is necessary; in addition, a reading of the policy papers also in terms of definitions of concepts that they provide reveals a lot about the state of the art of CI(I)P and the topic more generally.

In an ideal world, strategies "guide the implementation of plans, programs, campaigns, and other activities" [5]. They refer to a plan of action designed to achieve a particular goal and should therefore be drafted before any policy action is taken. Strategies can also be seen as a pattern, "a consistency of behavior over time"[6]. Optimally, a strategy sets direction and focuses effort and provides consistency by sketching a path from a current state to a desired future end state. Therefore, strategic thinking is always about thinking about the future.

In a less ideal world, strategies come in a variety of forms. Very often, setting future goals and defining steps to get there are closely interwoven or not even separated at all. In a field as diverse as CI(I)P and as populated by so many players inside and outside of government, it is almost entirely impossible to define in theory what a strategy is and what it is not. Therefore, rather than just selecting documents that have the word "strategy" in the title, we drew from a broader document base. Without any claim for comprehensiveness, we looked at publicly available documents that contain a) definitions of CI(I)P and related concepts, b) the description of (protection) goals, c) statements about an object to be protected, d) statements about the type of threat to which these objects are subject, and e) the means by which these objects are to be protected. In short, we were mainly interested in statements about a desired state of security of an identifiable object that is seen in need of protection from one or a variety of threats as well as statements about the type of countermeasures to be taken. In short, we mainly focus on protection goals. However, the constant and sometimes rapid advancement of existing policies shows that many countries are still in the process of defining their own "CI(I)P identity". What we are looking at are snapshots of a dynamic policy field with fuzzy boundaries.

This chapter is structured as follows: First, it will be analyzed how CIIP is defined – or rather not defined – and that many countries focus not on CIIP but on cybersecurity. Second, we will identify and describe the definition of protection goals on different levels. It will be shown that these strategies and policies differ considerably with regard to the question what should be protected from which threat. Cyberthreats are often only vaguely defined and it remains unclear which is the most relevant threat to critical infrastructures. In order to understand the varying approaches in the documents, it is necessary to distinguish between different cyberthreats and to analyze which strategy focus on which threat. Furthermore, the chapter looks at the proposed responses to cyberthreats. Even though the policy and strategy papers on CIIP and cybersecurity differ with regard to the question who threatens what, they usually propose similar concepts to respond to cyber vulnerabilities. Common response strategies include the formation of Public-Private Partnerships (PPPs); efforts to strengthen coordination between the different agencies that are assuming tasks in the field of CIIP; campaigns to increase public awareness for cybersecurity; and attempts to improve international collaboration. It will be briefly discussed how these protection and prevention measures are defined and which are the most relevant challenges that need to be addressed in order to implement them. Third, we will take a step away from the content and look at the process of how these strategic elements are defined and then point out what an ideal strategy making process could look like.

2   Definitions and Demarcations

More than ten years after the beginning of the CIP debate, there still is little clarity with regard to a clear and stringent distinction between the two key terms "CIP" and

"CIIP". In official publications, the term CIP is frequently used even if the document is only referring to the information aspects of the issue. It will be shown in a first subsection how the two terms can be differentiated. In a second subsection, it will be shown that rather than focusing on CIIP specifically, most governments focus on strategies in the domain of cybersecurity instead.

2.1 Distinguishing the Critical 'I' from the Information 'I'

A focus on CIIP creates immediate difficulties for any researcher, since the basis for distinguishing between CIP and CIIP is unclear. A clear distinction between CIP and CIIP is lacking in most countries, and one finds both terms being used interchangeably. This reflects the continuing difficulties that arise from having to distinguish between physical and virtual aspects of critical infrastructures.

That the two concepts are closely interrelated is apparent from the current debate on protection necessities: The debate jumps from a discussion of defending critical physical infrastructure – telecommunications trunk lines, power grids, and gas pipelines – to talk of protecting data and software residing on computer systems that operate these physical infrastructures. This indicates that the two cannot and should not be discussed as completely separate concepts. Rather, CIIP seems an essential *part* of CIP: While CIP comprises all critical sectors of a nation's infrastructure, CIIP is only a subset of a comprehensive protection effort, as it focuses on the critical *information* infrastructure.

The definition of exactly what should be subsumed under CI, and what under CII, is another question: Generally, critical information infrastructures can be described as the part of the global or national information infrastructure that is essential for the continuity of critical infrastructure services. There is a *physical* component to it, consisting of high-speed, interactive narrow-band and broadband networks; satellite, terrestrial, and wireless communications systems; and the computers, televisions, telephones, radios, and other products that people employ to access the infrastructure. In addition, there is an equally important *immaterial*, sometimes very elusive component, namely the information and content that flows through the infrastructure, the knowledge that is created from this, and the services that are provided through them.

Due to their role in interlinking various other infrastructures and also providing new ways in which they can be targeted, (critical) information infrastructures are regarded as the backbone of critical infrastructures, given that the uninterrupted exchange of data is essential to the operation of infrastructures in general and the services that they provide. Thus, it comes as no surprise that many so-called CIP policies have a strong focus on the protection of specific information infrastructures rather than focusing on all CI sectors and aspects.

2.2 From CIIP to Cybersecurity

While it is uncontested that CIIP is an essential part of CIP, the protection of information and communication infrastructures or technologies (ICT) and of the information which is processed by these systems is not only crucial for critical infrastructures. ICTs have also become absolutely essential for societal and business relations across the board. Governments are therefore also developing policies with regard to the security of information infrastructures more generally – meaning not only for *critical* information infrastructures from a government perspective – with the aim to secure all interactions that are enabled by them and depend on them. These economic, social and cultural interactions take place in what is labeled cyberspace.[7] In accordance, the policies that aim to secure these interactions are usually called cyberspace security policies or, in short, cybersecurity policies.

One of the first national cybersecurity strategies, called "Defending America's Cyberspace", was issued by the Clinton administration in January 2000. Since then, cybersecurity is perceived as an integral part of national security and many countries have started to develop cybersecurity policies. Compared to CIIP policies, cybersecurity policies pursue a broader view on the security of ICTs and the protection of the information that is processed by them, but the protection of the essential information infrastructure remains an integral part of such policies. In order to examine the key concepts and policies with regard to CIIP, it is thus important not only to look at national security strategies or CIP policies, but also to analyze those documents that refer to cybersecurity.

There are many examples for recent policy documents in that area: in the last two years countries like the UK, Sweden, Japan, Estonia or Belgium released new strategies for cybersecurity (or information security which is used as an alternative label). In addition the administration Obama issued the widely noticed "Cyberspace Policy Review". Most of these publications include parts dedicated to CIIP and point to the fact that cybersecurity is crucial for CIP. The US Cyberspace Policy Review for example highlights that "…the growing connectivity between information systems, the internet, and other infrastructures creates opportunities for attackers to disrupt telecommunications, electrical power, energy pipelines, refineries, financial networks, and other critical infrastructures"[8] and the Estonian Cyber Security Strategy describes the formulation of a cybersecurity strategy as the first step "to protect the country's critical infrastructure and to ensure the country's information security"[9].

However, the cybersecurity strategies and policy papers studied rarely provide a clear definition of cybersecurity. The UK Cyber Security Strategy states that "[c]yber security embraces both the protection of UK interests in cyber space and also the pursuit of wider UK security policy through exploitation of the many opportunities that cyber space offers".[10] The US Cyberspace Policy Review defines cybersecurity policy broadly as the "strategy, policy, and standards regarding the security of and operations in cyberspace".[11] It can be observed, however, that all of these documents implicitly adhere to the following definition: Cybersecurity is the absence of a threat either via or to information and communication technologies and networks. Simply put, this means that cybersecurity is the security one enjoys in and from cyberspace. [12]

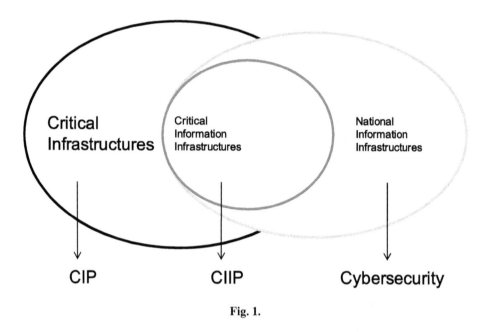

Fig. 1.

In sum, we will refer to CIP in this chapter when a document/strategy covers all relevant critical sectors of a country, to CIIP if the document/strategy just talks about one critical sector related to information infrastructures and to cybersecurity if the documents covers ICTs more generally, without just focusing on the critical part. With these general definition in mind, we will now move on to a depiction of the content of the various strategies.

3   Key Issues and Protection Goals in CI(I)P and Cybersecurity Strategy Documents

Protection goals – which according to our understanding contain statements about the object to be protected and the type of threat to which these objects are subjected – can be found on three hierarchically distinguishable levels and have different functions and purposes, which is shown in the first subsection. In a second subsection we will look at what is seen in need of protection and what is seen as the main threat. In a third, we look at the proposed countermeasures.

3.1   Protection Goals on Three Levels

We can distinguish between three levels on which protection goals can be found:

- First, protection goals are described on a strategic level in national security strategy documents.
- Second, protection goals are described in CIP, CIIP or cybersecurity strategies or similar documents.
- Third, protection goals are further defined and specified in sector-specific documents.

Not surprisingly, these goals become more concrete the further down one moves. We look at all three of them in separate subsections.

The analysis of CIP documents shows that 'protection goals' vary with regard to their specificity and purpose. On the level of national security strategies and policy papers, goals tend to use rather general terms such as 'prevention', 'mitigation of vulnerabilities', or 'protection of vital interests'. We believe it would be useful to label these kind of statements '*protection principles*' rather than protection goals, because they provide the general framework for CIP.

Slightly more specific protection goals are found on the second level of CIP strategies. They are more precise and specific than the protection principles, but still follow a systemic-abstract logic, as they refer to the totality of all CIs rather than to one sector or to one infrastructure. Examples for "protection goals" on this aggregated level are the goals of 'identifying critical infrastructures and key resources', 'enhancing resiliency', or 'analyzing interdependencies and vulnerabilities'. These goals, formulated for all CIs, can be described as '*protection policies*', as they define in a general way what must be protected from which threats in what way.

The third level is the sector-specific dimension. On this level, the "protection goals" are more concrete. Examples are the goals to ensure 'the availability, integrity and confidentiality of information and information technology' or 'sustain protection of public health and the environment'. They may be referred to as (sector-specific) '*protection goals*'.

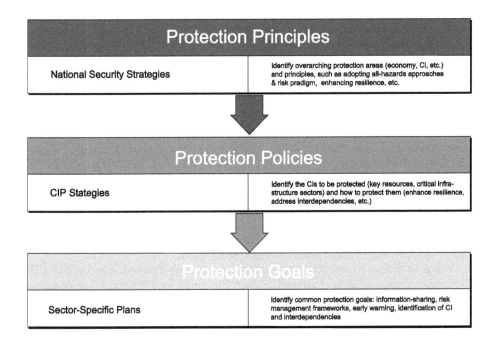

Fig. 2.

3.1.1   Level 1 (Protection Principles): National Security Strategies

Due to the high stakes if something went severely wrong with critical infrastructures, CIP is considered part of national security in most countries. However, in their national security strategies, different states focus on different aspects of CIP and define the protection goals of CIP in a different way. In order to highlight these differences, this section will provide an overview on the national security strategies of Canada, the Netherlands, the United Kingdom, and the United States and analyze how CIP is defined in these documents.

At the highest strategic level, the United States references the protection of critical infrastructures in its *National Strategy for Homeland Security*. The document calls for the 'Protection of the American people, our critical infrastructures, and key resources'[13] and outlines three specific goals for critical infrastructures protection: deter the terrorist threat; mitigate the vulnerabilities; and minimize the consequences. Furthermore, this document singles out the *National Infrastructure Protection Plan* (NIPP) – developed pursuant to the *Homeland Security Presidential Directive-7* – as the main guidance for the efforts to protect critical infrastructures. The NIPP is designated within this national strategy as the tool to 'ensure that our government, economy, and public services continue to function in the event of a man-made or natural disaster.'[14] This task is carried out through sector-specific plans developed within identified critical infrastructures and key resources (see below).

The general goal stated in the Netherlands' national security strategy is to protect the 'vital interests of the Netherlands in order to prevent societal disruption'. [15] CIP is seen as the operational tool to ensure this. *The Dutch National Security Strategy* depicts critical infrastructures protection as risk management and positions it on a par with crisis management; the two concepts together cover the operational aspects of security, while national security covers the strategic aspects. Moreover, it specifies that 'with critical infrastructures the emphasis is primarily on prevention (measures for better security of the critical sectors), while with crisis management the emphasis is on preparation (preparation for incidents), response (if an incident has occurred) and after-care.'[16]

While the Dutch strategy locates CIP in to the context of both national security and crisis management, Canada and the United Kingdom view critical infrastructure vulnerability (i.e., the threat) and its protection (i.e., the countermeasure) as a main challenge of emergency management.[17] In the UK, it is defined as the 'single overarching national security objective' to protect 'the United Kingdom and its interests, enabling its people to go about their daily lives freely and with confidence, in a more secure, stable, just and prosperous world'.[18] Furthermore, the British national security strategy identifies critical infrastructures among the key assets to be protected, stating the goal as 'to improve the protection of critical infrastructures, hazardous sites and materials, and crowded places'.[19]

These examples reveal the interrelationship between national security and CIP: National security is often described as being in some way related to ensuring the continuity of life – and CIP is the way to ensure this on an operational level. In other words, because CI are regarded as the fabric of society, the protection of society is equated with the protection of CI. This has several implications: a) Because CIP is a national security issue, there is a level of secrecy when it comes to concrete aspects such as protection goals; b) protection goals are directly linked to human survival. The stakes are thus very high. If the security of entire nations depends on CIP measures, then protection goals in CIP are – or should have to be – top-level strategic-political decisions. This is an important aspect that will be addressed in some more detail in the concluding section.

3.1.2   Level 2 (Protection Policies): CI(I)P Strategies

Protection goals formulated in CI(I)P and cybersecurity strategy papers (usually at the national/federal level) tend to be very general as well; rather than being specific mandates or measurable values, they are guiding principles, or mission statements. Nevertheless, on the second level, much more information can be found about the objects to be protected, the measures, and the threats.

There are many similarities between CI(I)P strategy documents: One common element is the importance of the concepts of resilience and of public-private partnerships, in different combinations. For example, the overarching goal of the United States' *National Infrastructure Protection Plan* (NIPP), one of the more elaborate strategies, is to '[b]uild a safer, more secure, and more resilient America by preventing, deterring, neutralizing, or mitigating the effects of deliberate efforts by terrorists to destroy, incapacitate, or exploit elements of our Nation's CIKR [Critical Infrastructures and Key Resources] and to strengthen national preparedness, timely response, and rapid recovery of CIKR in the event of an attack, natural disaster, or other emergency.'[20]

Similarly, in Canada, the document *National Strategy and Action Plan for Critical Infrastructure: Strategy* (2008) highlights the importance of enhancing resilience as a critical infrastructure protection goal that can be "achieved through the appropriate combination of security measures to address intentional and accidental incidents, human induced intentional threats, business continuity practices to deal with disruptions and ensure the continuation of essential services, and emergency planning to ensure adequate response procedures are in place to deal with unforeseen disruptions and natural disasters.'[21] Furthermore, this document reveals that partnerships, risk management, and information-sharing are viewed as key components of CI(I)P.

The recent Australian *Critical Infrastructure Resilience Strategy* (2010), finally, includes two main objectives of CIP. First, increasing the effectiveness of owners and operators of CI in managing foreseeable risks "through an intelligence and information led, risk informed approach", and secondly, "enhance their capacity to manage unforeseen or unexpected risk to the continuity of their operations, through an organizational resilience approach."[22]

There are many other national CI(I)P strategies that follow a similar approach, but in order to highlight the most important protection goals as formulated on the level of CI(I)P strategies, these three recent examples should be sufficient. They show that CI(I)P strategies usually pursue an all-hazard approach and include both human induced attacks and accidental failures of CIs. In addition, the goal of resilience of CIs has recently gained a lot of attention and is today perceived as one of the most important protection goals in CI(I)P. Resilience can be described as the ability of a system to recover quickly after experiencing a sudden shock or physical stress.[23] Since critical infrastructures are highly interdependent and complex, they cannot be protected against all potential threats. Accordingly, the ability to recover quickly after an incident – a high resiliency – is perceived as essential for ensuring the continuation of critical services.

3.1.3   Level 3 (Protection Goals): Sector-Specific Protection Goals

More tailored protection goals – very often tied specifically to definition and implementation of protection measures – can be found in sector-specific CIP plans. The case of the United States provides a good example for a CIP framework which is based on sector-specific protection approaches. The 2006 *National Infrastructure Protection Plan* (NIPP) allocates the responsibility for sector-specific protection plans to the respective federal agencies. The sector-specific federal agencies[24] became responsible for coordinating CIP efforts with relevant public and private stakeholders and developing sector-specific plans. All sector plans share a common framework; however, they also allow for flexibility and encourage customization.

Thus far, nine plans have been made available in the following areas: agriculture and food, banking and finance, communication, defense industrial base, energy, information technology, national monuments and icons, transportation systems, and water. In all of the sectors discussed, the respective plans list specific implementation measures used to achieve the goals.[25] The following protection goals have been identified for the IT sector:[26] 1) prevention and protection through risk management by identifying and assessing core functions, prioritizing risks and mitigating vulnerabilities; 2) improving situational awareness during normal operations; and 3) enhance the capabilities of public and private sector security partners to respond to and recover from realized threats and disruptions.

Another country that has a published sector-specific plan for CIIP is Germany. The documents *National Plan zum Schutz der Informationsinfrastruktur* (National Plan for Critical Information Infrastructure Protection) of 2005 and the subsequent 2007 report *Umsetzungsplan KRITIS* [27] (implementation plan KRITIS) outline the protection goals for CIIP. Similar to the IT-Sector-Specific-Plan of the US, prevention, reaction and sustainability are defined as generic goals of CIIP. In addition, the implementation strategy refers to the concepts of availability, integrity, and confidentiality, which are known form information assurance policies.

The examples of sector-specific protection goals for CIIP in the US and in Germany reveal that even on this specific level, the definitions of goals and objectives remain very broad. It is not described in further detail what exactly needs to be done in order to achieve the goals. The difficulties of formulating clear and unambiguous protection goals show that there is still a need for conceptual groundwork in the field of CI(I)P.

3.2   Referent Object and Threat Subject

Next to general protection principles, policies and goals, the documents studied also contain more specific information about that which is threatened and in need of protection (i.e., referent object) and the type of threat (i.e., threat subject). In this section, we will look at the referent object in one subsection, before turning to a discussion of the threats in the next.

3.2.1   Referent object: What Is Threatened?

When it comes to the referent object, there are two major issues: economic well-being and national security. The strategies and policy papers emphasize the importance of

ICTs for the national economy and point to the high costs of cyberattacks for the corporate sector.[28] These costs are deemed to have a negative impact on the growth of national economy.[29] The second referent object that is prominently discussed in the documents is national security. With reference to the large-scale attacks on Estonia in 2007, it is stressed that cyberattacks can compromise the functioning of critical infrastructures, which are considered to be crucial to national security.[30]

However, rather than being two clearly separable dimensions, economic well-being and national security are closely interconnected, since critical information infrastructures are essential for both dimensions at the same time. This interconnectedness is reflected in most of the documents. The United States, for example, claims that: "The continued exploitation of information networks and the compromise of sensitive data, especially by nations, leave the United States vulnerable to the loss of economic competitiveness and the loss of the military's technological advantages."[31] The Swedish Assessment of Information Security also mentions both dimensions: "Deficient information security can threaten [...] the capability to deal with serious disturbances and crises. Furthermore, it can have a negative impact on combating crime, trade and industry's profitability and growth, as well as the personal integrity of the country's citizens".[32]

The nexus between economic and national security interests is even more accentuated by the fact that many of the cyberstrategies view cybersecurity as being directly related to other governmental strategies, especially the respective countries' national security strategies (see section above). The UK realizes that: "Cyber security cuts across almost all the challenges outlined in the National Security Strategy, and interlinks with a wide range of Government policies, involving many departments and agencies"[33]. The US encourages the development of a new security strategy, noting that: "The national strategy should focus senior leadership attention and time toward resolving issues that hamper US efforts to achieve an assured, reliable, secure, and resilient global information and communications infrastructure and related capabilities"[34]. However, some of the strategies and policy papers also explicitly highlight the connection to information society and economic strategies. The Estonian Cyber Security Strategy, for example, states: "In developing the Cyber Security Strategy, the committee has taken into account national development plans that might also be relevant to information security and the information society, as well as plans relating to internal security and national defense."[35]

3.2.2 Malevolent Actors: Who Threatens Critical Information Infrastructures?

Two levels can be distinguished on which security in and from cyberspace can be at risk:

1. Technical level: While it is a commonplace that our societies are entirely and pervasively dependent upon ICT, the complexity and interconnectedness of this dependence is growing. With dependence comes vulnerability. On the first level, this vulnerability is linked to the danger of *system failures* that may have cascading effects affecting not only the individual use of ICT, but crippling the smooth functioning of entire branches of societal activity and security.

2. Actor level: Triggered by the pervasive societal dependence upon information and communication technology, the second area of vulnerability is the one linked to

potential *malevolent agency*. The panoply of malevolent agents deploying their activities in and/or through cyberspace is vast, but can be generally categorized into four elements. These include – in decreasing order of gravity – state-sponsored actors, ideological and politically extremist actors, frustrated insiders, organized criminal agents, and individual criminal agents.[36]

These two levels are interrelated: While the security challenge posed by potential systemic failure is inherent to the nature of the technological development in ICT, the dangers caused by and through malicious agents are conditioned by the nature of ICT. It is in fact the interaction between the two threat levels that makes the issue of cybersecurity such a complex challenge since it "is not simply that increasing dependence on ICT creates vulnerabilities and opportunities to be exploited by the unscrupulous, but also that ICT has an increasingly important enabling function for serious and organized crime, ideological and political extremism, and possibly even state-sponsored aggression."[37]

Despite the importance of technical vulnerabilities, there is an exclusive focus on the actor dimension of the threat spectrum in most of the CIP and cybersecurity strategies. This is not overly surprising, as cybersecurity is considered to be one of the key national security challenges of today; and in the context of national security, the possibility of a human attack is of special interest. Even though the immediate response to a cyberspace incident has to be tailored to the actual event on the technical level, mid- or long-term strategies work on a different level, and the identity of the attacker is crucial for calibrating the right response: If the attack was perpetrated by a state actor, military responses can be activated; when the threat originates from sub-state actors, the primary response should consist of law-enforcement measures. The question of who or what is threatening thus remains an important aspect of cybersecurity.

The recent policies and strategies with regard to cybersecurity and CIIP vary a lot with regard to the question who they consider to be the gravest threat in the domain of cyberspace. The UK Cyberspace Policy Review views the *"established capable states"* as the potentially most sophisticated threat,[38] the Estonian cyber security strategy notes that *"terrorist organizations, organized criminals and state-sponsored actors* already pose a serious global threat"[39], and the Swedish Information Security Strategy states that IT crimes "constitutes one of the largest threats to government agencies' electronic services being further developed and used by more people".[40]

This diversity shows that there are different perceptions and assessments of the threats to cyberspace. However, it has to be noted that the strategies and policy papers lack clear definitions and remain vague when it comes to the description and evaluation of the different threats. The terms "criminal activity" and "terrorist act" are not clearly defined. This vagueness can hardly be avoided, as it is a distinctive characteristic of cyberspace that it interlinks different actors and thus blurs the boundaries between different fields of activities. The Estonian cybersecurity strategy even explicitly acknowledges that "[t]here are no general regulations for the prevention and combating [sic] cyber threats, nor even a set of common definitions of these threats."[41]

Nevertheless, the strategies do differentiate between different threats. The most explicit delineation is made between state actors and non-state actors. The threats that are posed by states range from spreading disinformation to intelligence-gathering and large-scale attacks on critical infrastructures. In some documents, such activities are subsumed under the label "cyberwarfare".[42] Non-state actors, on the other hand, are described either as "cybercriminals" or as "cyberterrorists", depending on their motivation or their targets.

Despite this categorization of malicious actors into state and non-state actors, it remains unclear who poses the biggest threat, since there is not enough information on the capabilities and motivations of potential perpetrators. The difficulty of assessing the level and origin of threats to cybersecurity is acknowledged in most of the strategy and policy papers, and they avoid ranking the threats according to likelihood or severity.

The differences between the strategies show that there are different perceptions concerning the questions of who is threatening and what is threatened in cyberspace. Figure 3 summarizes four categories of threats that are referenced in the documents, arranged by the differences between those two questions.

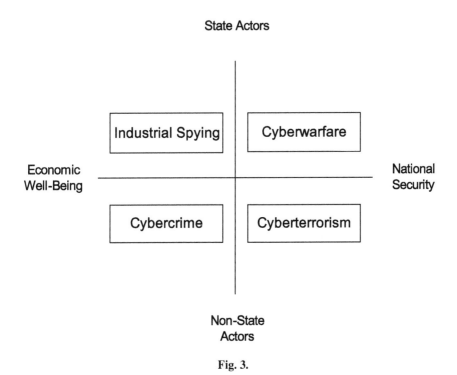

Fig. 3.

In theory, what one perceives as threatening and what one perceives as being threatened generates the focus of what is perceived to be in need of protection. A clear prioritization of the threats would therefore lead to a prioritization of response strategies. However, as mentioned above, in the case of CIIP cybersecurity, it is neither possible to define which actor poses the biggest threat, nor can the two dimensions of economy and national security be viewed in isolation. In consequence, the link between threat perceptions and countermeasures is far less clear. In fact, even though the strategies do differ in their assessments of key threats, they arrive at very similar countermeasures, as is shown in the next section.

3.3   Responding to the Threat: Protection Policies

In the absence of a clear picture of the severity and likelihood of different threats to cybersecurity, most strategy and policy papers define response strategies that reduce vulnerability to all forms of cyberattacks. Despite the differences between various kinds of attacks, there are also similarities that can be used to define general response strategies. For example, cybercriminals and cyberterrorists may exploit the same vulnerabilities to intrude into IT systems. Furthermore, both types of actors benefit from the lack of knowledge of many users and from the fact that they can start their attacks from the location of their choice, which can make it hard to prosecute them.

It is thus possible to mitigate the risk of all kinds of attacks by reducing vulnerabilities and improving national and international coordination and prosecution. Thus, even though strategies and policy papers sometimes differ in their threat description, they all identify similar response strategies: they promote an increase of public-private collaboration to enable a better exchange of information; they call for more coordination within the public sector in order to foster coherent responses; they highlight the importance of public awareness campaigns; and they point to the need for more international cooperation. These response strategies shall be briefly discussed.

3.3.1   Public-Private Partnerships/Information-Sharing

The idea of public-private partnerships (PPPs) for CIIP is by no means a new development. In fact, the 1997 US Report on Critical Infrastructure Protection clearly states that "coping with increasingly cyber-based threats demands a new approach to the relationship between government and the private sector."[43] Already more than a decade ago, governments realized the crucial role of the private sector in information infrastructure protection, as it is the private companies that own most of the critical infrastructure and can therefore be crucial in sharing information that is required for the effective protection of such infrastructure elements. Considering that PPPs have been continuously promoted for many years, it is clear that so far, this concept has not reached its full efficiency potential. This is reflected in the current strategies and policy reviews – especially in the latest US Cyberspace policy review. According to this document, "these groups perform valuable work, but the diffusion of effort has left some participants frustrated with unclear delineation of roles and responsibilities, uneven capabilities across various groups, and a proliferation of plans and recommendations."[44]

The crux of public-private partnership is that their implementation is demanding and that there is no single best way how to establish them. The design of partnerships must be in line with their function as well as with the specific characteristics of the public and private partners involved. [45] A partnership approach must therefore be flexible in order to allow various ways of implementation, and it makes no sense to define the structure of partnerships on the level of a strategy paper. On the other hand, it is unsatisfactory to promote better PPPs without describing how the difficulties in their implementation shall be addressed. A potential solution is the definition of frameworks and programs for PPPs. Such frameworks are, for example, proposed by the US Cyberspace Policy Review[46] or by the Communication from the EU Commission on Critical Information Infrastructure Protection.[47]

3.3.2 Better Coordination and Integration

A second measure that is proposed in almost all strategies is better coordination and a more integrated approach on the domestic front, which would offer clear allocations of responsibilities and thus improve the efficiency of cybersecurity measures. The Estonian Cyber Security Strategy for example notes: "It is necessary to acknowledge cyber threats much more widely, and to improve interdepartmental coordination system related to the prevention and combating of cyber attacks on a national level."[48] And the UK Cyber Security Strategy highlights that the "[g]overnment must lead a coherent UK response to the security challenges that arise from these threats and risks and a strategic approach is fundamental to achieving this aim."[49]

In order to implement greater coordination at the practical level, many strategies suggest the development of new structures or offices that would be responsible for overseeing the activities of all of the agencies that deal with cybersecurity-related issues. This trend is particularly observable in the cases of the United States and the United Kingdom. The United States Cyberspace policy review suggests that the President appoints a cybersecurity policy official at the White House (a so-called "cyber czar"), who would coordinate all of the national cybersecurity related policies and activities.[50] Likewise, the UK Cyber Security Strategies also recommends more centralization and proposes the establishing of a *Cyber Security Operations Center* involving representatives from across the government and key stakeholders.[51] The goal of this center would then be to "provide policy guidance, expertise and situational awareness to those elements of government that deal directly with national security threats, and to the private sector and the public."[52]

By defining new structures, the strategies can be useful for achieving better coordination in cybersecurity and CIIP. Often, there are too many governmental agencies involved. In consequence, it has often been impossible to attribute responsibilities, which hindered the effective response. At the same time, however, it should be noted that the implementation of new structures is a cumbersome process and reorganization could also destroy mechanisms that have been working quite effectively. While new developments may require institutional reforms, it is also important to ensure a certain degree of stability and continuity. A cybersecurity strategy should therefore try to define an institutional framework for cybersecurity that is not only able to tackle the short-term problems, but is also flexible enough to deal with potential new problems.

3.3.3   Awareness Campaigns and the Promotion of Education, Training, and Research

As a third response strategy to cyberthreats many strategies and policy papers highlight the importance of awareness rising. They argue that cybersecurity can only be improved if the whole society becomes more aware of the problem. Therefore, in order to recognize the public vulnerability to cyberthreats and the importance of public participation in building cybersecurity policies, awareness-raising campaigns as well as education, training, and research have been continuously emphasized in strategy and policy papers. The 1997 report on critical infrastructure protection in the United States already includes a clear call for ingraining infrastructure protection "in our culture, beginning with a comprehensive program of education and awareness",[53] and the Cyberspace Policy Review of 2009 recommends that "[t]he Federal government, in partnership with educators and industry, should conduct a national cyber security public awareness and education. The strategy should involve public education about the threat and how to enhance digital safety, ethics, and security."[54]

While many strategies emphasize the importance of awareness and education programs, they rarely specify how or by whom such programs should be implemented. Some refer to previous established and still ongoing programs,[55] while others refer to implementation plans that will be issued later.[56] It also often remains unclear who should be targeted by such campaigns (the strategies and policy papers mention company leaders, students, government officials, or the general public as potential addressees). Although it is not necessary to define every detail of awareness and education programs at the level of a strategy, it would still be beneficial to have better specifications, which would make it possible to analyze which programs are already implemented (and by whom) and which have still to be developed.

3.3.4 International Cooperation

Despite the fact that international cooperation is in many ways already taking place,[57] virtually all of strategies and policy papers in the field of cybersecurity and CIIP underscore the need for expanded and more efficient cooperation, realizing that cyberthreats and the perpetrators of cybercrimes do not recognize national boundaries.

There are several international initiatives regarding cyber space. The Council of Europe Convention on Cyber Crime was opened for signature in 2001 and entered into force in 2004. The Forum of Incident Response and Security Teams (FIRST) brings together a variety of Computer Security Incident Response Teams (CSIRTs) from national governments as well as commercial and education organizations; the European Network and Information Security Agency (ENISA) promotes cooperation on the level of EU members and institutions; the International Telecommunication Union is a UN agency for information and communication technology issues; and the Meridian Process is a platform providing governments worldwide with a means of discussing and working together on policies regarding critical information infrastructure protection.

Such international initiatives and organizations play a very important role in CIIP, since information and communication infrastructures are international and cyberthreats are therefore not territorially based. It should be noted however, that one of the reasons for the lack of efficient cooperation is the difference in perceptions of terms such as 'cyberterrorism,' 'cyberattack', 'cyberwarfare', etc. This contributes to the status quo, which is characterized by a lack of coherent international approach. There are also different perceptions of cooperation from different international actors. While some countries would like to treat information system attacks merely as criminal offences against public and private property, as suggested in the Council of Europe's Convention on Cybercrime, other actors would like to see the response to such offences to be escalated to the level of a national security issue. Other differences include the distinction between small- and large-scale attacks as well as ordinary computer systems and critical infrastructure systems.[58] Therefore, while the demands for more international cooperation constitute a positive phenomenon, international cooperation will continue to be insufficient unless there is a real will for unity concerning these essential terms and basic regulations.

4   The Strategy Making Process

In the section above, we have outlined several points that can be found in CI(I)P and cybersecurity strategies. If we compare them, it can be shown that recent documents contain thoughts that are already well established, rather than any new ideas. In addition, these documents are quite alike with regard to their description of the threat. First, the documents are all rather vague in describing the threats, since they aim to avoid excluding certain types of threats. Second, they all take into account the fact that cybersecurity concerns both national security and the national economy. Third, they unanimously identify public-private partnerships, improved policy coordination, awareness campaigns, and international coordination as the most important measures for enhancing cybersecurity, but most of them fail to outline how such programs shall be implemented.

The similarities between the different strategy and policy papers show that most governments face similar problems in formulating and implementing CIIP policies. The underlying problem is that it remains unclear what is threatened, who is threatening, and what the potential consequences of attacks or failures could be. A CIIP strategy has to take into account very diverse types of threats, ranging from criminally motivated attempts to steal information to terrorist attacks on critical infrastructures with the goal to create as much damage as possible. The likelihood of occurrence for these threats varies greatly, as does their potential impact on the security of society. Would it thus make sense to include all these threats in one strategy, or should there rather be separate strategies for CIIP, cybercrime and cyberwar? The problem is that the different threats are interlinked and the connections between them are not clear. Treating different threats separately would be inconsistent with the so-called "all-hazards approach", which has proven to be a useful concept in CIP as well as in cybersecurity. It is thus not possible to separate the different kind of threats completely from each other, and CIIP strategies should take all of them into account.

More solid definitions would make it easier, however, to put the different countermeasures into context. The design of PPPs, for example, will vary depending on the function of the partnership. While PPPs for critical infrastructure protection are small and based on direct exchanges of information between the government and the private sector, PPPs for the fight against cybercrime require broader coalitions, as criminals may attack all kinds of companies (not only those operating critical infrastructures). Clearer definitions are also required in order to develop a coherent international approach for cybersecurity, as the different perceptions of threats still hinder collaborative efforts. Finally, a clear delineation of cyberthreats is required to define the responsibilities of different government agencies, which would be the first step towards better coordination of cybersecurity efforts. The inter-mixing of cybercrime with cyberwarfare and cyberterrorism, for example, often impedes a clear division of responsibility between military and civil agencies.

In sum, it can be noted that the vague definitions of threats in the strategy papers lead to rather vague concepts for countermeasures. Most strategies fail to set priorities and to provide well-defined cybersecurity programs. This clearly impairs their value and may even jeopardize the benefits of having a CIIP or a cybersecurity strategy. However, one should not jump to the conclusion that such strategies are completely unnecessary. Developing a CIIP strategy can be valuable for two reasons: First, the process of developing a strategy is valuable in its own right. The discussions about the existing policy that accompany the formulation of a strategy can be fruitful and may stimulate processes that lead to important advancements. Second, a strategy can help to raise awareness of cyberthreats in general, but can also underline the importance of individual countermeasures. The mention of PPPs as important instrument for more cybersecurity, for example, supports the existing public-private collaborations and can help to establish new PPPs. In this final section, we therefore want to sketch an optimal strategy making process.

4.1   Strategy Making: Top Down Meets Bottom Up

As mentioned above, public and private actors play specific roles in the formulation of protection principles, policies, or goals. We can distinguish between a top down and a bottom up part of the strategy making process.

4.1.1   The Definition of Principles and Policies in Political Processes
Political decision-makers set general goals – or principles – for CIP and thereby guide the development of more specific protection goals. They also decide what needs to be protected from which threats, and by which means. The question of 'what needs to be protected' is a key question in CIP that is closely related to the definition of protection goals. The criticality of infrastructures depends on factors such as the importance for other infrastructures, for the national economy, or for society at large. However, these factors are hard to quantify satisfactorily, so that the identification of CIs remains an inherently political decision. In consequence, the CIs are often listed in strategy papers or government directives.[59]

Another issue within CIIP that is highly influenced by political decisions is the question of which threats the CIs need to be protected from. The potential threat spectrum ranges from terrorist attacks to human error to technical failures. To avoid turf battles among agencies, it is therefore crucial to address the discussion on sources of threats at the political level. In response to that need, many strategies and policy papers emphasize the importance of the 'all-hazards approach' in CIP. This means that all relevant agencies need to be involved and that the concrete protection goals need to be formulated in a threat-neutral way.

Finally, there are also some decisions to be taken on the political level concerning the means by which a goal should be protected. This question is all the more important since many CIs are owned and operated by the private sector. Protection can only be achieved if all stakeholders act in concert. This means that concrete protection goals should be defined in collaboration with the private sector. Such an empowerment of non-state actors is not a routine process and needs to be anchored in political decisions. Hence, many strategies explicitly highlight the need for collaboration with the private sector. The important role of public-private partnerships in CIP is not only articulated in the documents reviewed in this report, but also evident in the establishment of state-sponsored partnership platforms such as Australia's Trusted Information Sharing Network (TISN), the United Kingdom's Centre for the Protection of National Infrastructure (CPNI), and the United States Critical Infrastructure Partnership Advisory Council (CIPAC), Sector Coordinating Councils (SCC), and Government Coordinating Councils (GCC). The principle of public-private collaboration is thus another important political decision that shapes the formulation of concrete protection goals for CIP.

4.1.2   The Definition of Protection Goals in Consultative Processes with Practitioners

As indicated above, decisions on the political level determine the room of maneuver for the definition of protection goals for CIP. However, these goals are not only influenced by top-down political decisions, but also by bottom-up consultations with the owners and operators of CIs.

The private sector influences the definition of protection goals in three different ways: First, the owners and operators of CI are represented in advisory boards for CIP and contribute directly to the development of national CIP policies. The best known historic example is the Advisory Committee to the President's Commission for Critical Infrastructure Protection (PCCIP), which was composed of 15 industry leaders and informed the work of the PCCIP.[60] Today, similar advisory bodies exist in many countries. Examples include the Strategic Board for CIP (SOVI)[61] in the Netherlands; the National Infrastructure Advisory Council (NIAC)[62] in the United States; or the Critical Infrastructure Advisory Council (CIAC)[63] in Australia. These advisory bodies are key actors in the development of CIP policies and thus have an important influence on the definition of general protection goals.

Secondly, private actors closely collaborate with sector-specific agencies to develop and implement protection goals for their individual sectors. While such collaborations are well-established across most sectors and in most countries, they often remain informal and only rarely publish reports identifying sector-specific protection goals. The Sector-Specific Plans in the United States,[64] which are mandated by the National Infrastructure Protection Plan (NIPP) and publicly available, are an exception. These plans list the sector-specific goals and identify the partners that contributed to the development of these goals. Another example of a jointly developed sector-specific plan that includes protection goals is the CIP Implementation Plan in Germany (UP KRITIS)[65] for the IT sector.

The third way in which private actors influence the definition of protection goals consists of what may be called lobbying activity. Industry groups try to shape CIP policies according to their interests by talking to politicians or by issuing white papers and press releases. The goals of lobbying in CIP can be to highlight the importance of the own sector or to push for government initiatives. The Information Technology Association of America (which is a leading industry group for United States IT and electronics businesses), for example, writes in its Mission Statement on Information Security Policy that it is the organization's goal to 'ensure that cyber security is an integral part of critical infrastructure protection.'[66]

4.2   Combining the Three Levels with a Top-Down / Bottom-Up Interaction

Of course, the top-down and bottom-up processes cannot be regarded as being independent, since they influence each other: Protection principles, policies and goals as described above are usually the result of both political decisions and consultations with the private sector. Nevertheless, the public and private sectors do have different responsibilities when it comes to protection goals. It is the role of the public actors to ensure that protection goals developed on the third level are in line with the protection principles and policies defined on the first and second levels, and it is the role of the private actors to ensure that the protection goals are realizable and meaningful for the specific demands of their sector.

We can therefore sketch a process that combines the top-down and the bottom-up approach and integrates the three levels of protection principles, policies and goals. As mentioned, protection principles (Level 1) are formulated in political processes and formulated in national security strategies. They can provide guidance to the administrative bodies in charge of CIP by describing potential threats and risks and by highlighting the necessity to tackle them. The national security strategies and policy papers provide the framework for the risk analysis and management processes. Protection principles are very important in a complex field such as CIP, since they ensure a necessary level of coherence between different levels of government and help in developing measures to ensure security.

In order to analyze and manage the risks in the field of CIP, protection principles need to be translated into less abstract concepts. This translation process happens on Level 2, the level of protection policies. Protection policies specify what protection principles such as 'prevention' or 'resilience' mean for CIP and identify means for identifying, assessing, and managing the risks to CI. Such protection policies state, for example, that prevention shall be improved by public-private collaboration or that the resilience of CI (understood as the entity of CIs, not as individual infrastructures) shall be strengthened by information-sharing between the owners and operators of CIs. These policies are necessarily broad, because it is not possible to determine criteria for all sectors of CIs: the differences are too big. But at the same time, the interdependencies between the different CIs make a coherent approach indispensable. One sector cannot be secure if another sector on which it depends is not. The development of shared frameworks for risk analysis and management is a crucial step in CIP, as it allows the formulation of sector-specific protection goals without risking a loss of coherence within CIP as a whole. The function of protection policies (Level 2) is therefore to connect these top-down and bottom-up processes and incorporate them into one coherent approach to CIP.

Sector-specific protection goals (Level 3) are formulated in collaboration with the owners and operators of CI. The goals need to be sufficiently specific to enable implementation (cf. the concept of operational protection goals in the German case). On this level, there needs to be clarity with regards to the overall aim and purpose of protection efforts, including what risks to focus on.

5   Conclusion

In this chapter, it was first shown how the terms CIIP and cybersecurity relate to each other to bring some clarity into the terminological muddle that exists in the field and to show why many countries have begun focusing on cybersecurity more recently. Second, the chapter looked at statements about the object to be protected and the type of threat to which these objects are subjected in recent policy papers. It was shown how such 'protection goals' vary with regard to their specificity and purpose. The chapter then introduced three labels for three different types of such goals: *protection principles* for the level of national security strategies and policy papers, *protection policies* for more specific CI(I)P strategies, and (sector-specific) *protection goals* for the most concrete form of such statements in sector-specific protection plans. Furthermore, the chapter compared what is said about that which is threatened and in need of protection (i.e., referent object) and the type of threat (i.e., threat subject). It was shown that the strategies and policies differ considerably with regard to these two issues, but that despite these discrepancies, they usually propose similar concepts to respond to cyber vulnerabilities: Public-Private Partnerships (PPPs); efforts to strengthen coordination between the different agencies that are assuming tasks in the field of CIIP; campaigns to increase public awareness for cybersecurity; and attempts to improve international collaboration.

The similarities between the different strategy and policy papers can be seen as an indication that most governments face the same problems in formulating and implementing CIIP policies: Specifically, the vague definitions of threats in the strategy papers lead to rather vague concepts for countermeasures. As a consequence, most strategies do not succeed in setting priorities or in providing sufficiently defined cybersecurity programs, which impairs their value. To move beyond this problem, an optimal strategy making process was outlined in the section above. This process combines a top-down with a bottom-up approach and integrates the three levels of protection principles, policies and goals in an optimal way.

The three-level model in combination with the description of the combined top-down/bottom-up process outlined above provides a useful framework for the definition and use of protection goals in critical infrastructure protection, as it ensures coherence between the protection goals in different sectors and a sufficient level of specification of protection goals within the individual sectors. Beginning at the political level, protection goals are first identified at the highest strategic levels and articulated in a national security framework/strategy. In this phase, overarching protection principles and goals, such as the protection of critical infrastructure, are addressed. The next step is the creation of CIP strategies where specific sectors and sub-sectors are highlighted and protection principles (such as promoting information-sharing, utilizing a risk framework, creating public-private partnerships, etc.) are applied and further refined. This step leads to a process of policy transfer, with protection goals developed in the political level being applied at the sector-specific level, and the beginning of an exchange between specialized public agencies and CI operators in the private sector. The sector-specific level is where protection goals become customized based on the particular needs of an identified CI sector – resulting in the construction of sector-specific plans. At this stage, the role of the private sector is to manage CI, liaise with the public sector, and articulate goals and measures to achieve protection. Within the public sector, specialized agencies work to communicate federal mandates to CI operators and create platforms for information-sharing and partnerships.

While the CIP framework described herein points to a traditional top-down process – with the top level setting the agenda – there are bottom-up forces that inform the political level, creating feedback loops. At both levels, a broader informing environment provides insights and influence to those identifying goals and means of protection, for example. This informing environment includes public officials and local/regional state agencies as well as those operating in the private sector and in academia/think-tanks. Overall, this framework exemplifies a dynamic, interactive process where each sphere of influence has a key role to play in defining and refining protection goals.

References

1. Collier, S., Lakoff, A.: The Vulnerability of Vital Systems: How 'Critical Infrastructure' Became a Security Problem. In: Dunn Cavelty, M., Kristensen, K.S. (eds.) The Politics of Securing the Homeland: Critical Infrastructure, Risk and Securitisation, pp. 40–62. Routledge, London (2008)
2. Dunn Cavelty, M.: Cyber-Security. In: Burgess, P. (ed.) The Routledge Handbook of New Security Studies, pp. 154–162. Routledge, London (2010)
3. President's Commission on Critical Infrastructure Protection. Critical Foundations. Protecting America's Infrastructures, US Government Printing Office, Washington DC (1997)
4. Brunner, E.M., Suter, M.: International CIIP Handbook 2008/2009. Center for Security Studies, Zurich (2008)
5. Claudle, S.L.: National Security Strategies: Security from What, from Whom, and by What Means. Journal of Homeland Security and Emergency Management 6(1), 10 (2009)
6. Mintzberg, H., Ahlstrand, B., Lampel, J.: Strategy Safari: A Guided Tour Through the Wilds of Strategic Management, p. 9. The Free Press, New York (1998)
7. Schneider, V., Hyner, D.: Security in Cyberspace. In: Koenig-Archibougi, M., Zürn, M. (eds.) New Modes of Governance in the Global System. Exploring Publicness, Delegation and Inclusiveness, Palgrave MacMilllan, pp. 154–176 (2005)
8. US Government. Cyberspace Policy Review. Assuring a Trusted and Resilient Information and Communication Infrastructure. US Government Printing Office, Washington DC (2009)

9. Ministry of Defence of Estonia. Cyber Security Strategy. Cyber Security Strategy Committee, Tallinn, p. 8 (2008)
10. Cabinet Office of the United Kingdom. Cyber Security Strategy of the United Kingdom. Safety, Security and Resilience in Cyber Space. The Stationery Office, London, p. 9 (2009)
11. US Government, Cyberspace Policy Review, p. 2
12. Cornish, P., Hughes, R., Livingstone, D.: Cyberspace and the National Security of the United Kingdom. Threats and Responses. Chatham House, London (2009)
13. Homeland Security Council. National Strategy for Homeland Security. US Government Printing Office, Washington DC, p. 1 (2007)
14. Ibid, p. 26
15. Dutch Ministry of the Interior and Kingdom Relation. National Security Strategy and Work Programme 2007-2008. Broese & Peereboom, The Hague, p. 16 (2007)
16. Ibid, p.13
17. Her Majesty the Queen in Right of Canada. National Strategy for Critical Infrastructure. Public Safety Canada, Ottawa, p. 25 (2009)
18. Cabinet Office of the United Kingdom. The National Security Strategy of the United Kingdom. Security in an Interdependent World. The Stationery Office, London p. 5 (2008)
19. Ibid, p. 26
20. Department of Homeland Security. National Infrastructure Protection Plan. Partnering to Enhance Protection and Resiliency. Government Printing Office, Washington DC, p. 1 (2009)
21. Her Majesty the Queen in Right of Canada. National Strategy for Critical Infrastructure p. 1 (2008)
22. Australian Government. Critical Infrastructure Resilience Strategy. Commonwealth of Australia, Barton, pp. 3ff (2010)
23. Brunner, E., Giroux, J.: Resilience: A Tool for Preparing and Managing Emergencies. CSS Analyses in Security Policy, No. 60, p. 1 (2009)
24. For a complete list of the sector-specific agencies, see: Department of Homeland Security, National Infrastructure Protection Plan, p. 19
25. Other plans can be retrieved,
    http://www.dhs.gov/files/programs/gc_1179866197607.shtm
26. Department of Homeland Security. Information Technology. Critical Infrastructure and Key Resources Sector-Specific Plan as Input to the National Infrastructure Protection Plan. Government Printing Office, Washington DC, p. 11ff (2007)
27. Bundesministerium des Innern. Umsetzungsplan KRITIS des nationalen Plans zum Schutz der kritischen Informationsinfrastrukturen. Publikationsversand der Bundesregierung, Rostock (2007)
28. Cabinet Office of the United Kingdom, Cyber Security Strategy, pp. 12f
29. Swedish Civil Contingency Agency. Information Security in Sweden: Situational Assessment 2008. MSB, Karlstad, p. 3 (2008)
30. US Government, Cyberspace Policy Review, p. 2; Ministry of Defence of Estonia, Cyber Security Strategy of Estonia, p.10
31. US Government, Cyberspace Policy Review, p. 1
32. Swedish Civil Contingency Agency, Information Security in Sweden, p. 3
33. Cabinet Office of the United Kingdom , Cyber Security Strategy, pp. 14
34. US Government, Cyberspace Policy Review, p. 8
35. Ministry of Defence of Estonia, Cyber Security Strategy of Estonia, p.8
36. Ibid
37. Ibid.: p. vii

38. Cabinet Office of the United Kingdom, Cyber Security Strategy, pp. 12ff
39. Ministry of Defence of Estonia, Cyber Security Strategy of Estonia, p.10
40. Swedish Civil Contingency Agency, Information Security in Sweden, p. 17
41. Ministry of Defence of Estonia, Cyber Security Strategy of Estonia, p.17
42. Cabinet Office of the United Kingdom, Cyber Security Strategy, p. 12; Ministry of Defence of Estonia, Cyber Security Strategy of Estonia, p.10; Swedish Civil Contingency Agency, Information Security in Sweden, p. 17
43. President's Commission on Critical Infrastructure Protection, Critical Foundations, p. x
44. US Government, Cyberspace Policy Review, p. 18
45. Dunn Cavelty, M., Suter, M.: Public-Private Partnerships are no Silver Bulled: An Expanded Governance Model For Critical Infrastructure Protection. International Journal of Critical Infrastructure Protection 2(4), 179–187 (2009)
46. US Government, Cyberspace Policy Review, p. 38
47. Commission of the European Communities. Protecting Europe from Large Scale Cyber-attacks and Disruptions: Enhancing Preparedness, Security and Resilience. Communication from the Commission to the European Parliament, the Council, the European Economic and Social Committee and the Committee of Regions, Brussels, p. 6. (2009)
48. Ministry of Defence of Estonia, Cyber Security Strategy of Estonia, p.15
49. Cabinet Office of the United Kingdom , Cyber Security Strategy, p. 9
50. Obama followed this suggestion and appointed Howard Schmidt as the first cybersecurity coordinator of the White House in December 2009. Cf. The White House Blog (December 22, 2009),
    http://www.whitehouse.gov/blog/2009/12/22/introducing-new-cybersecurity-coordinator
51. Up to now (Spring 2010) this center is still planned but not yet implemented. Cf. Infosecurity Magazine (March 12 2010),
    http://www.infosecurity-magazine.com/view/8020/uk-government-cyber-security-operations-centre-going-live-soon/
52. Cabinet Office of the United Kingdom , Cyber Security Strategy, p. 16
53. President's Commission on Critical Infrastructure Protection, Critical Foundations, p. xi
54. US Government, Cyberspace Policy Review, pp. 13f
55. Cabinet Office of the United Kingdom, Cyber Security Strategy, p. 18
56. Ministry of Defence of Estonia, Cyber Security Strategy of Estonia, p. 34
57. Portnoy, M., Goodman, S.: Global Initiatives to Secure Cyberspace. An Emerging Landscape. Springer, New York (2009)
58. NATO Parliamentary Assembly. NATO and Cyber Defence. Committee Report of the 2009 Annual Session, Bruxelles, §38 (2009)
59. Such as, e.g: Department of Homeland Security. Homeland Security Presidential Directive 7: Critical Infrastructure Identification, Prioritization and Protection. US Government Printing Office, Washington DC (2003)
60. Ann Brown, K.: Critical Path. A Brief History of Critical Infrastructure Protection in the, p. 82. George Mason University, Washington DC (2006)
61. https://www.navi-online.nl/content/24/SOVI+werkgroep (in Dutch)
62. http://www.dhs.gov/files/committees/editorial_0353.shtm
63. http://www.tisn.gov.au/www/tisn/content.nsf/Page/The_TISN
64. http://www.dhs.gov/files/programs/gc_1179866197607.shtm
65. Bundesministerium des Innern, Umsetzungsplan KRITIS.
66. http://www.itaa.org/information-security

Infrastructure Sectors and the Information Infrastructure[*]

Andrea Glorioso and Andrea Servida

European Commission, DG Information Society and Media, Unit A3 – Internet,
Network and Information Security

The protection of Critical Information Infrastructures (CIIs) is usually framed in the larger context of protecting all the Critical Infrastructures (CIs) that a Nation or a group of Nations (as is the case of the European Union) consider as essential for the maintenance of vital societal functions, health, safety, security, economic or social well-being of citizens.

There is no globally accepted definition of what constitutes a CII – various organisations have provided their own view on the matter, including among others the OECD (2008), according to which CIIs are "those interconnected information systems and networks, the disruption or destruction of which would have a serious impact on the health, safety, security, or economic well-being of citizens, or on the effective functioning of government or the economy", and the European Commission (2005), according to which they are "ICT systems that are critical infrastructures for themselves or that are essential for the operation of critical infrastructures (telecommunications, computers/software, Internet, satellites, etc.)". Similar terminological differences can be found in the definitions of CIs, which, for the purposes of this discussion, will be understood as "those physical resources, services, and information technology facilities, networks and infrastructure assets which, if disrupted or destroyed, would have a serious impact on the health, safety, security or economic well-being of Citizens or the effective functioning of governments. There are three types of infrastructure assets: public, private and governmental infrastructure assets and interdependent cyber & physical networks; procedures and where relevant individuals that exert control over critical infrastructure functions; objects having cultural or political significance as well as "soft targets" which include mass events (i.e. sports, leisure and cultural)" (European Commission 2005).

Although semantic divergences should not be underestimated for their potential impact on harmonized or at least coherent approaches to regional and often global challenges, it is essential to keep in mind that no matter which definition is used, the operational goal is to further and promote a holistic perspective towards the resilience of infrastructures that are vital to the well-being of very large number of citizens.

Policies related to CIIs usually "live" in taxonomy of various categories or sectors of CIs and related policies.

Such an approach is based on the assumption that, notwithstanding the importance of Information and Communication Technologies (ICTs) in contemporary societies,

---

[*] The views expressed in this contribution are purely those of the writers and may not in any circumstances be regarded as stating an official position of the European Commission. The authors would like to thank Ms. Camino Manjon for her editorial support.

J. Lopez et al. (Eds.): Critical Information Infrastructure Protection, LNCS 7130, pp. 39–51, 2012.
© Springer-Verlag Berlin Heidelberg 2012

there are certain vital functions which ICTs alone are not able to satisfy. To put it in perhaps oversimplifying but certainly clear terms, citizens can not eat computer chips or drink web pages.

Dividing CIs in different categories or sectors is also an answer to the recognition that different kinds of CIs potentially require different types of policy interventions, in terms of instruments, scope, speed, target stakeholders and expertise. Consequently, there is a clear advantage in positively identifying different CIs sectors to allow different entities to take responsibility for the practical implementation of the strategies put forth by decision-makers. This approach is obviously without prejudice to the possibility, indeed the desirability, to have a single entity providing the necessary high-level coordination functions between the activities conducted in different CI sectors; but even in those situations where the legal and political environment allows and/or pushes for a clear top-down approach to CI protection, it is unsurprising to see that different bodies, or departments within a body, take the lead for different CI sectors.

On the other hand, as suggested with the reference to the need of an overall strategic approach, the division of CI protection into different sectors should be handled with care: the abstract nature of any taxonomy, as well as the potential challenges deriving from an over-segmentation of CIs (whether deriving from conceptualisation excesses or internal power struggles between different stakeholders or different groups within a single stakeholder) should be identified, prevented and corrected as quickly and effectively as possible.

Notwithstanding the simplifying, but nonetheless true, remark made above concerning the importance of other sectors than the ICT one, in our contemporary and "information intensive" societies ICTs have come to constitute the backbone and enabling infrastructure for a number of other sectors.

Many parts of the supply chain for food production and distribution crucially depend on the collection, processing and transmission of information. It is hard to imagine the food supply of a country being able to withstand the breakdown of communication infrastructures or a general, widespread malfunctioning of information processing equipment. Similar remarks can be made for other sectors which are normally identified as critical, such as the energy sector (even more so, given the recent trend towards "smart metering" and the shifts of the sector towards real-time, information-intensive processes, sometimes collectively referred to a the "smart grid"[1]), the financial sector (with ICTs constituting one of the most essential tools for the daily exchanges taking place at the national and international level), the transportation sector, and others.

It is also necessary to recognise that the ICT sector, and therefore CIIs, depends on other sectors for the correct functioning of its most vital functions. Computers and networks need electricity to work; replacement parts must be quickly transported in case of malfunctions; last, not least (and limiting ourselves only to a few sectors)

---

[1] European Technology Platform "SmartGrids", http://www.smartgrids.eu/;
The SuperSmartGrid Project, http://www.supersmartgrid.net/
and The Smart Grid Interoperability Standards Project,
http://www.nist.gov/smartgrid/

human beings which still operate – and, considering the limits of automated technologies,[2] will hopefully continue to operate at least some parts of – CIIs need at least some basic biological needs (e.g. eating) to be catered for.

These mutual dependencies are not merely bidirectional – the ICT sector depends on sector A, B, C, etc, and sectors A, B, C, etc depends each on the ICT sector – but should be rather seen as a complex graph of relationships in which each and every sector depends from and satisfies the dependency of another sector. In simpler terms: to properly function, the food sector needs (at least) the transport, energy and ICT sector to work correctly, but the transport sector crucially depends on the energy and food sector (drivers need to eat at least as much as computer operators, after all) and, although perhaps less so for the time being, on the ICT sector; the energy sector is becoming more and more dependent on the ICT sector and is, for the same biologic reasons outlined just above, may prove to be rather dependent on the food sector – and so on and so forth.

The bottom line is that no sector lives in a vacuum and therefore a "silo approach" to the protection of CIs risks to become counter-productive. On the other hand, modelling, managing and mastering the interdependencies between each and every CIs sector is a daunting task and goes well beyond the space allotted to this chapter, which will focus specifically on the role of the ICT sector and CIIs – keeping in mind that this would be but the first step in a more thorough and holistic understanding of the functional and non-functional requirements for any policy for the protection of CIs. The European Commission has devoted part of its R&D funds to better understand how to model interdependencies between CI sectors, for example via the DIESIS project the goal of which is to establish the basis for a European modelling and simulation e-Infrastructure based upon open standards to foster and support research on all aspects of critical infrastructures with a specific focus on their protection.[3]

1   The Situation in the EU

The EU experience may serve as a useful, although certainly not the only, example of the way in which taxonomy of CIs is constructed, as well as the peculiar role that ICTs play in this context.

In June 2004, following *inter alia* the terrorist attack in Spain, the European Council (composed of the Heads of State and Government of the Member States of the European Union, which highlights the political relevance of the topic) asked for the preparation of an overall strategy to protect critical infrastructures (European

---

[2] The implications of the growing dependence of many sectors on automated processes based on ICTs are a clear example of the complexities we have to face. The recent allegations that algorithmic exchanges were to blame for erratic and/or unexpected behaviours of stock exchanges are a useful reminder of this (Mackenzie 2010).

[3] Design of an Interoperable European federated Simulation network for critical Infrastructures, http://www.diesis-project.eu/

Council 2004). In response, on 20 October 2004, the Commission adopted a Communication on Critical Infrastructure Protection in the Fight against Terrorism (European Commission 2004) which put forward suggestions as to what would enhance European prevention of, preparedness for and response to terrorist attacks involving critical infrastructures. Furthermore, on 17 November 2005, the Commission adopted the above-mentioned Green Paper on a European Programme for Critical Infrastructure Protection (EPCIP) which provided policy options on the establishment of the programme and the Critical Infrastructure Warning Information Network (CIWIN), the specific objective of which is to enable co-ordination and co-operation concerning the information on the protection of critical infrastructure at EU level, as well as to ensure secure and structured exchange of information and thus allow its users to learn about best practices in other EU Member States in a quick and efficient way (CIWIN) (European Commission 2008).

The responses received to the Green Paper emphasised the added value of a Community[4] framework – as opposed to a purely inter-governmental one – concerning CIs protection. The need to increase the European protection capability and to help reduce vulnerabilities concerning critical infrastructures was acknowledged. The importance of the key principles of subsidiarity (implying that efforts would focus on infrastructure that is critical from a European, rather than a national or regional perspective, notwithstanding the possibility for the Commission, where requested and taking due account of its competences, to provide support to Member States concerning National Critical Infrastructures), proportionality (implying that measures would only be proposed where a need has been identified following an analysis of existing security gaps and would be proportionate to the level of risk and type of threat involved) and complementarity (implying that the Commission would avoid duplicating existing efforts, whether at EU, national or regional level, where these have proven to be effective in protecting critical infrastructure, rather complementing and building on existing sectoral measures), as well as of stakeholder dialogue was emphasised (European Commission 2006). In December 2005 the Justice and Home Affairs Council called upon the Commission to make a concrete proposal for EPCIP and decided that it should be based on an all-hazards approach while countering threats from terrorism as a priority. Under this approach, man-made, technological threats and natural disasters should be taken into account in the CI protection process, but the threat of terrorism should be given priority.

On 12 December 2006, the European Commission adopted the "Communication on a European Programme for Critical Infrastructure Protection" (European Commission 2006), which sets out the principles, processes and instruments proposed to implement EPCIP, to be supplemented where relevant by sector specific instruments setting out the Commission's approach concerning particular critical infrastructure sectors.

---

[4] Following the entry into force of the Treaty of Lisbon on 1 December 2009, the term "Community" does not have a legal meaning anymore and should be replaced by the term "Union". The term will nonetheless be used in the document when it is appropriate in its historical context.

The so-called "EPCIP framework" consists of a number of elements, including (1) a proposal for a procedure for the identification and designation of European Critical Infrastructures (ECI), and a common approach to the assessment of the needs to improve the protection of such infrastructures, which would be later implemented by way of Council Directive 2008/114/EC of 8 December 2008 on the identification and designation of European critical infrastructures and the assessment of the need to improve their protection; (2) measures designed to facilitate the implementation of EPCIP, including an Action Plan, the Critical Infrastructure Warning Information Network (CIWIN – see above), the use of CIP expert groups at EU level, CIP information sharing processes and the identification and analysis of interdependencies; (3) support for Member States concerning National Critical Infrastructures which may optionally be used by a particular Member State; (4) accompanying financial measures and in particular the EU programme on "Prevention, Preparedness and Consequence Management of Terrorism and other Security Related Risks".

EPCIP is a sectoral programme: since "various sectors possess particular experience, expertise and requirements" concerning the protection of CIs, "EPCIP will be developed on a sector-by-sector basis and implemented following an agreed list of […] sectors".

2   The Peculiarities of the ICT Sector

The ICT sector is characterised by a high degree complexity both in terms of its relationships with other sectors and, perhaps even more importantly, in terms of the difficulties in understanding what should exactly be "counted in" as a part of the sector and, more specifically, what would constitute a "critical infrastructure" in this sector.

These challenges are clearly visible in Council Directive 2008/114/EC (the "ECI Directive"). The purpose of this Directive is to define a common framework for identifying and designating European Critical Infrastructures, i.e. a critical infrastructure (defined as an asset, system or part thereof located in Member States, which is essential for the maintenance of vital societal functions, health, safety, security, economic or social well-being of people, and the disruption or destruction of which would have a significant impact in a Member State as a result of the failure to maintain those functions) located in a Member State, the disruption or destruction of which would have a significant impact on at least two other Member States. The ECI Directive also states that the significance of the impact shall be assessed in terms of cross-cutting criteria and that such effects include those resulting from cross-sector dependencies on other types of infrastructure.

The Directive is based on an "all hazards" approach – intentional attacks are only one of the potential threats to be considered – and is designed alongside the "sectoral" approach followed in the overall EPCIP programme. The initial proposal by the Commission was based on a list of eleven sectors, namely energy (including the sub-sectors of oil and gas production, refining, treatment, storage and distribution by pipelines; electricity generation and transmission), nuclear industry, ICT (including the sub-sectors of information system and network protection; instrumentation automation and control systems; Internet; provision of fixed telecommunications; provision of mobile telecommunications; radio communication and navigation; satellite communication; broadcasting), water (including the sub-sectors of provision of drinking water; control of water quality; stemming and control of water quantity), food, health (including the sub-sectors of medical and hospital care; medicines, serums, vaccines and pharmaceuticals; bio-laboratories and bio-agents), financial (including the sub-sectors of payment and securities clearing and settlement infrastructures and systems; regulated markets), transport (including the sub-sectors of road transport; rail transport; air transport; inland waterways transport; ocean and short-sea shipping), chemical industry (including the sub-sectors of production and storage/processing of chemical substances; pipelines of dangerous goods), space and research facilities.

However, the final Directive that was adopted by the Council referred only to two sectors, namely transport and energy; notwithstanding a common consensus that the ICT sector is, from many points of view, vital in and by itself and as a support for other sectors, the Directive considers the ICT sector as potentially in the scope when the Directive will be reviewed in 2011. The distance between the overall recognition of the importance of the ICT sector – as visible in other policy initiatives of the EU and of its Member States – and the lack of immediate action in the ECI Directive can be explained by the fact that finding an agreement on what would be the appropriate criteria to identify critical infrastructures in this sector is indeed a major challenge.

On top of this, it is necessary to keep into account that policies related to Critical Information Infrastructure Protection do not live in a vacuum, but should be framed in the context of the policy framework of the European Union in the field of Network and Information Security (European Commission 2006a, Council of the EU 2007). The overarching goal of such framework is to strengthen a dynamic, global strategy in the European Union, based on a culture of security and founded on dialogue, partnership and empowerment, through an inclusive an cooperative approach that would recognise the vital importance of resilience of ICT infrastructures for European economy and society.

3   The Action Plan on Critical Information Infrastructure Protection

It is in this context that, on 30 March 2009, the Commission adopted its Communication on Critical Information Infrastructure Protection – Protecting Europe from large scale cyber-attacks and disruptions: enhancing preparedness, security and resilience (European Commission 2009). The Communication sets forth an action plan until 2011, which constitutes the concrete implementation of the most urgent challenges that the ICT sector needs to address in the context of the European Programme on Critical Infrastructure Protection, as well as the stepping up of the strategic framework for Network and Information Security already proposed in 2006 (European Commission 2006a).

The CIIP action plan is based on the recognition that ICTs are increasingly intertwined in our daily activities and that some of these ICT systems, services, networks and infrastructures (in short, ICT infrastructures) form a vital part of European economy and society, either providing essential goods and services or constituting the underpinning platform of other critical infrastructures. However, the risks due to man-made attacks – which have risen in sophistication and are now often performed for commercial or political reasons – natural disasters or technical failures are often not fully understood and/or sufficiently analysed.

Therefore, the CIIP Communication and action plan should be seen as an attempt to view network and information security, and more specifically the development of a true resilience and preparedness capability throughout the European Union, in a holistic manner. ICT infrastructures – and the resilience thereof – are considered not as "autonomous entities", but as an essential driver and condition for the resilience of society, in all its constituting elements and sectors, as a whole.

The CIIP action plan is complementary to the regulatory approach pursued by the Commission, including via the reform of the regulatory framework for Electronic Communications, which includes new provisions on security and integrity, in particular to strengthen operators' obligations to ensure that appropriate measures are taken to meet identified risks, guarantee the continuity of supply of services and notify security breaches. The proposed actions are also complementary to existing and prospective measures in the area of police and judicial cooperation to prevent, fight and prosecute criminal and terrorist activities targeting ICT infrastructures; they also take into account of international policy developments, such as the G8 principles on CIIP (G8 2003); the UN General Assembly Resolution 58/199 on the creation of a global culture of cybersecurity and the protection of critical information infrastructures and the OECD Recommendation on the Protection of Critical Information Infrastructures.

The Commission, on the basis of extensive consultations with stakeholders and of its own Impact Assessment to the action plan (Europena Commission 2009a) – identifies four major challenges for an efficient and effective protection of Critical Information Infrastructure and an enhanced level of Network and Information Security throughout Europe: the presence of uneven and uncoordinated national approaches, the peculiar governance arrangements that characterise CIIs, a limited early-warning and incident response capability and the need for international cooperation.

First of all, the Commission is of the opinion that although challenges are for the most part common across the EU, measures and regimes to ensure the security and resilience of CIIs, as well as the level of expertise and preparedness, differ across Member States. On the other hand, there is a real risk that different national approaches would produce fragmentation and inefficiency, in particular because of the lack of systematic cross-border cooperation – in the face of interconnectedness of CIIs, which might produce "negative externalities" when vulnerabilities in one Member State can increase risks in other ones. Developing common awareness and understanding of the challenges, adopting shared policy objectives and priorities and reinforcing cooperation are key instruments to overcome this challenge.

Secondly, it is clear that the governance of ICT infrastructures, in particular those that may be categorised as CIIs, poses peculiar challenges. The private sector owns or controls most of these infrastructures, but public authorities have a clear responsibility to prevent large-scale disruptions or act when they take place. Furthermore, markets are not always the best mechanism to provide the necessary level of resilience and security, not least because of the "negative externalities" mentioned above and the lack of market-based incentives for the private sector (Anderson et al 2008). Public-private partnerships (PPPs) have emerged at the national level as a useful governance tool in this area, but the lack of a European approach risks creating similar problems to the ones highlighted above. It is important to note that the concept of PPPs used in this field has a different meaning than the technical term used in the field of EU public procurement (European Commission 2007). The concept of PPPs in the field of network and information security and CIIP can perhaps be better understood with reference to the concept of "co-regulation", understood as "the mechanism whereby a Community legislative act entrusts the attainment of the objectives defined by the legislative authority to parties which are recognised in the field (such as economic operators, the social partners, non-governmental organisations, or associations)" (European Parliament, Council and Commission 2003).

Thirdly, any cooperation or governance mechanism is effective only in the presence of reliable information to act upon. However, as suggested above, policies, processes and practices for monitoring, reporting and sharing of information differ greatly among Member States. Furthermore, the presence of relevant EU-wide – as opposed to bilateral or limitedly multilateral, as is the case today – agreements, it is necessary to assess the practical ability to react to disruptions in a cooperative fashion: in this sense, pan-European exercises would constitute a most useful tool to assess the effective capability of cooperation and address any "weak spot". Last, not least, a European early-warning and incident response capability has to rely on well-functioning National/Governmental Computer Emergency Response Teams (CERTs, also known as Computer Security Incidents Response Teams or CSIRTs): the development of a common baseline of capabilities is an essential precondition for ensuring true cooperation – possibly leveraging existing organisations, such as the European Governmental CERTs Group, an informal group of governmental CSIRTs that is developing effective co-operation on incident response matters between its members, building upon the similarity in constituencies and problem sets between governmental CSIRTs in Europe[5] – among these key entities.

Last, not least, the rise of globally interconnected ICT infrastructures – of which the Internet is perhaps the most widely known, but certainly not the only one, example – raises a challenge in terms of global cooperation. The Internet has proven to be a remarkably robust infrastructure, not least because of its distributed nature and the bottom-up approach to its management, including for what concerns its stability and resilience. Nonetheless, the European Commission believes it is fair to analyse the capability of Internet stakeholders – at a very high level of categorisation: the private sector, public authorities, civil society – to properly and quickly coordinate

---

[5] European Government CERTs group, http://www.egc-group.org/

their reactions in the face of major disruptions, as well as to ensure that continuous technological developments and organisational arrangements, including for what concerns the supply chain of vital components of the Internet infrastructure (e.g. routers), are conducive to maintaining the stability and resilience of this global resource. Furthermore – and perhaps most importantly – the priorities of different stakeholders at the global level differ. While some consider State security of the utmost importance, others developed a particular sensitivity towards fundamental rights such as privacy and freedom of expression. It is clear that policies towards maintaining and enhancing the stability and resilience of the Internet do and will differ accordingly. On the other hand, it is essential to avoid a fragmentation - and the inherent risks that local approaches would entail – of the Internet into many "national internets". Developing a common set of principles and guidelines on how to ensure the stability and resilience of the Internet, based on existing and recognised principles, such as those agreed upon as an output of the World Summit on the Information Society[6] and having them accepted first at the EU level and then by all global stakeholders, but especially by public authorities – which are bound to play an increasing role in all matters related to the Internet – would be, in the opinion of the Commission, a most useful instrument. The European Commission has clearly stated that while continuing to pursue an exclusively 'back-set' approach for public authorities is clearly not an option, this does not mean that they should have any stronger role in managing or controlling the day-to-day operations of the Internet, an activity which has been successfully performed by the private sector (European Commission 2009b). Nonetheless, not all countries necessarily share this view; furthermore, in almost all areas of relevance to the Internet, but especially for what concerns security, stability and resilience, it is sometimes difficult to identify the dividing lines between public and private responsibilities. In this context, globally accepted principles could help.

To address these challenges, the CIIP action plan focuses on five main pillars: preparedness and prevention (to ensure preparedness at all levels), detection and response (to provide adequate early warning mechanisms), mitigation and recovery (to reinforce EU defence mechanisms for CIIs), international cooperation (to promote EU priorities internationally) and criteria for European Critical Infrastructures in the ICT sector (to support the implementation of the Directive on the Identification and Designation of European Critical Infrastructures).

The actions envisaged under the first pillar are developing a baseline of capabilities and services for pan-European cooperation (the Commission invites Member States and concerned stakeholders to define, with the support of the European Network and Information Security Agency – ENISA, a minimum level of capabilities and services for National/Governmental CERTs and incident response operations, as well as to make sure that these CERTs act as the key component of national capability for preparedness, information sharing, coordination and response) and creating a European Public-Private Partnership for Resilience and a European Forum of Member States (see below).

---

[6] World Summit on the Information Society, http://www.itu.int/wsis/

Under the second pillar the Commission supports the development of a European Information Sharing and Alert System (EISAS), based on national and private sector information and alert sharing systems, capable to reach out to citizens and Small/Medium Enterprises.

The actions comprised in the third pillar include the development, by Member States, of national contingency plans and the organisations of regular exercises for large scale networks security incident response and disaster recovery, possibly with the involvement of National/Governmental CERTs; the organisation, with the financial support of the European Commission, of pan-European exercises on Internet security incidents, with a view to participate in international network security incidents exercises, such as the US Cyber Storm exercise; and the reinforcement of cooperation among National/Governmental CERTs, with the active support of ENISA.

For what concerns the fourth pillar, the Commission supports the identification, via a Europe-wide debate, of the European priorities for the long-term resilience and stability of the Internet; the definition of principles and related guidelines, focusing inter alia on regional remedial actions, mutual assistance agreements, coordinated recovery and continuity strategies, geographical distribution of critical Internet resources, technological safeguards in the architecture and protocols of the Internet, replication and diversity of services and data; the international promotion of the European principles identified via this process, with a view to agree on a shared set of principles with third countries, in particular with the strategic partners of the EU; the extension at the global level of the exercises conducted under the "mitigation and recovery" pillar.

Last, not least, the fifth pillar focuses on the development of the criteria for identifying European Critical Infrastructures for the ICT sector, also on the basis of a study funded by the Commission under the Under the Programme "Prevention, Preparedness and Consequence Management of terrorism and other Security Related Risks".

Although reasons of space prevent a thorough presentation of all the actions under these five pillars, it appears nonetheless useful to highlight the role of three key instruments in achieving the goals of the action plan and in general to further the objectives of enhancing the capabilities of the European Union in the field of network and information security, as an essential element to further the protection of vital ICT infrastructures – not only as stand-alone objectives, but as essential elements to support the operations in other critical sectors of European economy and society: the European Public-Private Partnership for Resilience (EP3R), the European Forum of Member States (EFMS) and the European Network and Information Security Agency (ENISA).

EP3R aims to provide a flexible European-wide governance framework to involve relevant public and private stakeholders in public policy and strategic decision making discussions to strengthen the security and resilience of CIIs in Europe. EP3R focuses on prevention and preparedness matters with a European dimension and in view of a global outreach. More specifically, EP3R aims to provide a platform for information sharing and stock taking of good policy and industrial practices in order to foster a common understanding on the economic and market dimensions of security and resilience of CIIs as well as on the roles and responsibilities of public and private stakeholders; discuss public policy priorities, objectives and measures with a view to define framework conditions and socio-economic incentives to improve the coherence and coordination of policies for security and resilience of CIIs in Europe; identify and promote the adoption of good baseline practices for the security and resilience of CIIs, with a view to pursue minimum security and resilience standards and coordinated risk assessment approaches. Considering that enhancing security and resilience of CIIs is a joint responsibility which is shared among a multiplicity of public and private stakeholders, the success of EP3R would depend decisively on the active participation and strong commitment of all relevant stakeholders. A bottom-up approach, seeking the active contribution of all relevant stakeholders and building upon national initiatives, seems to be the best way to ensure EP3R would be designed and then operated to address the actual needs of the EU public and private stakeholders. Besides being proposed in the CIIP Action Plan, the idea of creating a European Public-Private Partnership in the area of resilience was also supported by the Council Resolution on "a collaborative European approach to network and information security" of 18 December 2009. The Council recognises "the importance of multi-stakeholder models such as Public Private Partnerships (PPPs), built on a long term, bottom-up model", and if further invites the Commission to "encourage and improve multi-stakeholder models, which need to have a clear added value benefiting end-users and industry".

The EFMS has a similar high-level objective – to support a cooperative approach to the challenges under examination – but its membership is restricted to national public authorities, in order to allow for a more direct exchange of information and good public policy practices and to reinforce the cooperation between Member States, integrating national policies in a more European and global dimension. The scope of the discussions in the EFMS is obviously up to its members, but so far a number of topics – the criteria to identify and designate European Critical Infrastructures in the ICT sector, the principles for Internet resilience and stability and the organisation of pan-European exercises – have been chosen as key elements of discussion.

ENISA – a regulatory agency of the European Union – was founded in 2004 to enhance the capacity of the Union, the Member States and the business community to prevent, address and respond to major network and information security risks. The Agency focuses on fostering the dialogue between stakeholders to facilitate exchanges of good practices on an operational level and to pro-actively engage stakeholders to play their role in improving network and information security. In the context of the CIIP action plan, ENISA has been a key tool to support the development of pan-European exercises, enhance the level of collaboration among CERTs and provide expertise for stakeholders in the context of their exchanges via EP3R and the EFMS.

4   Conclusions: A Digital Agenda for Europe

It is clear that summarising in a few pages the approach of the European Union towards Critical Information Infrastructures is a daunting task. This contribution tried, and hopefully succeeded, to summarise the main elements of this complex picture. In order to give the proper context, it focused extensively on the past – it seems therefore fit to conclude by pointing out that ensuring the protection of Critical Information Infrastructures and, more generally, the strengthening of the resilience of ICT infrastructures and of European society as a whole, is anything but a closed chapter. As someone said, it is very difficult to predict anything, but especially the future: nonetheless, as our society becomes more and more digital – and therefore our economy and social relationships become more and more dependent on information and communication technologies – we must step up our efforts to develop trust in all stakeholders, leaving no-one behind. This goal is clearly visible in the most recent (at the time of writing) policy initiative of the European Commission in the ICT field, its "Digital Agenda for Europe" (European Commission 2010), itself one of the flagship initiatives of the "Europe 2020" strategy (European Commission 2010b). Trust and security play a central role in achieving all the objectives that the Commission has put on the table for the next ten years. The protection of Critical Information Infrastructures will undoubtedly continue to be a vital object of theoretical discussion, policy development and operational practice.

References

Anderson, R., Bohme, R., Clayton, R., Moore, T.: Security, Economics and the Internal Market, Report to the European Network and Information Security Agency, ENISA (2008)

Council of the EU, Resolution on a Strategy for a Secure Information Society in Europe, 2007/C 68/01 (2007)

European Commission, Communication from the Commission on Critical Infrastructure Protection in the fight against terrorism, COM(2004) 702 final (2004)

European Commission, Green Paper on a European Programme for Critical Infrastructure Protection, COM(2005) 576 final (2005)

European Commission, Communication from the Commission on a European Programme for Critical Infrastructure Protection, COM(2006) 786 final (2006)

European Commission, Communication on A strategy for a secure information society: dialogue, partnership and empowerment, COM(2006) 251 final (2006a)

European Commission, Communication on the application of Community law on Public Procurement and Concessions to Institutionalised Public-Private Partnerships, C(2007) 6661 (2007)

European Commission, Commission staff working document - Accompanying document to the proposal for a Council decision on creating a Critical Infrastructure Warning Information Network (CIWIN), SEC(2008) 2701 (2008)

European Commission, Communication on Critical Information Infrastructure Protection – Protecting Europe from large scale cyber-attacks and disruptions: enhancing preparedness, security and resilience, COM(2009) 149 (2009)

European Commission, Impact Assessment of the Commission Communication on Critical Information Infrastructure Protection, SEC(2009) 399 (2009a)

European Commission, Communication on Internet Governance: the next steps, COM(2009) 277 (2009b)

Europenan Commission, Communication on a Digital Agenda for Europe, COM(2010) 245 (2010)

European Commission, Communication on a Strategy for smart, sustainable and inclusive growth, COM(2010) 2020 (2010b)

European Parliament, Council and Commission, Interinstitutional Agreement between the European Parliament, Council and Commission on Better Law-Making, 2003/C 321/01 (2003)

G8 Principles for Protecting Critical Information Infrastructure. In: G8 Justice and Interior Ministers Meeting, Paris (2003)

Mackenzie, M.: Vital lessons of the 'flash crash'. Financial Times online (2010)

OECD Recommendation of the Council on the protection of Critical Information Infrastructures. In: OECD Ministerial Meeting on the Future of the Internet Economy, Seoul, Korea, (2008); Organization for Economic Co-operation and Development, http://www.oecd.org/dataoecd/1/13/40825404.pdf

Presidency Conclusions of the Council of the European Union, 10679/2/04 REV 2, pp. 4 (2004)

Understanding Cyber Threats and Vulnerabilities

Eric Luiijf

Netherlands Organisation for Applied Scientific Research TNO
P.O. Box 96864, 2509 JG The Hague, The Netherlands
eric.luiijf@tno.nl

Abstract. This chapter reviews current and anticipated cyber-related threats to the Critical Information Infrastructure (CII) and Critical Infrastructures (CI). The potential impact of cyber-terrorism to CII and CI has been coined many times since the term was first coined during the 1980s. Being the relevance to consider possible threats and their impact, this paper provides a systematic treatment of actors, tools and potential effects. Some future risk to the CII is discussed as well.

Keywords: actor, cyber crime, cyber terrorism, cyber threat, cyber vulnerabilities, critical infrastructure

1 Introduction

The disruption or destruction of certain infrastructures such as energy supply, drinking water supply, telecommunication and various modes of transport may have a serious impact on the health, safety, security or economic well-being of citizens or the effective functioning of governments. Such infrastructures are therefore denoted as Critical Infrastructures (CI).

The functioning of critical processes in most CI increasingly depends on information and communication technologies (ICT). Therefore, the undisturbed functioning of CI depends on the security of information assets, hardware, software, information-based processes, and internal and external communication networks and links. These assets include process control systems and networks which monitor and control physical processes of CI. The notion Critical Information Infrastructure (CII) is used to pinpoint this critical part of 'cyber space': the cross-sector set of ICT assets that has a critical meaning to society. From the above, it will be obvious that a disturbance or a disruption of the CII may seriously affect society, may have a significant impact on a national economy, and may affect the trust of citizens in ICT services at large.

In this chapter a systematic taxonomy of threats, attack actors and their motives is proposed with a specific reference to CII. The aim is to provide a common vocabulary for this complex and multi-disciplinary framework.

2 Definitions

The following definitions will be used in the remainder of this chapter.

J. Lopez et al. (Eds.): Critical Information Infrastructure Protection, LNCS 7130, pp. 52–67, 2012.

Critical Infrastructure (CI) is defined as an asset, system or part thereof located in a nation which is essential for the maintenance of vital societal functions, health, safety, security, economic or social well-being of people, and the disruption or destruction of which would have a significant impact in that nation as a result of the failure to maintain those functions. [1]

Critical Information Infrastructure (CII) is defined as those interconnected information systems and networks, the disruption or destruction of which would have a serious impact on the health, safety, security, or economic well-being of citizens, or on the effective functioning of government or the economy. [2]

At a first glance, this definition seems to point at critical computer servers and services and large-scale networks such as the public telephone network, the Internet, and terrestrial and satellite links. This definition, however, encompasses all ICT that monitor, control or interact with other CI and our physical world: process control systems, ATMs and e-payment systems, logistic transponder infrastructures, cars communicating with each other and/or the road, systems for remote surgery, etceteras.

Cyber is a prefix to other terms. It refers to the automation and information processing domain. The Greek word kybernetes (steersman; governor) is the root of the word cyber. In 1948, the term cyber was connected to the automation and information processing domain when Wiener used the term cybernetics in the title of his book on control and communication. [3]

Cyber Crime. There does not exist an internationally accepted definition for cyber crime. An obvious source would be the Convention on Cybercrime [4] by the Council of Europe, as this treaty has been signed, and ratified by many nations in Europe and abroad. The treaty intends to harmonize how nations deal with cross-border cyber-related offenses. Interestingly, the treaty pre-amble and articles often refer to cyber-crime without defining it.

The EU has defined in [5] the interchangeable terms *cyber crime*, *computer crime*, and *high-tech crime* as criminal acts committed using electronic communications networks and information systems or against such networks and systems. Three categories of criminal activities are recognised by [5]: (1) traditional forms of crime such as fraud or forgery using electronic communication networks and information systems; (2) the publication of illegal content over electronic media (i.e., child sexual abuse material or incitement to racial hatred); and (3) crimes unique to electronic networks, i.e. attacks against information systems, denial of service and hacking. These types of attacks can also be directed against the CI in Europe in many areas, with potentially disastrous consequences for the whole society. Common to each category of ICT-related crime is that they may be committed on a mass-scale and with a great geographical distance between the criminal act and its effects.

Recently, [6] defined cyber crime as the use of cyberspace for criminal purposes as defined by national and international law. Below we will use this definition as it more clearly encompasses cyber crimes which have effects on the physical world, e.g. a deliberate shut down of a refinery by hacking into the process control systems.

Cyber Activism (also known as hacktivism), is the deliberate act or threat with illegal actions - either by a single person or in conspiracy - against the integrity, confidentiality and/or availability of information, and of information processing systems and networks - with the intent to influence the societal and political mindset on a specific cause or issue.

Cyber Espionage. Cyber or electronic espionage is the intentional use of information processing systems and networks activities in an effort to gain access to sensitive information about an adversary or competitor for the purpose of gaining an advantage or selling the sensitive information for monetary reward. [7]

Cyber Operations are actions taken to achieve a goal by influencing and controlling the information, computer processes and information systems of an adversary, while protecting one's own information, computer processes and information systems. [8]

Cyber Sabotage (also known as cybotage) is the act of deliberately hampering, deliberating subverting, or destroying the integrity, confidentiality and/or availability of information, information processing systems and networks, or the physical processes controlled by such systems.

Cyberspace is defined by [6] as an electronic medium through which information is created, transmitted, received, stored, processed, and deleted. According to [8], cyberspace is a digital world, generated by computers and computer networks, in which people and computers coexist and which includes all aspects of online activity. The understanding of cyberspace in this chapter comprises the 'whole digital world' which extends both definitions above with the digital worlds of non-internet connected systems and networks, traditional telephony systems, embedded processors, EMV-chips etceteras.

Cyber Terror. Until now, no attacks on information assets which can be qualified as cyber terror have been seen. Nevertheless, literature and press discuss the threat and potential impact of cyber terrorism at large since the mid of the eighties. Many definitions have been coined from a lot of different angles by for instance information operation experts, terrorism fighters, information security experts, CI protection professionals, lawyers, and the popular press. These definitions diverge largely as they are specifically focused based on the field of expertise [6, 9, 10, 11, 12, and 13]. In the remainder of this chapter we will use the definition derived from [14]:

Cyber terror is the deliberate act or threat with illegal actions - either by a single person or in conspiracy - against the integrity, confidentiality and/or availability of information, and of information processing systems and networks - leading to one or more of the following consequences:

— suffering, serious injuries, or death of people,
— serious psychological effects to people and the population,
— serious, societal disruptive economic loss,
— serious breach of ecological safety,
— serious breach of the social and political stability and cohesion,

with the intent:
- to cause changes to the societal *structure*, and/or
- to influence political decisions of a nation.

3   Threats

Threats may potentially disrupt the normal operation of ICT and ICT-monitored and controlled processes in a number of ways on the one hand, and disrupt the trust of people in ICT and information on the other hand. In this section we will explore the threats that may cause the disturbance or even the destruction of CII. Before doing so, one should realise that popular press and literature often confuses a threat - the expressed potential for the occurrence of a harmful event - with intent. Examples are terms like terror threat and sabotage. The European VITA project created an extensible threat taxonomy with a large set of threats to CI. The VITA approach made a clear distinction between threat and intent [15]. The reason is that the same threat - vulnerability combination that disrupts CI may either be triggered or 'exploited' by nature, unintentionally by a human, or deliberately by a malicious actor.

For the purpose of this book, only a subset of the over 320 threats to CI identified by the VITA project is relevant. Nevertheless, the list of threats that may have serious effects upon CII is still large. For that reason, we will cluster them. This is less easy than it seems as there are a number of ways to do this, each having its pros and cons. For instance, one may distinguish (1) threats to the operational environment of ICT, and (2) ICT-specific threats that affect CII (and CI). The first category comprises a large range of threats such natural threats, technical threats, human error, organisational issues, and deliberate external physical threats. The second category includes for instance malware, denial-of-service attack, hacking, and electro-magnetic disturbance such as jamming.

Another way is to look at the set of threats from the viewpoint of CII disruption effects. That is an approach well-known to information security experts. They try to manage the ICT-risk for the organisation by balancing the protection of the three so-called CIA-aspects: confidentiality, integrity, and availability. Note that availability is a less straightforward concept than the word suggests. ICT availability spans the notions of existence (e.g., physical connectivity), functional service (e.g., sent bytes reach the destination), and quality (e.g., meeting an expected performance or service level). Moreover, at societal level, ICT-related CII disruptions are often classified by society as the failure to secure one or more of the confidentiality, integrity and availability (CIA)-aspects resulting in a major impact: loss of service, loss of privacy, loss of trust in ICT-services, and loss of trust in ICT at large.

In the next section we will use the cluster threats according to the first approach and point at the CIA-aspects where appropriate.

3.1   Threats to the CII Environment

Nature. Nature may disrupt the availability of ICT in several ways. A large subset of threats from [15] have the potential to affect the structural integrity of equipment enclosures, communication lines, and large set of end-user locations [16]: earth quake, land slide, mud stream, various forms of strong wind (storm, hurricane, typhoon, cyclone), water (flooding, piling up of snow, black ice), electromagnetic impact (lightning, geo-magnetically induced current (GIC)), and natural fire (e.g., bush fire, forest fire).

Another threat subset is nature which becomes in conflict with human built infrastructures and equipment: growing tree roots that cause communication lines or pipelines to break, trees that topple, and a large set of animals that 'attack' ICT equipment and cables. A large set of animals that crawl, gnaw, drill holes, seek a hiding place in an equipment box for making love, etceteras, have seriously disrupted the functioning of CII in the past and will do that in future. Just some examples: ants, bald eagles, bats, cows, frogs, geese, possums, rodents, sharks, snakes, storks, and woodpeckers [17].

Considering these natural threats, major regional differences in frequency of occurrence of these threats are found across the world. Apart from the regional susceptibility for certain natural phenomena like hail, hurricane and Derecho storm alleys and geological fault areas, major differences in the impact of a CII disruption stem from technical design (e.g., overhead cables versus ones buried in soil), the level of preparedness to recover from disasters, and redundancy measures taken to protect the continuity of CII services.

Technical Threats. A set of technical threats may affect the environment of major CII nodes and links, e.g., wear and tear, mechanical failure, non-natural fire. Examples are a broken water main which downed a critical telecommunication node [18], and a tunnel fire affecting internet services globally [19].

External Human Activities. Human activities in the near environment of critical ICT nodes and (cable) links may unintentionally or intentionally disrupt CII. A major subset of these threats is disruption of communication links due to mechanical force. Daily, construction workers unintentionally cut fibre and copper cables which are part of the CII with backhoes and sheet piling equipment. Lorries and cars collide with telecommunication poles and bring the lines down. Anchors and trawl gears cut critical submarine cables. Although ring-architectures and rerouting provide measures to mitigate this type of threat, the alternate transport routes may fail as well causing the disruption CII services [20].

Deliberate threats to the CII premises and links involve the arson and bomb threats, theft of (copper) lines and equipment, the deliberate use of force to create damage including bird and pistol shots at communication lines [21, 22], and the external sabotage of the air-conditioning of a CII node by hacking.

Neighbours. Activities by neighbour organisations may lead to the risk of collateral damage of the CII node or the inaccessibility of the node because of threats to the neighbour. This set of threats includes dangerous activities which may lead to evacuation of the neighbourhood and the CII node in case of an incident: biological toxic and chemical spills, high explosive and fire risk. Business activities of a neighbouring organisation may cause activists to intimidate the organisation by arranging blockades and issuing bomb threats which may disrupt the free accessibility of the CII node for maintenance and repair. Note that the perpetrators may not intend to cause any CII disrupting consequences at all.

3.2   Internal Human Threats to CII Operations

The continuity of CII operations may be seriously disturbed by threats that cause operators and engineers not performing their job in a proper way to safeguard the continuity of CII. External threats include strikes and other types of labour unrest as well as civil disorder which cause operators and engineers not being able to reach critical CII nodes like control rooms or switching nodes.

Internal organisational threats comprise insufficient training of CII operators and engineers, human error, lack of awareness about organisational, physical, cyber, electromagnetical, and personnel security, human neglect, lack of critically needed supplies.

A wide range of physical and operational threats can be used by disgruntled employees, employees with a psychological problem, and intruders to harm the undisturbed CII operation: cut cables, flood or smash equipment, unauthorised changing of parameters.

3.3   CI Dependency Threats to the Functioning of CII

The undisturbed functioning of CII highly depends on the availability of electric power, either by the direct supply of electrical power or by backup power. Proper cooling is often critical as well. The functioning of certain CII, such as the monitoring and control of energy systems, mobile communications, and internet routing depend on precise time which is often provided by the GPS time signal.

Non-normal of operation of CII, such as when a critical CI supply fails, a disaster situation, or during recovery may cause the CII to be critically dependent on other CI as under normal operational circumstances. For instance various transport modalities to move maintenance engineers and spare parts to critical nodes.

A large range of the aforementioned natural, technical, and human threats may affect the critical supply of these CI services to the CII. Especially a common mode failure affecting multiple CII and CI services at the same time may cause serious effects. Business continuity management across organisations and CI covering the whole supply chain of critical services is supposed to deliver a solution to this complex threat but is still in its infancy. One example of an end-to-end service that has to be provided by a number of competing CI operators with a high service quality is telephony. Mobile, plain old telephony service (POTS), CATV and voice-over-IP services connect end users from pole to pole, from East to West around the globe spanning a large number of operators and nations. The service level challenges are high and provide an increasing number of challenges as outlined by the ARECI report [23].

4   ICT-Specific Threats

As explained above, we decouple the threats from actors and their intent. Therefore, ICT-specific threats can be split into threats related to information-assets, hardware, basic software, applications and application level data, CII services, and authorised users.

Information Assets. The integrity, availability and confidentiality of information assets including software in the CII may be threatened by human error, configuration failure, failing applications, malware, and unauthorised access.

Hardware. The availability of critical hardware such as cables, processors, switches, routers, transmission equipment in the CII may be affected by hardware failure of power supply, chips, boards, and connectors; temperature and humidity problems (overheating, condensation, static discharge); and firmware errors.

The integrity of hardware components in critical CII elements such as network equipment is increasingly affected by counterfeit products which potentially may provide backdoors to unauthorised third parties and may fail under exceptional circumstances due to incompatibility issues [24]. CII hardware may be affected by electromagnetic pulses from e.g. a high-performance microwave inducing hardware defects or indeterminate hardware state changes leading to processor hangs. On the other hand, critical components in the CII may leak confidential and sensitive data via the electromagnetic spectrum.

Basic Software. The correct functioning of basic software such as operating system and protocol suites in key end-user systems, servers, software libraries, network components and process control systems is essential for the undisturbed functioning of the CII. Software design and implementation errors as well as configuration errors may give hackers and malware a path to unauthorised access to the CII and allow the breach of confidentiality, integrity and availability of CII components and information assets. Examples are the Zotob and Sasser worms. A targeted piece of malware was the Stuxnet worm which was crafted to attack process control systems in Iran's uranium enrichment installation at Natanz [25].

Applications. Certain CII, such as the CII provided by the financial and government sectors, provide application services which undisturbed availability, integrity and confidentiality are key to maintain the trust of the population in ICT-services. Failing integrity and confidentiality threaten the privacy of people and the trust in the institution or CI sector.

Software design and implementation errors as well as configuration errors may give hackers and targeted malware (e.g., phishing) unauthorised access to application level data. This allows theft and/or publication of confidential and sensitive data, unauthorised skimming of financial accounts, the provision of disinformation to the population or groups of customers, etceteras.

CII Services. The performance of CII services may deliberately be threatened by an overload of the available capacity of servers, applications, network components and links. Threats are denial-of-service (DoS) software, distributed denial-of-service (DDoS) attack means such as botnets which include a set of zombies - hijacked systems which often unknown to its owner take part in the botnet -, and a protocol error which unintentionally [26] or deliberately may result in a self replication of protocol requests causing overloading.

Increasingly, extortion of ICT service providers take place where cyber criminals shortly demonstrate their ability to disrupt the services. They extort the operator by threatening to disrupt the services for a long period of time. Such extortions in the U.K. alone may sum up to 0.5 to 2.7 billion Pounds per annum [27].

Communication links and protocols of the CII may be affected by electromagnetic threats such as jamming which is a denial-of-service attack to the frequency spectrum of communication links (including GPS time and location data).

Authorised Users. Authorised users of the CII may foremost affect the confidentiality and integrity of the CII, as well as its availability. The human factor threats comprise unintentional breaches of security: unsuspicious use of infected information media, giving away CII access information (social engineering), human sloppiness, human error. Deliberate data leakage may affect the trust in the protection of confidential and sensitive data in the CII. Recently, the Wikileaks' leaked sets of financial and government data prominently impact the trust in CI systems and organisational structures.

5   Actors

A wide spectrum of actors may threaten the undisturbed functioning of the CII. We recognise individuals, activists, criminals, terrorists, cyber spies, non-state and state actors.

5.1   Individuals

Individuals may have different reasons to cause an unintentional or deliberate disturbance of CII. First of all, individual insiders comprise disgruntled employees, employees with psychological problems, and employees that disagree with decisions of top-management. Examples of individual actions affecting CII are disconnecting safety circuits, cutting cables, setting a computer centre on fire, placing time bombs in software, manipulation of election results, and manipulation of normal operations of a sewage system. Under the outsiders belong script-kiddies using 'cyber knife' software without real understanding its functioning and individual hackers.

5.2   Activists

Activist groups which threat the operation of CII span a range of objectives and therefore intent in the way they want to affect the CII. A first group one can recognise are cyber volunteers ('hacktivists') supporting non-state and state actors during in a political conflict. Examples are the groups of hackers and DDoS attackers from both the People's Republic of China and the USA which showed their anger after the Hainan Island incident in 2001, and groups like the Young Intelligent Hackers Against Terror (YIHAT) mapping and attacking the CII in 'rogue states'. Another, almost spontaneous, set of attacks was raised by 'cyber volunteers' to various financial institutions and government services in multiple nations as protest to blocking bank accounts and the search by authorities for Julian Assange (Wikileaks) early 2011.

Some more organised activist groups which only want to show their protest in a non-destructive way may block certain CII services only for a short period of time (e.g., the Electronic Disturbance Theater protest in support of the Zapatista movement) using (D)DoS instruments only. Such activists which purely use cyber means are often called cyber activists. Other, more radicalized activist groups used both physical means and ICT-means to disrupt CII, e.g. as part of the protests against the World Economic Forum (WEF).

5.3   Criminals

One can distinguish crimes performed by individuals. They often use the cyber domain for 'old crimes' as swindling. An example is selling cheap goods via eBay and not delivering them. As long as mitigating measures reduce the risk to individual citizens such that it does not exceed a certain level, the trust in ICT for performing trade and business is not affected. Therefore it will not affect the trust in the CII.

Organised cyber crime, however, tries to move large sums from individual bank accounts of citizens and organisations as well as other valuables like for instance CO_2 certificates from companies to their own accounts by using a large range of innovative malware means (phishing, Trojans). A major high-tech crime industry and a black market supports the high-tech criminal organisations. Again, as long as the risk stays manageable and losses are largely covered by sector guarantees, the trust in ICT and thus the CII is not affected.

Apart from direct money, organised crime offers botnets for hire. Other criminals, non-state (but may be related to state) actors and cyber activists can hire such networks for performing DDoS attacks targeting CII, for spreading Trojans and spam messages, etcetera. For example, the Bredolab botnet had 143 control servers which could direct over 30 million computers in the world to perform DDoS and phishing attacks. At the end of 2009, some 3.6 billion emails were sent daily to unsuspecting computer users trying to infect them with an estimated success rate of three million computers a month. The cost for renting the 143 control servers amounted 20.000 euro a month. The estimated revenue for the Armenian criminal was factors higher until the police downed the network and captured him.

5.4   Terrorists

The only confirmed terror attacks to CII seen up worldwide until now is the use of physical bombs and Molotov cocktails to target telecommunication towers and premises, e.g. in Bhutan, Greece, Iceland, Philippines, and Tibet.

No cyber terror has been noticed (see definition above) until now despite the large set of news reports and scientific papers about cyber terror. Confirmed, however, is the increasing use of the CII by activist and terrorist groups as a tool for the communication, logistics, propaganda, recruitment, fund raising, and spreading of techniques about weapons and tactics [28]. At this moment, more and more nations regard cyber terror affecting their CII and CI a clear and present danger. They have started to develop operational capabilities to defend against a cyber terror attack and the potential threat posed by activist groups when they radicalise [29, 30]. When looking at CII from the perspective of a terror group, CII can be targeted, used as means in combination with a physical attack, and as a weapon affecting the functioning of CI and society. An example of a CII as target is unauthorised changes of hospital records that cause the loss of trust in the database. An example of a CII as a mean is feeding false information either to spread the fear of an imminent terror attack, or as force multiplier to a physical attack by, e.g., a DDoS-attack on information and emergency services. And last, but not least, CII may be used as a cyber attack means to cause disruption of CI and therefore society.

Table 1 shows the potential effects of cyber terror on casualty, economy, ecology, psychological well-being of the population, and the social and political stability of a nation. The main effects are denoted with an X; weaker effects are marked with a *.

Table 1. CII as terroristic target, means and weapon versus the intended effects

	Casualty	Economy	Ecology	Psychological effects	Social and political stability
CII as terroristic target					
- integrity of CII	*	X		X	
- confidentiality/privacy		*		*	*
- availability of CII		X		*	
- electromagnetic attack		X		*	
- physical attack to CII		X		*	
CII as terroristic mean					
- cause wrong decisions	X	*	X	*	*
- as force multiplier	*	*		X	*
CII as weapon for terrorism	X	X	X	X	

5.5   Cyber Espionage ('e-Spionage')

Increasingly, the CII of governments, multinationals and CI operators are under cyber espionage attack by foreign state actors and vague, possibly non-state but state-related actors. Large amounts of strategic, intellectual property (IP), and other information have been extracted from government, multinational operators and CI operator information assets. At the same time, a number of CI operators have noticed intrusion and network mapping attempts making them scared about unauthorised intrusion and disruption of the functioning of CII and CI during a major multi-national conflict. Examples of such CII intrusions are Moonlight Maze, Gh0stNet, Operation Aurora also known as the Trojan Hydraq attack, and Night Dragon. In the UK alone, an estimated value of 9.2 billion Pound per annum is lost by intellectual property theft [27], one third of the total cost of cyber crime in the nation.

5.6   Non-state and State Actors

States may perform Cyber Operations against other states and their CII. As attribution of attacks can be hidden, non-state – probably state-funded – actors may target the CII of an adversary for them probably helped by cyber volunteers who may add fog to such an attack. These actors may use both cyber and traditional espionage means to map network assets and create intrusion paths. A number of nations are known to have cyber operation units as part of their military, for example China, Germany, Israel, Russia, South Korea, Taiwan, and the United States (Cyber Command). The first glimpses of 'cyber warfare' have been seen during the 2008 Georgian–Ossetian conflict.

In 2010, a cybotage attack aimed at specific nuclear installations in Iran was worldwide headline news for weeks in the press. The Stuxnet worm is a carefully crafted attack mechanism affecting very specific process control systems. According to anti-virus specialists, the development of Stuxnet required a group of cyber specialists, some traditional human espionage assets, a long time for planning and code development, and a test bed with the process control equipment. The estimated development cost pinpoints to a state actor; some news sources even point to the Israeli Unit 8200 under the lead of General Ashkenazi. [25]

6   CII Attack Means

CII attack means may be used by an actor to cause a certain threat to become reality by exploiting a vulnerability in the defences of one or more CII. Attack means may target the CII environment, the CII hardware, software, and services, the CII operators, and the end-users. As shown above, attackers may use a large range of physical destruction means which cause mechanical force, kinetic force, fire damages, electromagnetic effects as Direct Energy Weapons (DEW), etceteras, to affect CII housing, CII nodes, links and equipment.

Attacks means to disrupt CII software comprise the use of knowledge about software or protocol vulnerabilities (such a 'zero days'), toolkits with Swiss knife sets of exploit code, malware and Trojans which exploit a specific (sub)set of vulnerabilities, targeted malware (e.g., Stuxnet), scanning software looking for vulnerabilities, using software backdoors purposely entered during coding by criminals or by manufacturers, etceteras.

Attack means to disrupt CII services comprise the use of botnets for DDoS attacks, exploitation of protocol weaknesses, electromagnetic jamming equipment, high-performance microwave equipment for affecting the availability of CII.

Attack means to breach the confidentiality of information assets in CII include malware, hacking tools, bribing and other ways to make use of insiders, listening in on electromagnetic emissions including war driving and war flying near CII nodes.

Attack to CII operations include the unauthorised use of backdoors such as not well secured modem entrances to the network, social engineering to elevate access for the intruder, and the unauthorised installation and use of stealthily hidden modems, and the hiding of configuration data [31].

Large-scale attacks on end-users to cause loss of trust in specific CII services such as offered by financial institutions or government agencies include crafted emails luring the end user to click a link with malware installation or stealthily redirected communications, phishing and ransomware attacks as a result.

7   Tomorrow Museum

The use of ICT in all kinds of new applications being part of the CII increase day by day. In the past as well as currently, a large number of organisational reasons have caused security to be added afterwards to CII when the vulnerability to natural phenomena, unintentional caused disruptions, and deliberate attacks have shown weaknesses that were beyond control and accepted (business) risk levels.

After the vulnerabilities of mainframes; later PCs and network components such as routers, the need to security such CII elements has become to the foreground in organisations. Since a number of years, it becomes clear that the same organisational disinterest found in the eighties to the security of mainframes, and in the nineteenths to the security of telecommunication switches, can be seen in the process control domain. Process control engineers are educated in safety and optimisation of (often CI) processes they monitor and control on a 24/7 basis; not in cyber security. The ICT department knows all about the security of internet access, servers and office networks but neglect process automation as that is "not ICT but just some electro-mechanical stuff pumps, valves, motors switches". History repeats itself. Major efforts in education of control engineers, system developers and manufacturers; the addition of security tools to process control networks; etceteras are currently on-going in a select set of nations which have noticed the vulnerability of the process control systems in their CII which monitors and controls most of their CI and important industrial processes. [32]

As said, history repeats itself. Unfortunately this is still true for the design and development phases of the next ICT waves. Insufficient security by design as part of new ICT give way to cyber activists, cyber criminals, cyber terror and state actors. In the 'Tomorrow Museum' we envision major cyber attack waves to new ICT developments by the whole range of actors mentioned above.

An example of such ICT developments is smart grids, the intelligent merger of energy grids and ICT. Smart grids promise to bring a lot of benefits to the users, the energy providers, the environment, and the economy. Smart grids range from intelligent appliances, e.g. dish washers, at home, via smart meters, to smart local grids, to FACTS-devices in transmission networks. A small cyber vulnerability may be exploited causing instability of the power grid, and distrust of hundreds if not millions of customers.

Another example is the set of on-going ICT-based innovations in the automotive industry. A current car or truck has between 30 to 100 intelligent processors which monitor and control engine performance parameters, airbags, brakes, traction, tyre pressure, the speedometer display, and so on. A closed system and secure? Car manufacturers already have called back cars to the garage to patch the car's software. Attacking these processors with malware injected via the wireless tyre pressure monitoring interface (TPMS), the radio and other interfaces has already been demonstrated [33].

By 2015, all new cars in Europe will be fitted with ecall which causes the car to call 1-1-2 in case the car is involved in a major car crash. Of course, such a wireless interface will be used for other services which may include hacker and malware 'access services'. Currently, no car manufacturer or car dealer educates its engineers in cyber security. They just connect their laptop to your car as soon as the car hood is opened … Scenarios like exploding air bags in MPVs of brand X when the car speed is above 80 km/h, the outside temperature is 0 C/32 F, the clock is between 16:30 and 18:30, it is darkening (light sensor) and raining (rain detector) then may become reality. Apart form the set of collisions at highways and major traffic jams, a major distrust in the MPVs of car brand X will be the result as well as a distrust in the in-car ICT developments.

New automotive industry innovations cause cars, buses and trucks to mutually exchange information about their speed, distance, etceteras. At the same time they acquire information from the road infrastructure about road surface temperature, the current speed limit, and so on. As such ICT-innovations focus on functionality and less on cyber security and resilience, such new innovations will likely be exploited by actors in future.

The development towards ubiquitous ICT services in the life of all citizens increases the need for protection and resilience of those ICT means as well as the CII which stores, processes and transports the critical information for those services. As our 'tomorrow museum' predicts, these new ICT services and inventions will be pushed to the market without proper cyber security resulting in cyber incidents with high consequences to life, ecology, economy, and distrust in ICT.

It is not only the technological innovation which brings new threats and vulnerabilities. It are also the operators and users as the ease of use often wins from a secure way of operations and use. As an example, despite security concerns in politics and press about cyber attacks, CII operators are known to monitor and control CI such as drinking water plants and sewage systems using their mobile phone.

8   Conclusions

This chapter covered the cyber threat to CII and CI. Both threats and actors have been discussed at length, as well as means attackers may use to disturb or destroy CII. The Tomorrow Museum section should have given you a head-ups on currently unmanaged CII risk which requires mitigation and control soon.

References

1. EC: Council Directive 2008/114/EC, of 8 December 2008 on the identification and designation of European critical infrastructures and the assessment of the need to improve their protection, EC, Brussels, Belgium (2008)
2. ENISA Glossary,
   http://www.enisa.europa.eu/act/res/files/glossary
3. Wiener, N.: Cybernetics or Control and Communication in the Animal and the Machine. The Technology Press John Wiley & Sons, Inc., New York (1948)
4. Council of Europe, Convention on Cyber-crime, CETS No.: 185, Budapest (November 23, 2001), http://conventions.coe.int (last visited May 08, 2011) Note: the CETS No.: 290 has changed the title into 'Convention on Cybercrime'
5. EC, Towards a general policy on the fight against cyber crime , Communications from the Commission to the European Parliament, the Council and the Committee of the Regions, COM(2007) 267 final, Brussels, Belgium (2007),
   http://eurlex.europa.eu/LexUriServ/LexUriServ.do?uri=COM:200
   7:0267:FIN:EN:PDF (last visited May 08, 2011)
6. Rauscher, K.F., Yashenko, V.: Russia-U.S. Bilaterial on Cyber Security: Critical Terminology Foundations, EastWest Institute (2011),
   http://www.ewi.info/system/files/reports/
   Russia-U%20S%20%20bilateral%20on%20terminology%20v76%20%282%
   29.pdf (last visited May 08, 2011)
7. Derived from, http://defensetech.org/2009/01/09/
   peeking-into-private-data (last visited May 08, 2011)
8. NATO: NATO MC0571, NATO Cyber Defence Concept, Brussels, Belgium (2008)
9. Scheuer, M.: Al-Quada Doctrine for International Political Warfare. Terrorism Focus III(42) (2006),
   http://jamestown.org/terrorism/news/uploads/tf_003_042.pdf
   (last visited May 08, 2011)
10. Denning, D.E.: Cyberterrorism. Testimony before the Special Oversight Panel on Terrorism Committee on Armed Services U.S. House of Representatives (2003),
    http://www.cs.georgetown.edu/~denning/infosec/
    cyberterror.html (last visited May 08, 2011)
11. Denning, D.E.: Is Cyber Terror Next?, Social Science Research Council (2001),
    http://www.ssrc.org/sept11/essays/denning.htm
    (last visited May 08, 2011)
12. Lewis, J.A.: Assessing the risk of cyber terrorism, cyber war and other cyber threats, Center for Strategic and International Studies (2002)
    http://www.csis.org/tech/0211_lewis.pdf (last visited May 08, 2011)

13. Pollitt, M.M.: Cyberterrorism: Fact or Fancy? In: Proceedings of the 20th National Information Systems Security Conference, Baltimore (1997)
14. Luiijf, H.A.M.: Cyberterrorisme. In: Muller, E.R., Rosenthal, U., de Wijk, R. (eds.) Bundel Terrorisme, pp. 149–168. Kluwer (2008)
15. Luiijf, H.A.M., Nieuwenhuijs, A.H.: Extensible Threat Taxonomy for Critical Infrastructures. Int'l Journal on Critical Infrastructures 4(4), 409–417 (2008)
16. Luiijf, H.A.M., Nieuwenhuijs, A.H., Klaver, M.H.A., van Eeten, M.J.G., Cruz, E.: Empirical findings on European critical infrastructure dependencies. Int. J. System of Systems Engineering 2(1), 3–18 (2010)
17. TNO's database on CI disruptions, version 334 (5110 events; 6922 CI disruptions) (last visited May 08, 2011)
18. Ciancamerla, E., Minichino, M.: A Mini Telco Blackout Scenario, in Tools and Techniques for Interdependency Analysis (IRRIIS Deliverable D2.2.2), IRRIIS Consortium, Fraunhofer Institute for Intelligent Analysis and Information Systems, Sankt-Augustin, Germany (2007),
http://www.irriis.org/File.aspx?lang=2&oiid=9138&pid=572
(last visited May 08, 2008)
19. Baltimore Howard Street Tunnel fire (July 2001),
http://en.wikipedia.org/wiki/Howard_Street_Tunnel_fire
(last visited May 08, 2011)
20. International Cable Protection Committee, http://www.icpc.org (last visited May 08, 2011)
21. Examples of cable cuts,
http://news.smh.com.au/thousands-hit-after-telstra-cable-cut/20080503-2am1.html,
http://www.icelandreview.com/icelandreview/daily_news/?cat_id=40764&ew_0_a_id=359600,
http://www.ksta.de/html/artikel/1137402866724.shtml
(last visited May 08, 2011)
22. Example of shooting fibre optic cables,
http://www.accessnorthga.com/detail.php?n=209108&c=10
(last visited May 08, 2011)
23. Availability and Robustness of Electronic Communication Infrastructures - The ARECI Study, Alcatel-Lucent (2007),
http://ec.europa.eu/information_society/policy/nis/strategy/activities/ciip/areci_study/index_en.htm (last visited May 08, 2011)
24. Counterfeit products,
http://www.andovercg.com/services/cisco-counterfeit-wic-1dsu-t1.shtml (last visited May 08, 2011)
25. Stuxnet dossier v 1.4, Symantec,
http://www.symantec.com/content/en/us/enterprise/media/security_response/whitepapers/w32_stuxnet_dossier.pdf
(last visited May 08, 2011)
26. http://www.networkworld.com/news/0414frame2.html (last visited May 08, 2011)
27. The Cost of Cyber Crime, Detica and U.K. Office of Cyber Security and Information Assurance (2011),
http://www.cabinetoffice.gov.uk/resource-library/cost-of-cyber-crime (last visited May 08, 2011)

28. Jihadists and the Internet, National Coordinator for Counterterrorism, The Hague (2010),
    `http://english.nctb.nl/Images/JihadismeUpdate2009-`
    `UK%20def_tcm92-279323.pdf?cp=92&cs=25496` (last visited May 08, 2011)
29. Williams, C., Gardham, D.: Great likelihood of Cyber attacks by terrorists, The Telegraph
    (February 1, 2011),
    `http://www.telegraph.co.uk/technology/8294023/`
    `Great-likelihood-of-cyber-attacks-by-terrorists.html`
    (last visited May 08, 2011)
30. Colarik, A.M.: Cyber Terrorism: Political And Economic Implications. Idea Group Pub-
    lishing, Hershey (2006)
31. The Terry Childs Case (2009),
    `http://www.techrepublic.com/blog/career/terry-childs-will-`
    `the-true-story-ever-be-told/555` (last visited May 08, 2011)
32. Luiijf, H.A.M. (ed.): Process Control Security in the Cybercrime Information Exchange,
    NICC (2010),
    `http://www.cpni.nl/publications/PCS_brochure-UK.pdf`,
    (last visited May 08, 2011)
33. Koscher, K., Czeskis, A., Roesner, F., Patel, S., Kohno, T., Checkoway, S., McCoy, D.,
    Kantor, B., Anderson, D., Shacham, H., Shacham, S.: Savage, Experimental Security
    Analysis of a Modern Automobile. In: 2010 IEEE Symposium on Security and Privacy,
    pp. 447–462 (2010),
    `http://www.autosec.org/pubs/cars-oakland2010.pdf`
    (last visited May 08, 2011)

Modelling Approaches

Nils Kalstad Svendsen and Stephen D. Wolthusen

Norwegian Information Security Laboratory, Gjøvik University College, Gjøvik, Norway
{nils.svendsen,stephen.wolthusen}@hig.no

Abstract. Understanding and mitigating risks and threats to critical infrastructures relies heavily on the ability to construct and validate models often involving physical systems or even human intervention. This, together with the wide range of scales from critical systems such as industrial process control systems of critical facilities to interactions among multiple sectors up to and including a global scale presents a very large problem space which can only be conquered by an equally broad range of modelling techniques commensurate to the infrastructure aspects being studied. Sophisticated domain-specific models do not necessarily provide the type of insight into dependencies and interactions, which are often driven by information and communication systems and necessitate the study of novel models. Similarly, however, conventional information security research is typically not concerned with interactions of information systems with physical environment, while at the same time conventional infrastructure models emphasise on well-understood statistical event models rather than considering adversarial behaviour.

1 Introduction

Although the formal identification and classification of critical infrastructures is relatively recent [89], the need to ensure robust infrastructure services even in the face of natural or man-made disruptions is neither new nor are the modelling techniques used to this end. Such models were, however, intended to solve relatively well-defined but more importantly well-circumscribed problems based mainly on physical and engineering problems and hence amenable to applying techniques such as statistical reliability models for physical systems and designing technical systems such as bridges or even an entire electrical power grid with parametric robustness against faults.

Current understanding of critical infrastructures, however, has identified several additional dimensions which must be captured by modelling efforts to ensure that the robustness of the overall infrastructure is adequate. One of the most important aspects is that of *dependencies* and *interdependencies* among infrastructures and their constituent elements and the fault conditions leading to infrastructure elements becoming unavailable, which is unlikely to become apparent without a sufficient degree of abstraction permitting a deeper understanding of such structural properties. Capturing such structural properties represents, as will be shown throughout the chapter, a severe challenge as these are not only limited to evident physical dependencies such as a water treatment plant depending on resources such as e.g. stocks of certain chemicals and electrical power, but also must include *information and communication* aspects which may induce logical dependencies. More importantly, however, is that both information-based

J. Lopez et al. (Eds.): Critical Information Infrastructure Protection, LNCS 7130, pp. 68–97, 2012.

mechanisms and conventional, physical vectors can be used by adversaries to degrade, damage, or destroy infrastructure elements with disproportionate effects. Such *adversarial* models are not common in many critical infrastructure sectors and can hence be a source of severe vulnerabilities where threats are not fully understood and because of this not adequately mitigated; modelling is therefore crucial in providing such insights so as to allow the development of more robust infrastructure elements. Conversely, information security has been successful in developing increasingly rigorous adversary models in studying the security properties of protocols and algorithms, but must rely on a closely circumscribed set of underlying axioms and assumptions to retain the respective models' validity.

A problem facing any description of models of critical infrastructure is the inherent broad scope as identified by Abele-Wigert *et al.* [3, 50] and subsequently expanded upon by Assaf [10]. When referring to models of critical infrastructure, this can refer to several layers of abstraction, necessarily also aiming to answer distinct types of questions to be addressed by the model as illustrated by Table 1.

Table 1. Critical infrastructure model hierarchy (adapted from Abele-Wigert *et al.* [3, 50])

Abstraction Level	Modelled Entities Model Actors Modelling Method Scope
National Security	Infrastructure sectors, state or supranational entities, general public
	Policy-makers, defence, and military organisations including national and international entities
	Qualitative analyses and macro-economic models
Legal	Infrastructure sectors and intra-sector actors, external entities
	Law enforcement, intelligence, and regulatory agencies
	Qualitative analyses and economic models
Technical	Trans-sector and sector-specific technical systems
	Technical systems, codified policies and mechanisms, management
	Qualitative and high-level quantitative models
System	Smaller-scale technical and organisational systems and their interactions, also across infrastructure sectors
	Management, engineers, and technicians
	Qualitative, but also quantitative models with substantial technical and organisational fidelity

In many cases the determination of constituent elements of critical infrastructures has been made based on the impact of events or chains of events affecting infrastructure elements; particularly for the case of technical infrastructure this can be traced back to analyses put forward by political scientists and sociologists such as Lagadec [76] and later Beck [16]. This understanding particularly of *risk* at different scales gives rise to a classification mechanism initially proposed by Perrow [108] in the context of modelling technical risks and subsequently refined by Rinaldi *et al.* [112] into a taxonomy of infrastructure *scale* as shown in Table 2. It is clear that the taxonomy does not provide detailed, prescriptive characteristics for bounding the individual layers of abstraction and rely on domain-specific conventions to perform such groupings. Particularly when comparing or even merging models from different sources or even domains, this can give rise to substantial mis-matches in the levels of abstraction captured.

The scales defined in Table 2 can be both logical (e.g. in the case of communication systems or financial services) and spatial (e.g. for electric power generation or transportation sectors). Although it appears plausible that the types of questions addressed at higher levels of the hierarchy described in Table 1 correspond to similar higher levels of abstraction in Table 2, it cannot necessarily be assumed that the objective of an analysis follows this alignment. However, as is evident throughout the following sections, model granularity varies sharply, and while it may often be possible to commit additional resources to permit the operation of a model at larger scales, aspects such as algorithmic complexity or the lack of reliable and available data underpinning more detailed models will limit the applicability of several types of particularly quantitative modelling approaches.

Similarly, the time-scales of questions posed to models vary considerably at different levels of abstraction. Policy formulation and implementation and the respective impact on infrastructure may take years and even decades (e.g. where planning permission and deployment of large-scale physical infrastructure such as roads or high-voltage transmission lines are concerned) while quantitative models at the part- or unit-level may require sub-millisecond resolution (e.g. when analysing the robustness of the aforementioned high-voltage transmission lines or related process control systems). It is, moreover, also clear that a policy-level model inherently can tolerate higher levels of uncertainty than a model used for automated behaviour such as state estimation and prediction.

Table 2. Taxonomy of scales in critical infrastructure models (adapted from Rinaldi *et al.* [112])

Model Scale	Definition
Part	The smallest component of a system identifiable in an analysis
Unit	Functionally related set of parts
Subsystem	Functionally related set of units
System	Grouping of subsystems
Infrastructure	Self-contained set of similar systems
Interdependent Infrastructures	National and supranational interconnected infrastructures

Many domains and infrastructure sectors can draw on sophisticated and mature models and accompanying analytical as well as simulation mechanisms for core aspects of their planning and operation. These models and the underlying techniques represent a substantial effort; however, it is not always clear whether the models can be adjusted or expanded in such a way as to permit the type of security-related questions described above. This is particularly problematic for quantitative models where models often rely on tacit assumptions e.g. about the probability density functions associated with parameters. In the underlying basic model, these assumptions will be backed by an in-depth understanding of the underlying processes such as physical characteristics of phænomena, while the same parameter may, in the case of an active adversary, be manipulated arbitrarily and hence will no longer conform to the assumptions made. As this and similar considerations may arise in multiple loci of a model which in turn may itself be constructed in a layered manner, validating the applicability of such models for security analysis represents a substantial effort even where the model may capture all parameters relevant to a security and dependability analysis.

For lower levels of abstraction detailed above it may be possible to derive and validate such assumptions and models explicitly from first principles (e.g. where physical, biological, or chemical processes must be captured within a model), but even under such restricted assumptions it may not always be possible to obtain results in closed form, forcing the use of approximations such as numerical solutions or even the use of experimental and simulation data in the verification and validation of models; at higher abstraction layers, this necessarily gives rise to uncertainty about model validity. Such uncertainty is already problematic when it cannot be easily determined whether the underlying problem itself is *ill-conditioned* (i.e. small variations in parameters leading to disproportionate changes in results), or whether this may merely represent an artifact of a given modelling technique, but is particularly difficult when the types of events and incidents of interest are by definition rare or difficult to observe.

This problem of incomplete models and their validation also arises in the context of conjoining multiple specialised models or models addressing different levels of abstraction; research in this area has been limited despite recent efforts e.g. by Casalicchio *et al.* [32], leaving models and their individual domains remain largely disjoint. Moreover, while in some cases the same mathematical methods can be applied at different abstraction levels, which is particularly notable for the case of game-theoretical models described in section 4.

2   Economic Models

Economic models serve mainly to identify high-level dependencies and can also highlight quantitative effects, albeit at what is necessarily a relatively coarse resolution. The majority of models used in the critical infrastructure domain are Input-Output models focusing primarily on either demand-driven or supply-driven aspects, respectively

The quantitative Input-Output model was developed by Leontief to study interrelations among industry sectors for a given region or nation in the form of a matrix where n sectors of an economic model are considered as variables of a set of linear equations with each sector i producing a single homogeneous good x_i. The model assumes that producing one such unit from sector i requires a_{ij} units of sector j, and that sectors are interdependent, producing and consuming outputs mutually as well as satisfying demand d_i. The output of sector i is then formulated as

$$x_i = a_{i1}x_1 + a_{i2}x_2 + \ldots + a_{in}x_n + d_i$$

giving a formulation for an entire economy under study as $x = \mathbf{A}x + d$, which not only allows efficient computation but also the determination of the required output for a given demand vector provided that $\mathbf{I} - \mathbf{A}$ is invertible [80] (a related model by Ghosh can be shown to reduce to the Leontief model [59], although its accounting and identities may in some cases be more convenient). The models have been studied and extended in multiple areas including in the study of spatial economic properties, also at different aggregation levels [45].

The basic concept of spatial interdependencies can also be extended naturally to physical systems as has been proposed by Rinaldi [111]. Although limited to certain well-conditioned problems where commodities are generated, transmitted, and consumed among infrastructure sectors, such as water resource systems and flood protection, the simplicity and ability to rapidly derive quantitative results allows to derive rapid insights even for large numbers of entities to be considered. Such models are, however, necessarily limited to an *equilibrium state*.

The application to critical infrastructures particularly for the case of failures or *inoperabilities* was, however, originally proposed by Haimes and Jiang [64]. Here, multiple interconnected systems, including intra-sector dependencies are considered, while instead of inputs for the production of goods, the objective is to identify inoperabilities caused by one or multiple failures. Such failures are not modelled further and can arise intrinsically or from external perturbations. In the model of Haimes and Jiang, inoperability is then defined as the level of a system's dysfunction as a fraction of its anticipated level of operation. Following the schema established for the Leontief model, the Inoperability Input-Output model (IIM) can be formulated straightforwardly as

$$q = \mathbf{A}q + c = (\mathbf{I} - \mathbf{A})^{-1}c \tag{1}$$

where q is the *inoperability vector* expressed as normalised economic loss, i.e. with elements of the vector representing unrealised production as opposed to a notional normal state; the matrix $\mathbf{A}$ is now used as an *interdependency matrix* explicitly denoting the coupling of sectors, with elements of a given row being interpreted as additional inoperability being contributed by a sector in a column. The vector c, finally, represents a *demand-side perturbation vector* and, analogous to q expresses the normalised degraded final demand (the notional baseline final demand less the actual final demand normalised by the notional production level).

As with the basic Input-Output model, the IIM was extended multiple times to study physical and regional aspects. However, so as to capture the aspect of perturbations, extensions to the IIM include the *Demand-Reduction IIM* as well as Dynamic IIM variants, which also seek to recapture recovery effects [63]. These models summarised by Haimes *et al.* in [63] are also reviewed and applied in multiple quantitative case studies at the regional and sector level [117], including [62] and studies at larger scales including those by Setola for the Italian economy [121]. The latter study is illustrative of the benefits found in IIM modelling as it can also demonstrate longer-term developments; reviewing economic data from 1995–2003, Setola showed that interdependencies among economic sectors were increasing and hence causing greater susceptibility of the overall economy to perturbations within individual sectors. Although initially developed with a focus on physical systems, both the Leontief model and the derivative IIM are not restricted to such systems and have also been applied successfully to information systems. Andrijcic and Horowitz applied the IIM to the case of damage sustained from industrial espionage [9], while earlier work by Haimes and Chittester [61] sought to apply the modelling technique to control systems by studying inoperability effects resulting from failures in supervisory control and data acquisition (SCADA) systems and, based on this, the derivation of metrics for the efficacy of risk management controls. The IIM approach has, moreover, been applied not only to the description and analysis of existing interdependencies and risks emanating from these, but also as the basis for minimising dependencies. One such approach was proposed by Crowther [39] and relies on matrix decompositions of the basic IIM, which can be mapped onto multi-objective optimisation problems.

More recently, Tanaka expanded the IIM model to capture both forward and backward linkage explicitly, and specifically studies the effects of information technology and information security-based dependencies for the Japanese economy [126], also deriving metrics for the identification of cross-sectoral dependencies caused by information security issues.

The model family by Haimes _et al._ was developed with a view to losses of physical capabilities and economic losses, but can readily be extended to assess the impact of failures to provide information. As with the basic Leontief model, the main purpose of the model is enhanced understanding of the impact of different failure types as well as the ability of a system to sustain operation and output levels under adverse conditions [63]. However, all variants of the Input-Output model are limited to larger-scale abstractions and hence are not well-suited to providing quantitative data for subsystems or units. This is also reflected in the mechanisms used for modelling adversary behaviour as well as recovery mechanisms; these typically are limited to simple stochastic processes such as in the Dynamic IIM variant studied by Lian and Haimes [83] where both perturbations caused by natural disasters and intentional agency as well as recovery mechanisms are described by simple Brownian processes.

In the Dynamic IIM, inoperability of an infrastructure i (as above) is further associated with a discrete time formulation, with inoperability remaining normalised, giving $q[i](k) \in [0, 1]$ at a point in time t.

$$q(t) = \mathbf{A}q(t) + c + \mathbf{B}(q(t+1) - q(t)) \tag{2}$$

Equation 2 hence provides a straightforward extension of the model described by equation 1 with the exception of the expression $\mathbf{B}$, which is used to capture the recovery coefficients and can be intuitively considered as the willingness to provide resources for accelerating recovery following an inoperability incident. Dynamic IIM do, moreover, allow to analyse parameters such as the optimisation of buffering in the form of inventories to ameliorate fluctuations in supply levels as discussed e.g. by Barker and

Santos [12]. A somewhat more robust formulation is the use of explicit probabilistic demand-side perturbation vectors c in the IIM (equation 1) as has been investigated by Santos [116] and Jung [71].

Considerations about the effectiveness of using such models for capturing perturbations also apply to cyber security aspects as discussed by Santos *et al.* [118] since it requires capturing both steady-state effects and knock-on effects which can arise both on supply and demand sides; although most models consider primarily the demand side, Leung *et al.* describe models based on the Ghosh formalism concentrating on demand-quantity and supply-price models, but showing that these models are equivalent [81, 82]. A related set of constraints arising from the Leontief equilibrium formulation is addressed by D'Agostino *et al.* [40] by casting the problem in the form of a Markov chain to capture time dependency, also using stochastic transitions between states.

A further constraint of IIM arising from the original Leontief formulation is the reliance on a single cost metric, which may not be appropriate in circumstances where multiple objectives must be optimised, but for which a mapping onto a single metric is inappropriate or infeasible [99]. In some cases such as in the work by Rosato *et al.*, this problem is approached by IIM parameter estimation for incommensurate entities based on parameter correlations found in more fine-grained models [113], while Panzieri and Setola similarly aim to build metrics and parameters based on both physical and cyber models of underlying infrastructures [104]. This is further extended in work by Setola *et al.* [122] which seeks to elucidate the role of individual infrastructures within the DIIM formulation, which is of particular interest in understanding the potential for cascading effects. Setola *et al.* also propose the use of qualitative parameter estimation similar to that originally proposed by Panzieri and Setola, and map these onto Type I fuzzy sets with convex membership functions. This has been further extended byOliva *et al.* [102] by introducing agent-based extensions, which decomposes sectors into explicit sub-units to which the IIM or DIIM formulations can then be applied analogously.

3   System Dynamics Approaches

Although Dynamic IIM can provide some insight into the behaviour of perturbed systems over time, it is often desirable to capture dependencies directly such as the flow of commodities among infrastructures [111]. As noted in section 2, however, it often difficult to obtain quantitative results particularly at higher abstraction levels as these often must rely on estimation. Where such uncertainty is unavoidable, qualitative methods can nevertheless provide insights by studying structural properties instead of quantitative metrics.

Abstracting core concepts from control systems theory, the *system dynamics* community seeks to capture dynamic behaviour through the mechanisms of feedback, explicit time models particularly represented by delays between events, and the accumulation of flows into stocks [56, 57]. This serves to capture causal relations, and allows the representation of both positive and negative reinforcement. The concepts are commonly captured in the form of diagrams, mainly causal-loop diagrams, and stock-and-flow diagrams (see figure 1 for a simple illustration). The former provides a high-level perspective of the relations, interactions, and feedback among entities, but does not yield insights into the flows of commodities or information itself; to this end, stock-and-flow diagrams are used, which can capture stocks as state variables or, in case of fungible commodities, as integrals. Flows can be both rates or derivatives, while the control of flows is mediated in addition to the provision of notional sources and sinks of infinite capacity where models are not closed.

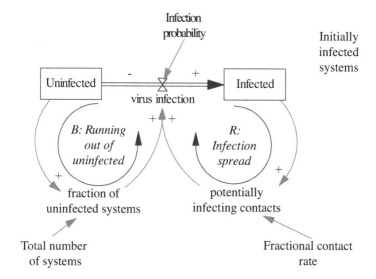

Fig. 1. A System Dynamics diagrammatic representation of computer virus epidemiological processes obtained from the Vensim environment (courtesy of J. Gonzalez)

As system dynamics was originally devised to understand organisational effects rather than physical systems, work including the results reported by Gonzalez *et al.* [60] provides insights into the types of threats posed to critical infrastructures, particularly the susceptibility of their ICT-based elements to *social engineering* type attacks. This provides a more abstract view of the type of intelligent adversary discussed in section 4 as the model only considers the relative effort and expenditure of an adversary to bypass or counter security or other organisational controls rather than concrete mechanisms. Under the assumption that such insider attacks, including ones based on social engineering rather than technical measures are difficult to avoid in their entirety, the design of control mechanisms can also focus on ways in which controls and interactions may at least induce delays in the adversaries' ability to achieve their objectives while subsequent work by Sarriegi *et al.* [119] sought to formalise similar aspects for the more general case of security management.

Despite this, the system dynamics approach is not solely limited to modelling organisational processes and has been applied to both targeted and large-scale critical infrastructure environments as was previously touched upon by Rinaldi [111]. Pasqualini *et al.* used such a model to capture the potable water distribution system within an urban area but also extended this model — rather than a more straightforward hydraulic physical model — with the cascading effects which disruptions would cause, studying the dynamics of coupled infrastructures [106].

Larger-scale applications of system dynamics to capture dynamic interactions often rely on simulations to aid the understanding of such interdependence and cascading effects, and can often also rely on sector-specific models which are subsequently coupled through a more qualitative system dynamics approach. One instance of such a modelling environment is the *Critical Infrastructure Protection Decision Support System* (CIP/DSS) developed by Bush *et al.* at the Los Alamos, Sandia, and Argonne National Laboratories [28, 78]. This environment relies on discrete event simulation, rule-based expert systems and coupled differential equations for sector sub-models, and has also been used in capturing explicit economic impacts and their dynamic remediation and mitigation by Dauelsberg and Outkin [41], permitting a direct juxtaposition with D-IIM. Although system dynamics models are necessarily qualitative, the fidelity of sub-models is not negligible as was demonstrated by LeClaire and O'Reilly for the case of a switched telecommunications network model [79]. The CIP/DSS model can also be considered as an archetype for the purpose to which system dynamics models are commonly put in critical infrastructure modelling, namely for consequence assessments and risk analyses involving multiple interacting entities with feedback behaviour, and at the same time to facilitate the communication of causal relationships and effects in an intuitive manner as is commonly the case for decision support systems. In the case of CIP/DSS the model is divided into regional or national-scale models of infrastructure sectors connected to more fine-grained metropolitan-scale sector models where necessary. Decision support is then provided by a further layer translating the qualitative effects obtained from the system dynamics model into consequence metrics and ultimately decision metrics affecting categories including human health and safety, economic parameters, environmental, socio-political, and national security. As the parameter space does not lend itself to a fully automated analysis, the modelling approach relies on the development of scenarios to be studied within the model framework, and similarly requires the explicit description of mitigation strategies.

A related system dynamics model was described by Min *et al.* [93], which used a functional modelling mechanism (IDEF0 [131]) to capture information exchange requirements and mechanisms. This permits the simulation of localised losses of function or capacity on the overall infrastructure, and subsequent application of a decision support system using non-linear optimisation. Although the overall model remains qualitative, suitable choice of initial parameters may still allow the identification of optimal resource allocation strategies.

Particularly for large-scale models as described in [93] and [28], however, the number of model elements can be on the order of 10^3, typically requiring an understanding of sector-specific aspects. System dynamics modelling attempts to address some of these issues through the use of so-called group model building [17], which seeks to integrate domain expert knowledge into the overall model; however, it is not necessarily clear that the participants in such efforts are aware of all interactions that may arise in the system being modelled while validation of qualitative models is itself an open problem [69].

4   Behavioural and Game-Theoretic Models

The high-level economic models described in section 2 rely on stochastic formulations for capturing perturbations. While this is a well-known and understood approach found in domains where events and risks can be modelled using stochastic processes, this is not necessarily suitable when confronted with active adversaries. Natural events or technical systems can typically be modelled by statistical analysis and reliability analysis models; where data sets are sparse such techniques usually rely on the combination of expert judgement and Bayesian statistics [20] or through explicit causal models, this is not helpful when one has to assume an adaptable and intelligent adversary as pointed out by Bier [19].

The need to capture *strategic interactions*, i.e. the incorporation of assessments of the state and likely lines of reasoning or courses of action that other interacting entities may take was originally formalised in an economics context by Morgenstern and von Neumann [96] based on earlier work by von Neumann [95]. Such models assume two or more agents whose interactions can be modelled under a variety of different constraints. Generally, however, these interactions include:

1. Agents have the ability to co-operate or to act against the interests of other agents
2. Agents can interact whilst having different levels of information about each other
3. Agents may interact in singular encounters, or their interactions and negotiations may take place over multiple rounds of engagement
4. Decisions and actions of agents can be reached simultaneously, or can occur sequentially

Morgenstern and von Neumann posited axioms of rationality as part of their original formulation, namely

Axiom 1 (Completeness). stating that an agent has well-defined preferences, i.e. for outcomes of games L, M, exactly one of the following holds: $L \prec M$, $M \prec L$, or $L = M$.

Axiom 2 (Transitivity). stating that preference is consistent across options, i.e. for outcomes L, M, N, $L \preceq M$, and $M \preceq N$, $L \preceq N$ holds.

Axiom 3 (Continuity). can be formulated in two variants, the weaker of which is also referred to as the *Archimedean property* and states that assuming $L \prec M \prec N$, there exists a probability $\varepsilon \in (0,1)$ such that $(1-\varepsilon)L + \varepsilon N \prec M \prec \varepsilon L + (1-\varepsilon)N$.

Axiom 4 (Independence). stating that if $L \prec M$, then for any N and $p \in (0,1]$, $pL + (1-p)N \prec pM + (1-p)N$.

which is commonly referred to as the condition for VNM-rational agents. For such agents, the key result of von Neumann and Morgenstern is the following theorem:

Theorem 1. *Von Neumann-Morgenstern Utility Theorem. For any VNM-rational agent satisfying axioms 1-4 above, there exists a utility function u assigning to each outcome A a real number $u(A)$ such that for any two outcomes $L \prec M \iff Eu(L) < Eu(M)$, $Eu(p_1, A_1 + \cdots + p_n A_n) = p_1 u(A_1) + \cdots + p_n u(A_n)$ where $Eu(L)$ denotes the expected value of u in L.*

This allows the determination of u by preferences between game outcomes (in the simplest case with only two outcomes). The model assumes that agents are *rational* in the sense that they will act to maximise their utility by assessing outcomes, calculating paths to outcomes, and selecting actions from the sets of alternatives yielding the most-preferred outcomes whilst considering the actions of other players. Such programmes specifying the actions to take in response to other players are referred to as *strategies*. A set of strategies which provides the best outcome for each agent considering all strate-gies of other agents is referred to as a *Nash Equilibrium*, where the existence of unique equilibria depends among other parameters on whether a game is a *zero-sum* or *non-zero-sum* game. In the latter, outcomes of agents are not necessarily opposed to each other, resulting in multiple possible equilibria.

Although a large number of formulations for games exist, several key parameters can be identified; of particular interest for the consideration of adversarial behaviour is the assumption of *complete information*; in the simplest game-theoretic models, this states that agents have full information on all events in a game up to the point of their current decision. Conversely, in games under *incomplete information* agents are not certain of the state and hence likely actions of their adversaries. While in complete information games one can decide on outcomes of highest utility through backwards induction, this is not possible in the latter case. A similar distinction must be made with regard to *sequential-move* and *simultaneous-move* games as agents are not aware of other agents' actions when having to decide on their own actions in the latter case [58, 103]. Moreover, while the above is restricted to single-round games, significant differences also arise in the case of *repeated games* where agents can, expecting to face the same adversaries repeatedly, reach different strategies, or may learn, resulting in adaptive behaviour. Such strategies include the possibility of cooperation, which can in turn be *crisp* with fully involved or *fuzzy* where participation levels can vary [26].

Game-theoretic modelling found early applications in the security domain including for both strategic military models such as proposed by Haywood [68] and in the tactical domain in work including by Hamilton and Mesic [65], but also in the political science domain where applications include arms control strategies as summarised in the work by Brams and Kilgour [25]. More specifically, the applicability to information warfare has been investigated by work including Burke [27], although a substantial body of literature focuses on economic aspects studying aspects such as cost effectiveness mod-els for security controls, while both Major as well as Sandler and Arce model terrorist activities and corresponding defences or resource allocation strategies [88, 114, 115].

The application of game-theoretical models to the defence of critical information in-frastructures has been limited; beyond the work by Burke [27], examples include the use of two-player stochastic games by Liu *et al.* [84] to capture the behaviour of insider attackers, which lends itself to a simple Nash equilibrium derivation as noted above. One model proposed by Jenelius *et al.* explicitly seeks to capture also the *perception* of attackers in a game-theoretic framework as well as parameters including the allocation of resources [70]. It is clear that many of the problems studied for physical security and in the counter-terrorism domain require a careful analysis given the different assump-tions; this includes the rigorous modelling of substitution effects, and the amount of mutual information [138]. Existing models such as those proposed by Major [88] and subsequent developments [77, 136] are not only estimating parameters but also assume simultaneous plays by attackers and defenders, which does not allow for hedging at equilibrium [18, 115].

5   Graph- and Network-Based Models

Graph and network-based models provide a well-understood rigorous formalism [21] for capturing particularly aspects such as dependencies and are also readily adapted to grid- or network-based infrastructure sectors such as telecommunications, pipelines, and power distribution. By assigning a set of properties to nodes and edges and allowing flow of different commodities along the edges of a graph, numerous aspects of critical infrastructures and their interconnections can be captured both for physical assets and information flows.

One main purpose of such models is typically to capture physical and logical dependencies between network components, which may themselves also belong to multiple different infrastructure sectors. Except for high-level trans-sectoral models, this generally requires that a graph-based model serves mainly as an aggregation mechanism for system- or subsystem-level models rather than providing a comprehensive model at all scales. However, to permit the capturing of relevant relevant physical and logical interdependencies, e.g. interaction of different types between the network components and resource buffering so as to be able to derive quantitative information, the aggregation must provide for parameters to be commensurate. In other instances, research seeks to identify dynamic or emergent properties, particularly of large structures that have not been the subject of rigorous design. As a result, a broad spectrum of methods has been investigated.

A relatively fine-grained model focused on the identification of *dynamic* effects within interdependent infrastructures using graph formalisms and flow algorithms is discussed in section 5.1 based on work by the authors [124, 125]. However, critical infrastructures are often characterised by their very large extent with even some individual infrastructures such as telecommunications networks or electric power grids encompassing in excess of 10^5 elements. This has led to an interest in studying graph-theoretical concepts for insights into how graph or — in this application — interaction and dependence structures can be used to characterise infrastructure network robustness.

Random graphs have been studied intensively in recent decades given the relative simplicity and paucity of required assumptions as in the case Erdös-Renyi graphs [21, 51]; the handbook edited by Bollobás *et al.* [22] collects key results in random graph theory and related fields with a particular focus on large graphs, although in the application domain considered here results in extremal graph theory are of limited utility.

In the case Erdös-Renyi graphs one assumes that every edge (arc) of a graph is independently formed of every other node with a given probability p. It can be seen that the number of edges is a random variable, but one which is tightly concentrated around its mean for large numbers of vertices.

Graph properties of interest include the diameter of a graph (for the shortest *path* $l(i, j)$ between vertices i and j, this is defined as $\max_{i,j} l(i, j)$), the average path length as the distance between any two nodes in a graph

$$\text{average path length} = \frac{\sum_{i \geq j} l(i,j)}{\frac{n(n-1)}{2}}$$

which is obviously bounded by the diameter, but provides important insights e.g. where dependency paths are analysed. A further parameter of interest is the degree distribution of a graph; this describes the relative frequencies of vertices with different degrees d. In case of an Erdös-Renyi graph, the degree of nodes can be again represented as a random variable. As D is a binomial random variable with $\mathbb{E}(D) = (n-1)p$, i.e. $\mathbb{P}(D = d) = \binom{n-1}{d} p^d (1-p)^{n-1-d}$. For constant expected degree D, this can be approximated (for $n \to \infty$) with a Poisson variable with $\lambda = (n-1)p$ as $\mathbb{P}(D = d) = \frac{e^{-\lambda} \lambda^d}{d!}$.

A number of questions arise regarding graph properties such as whether graphs have cycles (or cycles with specific properties) and whether subgraphs are connected; for many of these questions, however, the problem will be intractable. A common approach is therefore to resort to asymptotic analysis; showing that thresholds exist at which graph parameters influence probabilities of properties approaching either 0 or 1 was one of the seminal contributions in the original work by Erdös and Réyni [51]; as an example consider that in a Erdös-Réyni random graph the threshold for connectivity can be shown to be $t(n) = \frac{\log(n)}{n}$ [52].

Most critical infrastructure components are, however, not necessarily best modelled by random graphs. These may be subject to rigorous design and hence exhibit considerable regularity, but more frequently will have been evolving over longer time-frames without the benefit of an overarching design e.g. in response to population developments and responding to external constraints, particularly where physical infrastructure is concerned (see also section 7).

One possible way to model such graphs and networks that has been found to apply in a large number of domains is to consider the probability of edge formation. An early example of such a study was the quantitative analysis of bibliometric information conducted by de Solla Price [44], although the concept of *small worlds*, i.e. graph diameters in social networks was popularised by Milgram [92] somewhat later including experimental validation of the initial results by Travers and Milgram [130]. This work was taken up again in seminal work by Watts and Strogatz [134] (see also the later popular exposition by Watts [133]), which validated the findings of Milgram for a number of other disparate networks, but also identified local properties of such graph.

Based on these findings, Watts and Strogatz proposed a model for graphs exhibiting a limited amount of randomness. To this end, they assumed a ring lattice of n vertices with degree k and modifying each edge to direct to other vertices with a given probability p, which was investigated as the key parameter of such graphs. The characteristic path length $L(p)$ and clustering coefficients $C(p)$ provide information on the separation between vertices as a global and clique formation as a local property. These are primarily of interest for relatively sparse graphs of $n \gg k \gg \ln(n) \gg 1$. A key characteristic of such graphs is that the existence of even a relatively small number of edges serving as "short cuts" can significantly reduce $L(p)$, providing an immediate intuitive model for the observations by Milgram as well as the starting point for a large and on-going body of research. This is particularly relevant as many networks, particularly also of critical infrastructures, have been shown to exhibit the properties of graphs identified by Watts and Strogatz; in their original research one of the examples analysed was in fact a portion of the U.S. power grid.

Empirical studies, however, identified that many networks both in nature and developed by humans do not exhibit either the Poisson distribution of degrees nor the small-world distribution, but rather are *scale-free*. In such networks, the degree distribution can be approximated or modelled asymptotically by a power law as

$$P(k) \sim k^{-\gamma}$$

This observation was explained by Albert and Barabási as being caused by the growth of graphs, and a mechanism of *preferential attachment* for new edges being added to the graph [5]. This seminal work has resulted in a number of techniques more commonly used in statistical mechanics being applied to complex networks including to critical infrastructures and their dependencies. A number of surveys including those of Albert and Barabási [6] and Newman [98], while the book by Newman *et al.* provides a somewhat wider perspective on complex networks in general [97].

It is noteworthy, however, that even with relatively simple graph-theoretic assumptions it is also possible to study the robustness of graphs to attack; Flaxman *et al.* describe a process where a dynamically evolving random graph is enlarged using preferential attachment to achieve scale-free properties, and considering an adversary with the ability to remove a fraction of vertices [55]. Similarly, to obtain otherwise intractable results some assumptions may need to be strengthened as in the case of the result on the diameter of scale-free random graphs by Bollobás and Riordan [23]. This is expanded upon in the recent survey of Magnien *et al.* [87], which also analyses the impact of differences between different degree distributions on the robustness of networks.

One area of interest arising from this ability to describe complex networks — of which critical infrastructure networks are only one instance — is to analyse the robustness of such networks to attacks. This has been studied under a number of assumptions; one early study by Albert *et al.* [7] considered general classes of vulnerabilities to errors as well as deliberate attacks, while a number of authors have analysed specific infrastructure sectors using methods from complex network theory. One sector of particular interest is the electric power grid; here, work by Albert *et al.* [4] on structural vulnerabilities in the North American power grid was subsequently broadened by a reliability analysis conducted by Chassin and Posse [35], while the Chinese and European power grids were later studied by Zhang *et al.* [139] and Solé *et al.* [123], respectively.

Other infrastructures can also be modelled as networks, but may exhibit somewhat different behaviour such as buffering (see section 5.1); for the case of gas pipelines, Carvalho *et al.* studied load patterns and the robustness of the European natural gas pipeline network using variants of the standard measures of betweenness centrality and flows [30]. Similarly, the case of water distribution networks was analysed by Yazdani and Jeffrey; here, the graph topology as well as buffering behaviour make a straightforward complex network analysis unsatisfactory. Instead, Yazdani and Jeffrey attempted to identify structural properties leading to vulnerabilities by investigating cut-sets and optimal-connectivity invariants [137].

One area of particular interest that has, however, not been fully explored but is crucial for understanding the effects of deliberate attacks on critical infrastructure networks are dynamic aspects of such graphs. Although analysis has been conducted on aspects such as individual failures as noted above [7] and cascading failures have been investigated by a number of researchers including early work by Cohen [38] as well as Motter and Lai [94]; in the work of Motter and Lai, the re-distribution of flows — mainly a characteristic of physical infrastructure networks — can lead to failures which are cascading and mutually reinforcing. Such cascading failures can, moreover, also be approximated efficiently using branching processes [75].

However, the modelling of disturbances itself has received less attention; a more static view was explored early on for the case of small-world networks by Barrat and Weigl [14], which was more recently elaborated by a study of dynamical processes in complex networks by Barrat et al. [13]. An alternative approach also arising from the statistical physics community has been the concept of fluctuations of flows in complex networks; this was studied e.g. by Kim and Motter [73, 74]. To address this issue partially, Wang et al. introduce cost models for attackers, however, as has been demonstrated in other contexts, the determination of such costs and weights is far from trivial [132].

Another area which has itself benefited greatly from the study of complex networks, but which are also of interest in understanding critical infrastructure robustness for a number of reasons are ocial networks and interactions on these, as models must often incorporate decisions and information flows which are not solely based on automated processes and can hence lead to incorrect results are omitted — a typical example being a failure warning being neglected if sender and receiver of information do not share a trust relationship. More generally, however, these aspects frequently relate to the need to understand information flows that may often be mediated by human interaction. The study of such networks employs graph-theoretical concepts to understand such relations, and can draw on a large body of modelling techniques specifically adapted for the analysis of social networks, see e.g. Borgatti for an introduction to the key concepts of centrality measures [24].

A further area drawing on complex networks seeks to integrate this with aspects of control systems theory. The latter generally must contend with hybrid systems, requiring a substantial degree of abstraction, but it is nevertheless possible to identify and reason about several core aspects of control systems. One such aspect is that of *controllability*, which is of particular importance in distributed systems as may be encountered in SCADA and distributed control systems (DCS). Modelling DCS as autonomous agents is a conservative assumption as both communication and actions of individual agents may be subject to faults [127]. In such a context, agents can be considered as executing distributed agreement protocols, where controlled nodes abide by the results of the protocol while some of these nodes do not, which can then be considered as the controlling nodes and captured in a graph abstraction as proposed by Rahmani et al. [110].

Liu et al. [85] utilised this model together with the Kalman controllability rank criterion, which requires edges to be weighted and edge weights to be known, to study the properties of what can be considered complex DCS networks. As edge weights are often unknowable or unknown, Liu *et al.* inferred parameters or relied on a subset of known parameters in their work; this reliance on a subset is also driven by the computational complexity of calculating the rank. Under these assumptions, however, it is possible to determine the controlling (or driver) nodes. Although many networks including control systems exhibit scale-free degree distributions, the results of Liu *et al.* somewhat counter-intuitively show that it is not necessarily the preferential attachment vertices in such a scale-free graph which are the controlling vertices [4, 46].

5.1 Interdependency Graph Model

The following provides a unified view of a model for interconnected infrastructures covering several levels in the scale model shown in table 2.

Infrastructure Components. Interconnected infrastructures can be formally modelled as an instance of a network $\mathcal{N}$ where vertices[1] are considered as representation of all components of the infrastructures that can produce, store, or consume services of fungible resource that flows through the network, e.g. transmission line segments, pipeline segments, and production facilities. The vertex set is defined by $\{v_1,\dots,v_k\}$, and denoted $V(\mathcal{N})$[2].

Pairwise dependencies between nodes are represented as arcs, where the head node is dependent on the tail node. So as to differentiate between different types of dependencies between nodes and different types of services or resources that these may exchange between each other, the notion of a *dependency type* is required.

Definition 1 (Dependency type). *A dependency type defines a type of interaction between two vertexes. The interaction can be delivery of a service or a fungible resource. The set of dependency types $\{d_1,\dots,d_m\}$ is denoted by $\mathcal{D}$.*

As the model is to reflect both logical and physical resources, dependency types are assumed to be scalar and are further constrained without loss of generality to integer values. The model allows for multiple dependencies between nodes in order to capture dependencies at multiple levels; however, loops are not allowed. While one can intuitively argue that a vertex can be considered dependent on itself if it is able to produce or store resources, but this is included in the model as a separate mechanism different from the graph model.

The i'th arc carrying dependency type d_j between the two vertices v_a and v_b is uniquely defined with the notation $(v_a, v_b)_i^j$, and can now define the arc set

$$\mathscr{A} = \{(v_1,v_2)_1^1,\dots,(v_{k-1},v_k)_{e_{(k-1,k,d)}}^m\},$$

where $e_{(k-1,k,d)}$ is the number of arcs from $v_{k-1,k}$ to v_k of dependency type d_m. From this it can be seen that the size of a given infrastructure representation is dependent to a

---

[1] Unless noted otherwise, the following refers to nodes and vertices interchangeably, except where explicit graph references make it necessary to refer to vertex properties.

[2] If there is no ambiguity with regard to which network is referred to, the vertex set will be denoted as V, as is the case for other sets in the following discussion.

considerable extent of the nature of the infrastructure, as the model does not impose any upper bound on the number of arcs between two vertices. However, unless otherwise specified, the assumption that $|\mathscr{A}| = O(|\mathscr{V}|)$ will be used in the following.

The m dependency types can now be further classified into *storable* and *non-storable* resources. Resources may be physical commodities, and in this case they have a mass and occupy a physical volume as well as exhibiting other physical characteristics, which can be captured by a model to establish constraints.

Definition 2 (Buffer). *A buffer is a volume of size V_a^j assigned to each node v_a for each dependency type d_j.*

Given a knowledge of the physical properties of given dependency type d_j and its density ρ_j, the available quantity N_a^j of d_j in v_a is easily derived. A natural extension here is to also allow for compressible commodities, and by this introduce the notion of pressure. This can be defined by using $P(v_a, d_j)$ as the pressure in the buffer assigned for dependency type d_j in node v_a. Further, such a buffer can be assigned a maximum pressure resistance, denoted $P_{\max}(v_a, d_j)$, an important safety related characteristic for several different types of physical infrastructure.

Based on the above discussion, dependency types may now be further subdivided into three classes: A dependency type is *ephemeral* if it cannot be stored. In this case there is no buffer volume assigned to the dependency type, i.e. $V_a^j = 0$ for all nodes v_a, and obviously $N_{\max}(v_a, d_j) = 0$. A resource may also be *storable and incompressible*. In this case the capacity of the buffer is given by $N_{\max}(v_a, d_j) = \rho V_a$, where ρ is the density of the resource. Finally, a dependency type can be *storable and compressible*. This characteristic is defined by the maximal pressure supported by a given buffer $N_{\max}(v_a, d_j) = P_{\max}(v_a, d_j)V_a$. $P_{\max}(v_a, d_j)$ is the maximum pressure supported in the storage of resource d_j in the node v_a. Further refinements such as multiple storage stages (e.g. requiring staging of resources from long-term storage to operational status) and logistical aspects are not covered at the abstraction level of the model described here, but are straightforward where such physical infrastructures are considered in greater detail.

Arcs may be similarly characterised further by properties. Depending on the nature of the dependency between two nodes there will be some flow, x, between then. This can be a binary, integer or continuous flow. Given these properties and constraints on the vertexes, it is natural to introduce some properties on the arcs of the graph. The value of x on a given arc $(v_a, v_b)_i^j$ is denoted $x_{a,b,i,j}$. As dependency problems can — similar to the Leontief and IIO models described in section 2 — be described in terms of flows, this includes the definition of the capacity $C_{\max}(e_i^j(v_a, v_b)) \in \mathbb{N}_0$ and the lower bound $C_{\min}(e_i^j(v_a, v_b)) \in \mathbb{N}_0$ are for each arc. Although typically required for modelling flow or similar optimisation problems, the basic model described here does not include cost or balance vectors for arcs. This simplified representation now allows the network $\mathscr{N}$ to be denoted by $(\mathscr{V}, \mathscr{A}, C_{\max}, C_{\min})$. For each instance of the networks, the state can now be characterized with two $g \times m$ matrices $C_{\max}$ and $C_{\min}$, where $g = |\mathscr{E}|$ and m is the number of dependency types.

Response Function: Representing Interaction between Components. Let $r_a^j(t)$ be the amount of dependency type j produced in node v_a at time t. $D(t)$ is defined to be a

$k \times m$ matrix over $\mathbb{Z}$ describing the amount of resources of dependency type j available at the vertex v_a at time t. It follows that the initial state of D is given by equation 3.

$$D_{aj}(0) = r_a^j(0). \tag{3}$$

For every edge in $\mathcal{E}$, a response function $R_i^j(v_a, v_b) :$ can then be defined as shown in equation 4.

$$D_{aj} \times V_a^j \times N_a^j \times N_{\max}(v_a, j) \times C_{\max} \times C_{\min} \longrightarrow \mathbb{N}_0 \tag{4}$$

Equation 4 determines the i-th flow of type j between the vertices v_a and ensures that v_b is defined. The function $R_i^j(v_a, v_b)$ w.l.o.g. is defined as a linear function, and may contain some prioritizing scheme over i and v_b. By constraining the response function to a linear function and discrete values for both time steps and resources, linear programming approaches can be employed for optimization of the relevant parameters; interior point methods for this type of problem such as [72, 120] exhibit computational complexity of the order of $O(n^{7/2})$, also permitting the efficient analysis of larger graphs.

Given the responses at time t, the amount of resource j available in any vertex v_a at time $t+1$ is given by equation 5.

$$D_{aj}(t+1) = r_a^j(t) + N_a^j(t) + \sum_{i,s|e_i^j(v_s,v_a)\in\mathcal{E}} R_i^j(v_s, v_a, t). \tag{5}$$

A node v_a is said to be *functional* at time t if it receives or generates the resources needed to satisfy its internal needs; that is, $D_{aj}(t) > 0$ for all dependency types j which are such that $e_i^j(v_b, v_a) \in \mathcal{E}$, where $b \in \{1, \ldots, a-1, a+1, \ldots k\}$. If this is the case for only some of the dependency types, the node is said to be partially functional, and finally, if non of the requirements are satisfied, the node is said to be *dysfunctional*.

As seen from equation 5, a single-step model with one state memory has been chosen for the sake of simplicity; the model can be naturally extended to arbitrary state memory retention. The model described here can be used to represent any topology given a set of infrastructures and their interconnections. It cannot, however, achieve the level of accuracy found in dedicated network simulators. Despite this, it has the advantage of being able to estimate the consequences of cascading failures through large-scale interconnected infrastructures.

The model outlined here serves mainly to the investigation of higher-level network effects (i.e. node functionality) and interrelations (connectivity of nodes) in interconnected infrastructures, identifying the effects of different attack scenarios as well as criteria and mechanisms for enhancing the robustness of the resulting interdependency multigraphs. This provides a natural progression from the initial studies of large complex networks which concentrated on evaluating the robustness of attacks towards the infrastructure based on static failures as proposed e.g. by Cohen *et al.* [37] or Callaway *et al.* [29], i.e. removing a fraction of nodes in the network and estimating how the performance or connectivity of network is affected by the induced failure. In dependency networks, as in the case of electric power distribution networks and the telephony transport network used in subsequent (purely illustrative) examples, the breakdown or partial degradation of a node may cause cascading failures and have other time-dependent dynamic effects through the network detectable only through a dynamic approach to the networks, which the model discussed in this section provides.

6   Agent-Based Models

Agent-based models are frequently used in interdependency and infrastructure analysis. Infrastructures or physical components are modeled as agents, allowing analysis of the operational characteristics and physical states of infrastructures, but also provide the ability to capture behavioural aspects including non-rational behaviour [111].

Such agent-based systems have been used extensively in other domains, which allowed to draw on a large body of existing work for capturing aspects such as physical behaviour. An early example of such models applied to critical infrastructures is the work by Barton and Stamber [15], concentrating mainly on describing physical agent interactions, while the early work by North drew on models of social agents interacting, but subsequently also integrated descriptions of physical interactions to capture the behaviour of agents in the electric power grid and natural gas markets [100]. In some cases modelling and particularly individual agents' behaviour may not be feasible, requiring the approximation of group behaviour. One example of such aggregate behaviour description was provided by Thomas et al. in linking the behaviour of agents in a multi-layer model to complex adaptive system aggregate descriptions [128].

However, most research focuses on utilising a smaller number of explicit agents to describe the behavior of interacting agents to capture interdependencies in infrastructures; this is exemplified by work such as the models of Panzieri et al. [105] or Balducelli et al. [11], which also relies on explicit discrete event simulations to obtain an understanding of dynamic interactions among agents. Agent-based mechanisms allow both the use of fine-grained internal models and also the effective encapsulation of different levels of detail; an example of such an agent-based modelling and simulation environment is the work by De Porcellinis et al. [43] as a follow-on effort of [105], which is a hybrid of interdependency analysis using qualitative techniques for identifying parameters inducing interdependencies and of system analysis, a semi-quantitative approach based on simulations. In this approach, the model is constructed from constituent elements, but with emergent properties, also referred to as *complex adaptive systems*. Agents are represented as entities with a geospatial location (see also section 7), a number of domain-specific capabilities, and internal memory, while events such as faults and the communication of operational status are exchanged via messaging protocols in a discrete event simulation.

Although highly detailed models of infrastructures in specific sectors may exist, this is not necessarily universal and, moreover, obtaining comprehensive and complete data sets may be difficult to obtain even if the analytical and simulation mechanisms exist. This has also given rise to several qualitative models and simulation environments whose main purpose is to allow an expert to visualise the interrelationships among sectors and infrastructure elements without necessarily providing predictive capabilities. One such environment was developed by Dudenhoeffer et al. [48, 49]; in the CIMS Critical Infrastructure Modeling System, entities are geo-referenced and linked through graphs representing interconnections and dependencies, while events arising from agents and from the environment such as fires or flooding were imposed within a discrete event simulation environment.

A related approach of explicitly using agent-based mechanisms to link (or federate) interactions among partial simulations with a formalism describing the local state, services provided, and services used on the part of agents with an explicit interdependency function based on service provision Casalicchio *et al.* [32]; this abstract formulation is, however, largely equivalent to the model described in section 5.1 as it does not ascribe autonomous agency explicitly and only provides a high-level abstraction of dependencies which is further analysed in [31] while Casalicchio *et al.* [33] subsequently also investigated the relative advantages of agent granularity. Both individual agents and, in the case of sub-models, the level of detail available to such models raise the question of overall model fidelity as described e.g. by Lunden *et al.* [86]. Flammini *et al.* discuss the use of formal modelling languages to interconnect models based on different formalisms, particularly for composing operations between different infrastructure models and layers in case of differing abstraction layers [54]. To this end, Flammini *et al.* propose the use of Generalised Stochastic Petri nets for composing sub-models based on earlier work by Ezell [53]; a similar approach is also described in work by De Porcellinis *et al.* [42].

As noted in section 2, moreover, it is also possible to extend the semantics of global models such as the IIM by explicitly casting it as an agent-based mechanism also allowing the propagation of faults to be modelled [102].

The representation of deterministic or probabilistic agent state in a discrete event simulation environment was also discussed by Cerotti *et al.* [34], utilising a finite-state continuous-time Markov chain to explicitly capture local state; by explicitly modelling entities as separate Markov chains and their interaction in the form of messages, which are transmitted using an explicit propagation function. This permits the analysis of both local state changes and also of messages being accepted by agents, providing the ability to determine the state probability distribution.

Agent-based mechanisms can, finally, also be utilised to capture explicit properties of interactions; while Cerotti *et al.* rely on a global distribution, work such as the model proposed by Hare and Goldstein seeks to investigate interactions based on a sparse interaction graph [67] as the ability to interact with other agents has a direct influence on decisions; where limited parameters are available, this allows the investigation of a larger state space also for structural properties. Hare and Goldstein use this approach to study dependencies of attacks on resource commitment based on combining the game-theoretical models described in section 4 at the agent level; this, however, can then be subjected to an analysis of how restricted (small-world, see section 5) interactions can cause "tipping" effects not identifiable when assuming a higher density of the interaction graph among agents.

7   Physical and Geospatial Models

The need to understand risks of failure and attack in physical systems and critical infrastructures substantially pre-dates the concept itself, and a large number of highly detailed and mature models for individual aspects of selected sectors such as electric power grids and pipeline systems exist to the component level (see table 2). However, such models are typically intended to solve smaller, well-defined problems within the individual sector or for a given component and may hence exhibit high computational complexity whilst varying considerably in the level of detail provided [111]. The level of detail may still, however, vary ranging from simple vulnerability and intra-sector dependency analyses to continuous physical models such as fluid dynamics, chemical and biological processes, or electrical networks.

Such models are necessary for the internal operation of infrastructures as e.g. exemplified for the case of gas pipelines by Zhu et al. [140] and Aalto [1], which permits the quantitative risk analysis for non-adversarial risks [66]. However, external influences on critical infrastructures such as fire, flooding, and explosions are of equal concern, while some sector models such as the aforementioned example of gas pipeline models must necessarily consider such events also as being generated within the model. A particular example of this approach is the case of fire dynamics and concomitant effects, which have been studied intensively; here, Drysdale provides a general introduction [47] while Olenick provides a recent review of models [101]. A model in widespread use for simulating fire and smoke propagation also in enclosed spaces is the U.S. National Institute of Standards and Technology's *Fire Dynamics Simulator* [91]. Similarly, explosions and blast damage, particularly blast overpressure damage has been studied both experimentally and using different types of first-principle models [8, 36].

Spatial proximity provides an important parameter when studying interdependencies and physical effects, which is not always clear from an analysis of logical dependencies alone [111]; a number of efforts have therefore sought to base models of critical infrastructures and their interdependencies around geospatial information systems (GIS) [135]. Examples of the use of GIS features in the critical infrastructure domain include Patterson and Apostolakis' Monte Carlo approach based on multi-attribute utility theory to predict locations of interest e.g. to targeted attacks incorporating GIS features. Other models also take multiple infrastructure types into account, as exemplified by the work of Patterson and Apostolakis [107]. Application areas for selected critical infrastructures are the integration of geospatial and hydraulic models Ingedluld [109] to enable real time response and contingency planning within the water distribution system. Water distribution systems are highly vulnerable to degradation of quality and reliability of supply, and multiple threats can be identified (natural, accidental, and intentional). Rapid recognition of the nature and location of an occurrence is vital to protect the integrity of the water supply, and it is claimed that the proposed tool in combination with a SCADA system for water treatment plants, active element control, and monitoring of critical points in the distribution system are invaluable resources for operators for real time response and contingency planning. An example of a model which also introduces geological sub-models in an effort to assess risks to different infrastructure types and sectors is the network-centric GIS application developed by Abdalla et al. [2]; here, a a framework GIS is employed to provide the interconnection and ability to correlate sub-models of different detail gradations. Moreover, although such models are typically quantitative, they also can provide further benefits in the form of visualisation as in the case of work by Lunden et al. [86] for small-scale environments such as built-up areas and Tolone [129] for larger geographical areas.

8   Conclusion

As both the scale and nature of critical infrastructures often does not permit experiments, much of the burden in understanding critical infrastructure, particularly also
their interconnections, emergent properties, and robustness to adversarial action falls
on model-building efforts. This chapter has attempted to highlight several techniques
which have been used extensively or are the subject of on-going research efforts. Even
so it can only be a somewhat arbitrary selection of techniques and mechanisms as the
exact choice of question posed to a model is necessarily driving the choice of modelling technique as much as the ability to represent such models in a way as to obtain
predictive results.

One of the key challenges particularly for large-scale systems with no clear boundaries as is the case for critical information infrastructures is the ability to describe
agency, particularly of adversaries; while the study of complex networks is able to describe the behaviour of very large networks, such models are necessarily restricted to
aggregate or phase-transition mechanisms, while the fine-grained physical models exemplified in section 7 can capture intricate detail including detailed modelling of physical and logical manipulation of small-scale entities including agent behaviour. However,
the modelling of adversaries and adversary behaviour itself in this context remains an
area of ongoing research [90].

References

1. Aalto, H.: Real-Time Receding Horizon Optimisation of Gas Pipeline Networks. Ph.D.
   thesis, Department of Automation and Systems Technology, Helsinki University of Technology, Espoo, Finland (2005)
2. Abdalla, R.M., Niall, K.M.: Location-Based Critical Infrastructure Interdependency
   (LBCII). Tech. Rep. TR 2009-130, Defence Research and Development Canada, Toronto,
   Ontario, Canada (2010)
3. Abele-Wigert, I., Dunn, M., Wenger, A., Mauer, V. (eds.): International CIIP Handbook
   2006: An Inventory of 20 National and 6 International Critical Information Infrastructure Protection Policies, 3rd edn. Center for Security Studies, vol. I. ETH Zurich, Zurich,
   Switzerland (2006)
4. Albert, R., Albert, I., Nakarado, G.L.: Structural Vulnerability of the North American Power
   Grid. Physical Review E – Statistical, Nonlinear, and Soft Matter Physics 69(2), 025103
   (2004), doi:10.1103/PhysRevE.69.025103
5. Albert, R., Barabási, A.L.: Emergence of Scaling in Random Networks. Science 286(5439),
   509–512 (1999), doi:10.1126/science.286.5439.509
6. Albert, R., Barabási, A.L.: Statistical Mechanics of Complex Networks. Reviews of Modern
   Physics 74(1), 47–97 (2002), doi:10.1103/RevModPhys.74.47
7. Albert, R., Jeong, H., Barabási, A.L.: Error and Attack Tolerance of Complex Networks.
   Nature 406, 378–382 (2000), doi:10.1038/35019019
8. Alonso, F.D., Ferradása, E.G., Sánchez Péreza, J.F., Miñana Aznara, A., Ruiz Gimenoa,
   J., Martínez Alonso, J.: Characteristic Overpressure-Impulse-Distance Curves for Vapour
   Cloud Explosions Using the TNO Multi-Energy Model. Journal of Hazardous Materi-
   als 137(2), 734–741 (2006), doi:10.1016/j.jhazmat.2006.04.005

9. Andrijcic, E., Horowitz, B.: A Macro-Economic Framework for Evaluation of Cyber Security Risks Related to Protection of Intellectual Property. Risk Analysis 26(4), 907–923 (2006), doi:10.1111/j.1539-6924.2006.00787.x
10. Assaf, D.: Models of Critical Information Infrastructure Protection. International Journal of Critical Infrastructure Protection 1(1), 6–14 (2008), doi:10.1016/j.ijcip.2008.08.004
11. Balducelli, C., Bologna, S., Di Pietro, A., Vicoli, G.: Analysing Interdependencies of Critical Infrastructures using Agent Discrete Event Simulation. International Journal of Emergency Management 2(4), 306–318 (2005), doi:10.1504/IJEM.2005.008742
12. Barker, K., Santos, J.R.: Measuring the Efficacy of Inventory with a Dynamic Input-Output Model. International Journal of Production Economics 126(1), 130–143 (2010), doi:10.1016/j.ijpe.2009.08.011
13. Barrat, A., Barthélemy, M., Vespignani, A.: Dynamical Processes on Complex Networks. Cambridge University Press, Cambridge (2008)
14. Barrat, A., Weigl, M.: On the Properties of Small-World Network Models. The European Physical Journal B — Condensed Matter and Complex Systems 13(3), 547–560 (2000), doi:10.1007/s100510050067
15. Barton, D.C., Stamber, K.L.: An Agent-Based Microsimulation of Critical Infrastructure Systems. Tech. Rep. SAND2000-0808C, Sandia National Laboratories, Albuquerque, NM, USA (2000)
16. Beck, U.: Risikogesellschaft: Auf dem Weg in eine andere Moderne. Edition Suhrkamp. Suhrkamp, Frankfurt, Germany (1986)
17. Bérard, C.: Group Model Building Using System Dynamics: An Analysis of Methodological Frameworks. Electronic Journal of Business Research Methods 8(1), 35–45 (2010)
18. Bier, V., Oliveros, S., Samuelson, L.: Choosing What to Protect: Strategic Defensive Allocation against an Unknown Attacker. Journal of Public Economic Theory 9(4), 563–587 (2007), doi:10.1111/j.1467-9779.2007.00320.x
19. Bier, V.M.: Game Theoretic Models for Critical Infrastructure Protection. Abstracts of the 2001 Society for Risk Analysis Annual Meeting "Risk Analysis in an Interconnected World" (2001)
20. Bier, V.M., Ferson, S., Haimes, Y.Y., Lambert, J.H., Small, M.J.: Risk of Extreme and Rare Events: Lessons from a Selection of Approaches. In: Risk Analysis and Society: An Interdisciplinary Characterization of the Field, pp. 74–118. Cambridge University Press, Cambridge (2004)
21. Bollobás, B.: Modern Graph Theory. Graduate Texts in Mathematics, vol. 184. Springer, Berlin (1998)
22. Bollobás, B., Kozma, R., Miklós, D. (eds.): Handbook of Large-Scale Random Networks. Bolyai Society Mathematical Studies, vol. 18. János Bolyai Mathematical Society and Springer, Budapest (2009)
23. Bollobás, B., Riordan, O.: The Diameter of a Scale-Free Random Graph. Combinatorica 24(1), 5–34 (2004), doi:10.1007/s00493-004-0002-2
24. Borgatti, S.P.: Centrality and Network Flow. Social Networks 27(1), 55–71 (2005), doi:10.1016/j.socnet.2004.11.008
25. Brams, S., Kilgour, M.D.: Game Theory and National Security. Basil Blackwell, Oxford (1988)
26. Branzel, R., Dimitrov, D., Tijs, S.: Models in Cooperative Game Theory, 2nd edn. Springer, Heidelberg (2008)
27. Burke, D.A.: Towards a Game Theory Model of Information Warfare. Ph.D. thesis, Faculty of the Graduate School of Engineering and Management, Air Force Institute of Technology, Wright-Patterson Air Force Base, OH, USA (1999)

28. Bush, B.B., Dauelsberg, L.R., LeClaire, R.J., Powell, D.R., DeLand, S.M., Samsa, M.E.: Critical Infrastructure Protection Decision Support System (CIP/DSS) Project Overview. Tech. Rep. LA-UR-05-1870, Los Alamos National Laboratory, Los Alamos, NM, USA (2005)

29. Callaway, D.S., Newman, M.E.J., Strogatz, S.H., Watts, D.S.: Network Robustness and Fragility: Percolation on Random Graphs. Physical Review Letters 85(25), 5468–5471 (2000), doi:10.1103/PhysRevLett.85.5468

30. Carvalho, R., Buzna, L., Bono, F., Gutiérrez, E., Just, W., Arrowsmith, D.: Robustness of trans-European Gas Networks. Physical Review E – Statistical, Nonlinear, and Soft Matter Physics 80(1), 016106 (2009), doi:10.1103/PhysRevE.80.016106

31. Casalicchio, E., Galli, E.: Metrics For Quantifying Interdependencies. In: Papa, M., Shenoi, S. (eds.) Critical Infrastructure Protection II: Proceedings of the Second Annual IFIP Working Group 11.10 International Conference on Critical Infrastructure Protection. IFIP, vol. 290, pp. 215–227. Springer, Arlington (2008), doi:10.1007/978-0-387-88523-0_16

32. Casalicchio, E., Galli, E., Tucci, S.: Modeling and Simulation of Complex Interdependent Systems: A Federated Agent-Based Approach. In: Setola, R., Geretshuber, S. (eds.) CRITIS 2008. LNCS, vol. 5508, pp. 72–83. Springer, Heidelberg (2009), doi:10.1007/978-3-642-03552-4_7

33. Casalicchio, E., Galli, E., Tucci, S.: Macro and Micro Agent-Based Modeling and Simulation of Critical Infrastructures. In: Rizzo, A. (ed.) Complexity in Engineering (COMPENG 2010), pp. 79–81. IEEE Press, Rome (2010), doi:10.1109/COMPENG.2010.20

34. Cerotti, D., Gribaudo, M., Bobbio, A.: Disaster Propagation in Heterogeneous Media via Markovian Agents. In: Setola, R., Geretshuber, S. (eds.) CRITIS 2008. LNCS, vol. 5508, pp. 328–335. Springer, Heidelberg (2009), doi:10.1007/978-3-642-03552-4_31

35. Chassin, D.P., Posse, C.: Evaluating North American Electric Grid Reliability using the Barabási-Albert Network Model. Physica A: Statistical Mechanics and Its Applications 355(2-4), 667–677 (2005), doi:10.1016/j.physa.2005.02.051

36. Cleaver, R.P., Humphreys, C.E., Morgan, J.D., Robinson, C.G.: Development of a Model to Predict the Effects of Explosions in Compact Congested Regions. Journal of Hazardous Materials 53(1–3), 35–55 (1997), doi:10.1016/S0304-3894(96)01817-1

37. Cohen, R., Erez, K., ben Avraham, D., Havlin, S.: Resilience of the Internet to Random Breakdowns. Physical Review Letters 85(21), 4626–4628 (2000), doi:10.1103/PhysRevLett.85.4626

38. Cohen, R., Erez, K., ben Avraham, D., Havlin, S.: Breakdown of the Internet under Intentional Attack. Physical Review Letters 86(16), 3682–3685 (2001), doi:10.1103/PhysRevLett.86.3682

39. Crowther, K.G.: Decentralized Risk Management for Strategic Preparedness of Critical Infrastructure through Decomposition of the Inoperability Input–Output Model. International Journal of Critical Infrastructure Protection 1(1), 53–67 (2008), doi:10.1016/j.ijcip.2008.08.009

40. D'Agostino, G., Cannata, R., Rosato, V.: On Modelling of Inter-dependent Network Infrastructures by Extended Leontief Models. In: Rome, E., Bloomfield, R. (eds.) CRITIS 2009. LNCS, vol. 6027, pp. 1–13. Springer, Heidelberg (2010), doi:10.1007/978-3-642-14379-3_1

41. Dauelsberg, L., Outkin, A.: Modeling Economic Impacts to Critical Infrastructures in a System Dynamics Framework. In: Sterman, J.D., Repenning, N.P., Langer, R.S., Rowe, J.I., Yanni, J.M. (eds.) Proceedings of the 23rd International Conference of the System Dynamics Society, p. 63. System Dynamics Society, Boston (2005)

42. De Porcellinis, S., Oliva, G., Panzieri, S., Setola, R.: A Holistic-Reductionistic Approach for Modeling Interdependencies. In: Palmer, C., Shenoi, S. (eds.) Critical Infrastructure Protection III: Proceedings of the Third Annual IFIP Working Group 11.10 International Conference on Critical Infrastructure Protection. IFIP AICT, vol. 311, pp. 215–227. Springer, Hanover (2009), doi:10.1007/978-3-642-04798-5_15

43. De Porcellinis, S., Panzieri, S., Setola, R., Ulivi, G.: Simulation of Heterogeneous and Interdependent Critical Infrastructures. International Journal of Critical Infrastructures 4(1/2), 110–128 (2008), doi:10.1504/IJCIS.2008.016095

44. de Solla Price, D.J.: Networks of Scientific Papers. Science 149(3683), 510–515 (1965), doi:10.1126/science.149.3683.510

45. Dietzenbacher, E., Lahr, M.L. (eds.): Wassily Leontief and Input-Output Economics. Cambridge University Press, Cambridge (2004)

46. Dorogovtsev, S.N., Goltsev, A.V., Mendes, J.F.F.: Critical Phenomena in Complex Networks. Reviews of Modern Physics 80(4), 1275–1335 (2008), doi:10.1103/RevModPhys.80.1275

47. Drysdale, D.: An Introduction to Fire Dynamics, 2nd edn. John Wiley & Sons, Chichester (2002)

48. Dudenhoeffer, D.D., Permann, M.R., Manic, M.: CIMS: A Framework for Infrastructure Interdependency Modeling and Analysis. In: Proceedings of the 2006 Winter Simulation Conference (WSC 2006), p. 478. IEEE Press, Phoenix (2006), doi:10.1109/WSC.2006.323119

49. Dudenhoeffer, D.D., Permann, M.R., Sussman, E.M.: A Parallel Simulation Framework for Infrastructure Modeling and Analysis. In: Proceedings of the 34th Winter Simulation Conference (WSC 2002), p. 1971. IEEE Press, San Diego (2002), doi:10.1109/WSC.2002.1166498

50. Dunn, M., Mauer, V., Abele-Wigert, I. (eds.): Inetnational CIIP Handbook 2006: Analyzing Issues, Challenges, and Prospects, 3rd edn. Center for Security Studies, vol. II. ETH Zurich, Zurich (2006)

51. Erdős, P., Rényi, A.: On Random Graphs. Publicationes Mathematicae (Debrecen) 6, 290–297 (1959)

52. Erdős, P., Rényi, A.: On the Evolution of Random Graphs. Publications of the Mathematical Institute of the Hungarian Academy of Sciences 5, 17–61 (1960)

53. Ezell, B.C.: Infrastructure Vulnerability Assessment Model (I-VAM). Risk Analysis 27(3), 571–583 (2007), doi:10.1111/j.1539-6924.2007.00907.x

54. Flammini, F., Vittorini, V., Mazzocca, N., Pragliola, C.: A Study on Multiformalism Modeling of Critical Infrastructures. In: Setola, R., Geretshuber, S. (eds.) CRITIS 2008. LNCS, vol. 5508, pp. 336–343. Springer, Heidelberg (2009), doi:10.1007/978-3-642-03552-4_32

55. Flaxman, A.D., Frieze, A.M., Vera, J.: Adversarial Deletion in a Scale-Free Random Graph Process. Combinatorics, Probability and Computing 16(2), 261–270 (2007), doi:10.1017/S0963548306007681

56. Forrester, J.W.: Industrial Dynamics. Pegasus Communications, Waltham, MA, USA (1961)

57. Forrester, J.W.: Principles of Systems, 2nd edn. Pegasus Communications, Waltham, MA, USA (1961)

58. Fudenberg, D., Tirole, J.: Game Theory. MIT Press, Cambridge (1991)

59. Ghosh, A.: Input-Output Approach in an Allocation System. Economica 25(97), 58–64 (1958)

60. Gonzalez, J.J., Sarriegi, J.M., Gurrutxaga, A.: A Framework for Conceptualizing Social Engineering Attacks. In: López, J. (ed.) CRITIS 2006. LNCS, vol. 4347, pp. 79–90. Springer, Heidelberg (2006), doi:10.1007/11962977_7

61. Haimes, Y.Y., Chittester, C.G.: A Roadmap for Quantifying the Efficacy of Risk Management of Information Security and Interdependent SCADA Systems. Journal of Homeland Security and Emergency Management 2(2), 1–23 (2005), doi:10.2202/1547-7355.1117

62. Haimes, Y.Y., Horowitz, B.M., Lambert, J.H., Santos, J.R., Crowther, K.G., Lian, C.: Inoperability Input-Output Model for Interdependent Infrastructure Sectors II: Case Studies. Journal of Infrastructure Systems 11(2), 80–92 (2005), doi:10.1061/(ASCE)1076-0342(2005)11:2(80)

63. Haimes, Y.Y., Horowitz, B.M., Lambert, J.H., Santos, J.R., Lian, C., Crowther, K.G.: Inoperability Input-Output Model for Interdependent Infrastructure Sectors I: Theory and Methodology. Journal of Infrastructure Systems 11(2), 67–79 (2005), doi:10.1061/(ASCE)1076-0342(2005)11:2(67)

64. Haimes, Y.Y., Jiang, P.: Leontief-Based Model of Risk in Complex Interconnected Infrastructures. Journal of Infrastructure Systems 7(1), 1–12 (2001), doi:10.1061/(ASCE)1076-0342(2001)7:1(1)

65. Hamilton, T., Mesic, R.: A Simple Game-Theoretic Approach to Suppression of Enemy Defenses and Other Time Critical Target Analyses. Tech. Rep. DB-385-AF, RAND Corporation, Santa Monica, CA, USA (2004)

66. Han, Z.Y., Weng, W.G.: An Integrated Quantitative Risk Analysis Method for Natural Gas Pipeline Network. Journal of Loss Prevention in the Process Industries 23(3), 428–436 (2010), doi:10.1016/j.jlp.2010.02.003

67. Hare, F., Goldstein, J.: The Interdependent Security Problem in the Defense Industrial Base: An Agent-Based Model on a Social Network. International Journal of Critical Infrastructure Protection 3(3–4), 128–139 (2010), doi:10.1016/j.ijcip.2010.07.001

68. Haywood Jr., O.G.: Military Decision and Game Theory. Operations Research 2(4), 365–385 (1954), doi:10.1287/opre.2.4.365

69. Hernantes, J., Lauge, A., Labaka, L., Rich, E.H., Sveen, F.O., Sarriegi, J.M., Martinez-Moyano, I.J., Gonzalez, J.J.: Collaborative Modeling of Awareness in Critical Infrastructure Protection. In: Proceedings of the 44th Hawaii International International Conference on Systems Science (HICSS-44 2011), pp. 1–10. IEEE Press, Koloa (2011), doi:10.1109/HICSS.2011.113

70. Jenelius, E., Westin, J., Holmgren, Å.J.: Critical Infrastructure Protection under Imperfect Attacker Perception. International Journal of Critical Infrastructure Protection 3(1), 16–26 (2010), doi:10.1016/j.ijcip.2009.10.002

71. Jung, J.: Probabilistic Extension to the Inoperability Input-Output Model: P-IIM. Ph.D. thesis, University of Virginia, Department of Systems and Information Engineering, Charlottesville, VA, USA (2009)

72. Karmarkar, N.: A New Polynomial-Time Algorithm for Linear Programming. Combinatorica 4(4), 373–395 (1984), doi:10.1007/BF02579150

73. Kim, D.H., Motter, A.E.: Fluctuation-Driven Capacity Distribution in Complex Networks. New Journal of Physics 10, 053022 (2008), doi: 10.1088/1367-2630/10/5/053022

74. Kim, D.H., Motter, A.E.: Resource Allocation Pattern in Infrastructure Networks. Journal of Physics A: Mathematical and Theoretical 41(22), 224019 (2008), doi: 10.1088/1751-8113/41/22/224019

75. Kim, J., Dobson, I.: Approximating a Loading-Dependent Cascading Failure Model With a Branching Process. IEEE Transactions on Reliability 59(4), 691–699 (2010), doi:10.1109/TR.2010.2055928

76. Lagadec, P.: La Civilisation du Risque: Catastrophes Technologiques et Responsabilité Sociale. Science Ouverte. Éditions du Seuil, Paris, France (1981)

77. Lakdawalla, D.N., Zanjani, G.: Insurance, Self-Protection, and the Economics of Terrorism. Tech. Rep. WR-171-ICJ, RAND Corporation, Santa Monica, CA, USA (2004)

78. LeClaire, R., Bush, B., Dauelsberg, L., Powell, D.: Critical Infrastructure Protection Decision Support System. In: Sterman, J.D., Repenning, N.P., Langer, R.S., Rowe, J.I., Yanni, J.M. (eds.) Proceedings of the 23rd International Conference of the System Dynamics Society, p. 97. System Dynamics Society, Boston (2005)

79. LeClaire, R., O'Reilly, G.: Leveraging a High Fidelity Switched Network Model to Inform a System Dynamics Model of the Telecommunications Infrastructure. In: Sterman, J.D., Repenning, N.P., Langer, R.S., Rowe, J.I., Yanni, J.M. (eds.) Proceedings of the 23rd International Conference of the System Dynamics Society, p. 97. System Dynamics Society, Boston (2005)

80. Leontief, W. (ed.): Input-Output Economics, 2nd edn. Oxford University Press, Oxford (1986)

81. Leung, M., Haimes, Y.Y., Santos, J.R.: Supply- and Output-Side Extensions to the Inoperability Input-Output Model for Interdependent Infrastructures. Journal of Infrastructure Systems 13(4), 299–310 (2007), doi:10.1061/(ASCE)1076-0342(2007)13:4(299)

82. Leung, M.F.P.: Supply- and Output-Side Extensions to Inoperability Input-Output Model (IIM) with Application to Interdependencies of Road Transportation System. Ph.D. thesis, University of Virginia, Department of Systems and Information Engineering, Charlottesville, VA, USA (2006)

83. Lian, C., Haimes, Y.Y.: Managing the Risk of Terrorism to Interdependent Infrastructure Systems through the Dynamic Inoperability Input-Output Model. Systems Engineering 9(3), 241–258 (2006), doi:10.1002/sys.20051

84. Liu, D., Wang, X.F., Camp, J.: Game-Theoretic Modeling and Analysis of Insider Threats. International Journal of Critical Infrastructure Protection 1(1), 75–80 (2008), doi:10.1016/j.ijcip.2008.08.001

85. Liu, Y.-Y., Slotine, J.-J., Barabási, A.-L.: Controllability of Complex Network. Nature 473, 167–173 (2011), doi:10.1038/nature10011

86. Lunden, N., Sveen, R., Lund, H., Svendsen, N., Wolthusen, S.: Interactive Visualization of Interdependencies and Vulnerabilities in Constrained Environments. In: Moore, T., Shenoi, S. (eds.) Critical Infrastructure Protection IV: Proceedings of the Fourth Annual IFIP Working Group 11.10 International Conference on Critical Infrastructure Protection. IFIP AICT, vol. 342, pp. 171–183. Springer, Washington D.C (2010), doi:10.1007/978-3-642-16806-2_12

87. Magnien, C., Latapy, M., Guillaume, J.L.: Impact of Random Failures and Attacks on Poisson and Power-Law Random Networks. ACM Computing Surveys 43(3), 13 (2011), doi:10.1145/1922649.1922650

88. Major, J.A.: Advanced Techniques for Modeling Terrorism Risk. The Journal of Risk Finance 4(1), 15–24 (2002), doi:10.1108/eb022950

89. Marsh, R.T. (ed.): Critical Infrastructures: Protecting America's Infrastructures. United States Government Printing Office, Washington D.C., USA (1997); Report of the President's Commission on Critical Infrastructure Protection

90. McEvoy, T.R., Wolthusen, S.D.: A Formal Adversary Capability Model for SCADA Environments. In: Xenakis, C., Wolthusen, S. (eds.) CRITIS 2010. LNCS, vol. 6712, pp. 93–103. Springer, Heidelberg (2011)

91. McGrattan, K., Baum, H., Rehm, R., Mell, W., McDermott, R., Hostikka, S., Floyd, J.: Fire Dynamics Simulator (Version 5) Technical Reference Guide Volume 1: Mathematical Model. National Institute of Standards and Technology, Gaithersburg, MD, USA, NIST Special Publication 1018-5 (2009)

92. Milgram, S.: The Small World Problem. Psychology Today 1(1), 60–67 (1967)

93. Min, H.S.J., Beyeler, W., Brown, T., Son, Y.J., Jones, A.T.: Toward Modeling and Simulation of Critical National Infrastructure Interdependencies. IIE Transactions 39(1), 57–71 (2007), doi:10.1080/07408170600940005

94. Motter, A.E., Lai, Y.C.: Cascade-Based Attacks on Complex Networks. Physical Review E – Statistical, Nonlinear, and Soft Matter Physics 66(6), 378–382 (2002), doi:10.1103/PhysRevE.66.065102

95. von Neumann, J.: Zur Theorie der Gesellschaftsspiele. Mathematische Annalen 100(1), 295–320 (1928), doi:10.1007/BF01448847

96. von Neumann, J., Morgenstern, O.: Theory of Games and Economic Behavior, 2nd edn. Princeton University Press, Princeton (1947)

97. Newman, M., Barabási, A.L., Watts, D.J. (eds.): The Structure and Dynamics of Networks. Princeton Studies in Complexity. Princeton University Press, Princeton (2006)

98. Newman, M.E.J.: The Structure and Function of Complex Networks. SIAM Review 45(2), 167–256 (2003), doi:10.1137/S003614450342480

99. Nieuwenhuijs, A., Luiijf, E., Klaver, M.: Modeling Dependencies In Critical Infrastructures. In: Papa, M., Shenoi, S. (eds.) Critical Infrastructure Protection II: Proceedings of the Second Annual IFIP Working Group 11.10 International Conference on Critical Infrastructure Protection. IFIP, vol. 290, pp. 205–213. Springer, Heidelberg (2008), doi:10.1007/978-0-387-88523-0

100. North, M.: Agent-Basd Modeling of Complex Infrastructures. In: Sallach, D., Wolsko, T. (eds.) Proceedings of the Workshop on Simulation of Social Agents: Architectures and Institutions, pp. 239–250. University of Chicago and Argonne National Laboratory, Chicago (2000); ANL/DIS/TM-60

101. Olenick, S.M., Carpenter, D.J.: An Updated International Survey of Computer Models for Fire and Smoke. Journal of Fire Protection Engineering 13(2), 87–110 (2003), doi:10.1177/1042391503013002001

102. Oliva, G., Panzieri, S., Setola, R.: Agent-Based Input–Output Interdependency Model. International Journal of Critical Infrastructure Protection 3(2), 76–82 (2010), doi:10.1016/j.ijcip.2010.05.001

103. Osborne, M.J., Rubinstein, A.: A Course in Game Theory. MIT Press, Cambridge (1994)

104. Panzieri, S., Setola, R.: Failure Propagation in Critical Interdependent Infrastructures. International Journal of Modelling, Identification, and Control 3(1), 69–78 (2008), doi:10.1504/IJMIC.2008.018186

105. Panzieri, S., Setola, R., Ulivi, G.: An Agent Based Simulator for Critical Interdependent Infrastructures. In: Proceedings of the 2nd International Conference on Critical Infrastructures (CRIS 2004), Grenoble, France (2004)

106. Pasqualini, D., Witkowski, M.S., Klare, P.C., Patelli, P., Cleland, C.A.: A Model for a Water Potable Distribution System and its Impacts resulting from a Water Contamination Scenario. In: Größler, A., Rouwette, E.A.J.A., Langer, R.S., Rowe, J.I., Yanni, J.M. (eds.) Proceedings of the 24th International Conference of the System Dynamics Society, pp. 99–100. Wiley, Nijmegen (2006)

107. Patterson, S.A., Apostolakis, G.E.: Identification of Critical Locations Across Multiple Infrastructures for Terrorist Actions. Reliability Engineering & System Safety 92(9), 1183–1203 (2007), doi:10.1016/j.ress.2006.08.004

108. Perrow, C.: Normal Accidents: Living with High-Risk Technologies. Basic Books, New York (1984)

109. Ingeduld, P.: Real Time Analysis for Early Warning Systems. In: Pollert, J., Dedus, B. (eds.) Security of Water Supply Systems: From Source to Tap. NATO Science for Peace and Security Series C: Environmental Security, vol. 8, pp. 65–84. Springer, Heidelberg (2006), doi:10.1007/1-4020-4564-6_7

110. Rahmani, A., Ji, M., Mesbahi, M., Egerstedt, M.: Controllability of Multi-Agent Systems from a Graph-Theoretic Perspective. SIAM Journal on Control and Optimization 48(1), 162–186 (2009), doi:10.1137/060674909

111. Rinaldi, S.M.: Modeling and Simulating Critical Infrastructures and Their Interdependencies. In: Proceedings of the 37th Annual Hawaii International Conference on System Sciences (HICSS 2004), pp. 1–8. IEEE Computer Society Press, Big Island (2004), doi:10.1109/HICSS.2004.1265180

112. Rinaldi, S.M., Peerenboom, J.P., Kelly, T.K.: Identifying, Understanding, and Analyzing Critical Infrastructure Dependencies. IEEE Control Systems Magazine 21(6), 11–25 (2001), doi:10.1109/37.969131

113. Rosato, V., Issacharoff, L., Tiriticco, F., Meloni, S., De Porcellinis, S., Setola, R.: Modelling Interdependent Infrastructures using Interacting Dynamical Models. International Journal of Critical Infrastructures 4(1/2), 63–79 (2008), doi:10.1504/IJCIS.2008.016092

114. Sandler, T., Arce, D.G.: Terrorism & Game Theory. Simulation & Gaming 34(3), 319–337 (2003), doi:10.1177/1046878103255492

115. Sandler, T., Siqueira, K.: Games and Terrorism. Simulation & Gaming 40(2), 164–192 (2009), doi:10.1177/1046878108314772

116. Santos, J.R.: Interdependency Analysis with Multiple Probabilistic Sector Inputs. Journal of Industrial and Management Optimization 4(3), 489–510 (2008), doi:10.3934/jimo.2008.4.489

117. Santos, J.R., Haimes, Y.Y.: Modeling the Demand Reduction Input-Output (I–O) Inoperability Due to Terrorism of Interconnected Infrastructures. Risk Analysis 24(6), 1437–1451 (2004), doi:10.1111/j.0272-4332.2004.00540.x

118. Santos, J.R., Haimes, Y.Y., Lian, C.: A Framework for Linking Cybersecurity Metrics to the Modeling of Macroeconomic Interdependencies. Risk Analysis 27(5), 1283–1298 (2007), doi:10.1111/j.1539-6924.2007.00957.x

119. Sarriegi, J.M., Santos, J., Torres, J.M., Imizcoz, D., Egozcue, E., Liberal, D.: Modeling and Simulating Information Security Management. In: López, J., Hämmerli, B.M. (eds.) CRITIS 2007. LNCS, vol. 5141, pp. 327–336. Springer, Heidelberg (2008), doi:10.1007/978-3-540-89173-4_27

120. Schrijver, A.: Combinatorial Optimization: Polyhedra and Efficiency. Springer, Heidelberg (2003); Three volumes

121. Setola, R.: Analysis of Interdependencies Between Italy's Economic Sectors. In: Goetz, E., Shenoi, S. (eds.) Critical Infrastructure Protection: Proceedings of the First Annual IFIP Working Group 11.10 International Conference on Critical Infrastructure Protection. IFIP, vol. 253, pp. 311–321. Springer, Hanover (2007), doi:10.1007/978-0-387-75462-8_22

122. Setola, R., De Porcellinis, S., Sforna, M.: Critical Infrastructure Dependency Assessment using the Input–Output Inoperability Model. International Journal of Critical Infrastructure Protection 2(4), 170–178 (2009), doi:10.1016/j.ijcip.2009.09.002

123. Solé, R.V., Rosas-Casals, M., Corominas-Murtra, B., Valverde, S.: Robustness of the European Power Grids under Intentional Attack. Physical Review E – Statistical, Nonlinear, and Soft Matter Physics 77(2), 026102 (2008), doi:10.1103/PhysRevE.77.026102

124. Svendsen, N., Wolthusen, S.: Multigraph Dependency Models for Heterogeneous Infrastructures. In: Goetz, E., Shenoi, S. (eds.) Critical Infrastructure Protection: Proceedings of the First Annual IFIP Working Group 11.10 International Conference on Critical Infrastructure Protection. IFIP, vol. 253, pp. 337–350. Springer, Hanover (2007), doi:10.1007/978-0-387-75462-8_24

125. Svendsen, N.K., Wolthusen, S.D.: An Analysis of Cyclical Interdependencies in Critical Infrastructures. In: Lopez, J., Hämmerli, B.M. (eds.) CRITIS 2007. LNCS, vol. 5141, pp. 25–36. Springer, Heidelberg (2008), doi:10.1007/978-3-540-89173-4_3

126. Tanaka, H.: Quantitative Analysis of Information Security Interdependency between Industrial Sectors. In: Proceedings of the 3rd International Symposium on Empirical Software Engineering and Measurement (ESEM 2009), pp. 574–583. IEEE Computer Society Press, Lake Buena Vista (2009), doi:10.1109/ESEM.2009.5314218

127. Tanner, H.G.: On the Controllability of Nearest Neighbor Interconnections. In: Cassandras, C.G. (ed.) Proceedings of the 43rd IEEE Conference on Decision and Control (CDC 2004), p. 2467. IEEE Press (2004), doi:10.1109/CDC.2004.1428782

128. Thomas, W.H., North, M.J., Macal, C.M., Peerenboom, J.P.: From Physics to Finances: Complex Adaptive Systems Representation of Infrastructure Interdependencies. United States Naval Surface Warfare Center, Dahlgren, VA, USA (2003); Naval Surface Warfare Center Technical Digest

129. Tolone, W.J.: Interactive Visualizations for Critical Infrastructure Analysis. International Journal of Critical Infrastructure Protection 2(3), 124–134 (2009), doi:10.1016/j.ijcip.2009.07.004

130. Travers, J., Milgram, S.: An Experimental Study of the Small World Problem. Sociometry 32(4), 425–443 (1969)

131. United States Department of Commerce, National Institute of Standards and Technology, Computer Systems Laboratory: Integration Definition for Function Modeling (IDEF0). United States Draft Federal Information Standard 183 (1993)

132. Wang, X., Guan, S., Lai, C.H.: Protecting Infrastructure Networks from Cost-Based Attacks. New Journal of Physics 11, 033006 (2009), doi: 10.1088/1367-2630/11/3/033006

133. Watts, D.J.: Small Worlds: The Dynamics of Networks Between Order and Randomness. Princeton University Press, Princeton (1999)

134. Watts, D.J., Strogatz, S.H.: Collective Dynamics of 'Small-World' Networks. Nature 393, 440–442 (1998), doi:10.1038/30918

135. Wolthusen, S.D.: GIS-based Command and Control Infrastructure for Critical Infrastructure Protection. In: Proceedings of the First IEEE International Workshop on Critical Infrastructure Protection (IWCIP 2005), pp. 40–47 (2005), doi:10.1109/IWCIP.2005.12

136. Woo, G.: Quantitative Terrorism Risk Assessment. The Journal of Risk Finance 4(1), 7–14 (2002), doi:10.1108/eb022949

137. Yazdani, A., Jeffrey, P.: Complex Network Analysis of Water Distribution Systems. Chaos 21(1), 016111 (2011), doi:10.1063/1.3540339

138. Yoshida, M., Kobayashi, K.: Disclosure Strategies for Critical Infrastructure against Terror Attacks. In: Proceedings of the 2010 IEEE International Conference on Systems Man and Cybernetics (SMC 2010), pp. 3194–3199. IEEE Press, Istanbul (2010), doi:10.1109/ICSMC.2010.5642277

139. Zhang, G., Wang, C., Zhang, J., Yang, J., Zhang, Y., Duan, M.: Vulnerability Assessment of Bulk Power Grid Based on Complex Network Theory. In: Proceedings of the 3rd International Conference on Electric Utility Deregulation and Restructuring and Power Technologies (DRPT 2008), pp. 1554–1558. IEEE Press, Nanjing (2008), doi:10.1109/DRPT.2008.4523652

140. Zhu, G.Y., Henson, M.A., Megan, L.: Dynamic Modeling and Linear Model Predictive Control of Gas Pipeline Networks. Journal of Process Control 11(2), 129–148 (2001), doi:10.1016/S0959-1524(00)00044-5

Anomaly Detection in Water Management Systems

Massimiliano Raciti, Jordi Cucurull, and Simin Nadjm-Tehrani

Department of Computer and Information Science
Linköping University, Sweden
name.surname@liu.se

Abstract. Quality of drinking water has always been a matter of concern. Traditionally, water supplied by utilities is analysed by independent laboratories to guarantee its quality and suitability for the human consumption. Being part of a critical infrastructure, recently water quality has received attention from the security point of view. Real-time monitoring of water quality requires analysis of sensor data gathered at distributed locations and generation of alarms when changes in quality indicators indicate anomalies. The event detection system should produce accurate alarms, with low latency and few false positives.

This chapter addresses the application of data mining techniques developed for information infrastructure security in a new setting. The hypothesis is that a clustering algorithm ADWICE that has earlier been successfully applied to n-dimensional data spaces in IP networks, can also be deployed for real-time anomaly detection in water management systems. The chapter describes the evaluation of the anomaly detection software when integrated in a SCADA system. The system manages water sensors and provides data for analysis within the Water Security initiative of the U.S. Environmental Protection Agency (EPA). Performance of the algorithm is illustrated and improvements to the collected data to deal with missing and inaccurate data are proposed.

1 Introduction

Water management systems deserve a special attention in critical infrastructure protection due to a number of factors. First, the quality of distributed water affects every single citizen with obvious health hazards. Second, in contrast to some other infrastructures where the physical access to the critical assets may be possible to restrict, in water management systems there is a large number of remote access points difficult to control and protect from accidental or intentional contamination events. Third, in the event of contamination, there are few defence mechanisms available. Water treatment facilities are typically the sole barrier to potential large scale contaminations and distributed containment of the event leads to widespread water shortages. Techniques to model the spatial and temporal distribution of the contaminants [30] can be used, but because the scale of the distribution network they are complex to apply.

A recent health hazard was identified in France where 30 cubic metres of fluid containing 12g per litre of low-grade uranium were spilt at the Tricastin facility near Marseilles [1]. In the USA a major initiative has been established by the US Environmental Protection Agency (EPA) in response to Homeland Security Presidential Directive 9, under which the Agency must "develop robust, comprehensive, and fully

J. Lopez et al. (Eds.): Critical Information Infrastructure Protection, LNCS 7130, pp. 98–119, 2012.

coordinated surveillance and monitoring systems, including international information, for water quality that provides early detection and awareness of disease, pest, or poisonous agents." [2].

Supervisory control and data acquisition (SCADA) systems provide a natural opportunity to increase vigilance against water contaminations. Specialised event detection mechanisms for water management can be included such that 1) a contamination event is detected as early as possible and with high accuracy with few false positives, and 2) predictive capabilities ease preparedness actions in advance of full scale contamination in a utility.

While research on protection of SCADA systems have seen an increased attention in the past decade, most of the reported works focus on how to deploy detection and mitigation mechanisms in the event of an adversary attack on the power networks or the information and communication (ICT) network on which the SCADA system depends [15]. Published literature in which water management systems is the application area, covers the protection of the ICT related security issues for SCADA in water management systems [29], but little work has been published on detection and anticipation of water contaminations using ICT techniques.

The analogy with ICT threats is however not vacuous. Recent advances in intrusion detection target complex ICT environments where large scale systems are integrated with Internet with no well-determined perimeter. Increase in both accidental and malicious activity creates a changing landscape for emergent information infrastructures; hence the difficulty of modelling the system and the attack patterns statically. In these networks, intrusion detection is either based on modelling and recognising the attacks (misuse detection) or modelling the normal behaviour of the system and detecting potential intrusions as a deviation from normality (anomaly detection) [32,24]. While misuse detection provides immediate diagnosis when successful, it is unable to detect cases for which no previous data exists (earlier similar cases in history, a known signature, etc.). Anomaly detection, on the other hand, is able to uncover new attacks not seen earlier, but it is dependent on a good model of normality. Misuse detection requires exact characterisation of known constraints on the historical data set and gives accurate matches for those cases that are modelled. Anomaly detection is most often based on learning techniques which creates an approximate model of normality. A typical problem is the high rate of false positives if attacks and normality data are similar in subtle ways.

The available data from water management system sensors are based on biological, chemical and physical features of the environment and the water sources. Sinche these change over seasons, the normality model is rather complex. Also, it is hard to create a static set of rules or constraints that clearly capture all significant attacks since these can affect various features in non-trivial ways and we get a combinatorial problem. Therefore, we propose the application of learning based anomaly detection techniques as a basis for contamination event detection in water management systems.

Since anomaly detection needs a model of normality one could imagine using classification based techniques to extract models of benign and contaminated data samples automatically. However, the clustered data sets would then have to be individually examined by experts to verify the suitability of the normality clusters (representation of benign data). Another approach would be to get the anomaly detector to only learn normality from data that is known to be benign. In water management systems since it may be possible to analyse water quality in test beds and prepare a calibration a normality model based on benign data can be built. In this paper we explore this direction. An interesting question is then whether the detection technique provides fast enough recognition of the contamination events and whether it can be accurate and reliable enough.

The contributions of this chapter are as follows.

- Application of a method for Anomaly Detection With fast Incremental ClustEring (ADWICE) [8] in a water management system based on measured sensor values from the EPA database.
- Analysis of the performance of the approach for two stations using performance metrics such as detection rate, false positives, detection latency, and sensitivity to the contamination level of the attacks.
- Discussion of reliability of the analysis when data sets are not perfect (as seen in real life scenarios), where data values may be missing or less accurate as indicated by sensor alerts.

The chapter is composed of six sections. Section 2 describes the background. Section 3 describes ADWICE, an existing anomaly detection tool. Section 4 describes the application of ADWICE on a water management system, presents the results obtained, and proposes a technique to deal with unreliable data. Section 5 presents related work in this field. The paper is concluded in Section 6, with description of future works.

2 Background

The monitoring of water quality in a distribution system is a highly complex and sensitive process that is affected by many different factors. The different water qualities coming from multiple sources and treatment plants, the multiplicity of paths that water follows in the system and the changing demand over the week from the final users make it difficult to predict the water quality at a given point of the system life time. Water quality is determined by the analysis of its chemical composition: to be safe to drink some water parameters can vary within a certain range of values, and typically the maximum and the minimum values are established by law. Water from different sources have different compositions. Before entering the distribution system, water is treated first in the treatment plants, in order to ensure its safety. Once processed by the treatment plant, water enters the distribution system so it can be directly pumped to the final user, or stored in tanks or reservoirs for further use when the demand on the system is greater than the system capacity. System operations have a consistent impact on water quality. For instance, pumping water coming from two or more different sources can radically modify the quality parameters of the water contained in a reservoir. In general, the water quality (WQ) is measured by the analysis of some parameters, for example:

- *Chlorine (CL2) levels*: free chlorine is added for disinfection. Free chlorine levels decrease with time, so for instance levels of CL2 in water that is stagnant in tanks is different from levels in water coming from the treatment plants.
- *Conductivity*: estimates the amount of dissolved salts in the water. It is usually constant in water from the same source, but mixing waters can cause a significant change in the final conductivity.
- *Oxygen Reduction Potential (ORP)*: measures the cleanliness of the water.
- *PH*: measures the concentration of hydrogen ions.
- *Temperature*: is usually constant if measured in short periods of time, but it changes with the seasons. It differs in waters from different sources.
- *Total Organic Carbon* (TOC): measures the concentration of organic matter in the water. It may decrease over the time due to the decomposition of organic matters in the water.
- *Turbidity*: measures how clear the water is.

In normal conditions, it is possible to extract some usage patterns from the system operations relating the changes of WQ parameters with changes of some system configurations: for example the cause of a cyclic increment of conductivity and temperature of the water contained in a reservoir can be related to the fact that water of a well known characteristic coming from a treatment plant is cyclically being pumped into the reservoir. This information must be taken into account to avoid false alarms raised by the Event Detection System (EDS).

The situation changes dramatically when some contaminants are intentionally or accidentally injected in some points of the distribution system. Contaminants cause changes in one or more water parameters at the same time, so event detection systems must be able to detect and classify events caused by normal system operations as well as events caused by contaminants. This makes the monitoring of water quality more complex, and effective tools must be applied for this new situation.

The United States Environmental Protection Agency has launched an Event Detection System challenge to identify the best tools applicable to event detection in the water quality domain. In particular, EPA is interested in the development of Contaminant Warning Systems (CWS) that in real-time proactively detect the presence of contaminants in the distribution system. The goal to take the appropriate countermeasures upon unfolding events to limit or cut the supply of contaminated water to users.

The challenge is conducted by providing water quality data from sensors of six monitoring stations from four US water utilities. Data comes directly from the water utilities without any alteration from the evaluators, in order to keep the data in the same condition as if it would come from real-time sensing of the parameters. Data contains WQ parameter values as well as other additional information like operational indicators (levels of water in tanks, active pumps, valves, etc.) and equipment alarms (which indicate whether sensors are working or not). Each station differs from the others in the number and type of those parameters. A baseline data is then provided for each of the six stations. It consists of 3 to 5 months of observations coming from the real water utilities. Each station data has a different time interval between two observations, ranging in the order of few minutes. The contaminated testing dataset is obtained from the baseline data by simulating the superimposition of the contaminant effects on the WQ parameters. Figure 1 [4] is an example of effects of different types of contaminants on the WQ values.

Class	Description	TOC	Cl2	ORP	COND	pH	TURB
1	Petroleum products	↑	—	—	—	—	—
2	Pesticides (reactive)	↑	↓	↓	—	—	—
3	Inorganic compounds	—	↓	↓	↑	—	—
4	Metals	—	—	—	↑	↓	—
5	Pesticides (non-reactive)	↑	—	—	↑	—	—
6	Chemical warfare agents	↑	—	—	—	—	—
7	Radionuclides (metal-salt)	—	—	—	↑	—	—
8	Bacterial toxins (with dechlor agent)	—	↓	↓	↑	—	—
9	Plant toxins	↑	—	—	—	—	—
10	Pathogen (clean with dechlor agent)	—	↓	↓	↑	—	—
11	Pathogen (dirty with growth media)	↑	↓	↓	—	—	↑
12	Persistent chlorinated organics	↑	—	—	—	—	—

Fig. 1. Effect of contaminants on the WQ parameters

EPA has provided a set of 14 simulated contaminants, denoting them contaminant A to contaminant N. Contaminants are not injected along the whole testing sequence, but the attack can be placed in a certain interval inside the testing data, with a duration limited to a few timesteps. Contaminant concentrations are added following a certain profile, which define the rise, the fall, the length of the peak concentration and the total duration of the attack. Figure 2 shows some examples of profiles.

To facilitate the deployment and the evaluation of the EDS tools, a software called EDDIES has been developed and distributed by EPA to the participants. EDDIES has four main functionalities:

- Real-time execution of EDS tools in interaction with SCADA systems (collecting data from sensors, analysing them by the EDS and sending the response back to the SCADA tool to be viewed by the utility staff).
- Offline evaluation of EDS tool by using stored data.
- Management of the datasets and simulations.
- Creation of new testing datasets by injection of contaminants.

Having the baseline data and the possibility to create simulated contaminations, EDS tools can be tuned and tested in order to see if they suite this kind of application. In the next sections we will explain how we adapted an existing anomaly detection tool and we will present the results obtained by applying ADWICE to data from two monitoring stations.

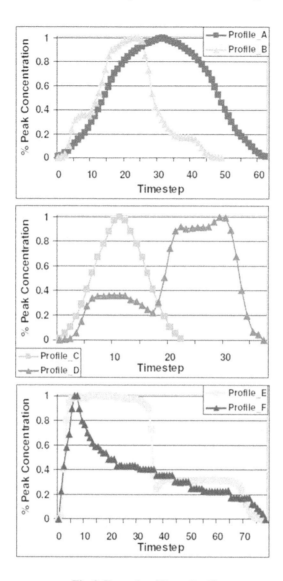

Fig. 2. Example of Event Profiles

3   Anomaly Detection with ADWICE

ADWICE is an anomaly detector that has been developed in an earlier project targeting infrastructure protection [7]. The basic idea is that a normality model is constructed as a set of clusters that summarise all the observed normal behaviour in the learning process. Each cluster comprises a set of points and it is represented through a summary denoted cluster feature (CF). The points are multidimensional numeric vectors where each dimension represents a feature in data. CF is a data structure that has three fields: the number of points in the cluster, the sum of the points in the cluster, and the sum of the squares of the points. The first and second element can be efficiently used to compute the average for the points in the cluster used to represent the centroid of the cluster. The third element, the sum of points can be used to check how large is a circle that would cover all the points in the cluster, and using this radius, how far is a new point from the centre of the cluster. This is used for both building up the normality model (is the new point close enough to any existing clusters or should it form a new cluster?), and during detection (is the new point close enough to any normality clusters or is it an outlier?).

In both cases, and more specifically during detection, the search through the existing clusters needs to be efficient (and fast enough for the application). In order to find the closest cluster we need an index that helps to find the closest cluster to a given point efficiently. The cluster summaries, that constitute the normality observations, are therefore organised in a tree structure. Each level in the tree summarises the CFs at the level below by creating a new CF which is the sum of them.

ADWICE uses an adaptation of the original BIRCH data mining algorithm which has been shown to be fast for incremental updates to the model during learning, and efficient when searching through clusters during detection. The difference is the indexing mechanism used in one of its adaptations (namely ADWICE-Grid), which has been demonstrated to give lower false positive rates due to fewer indexing errors [8].

The implementation of ADWICE consists of a Java library that can be embedded in a new setting by feeding the preprocessing unit (e.g. when input are alphanumeric and have to be encoded into numeric vectors) from a new source of data. The algorithm has three parameters that have to be tuned during the pre-study of data (with some detection test cases) in order to "optimise" the search efficiency: the maximum number of clusters (M), and the threshold for comparing the distance to the centroid (E). The threshold implicitly reflects the maximum size of each cluster. The larger a cluster (with few points in it) the larger the likelihood that points *not* belonging to the cluster are classified as part of the cluster – thus decreasing the detection rate. Too small clusters, on the other hand, lead to overfitting and increase the likelihood that new points are considered as outliers, thus adding to the false positive rate.

In the experiments for this application we have used ADWICE with a setting in which M has been set to 150 in one case and 200 in another one, and E has been varied between 1 and 2.5 as it will be shown in the RoC curves in the results section.

While deploying machine learning based anomaly detectors for detection of attacks in networks is known to face considerable challenges [35], we show in this chapter that it is worth exploring the technique in data collected from sensors in critical infrastructures such as water management systems.

4   Training and Detection

4.1   Training

The training phase is the first step of the anomaly detection. It is necessary to build a model of normality of the system to be able to detect deviations from normality.

ADWICE uses the approach of pure anomaly detection, meaning that training data is supposed to be unaffected by attacks. Training data should also be long enough to capture as much as possible the normality of the system. In our scenario, the data that EPA has provided us is clean from contaminants, the baseline data contains the measurements of water quality parameters and other operational indicators over a period of some months. Pure anomaly detection is thereby applicable.

For our purpose, we divided the baseline data into two parts: the first is used to train the anomaly detector, while the second one is first processed to add the contaminations and then used as testing data. To see how the anomaly detector reacts separately to the effect of each contaminant, 14 different testing datasets, each one with a different contaminant in the same timesteps and with the same profile, are created.

4.1.1 Feature Selection

A feature selection is made to decide which parameters have to be considered for the anomaly detection. In the water domain, one possibility is to consider the water quality parameters as they are. Some parameters are usually common to all the stations (general WQ parameters), but some other station-specific parameters can be helpful to train the anomaly detector on the system normality. The available parameters are:

- *Common WQ Parameters*: Chlorine, PH, Temperature, ORP, TOC, Conductivity, Turbidity
- *Station-Specific Features:* active pumps or pumps flows, alarms, CL2 and PH measured at different time points, valve status, pressure.

Sensor alarms are boolean values which indicate whenever sensors are working properly or not. The normal value is 1, while 0 means that the sensor is not working or, for some reason, the value is not accurate and should not be taken into account. The information regarding the pump status could be useful to correlate the changes of some WQ parameter with the particular kind of water being pumped to the station. There are other parameters that give information about the status of the system at different points, for example the measurement of PH and CL2 of water coming from other pumps.

Additional features could be considered in order to improve the detection or reduce the false positive rates. Those features can be derived from some parameters of the same observation, or they can consider some characteristic of the parameters along different observations. For instance, to emphasise the intensity and the direction of the parameter changes over the time, one possible feature to be added would be the difference of the value for a WQ parameter with the value in previous observations. This models the derivative function of the targeted parameter. Another feature, called sliding average, is obtained by adding for each observation a feature whose value is the average of the last n values of a WQ parameter. Feature selection and customisation must be made separately for each individual station, since they have some common parameters but they differ in many other aspects.

ADWICE assumes the data to be in numerical format to create an n-dimensional space state vector. So the timestep series of numerical data from water utilities suit the input requirements of ADWICE. This means that our testing data does not require any particular preprocessing phase before feeding it to the anomaly detector.

4.1.2   Challenges

The earlier application of ADWICE has been in IP networks. In its native domain, the main problem is finding a pure dataset, not affected by attacks, but the quantity and quality of data is always high. Network traffic generates a lot of data, which is good for having a reasonable knowledge of normality as long as resources for labelling the data are available. Feature selection from IP headers, for example, is easy and does not lead to many problems, while the difficult issues would arise if payload data would need to be analysed, where we would face privacy concerns and anonimisation. In a SCADA system, sensors could give inaccurate values and faults can cause missing observations. This makes the environment more complicated, thus feature selection and handling is complex. Dealing with inaccurate or missing data requires more efforts to distinguish whenever an event is caused due to those conditions or due to contamination. Furthermore, the result of the anomaly detection is variable depending on where the attack is placed. It is not easy, for example, to detect a contamination when at the same time some evaluations about some WQ parameters are inaccurate and some others are missing. Training the system with a limited dataset can result in a sub-optimal normality model, and this causes raising of a lot of false alarms when testing with data that resembles uncovered normality conditions of the system. In the next section we show some results that we obtained testing our anomaly detector with data from two different monitoring stations, proposing some possible solutions for the kinds of problems described.

4.2   Detection Results

Over six available stations, we have chosen to test our anomaly detection with the easiest one and the hardest one. As mentioned before, we have generated testing datasets by using the second half of the baseline data and adding one contamination per dataset. The contamination has been introduced in the middle of the dataset according to the profile A, depicted in Figure 2, which is a normal distribution of the concentration during 64 timesteps. Details about the single stations will be presented separately. Each testing dataset then contains just one attack along several timesteps. The detection classifies each timestep as normal or anomalous. The detection rate (DR) is calculated from the number of timesteps during the attack that are detected as anomalous, according to the following formula: $DR = TP/(TP + FN)$, where TP refers to the number of true positives and FN refers to the number of false negatives. The false positive rate (FPR) are the normal timesteps that are erroneously classified as anomalous according to the formula $FPR = FP/(FP + TN)$, where FP is the number of false positives and TN refers to the number of true negatives.

4.2.1   Station A

Station A is located at the entry point of a distribution system. It is the best station in terms of reliability of values. It only has the common features and three pump status indicators. Values are not affected by inaccuracies and there are no missing values both in the training and testing datasets. The baseline data consists of one observation

Table 1. Station A detection results of 1mg/L of concentration

Contaminant ID	False Positive Rate	Detection Rate
A	0.057	0.609
B	0.057	0.484
C	0.057	0
D	0.057	0
E	0.057	0
F	0.057	0
G	0.057	0
H	0.057	0.422
I	0.057	0
J	0.057	0.547
K	0.057	0
L	0.057	0.406
M	0.057	0.156
N	0.057	0.516

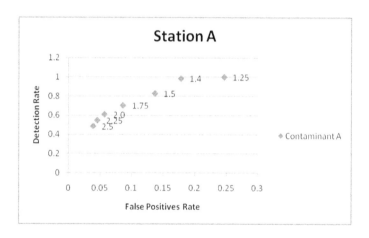

Fig. 3. Station A contaminant A ROC curve

every 5 minutes during the period of five months. The first attempt in generating a dataset is done by injecting contaminants according to the normal distribution during 64 timesteps, in which the peak contaminant concentration is 1 mg/L. Table 1 shows the results that we obtained doing a common training phase and then running a test for each of the contaminants. Training and testing have been carried out using a threshold value E set to 2 and the maximum number of clusters M is set to 150. Considering the fact that the amount of contaminant is the lowest possible the results from Table 1 are not discouraging. Some contaminants affect more parameters at the same time and their effect is more evident; some others only affect few parameters with slight changes. Contaminant F for instance only affects the ORP, which is not measured in this station, so this contaminant is undetectable in this case. The anomaly detector must be tuned in order to fit the clusters over the normality points and let the furthest points to be recognised as attacks. To determine the best threshold values the ROC curves can be calculated by plotting the detection rate as a function of the false positive rate while changing the threshold value. Evaluation of the ROC curves of all the contaminants can give hints to determine the best trade-off that gives good detection rates and false positives, but all of those curves refer to a contaminant concentration peak of 1 mg/L. As non-experts it was not clear to us whether this could be a significant level of contamination. For this reason we have tested the sensitivity of the anomaly detection by incrementally increasing the contaminant concentration. In our tests, we increased the concentration in steps of 4 mg/L a time, up to 24 mg/L. Figure 4 shows the variation of the detection rates of three significant contaminants with respect to the increase of the concentration. Contaminant A is the easiest to detect, Contaminant L is medium and Contaminant E is difficult to detect since it only sligthly affects the TOC.

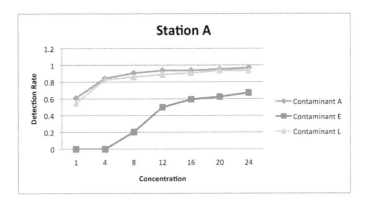

Fig. 4. Concentration Sensitivity of the Station A

In this figure the false positive rate is not considered since with the higher concentration of contaminants it is easier to detect the deviation from normality without any increase in the false alarms. These results confirm that even if ADWICE is not designed for this kind of application, by finding the optimal tradeoff between detection and false positive rates for 1mg/L, this anomaly detector would give good results for any other greater concentration. We conclude therefore that ADWICE is a good candidate tool to be applied as EDS for this station.

4.2.2 Station D

The situation becomes more complicated when a source of uncertainty is added to the system. Station D is located in a reservoir that holds 81 million gallons of water. The water quality in this station is affected by many operational parameters of co-located pump stations and reservoirs. Station D contains more parameters than station A and some sensors are affected by inaccuracy. In detail, Station D has the following parameters:

- *Common features*: PH, Conductivity, Temperature, Chlorine levels, TOC, Turbidity.
- *Alerts*: CL2, TOC and Conductivity; 1 means normal functioning, while 0 means inaccuracy.
- *System indicators*: three pump flows, two of them supply the station while the third is the pipe which the station is connected to.
- *Valves*: indicates the position of the key valve; 0 if open, 1 if closed.
- *Supplemental parameters*: Chlorine levels and PH measured in water coming from pump1 and pump2.

By checking the data that EPA has provided, we noted that the only sensor inaccuracy alert that is sometimes raised is the TOC alert, but in general we will assume that the other alerts could be raised as well. There are some missing values in different points scattered within the baseline file. The baseline data consists of one observation every 2 minutes during the period of three months. The same procedure for station A has then been applied to this station. Figure 5 shows the ROC curve obtained with the peak concentration of 1 mg/L and the same profile (profile A, Figure 2).

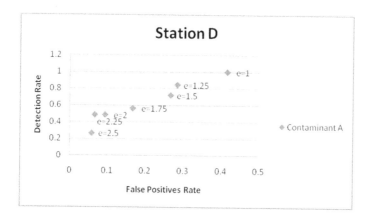

Fig. 5. ROC curve station D contaminant A

An accurate feature selection has been carried out to get reasonable results, since trying with all the station parameters the false positive rate is very high. This makes it not worthwhile to explore threshold variations with such bad results. To mitigate the effects of the missing data and the accuracy, the derivatives and sliding averages of the common parameters have been added as new features. The outcome was that the derivatives emphasise the intensity of the changes, thus improving the detection of the effects of the contaminations, while the sliding window averages mitigated the effect of the abrupt changes in data caused by the inaccuracies or missing data. Some parameters have been ignored, like the pumps flows and the key valve, since they caused lots of false positives if included as features. The same training and testing procedure for station A has then been applied to this station. Figure 6 shows the sensitivity of the detection with the increase of the concentrations. As in the case for station A, ADWICE was run with the parameter E=2. Since the dataset is more complex and there are more possible combinations of data to represent, the maximum number of clusters M was set to 200.

Data from from the above two stations have resulted in clustered models consisting of 115 clusters for station A and 186 clusters for station D.

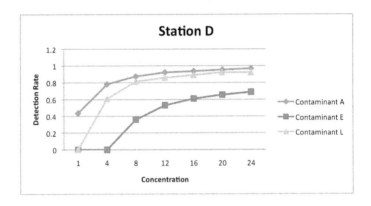

Fig. 6. Concentration sensitivity station D

4.3   Detection Latency

This section focuses on adequacy of the contaminants detection latency. As mentioned in section 2, the final goal of the EPA challenge is to apply the best EDS tools in real water utilities to proactively detect anomalous variations of the WQ parameters. Real-time monitoring allows to take opportune countermeasures upon unfolding contaminations. This makes the response time to be as crucial as the correctness of the detection in general, since even having a good detection rate (on average) a late response may allow contaminated water to leave the system and be delivered to users causing severe risks for their health.

The first issue that comes when measuring the detection latency is from when to start counting the elapsed amount of time before the first alarm is raised. This problem is caused by the fact that different event profiles make it necessary to consider the latency in different ways. In case of the normal distribution depicted as profile A (Figure 2), a possible approach could be counting the latency of the detection event from the initiation of the contamination event, since the concentration rapidly reaches its peak. If the peak concentration was reached very slowly, the evaluation of latency based on the first raised alarm from the beginning would result in an unnecessary pessimism (e. g. see profile D in Figure 2). In this case it would be more appropriate to start counting the reaction time from the time when the peak of the event has taken place. An earlier detection would then give rise to a negative delay and this would signal a predictive warning. For the purpose of our experiments, the normal distribution of profile A suits the computation of the latency based on counting the number of samples from the beginning of the event.

Since in the baseline data time is represented as discrete timesteps, we measure the latency by counting the number of timesteps elapsed before the first alarm is raised. Figure 7 and 8 show the measured latencies for Station A and Station D respectively, with respect to the detection of the three contaminants presented in the previous section.

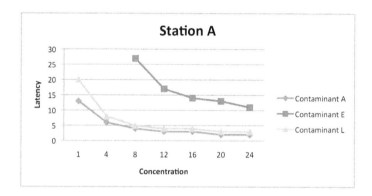

Fig. 7. Detection latency in station A

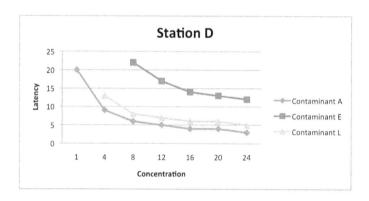

Fig. 8. Detection latency in station D

The curves indicate that in the case of the lowest concentration the latencies are high. For instance the detection of contaminant A and L in station A has a latency of 13 and 20 timesteps respectively. They are around one fourth and one third of the total duration of the contamination event (64 timesteps). Contaminant E is not detected at all, so its latency is not represented in the graph. The situation changes positively when the concentrations are gradually increased. The latencies of Contaminant A and L drop sharply until a concentration of 8 mg/L is reached, decreasing 60% and 75% respectively. At the same time, there are some detections of Contaminant E, characterised by a high latency. From this point the latencies of Contaminant A and L steadily drop, while the latency of Contaminant E decreases more rapidly. Latencies for the station D follow the same pattern, although the values are slightly higher.

Checking the results against reality, a latency of 13 discrete timesteps for Contaminant A in Station A would correspond to a latency of 65 minutes, which is quite a long time. One should note that time interval between two observations has a high impact on the real latency, since for example 20 timesteps of detection latency for Contaminant A in Station D with a concentration of 1 mg/L corresponds to 40 minutes of latency, 25 minutes less than the latency in Station A. Even in this case the results are definitely improved by the increases in the contaminant concentrations, but domain knowledge is required to evaluate whether the selected increments to a certain concentration are meaningful.

4.4   Missing and Inaccurate Data Problem

In Section 4.2 we have seen that data inaccuracies and missing data were a major problem in station D. Our approach for the tests carried out so far has been to use workarounds but not provide a solution to the original problem.

More specifically, our workaround for missing data was as follows. We have replaced the missing data values with a zero in the preprocessing stage. When learning takes place the use of a derivative as a derived feature helps to detect the missing data and classify the data points in its own cluster. Now, if training period is long enough and includes the missing data (e.g. inactivity of some sensors or other operational faults) as normality, then these clusters will be used to recognise similar cases in the detection phase as long as no other sensor values are significantly affected. During our tests we avoided injecting contaminants during the periods of missing data.

Sensor inaccuracies are indicated with a special alert in the provided data set (a 0 when the data is considered as inaccurate, i.e. the internal monitoring system warns for the quality of the data). According to our experiments it is not good to train the system during periods with data inaccuracies, even when workaround are applied. First, learning inaccurate values as normality may result in excessive false positives when accurate values are dominant later. Second, the detection rate can be affected if the impact of the contaminant is similar to some of the inaccurate values. Thus a more principled way for treating this problem is needed.

Our suggestion for reducing the impact of both problems is the classical approach in dependability, i.e. introducing redundancy. Consider two sensor values (identical or diversified technologies) that are supposed to provide measurements for the same data. Then the likelihood of both sensors being inaccurate or both having missing values would be lower than the likelihood of each sensor "failing" individually. Thus, for important contaminants that essentially need a given sensor value's reliability we could learn the normal value based on both data sets. When a missing data is observed (0 in the alert cell) the preprocessing would replace both sensor values with the "healthy" one. When one sensor value is inaccurate the presence of the other sensor has an impact on the normality cluster, and vice versa. So, on the whole we expect to have a better detection rate and lower false positive rate with sensor replicas (of course at the cost of more hardware).

In the experiments so far we have not yet been able to create the duplicate data sets since the generation of the base line requires domain knowledge of the water management experts. However, we are working towards incorporating a new base line with the replicated sensor and showing its impact on accuracy.

5   Related Work

In this section we first describe work that is closely related to ours (section 5.1), and then we continue with an overview of other works which are related to the big picture of water quality and monitoring (sections 5.2 to 5.6).

5.1   Water Quality Anomalies

The security issues in water distribution systems are typically categorised in two ways: hydraulic faults and quality faults [12]. Hydraulic faults (broken pipes, pump faults, etc.) are intrinsic to mechanical systems, and similar to other infrastructures, fault tolerance must be considered at design time to make the system reliable. Hydraulic faults can cause economic loss and, in certain circumstances, water quality deterioration. Online monitoring techniques are developed to detect hydraulic faults, and alarms are raised when sensors detect anomalous conditions (like a sudden change of the pressure in a pipe). Hydraulic fault detection is often performed by using specific direct sensors and it is not the area of our interest. The second group of security threats, water quality faults, has been subject to increased attention in the past decade. Intentional or accidental injection of contaminant elements can cause severe risks to the population, and Contamination Warning Systems (CWS) are needed in order to prevent, detect, and proactively react in situations in which a contaminant injection occurs in parts of the distribution system [5]. An EDS is the part of the CWS that monitors in real-time the water quality parameters in order to detect anomalous quality changes. Detecting an event consists of gathering and analysing data from multiple sensors and detecting a change in the overall quality. Although specific sensors for certain contaminants are currently available, EDS are more general solution not limited to a set of contaminants.

Byers and Carlsson are among the pioneers in this area. They tested a simple online early warning system by performing real-world experiments [9]. Using a multi-instrument panel that measures five water quality parameters at the same time, they collected 16.000 data points by sampling one measurement of tap water every minute. The values of these data, normalised to have zero as mean and 1 as standard deviation, were used as a baseline data. They then emulated a contamination in laboratories by adding four different contaminants (in specific concentrations) to the same water in beakers or using bench scale distribution systems. The detection was based on a simple rule: an anomaly is raised if the difference between the measured values and the mean from the baseline data exceeds three times the standard deviation. They evaluated the approach comparing normality based on large data samples and small data samples. Among others, they evaluated the sensitivity of the detection, and successfully demonstrated detection of contaminants at concentrations that are not lethal for human health. To our knowledge this approach has not been applied in a large scale to multiple contaminants at multiple concentrations.

Klise and McKenna [22] designed an online detection mechanism called multivariate algorithm: the distance of the current measurement is compared with an expected value. The difference is then checked against a fixed threshold that determines whether the current measurement is a normal value or an anomaly. The expected value is assigned using three different approaches: last observation, closest past observation in a multivariate space within a sliding time window, or by taking the closest-cluster centroid in clusters of past observations using k-mean clustering [17]. The detection mechanism was tested on data collected by monitoring four water quality parameters at four different locations taking one measurement every hour during 125 days. Their contamination has been simulated by superimposing values according to certain profiles to the water quality parameters of the last 2000 samples of the collected data. Results of simulations have shown that the algorithm performs the required level of detection at the cost of a high number of false positives and a change of background quality can severely deteriorate the overall performance.

A comprehensive work on this topic has been initiated by U.S. EPA resulting in the CANARY tool [18]. CANARY is a software for online water quality event detection that reads data from sensors and considers historical data to detect events. Event detection is performed in two online parallel phases: the first phase, called state estimation, predicts the future quality value. In the state estimation, history is combined with new data to generate the estimated sensor values that will be compared with actually measured data. In the second phase, residual computation and classification, the differences between the estimated values and the new measured values are computed and the highest difference among them is checked against a threshold. If that value exceeds the threshold, it is declared as an outlier. The number of outliers in the recent past are then combined by a binomial distribution to compute the probability of an event in the current time step.

While in our case the model of the system is based on observations from the training phase, CANARY integrates old information with new data to estimate the state of the system. Thus, their EDS is context-aware. A change in the background quality due to normal operation would be captured by the state estimator, and that would not generate too many false alarms. Singular outliers due to signal noise or background change would not generate immediately an alarm, since the probability of raising alarms depends on the number of outliers in the past, that must be high enough to generate an alarm. Sensor faults and missing data are treated in such way that their value does not affect the residual classification: their values (or lack thereof) are ignored as long as the sensor resumes its correct operational state.

CANARY allows the integration and test of different algorithms for state estimation. Several implementations are based on the field of signal processing or time series analysis, like time series increment models or linear filtering. However, it is suggested that artificial intelligence techniques such as multivariate nearest neighbour search, neural networks, and support vector machines can also be applied. A systematic evaluation of different approaches on the same data is needed to clearly summarise the benefits of each approach. This is the target of the current EPA challenge of which our work is a part.

So far, detection has been carried out on single monitoring stations. In a water distribution network, several monitoring stations could cooperate on the detection of contaminant event by combining their alarms. This can help to reduce false alarms and facilitate localisation of the contamination source. Koch and McKenna have recently proposed a method that considers events from monitoring stations as values in a random time-space point process, and by using the Kulldorffs scan test they identify the clusters of alarms [23].

5.2 Hydrodynamical Aspects and Distribution Network Topology

Modelling hydraulic water flow in distribution systems has always been an aspect of interest when designing and evaluating water distribution systems [36]. A water distribution system is an infrastructure designed to transport and deliver water from several sources, like reservoirs or tanks, to consumers. This infrastructure is characterised by the interconnection of pipes using connection elements such as valves, pumps and junctions. Water flows through pipes with a certain pressure, and valves and pumps are elements used to adjust this to desired values. Junctions are connection elements through which water can be served to customers. The flow of water through the distribution system can be described by mathematical formulation of fluid dynamics [14].

Water distribution networks are modelled using graphs where nodes are connection elements and edges represent pipes between nodes. Computer-based simulation has become popular to study the hydraulic dynamics as well as the water quality through the network. Notwithstanding the problem of intentional or accidental contaminations, water has always been monitored for quality, and the distribution system must be studied to compute the quality decay over the network [21]. System modelling has been performed for finding the appropriate location to place treatment facilities. The most popular tool to model and evaluate water quality in distribution systems is EPANET [3].

5.3 Contamination Diffusion

Modelling water quality in distribution networks allows the prediction of how a contaminant is transported and spread through the system. Using the equations of advection/reaction Kurotani et al. initiated the work on computation of the concentration of a contaminant in nodes and pipes [25]. They considered the topographical layout of the network, the changing demand from the users, and information regarding the point and time of injection. Although the model is quite accurate, this work does not take into account realistic assumptions like water leakage, pipes aging, etc. A more realistic scenario has been considered by Doglioni et al. [11]. They evaluate the contaminant diffusion on a real case study of an urban water distribution network that in addition to the previous hypothesis considers also water leakage and contamination decay.

5.4 Sensor Location Problem

The security problem in water distribution systems was first addressed by Kessler et al. [20]. Initially, the focus was on the accidental introduction of pollutant elements. The defence consisted of identifying how to place sensors in the network in such way that the detection of a contaminant can be done in all parts of the distribution network. Since the cost of installation and maintenance of water quality sensors is high, the problem consists of finding the optimal placement of the minimum number of sensors such that the cost is minimised while performing the best detection. Research in this field has been accelerated after 2001, encompassing the threat of intentional injection of contaminants as a terrorist action. A large number of techniques to solve this optimisation problem have been proposed in recent years [28,31,6,34,12].

Latest work in this area [13] proposes a mathematical framework to describe a wider number of water security faults (both hydraulic and quality faults). Furthermore, it builds on top of this a methodology for solving the sensor placement optimisation problem subject to fault-risk constraints.

5.5   Contamination Source Identification

Another direction of work has been contamination source identification. This addresses the need to react when a contamination is detected, and to take appropriate countermeasures to isolate the compromised part of the system. The focus is on identifying the time and the unknown location in which the contamination started spreading.

Laird et al. propose the solution of the inverse water quality problem, i.e. backtracking from the contaminant diffusion to identify the initial point. The problem is described again as an optimisation problem, and solved using a direct nonlinear programming strategy [27,26]. Preis and Ostfeld used coupled model trees and a linear programming algorithm to represent the system, and computed the inverse quality problem using linear programming on the tree structure [33].

Guan et al. propose a simulation-optimisation approach applied to complex water distribution systems using EPANET [16]. To detect the contaminated nodes, the system initially assumes arbitrarily selected nodes as the source. The simulated data is fed into a predictor that is based on the optimisation of a cost function taking the difference between the simulated data and the measured data at the monitoring stations. The output of the predictor is a new configuration of contaminant concentrations at (potentially new) simulated nodes, fed again to the simulator. This process in iterated in a closed-loop until the cost function reaches a chosen lower bound and the actual sources are found. Extensions of this work have appeared using evolutionary algoritms [37].

Huang et al. use data mining techniques instead of inverse water quality or simulation-optimisation approaches [19]. This approach makes possible to deal with systems and sensor data uncertainties. Data gathered from sensors is first processed with an algorithm to remove redundancies and narrow the search of possible initial contaminant sources. Then using a method called Maximum Likelihood Method, the nodes are associated with the probability of being the sources of injection.

5.6   Attacks on SCADA System

A further security risk that must be addressed is the security of the event detection system itself. As any other critical infrastructure, an outage or corruption of the communication network of the SCADA infrastructure can constitute a severe risk, as dangerous as the water contamination. Therefore, protection mechanisms have to be deployed in response to that threat, too. Since control systems are often sharing components and making an extensive use of information exchange to coordinate and perform operations, several new vulnerabilities and potential threats emerge [10]. This is a wide area of study and the reader is referred to several sources including other chapters in this book for further studies.

6 Conclusion

In this chapter an existing learning based anomaly detection technique has been applied to the detection of contamination events in water distribution systems. These systems are monitored by water quality sensors that provide chemical properties of the water which are processed and used to feed the detector.

The introduction of this system is challenging since the chemical properties of the water can change along the time depending on its source and can be confused as a contamination event. Nevertheless, the use of a learning based anomaly detection technique, which allows the characterisation of all the variations of the system normality, has proved to be effective. Besides, additional features based on sliding windows and derivatives of the data analysed have been introduced to improve the efficiency of the solution under certain circumstances.

The performance of the approach has been analysed using real data of two water stations together with synthetic contaminants superimposed with the EDDIES application provided by EPA. The first results, in terms of detection rate and false positive rate, have shown some contaminants are easier to detected than others. The sensitivity of the anomaly detector has also been been studied by creating new testing data sets with different contaminant concentrations. The results have shown that with more contaminant concentration the detector obtains higher detection rates with low false positive rates. The latency of the detection has also been analysed, showing reasonable results that are qualitatively improved as the contaminant concentration is increased. The inaccuracy of the data provided in one of the stations has negatively affected the performance, but the potential to improve the outcomes have been discussed.

Further research must be done in the analysis of the performance with different event profiles, since the current analysis has considered just one of them. Besides, in some cases a lack or inaccuracy of the monitored data from the chemical sensors has been observed. A solution based on redundancy of sensor values is proposed and it will be applied and evaluated in the future. Finally, the detector algorithm used has retraining and forgetting capabilities, which can be enabled to adapt the normality model to changes in the topology of the water distribution system. Further research must be done to evaluate the effects of the adaptability in this environment.

Acknowledgement. We would like to thank Katie Umberg, from EPA, for the provision of data, knowledge on water management systems and the review of our chapter. Support by Dan Joy, from Critigen, in connection with the EDDIES software, is gratefully acknowledged. The financial support of the CUGS graduate school during the preparation of this study is also acknowledged.

References

1. http://www.independent.co.uk/news/world/europe/contamination
   -fears-after-leak-from-french-nuclear-waste-plant-863928.html
   (accessed April 26, 2010)
2. http://cfpub.epa.gov/safewater/watersecurity/initiative.cfm
   (accessed April 26, 2010)
3. http://www.epa.gov/nrmrl/wswrd/dw/epanet.html
   (accessed November 19, 2010)
4. Allgeier, S.C., Umberg, K.: Systematic evaluation of contaminant detection through water quality monitoring. In: Water Security Congress Proceedings. American Water Works Association (2008)
5. ASCE: Interim voluntary guidelines for designing an online contaminant monitoring system. American Society of Civil Engineers, Reston,VA (2004)
6. Berry, J.W., Fleischer, L., Hart, W.E., Phillips, C.A., Watson, J.P.: Sensor placement in municipal water networks. Journal of Water Resources Planning and Management 131(3), 237–243 (2005)
7. Burbeck, K., Nadjm-Tehrani, S.: ADWICE – Anomaly Detection with Real-Time Incremental Clustering. In: Park, C., Chee, S. (eds.) ICISC 2004. LNCS, vol. 3506, pp. 407–424. Springer, Heidelberg (2005)
8. Burbeck, K., Nadjm-Tehrani, S.: Adaptive real-time anomaly detection with incremental clustering. Information Security Technical Report - Elsevier 12(1), 56–67 (2007)
9. Byer, D., Carlson, K.: Real-time detection of intentional chemical contamination in the distribution system. Journal American Water Works Association 97(7) (2005)
10. Cárdenas, A.A., Amin, S., Sastry, S.: Research challenges for the security of control systems. In: Proceedings of the 3rd Conference on Hot Topics in Security, pp. 6:1–6:6. USENIX Association, Berkeley (2008)
11. Doglioni, A., Primativo, F., Giustolisi, O., Carbonara, A.: Scenarios of contaminant diffusion on a medium size urban water distribution network, p. 84. ASCE (2008)
12. Eliades, D., Polycarpou, M.: Security of Water Infrastructure Systems. In: Setola, R., Geretshuber, S. (eds.) CRITIS 2008. LNCS, vol. 5508, pp. 360–367. Springer, Heidelberg (2009)
13. Eliades, D., Polycarpou, M.: A fault diagnosis and security framework for water systems. IEEE Transactions on Control Systems Technology 18(6), 1254–1265 (2010)
14. Friedlander, S., Serre, D. (eds.): Handbook of mathematical fluid dynamics, vol. 1. Elsevier B.V (2002)
15. Goetz, E., Shenoi, S. (eds.): Critical Infrastructure Protection. Springer, Heidelberg (2008)
16. Guan, J., Aral, M.M., Maslia, M.L., Grayman, W.M.: Identification of contaminant sources in water distribution systems using simulation–optimization method: Case study. Journal of Water Resources Planning and Management 132(4), 252–262 (2006)
17. Han, J.: Data Mining: Concepts and Techniques. Morgan Kaufmann Publishers Inc., San Francisco (2005)
18. Hart, D., McKenna, S.A., Klise, K., Cruz, V., Wilson, M.: Canary: A water quality event detection algorithm development tool, pp. 517–517. ASCE (2007)
19. Huang, J.J., McBean, E.A.: Data mining to identify contaminant event locations in water distribution systems. Journal of Water Resources Planning and Management 135(6), 466–474 (2009)
20. Kessler, A., Ostfeld, A., Sinai, G.: Detecting accidental contaminations in municipal water networks. Journal of Water Resources Planning and Management 124(4), 192–198 (1998)

21. Khanal, N., Speight, V.: Increasing application of water quality models, pp. 514–514. ASCE (2008)
22. Klise, K.A., McKenna, S.A.: Multivariate applications for detecting anomalous water quality, pp. 130–130. ASCE (2006)
23. Koch, M.W., McKenna, S.: Distributed sensor fusion in water quality event detection. To Appear in Journal of Water Resource Planning and Management 137(1) (2011)
24. Kruegel, C., Valeur, F., Vigna, G.: Intrusion Detection and Correlation Challenges and Solutions. Springer, Heidelberg (2005)
25. Kurotani, K., Kubota, M., Akiyama, H., Morimoto, M.: Simulator for contamination diffusion in a water distribution network. In: Proceedings of the 1995 IEEE IECON 21st International Conference on Industrial Electronics, Control, and Instrumentation, vol. 2, pp. 792–797 (1995)
26. Laird, C.D., Biegler, L.T., van Bloemen Waanders, B.G.: Mixed-integer approach for obtaining unique solutions in source inversion of water networks. Journal of Water Resources Planning and Management 132(4), 242–251 (2006)
27. Laird, C.D., Biegler, L.T., van Bloemen Waanders, B.G., Bartlett, R.A.: Contamination source determination for water networks. Journal of Water Resources Planning and Management 131(2), 125–134 (2005)
28. Lee, B.H., Deininger, R.A.: Optimal locations of monitoring stations in water distribution system. Journal of Environmental Engineering 118(1), 4–16 (1992)
29. Luiijf, E., Ali, M., Zielstra, A.: Assessing and Improving SCADA Security in the Dutch Drinking Water Sector. In: Setola, R., Geretshuber, S. (eds.) CRITIS 2008. LNCS, vol. 5508, pp. 190–199. Springer, Heidelberg (2009)
30. Murray, R., Uber, J., Janke, R.: Model for estimating acute health impacts from consumption of contaminated drinking water. J. Water Resource Planning and Management 132(4), 293–299 (2006)
31. Ostfeld, A., Salomons, E.: Optimal layout of early warning detection stations for water distribution systems security. Journal of Water Resources Planning and Management 130(5), 377–385 (2004)
32. Pietro, R.D., Mancini, L.V.: Intrusion Detection Systems. Springer, Heidelberg (2008)
33. Preis, A., Ostfeld, A.: Contamination source identification in water systems: A hybrid model trees–linear programming scheme. Journal of Water Resources Planning and Management 132(4), 263–273 (2006)
34. Propato, M.: Contamination warning in water networks: General mixed-integer linear models for sensor location design. Journal of Water Resources Planning and Management 132(4), 225–233 (2006)
35. Sommer, R., Paxson, V.: Outside the closed world: On using machine learning for network intrusion detection. In: 2010 IEEE Symposium on Security and Privacy (SP), pp. 305–316 (2010)
36. Walski, T.M., Chase, D.V., Savic, D.A., Grayman, W., Beckwith, S., Koelle, E. (eds.): Advanced water distribution modeling and management. Haestead Press (2004)
37. Zechman, E.M., Ranjithan, S.R.: Evolutionary computation-based methods for characterizing contaminant sources in a water distribution system. Journal of Water Resources Planning and Management 135(5), 334–343 (2009)

Security Aspects of SCADA and DCS Environments

Cristina Alcaraz[1], Gerardo Fernandez[1], and Fernando Carvajal[2]

[1] Computer Science Department - University of Malaga,
29071 - Malaga, Spain
{alcaraz,gerardo}@lcc.uma.es
[2] Indra Company,
28108 - Alcobendas, Madrid, Spain
jfcarvajalindra.es

Abstract. SCADA Systems can be seen as a fundamental component in Critical Infrastructures, having an impact in the overall performance of other Critical Infrastructures interconnected. Currently, these systems include in their network designs different types of Information and Communication Technology systems (such as the Internet and wireless technologies), not only to modernize operational processes but also to ensure automation and real-time control. Nonetheless, the use of these new technologies will bring new security challenges, which will have a significant impact on both the business process and home users. Therefore, the main purpose of this Chapter is to address these issues and to analyze the interdependencies of Process Control Systems with ICT systems, to discuss some security aspects and to offer some possible solutions and recommendations.

1 Introduction

As already commented in Chapter 4, *Process Control Systems* (PCS) are complex systems that perform some defined tasks as part of an industrial production process. In particular, they are considered the main control framework for other critical infrastructures. These systems monitor and supervise remote sensors deployed close to the critical infrastructure, managing automation operations and recording sensitive data measurements. In the existing literature, there are two types of PCSs [1]. They are differentiated by their geographical distribution, i.e.:

- *Supervisory Control and Data Acquisition* (SCADA) System. A SCADA system is a distributed network over large geographic areas where a set of industrial automation services are offered to control the performance and continuity of other critical infrastructures, such as: electric energy systems, nuclear energy systems, water and sewage treatment plants or transportation systems.

J. Lopez et al. (Eds.): Critical Information Infrastructure Protection, LNCS 7130, pp. 120–149, 2012.
© Springer-Verlag Berlin Heidelberg 2012

- *Distributed Control Systems* (DCS). These systems have the same functionality as a SCADA system but they are geographically closer to manufacturing operations and industrial facilities. It is very important to highlight that throughout this chapter, we will use the term SCADA to cover any monitoring and control procedure for both SCADA systems and DCS systems.

Historically, SCADA systems were composed of isolated networks without connection to public communication infrastructures, like the Internet. However, the need to remotely supervise and control critical industrial systems has meant the convergence of state-of-the-art information and communication technologies, such as the use of open software and hardware components (i.e., commercial off the shelf components (COTS)), the Internet and wireless technologies. These last two technologies are precisely the most demanded by today's Industry. Wireless technologies provide mobility and local control with a low installation and maintenance cost, whereas the Internet allows monitoring to take place from any place and at any time. Therefore, the TCP/IP standard is the main communication in SCADA transmissions and its commands and data streams are transmitted over a variety of specific IP-based protocols to facilitate automation and control in real-time over the Internet. On the other hand, the performance and survivability of a critical control system is also very dependent on the type of internal and external organization whose stakeholders (such as other critical systems, government and end users) may have a significant influence on monitoring processes.

From a security point of view, it is very important to take into account that technological convergence in critical control systems could give rise to new security risks, and challenges to resolve, some of them related to the secure management of ICT systems in both SCADA systems and corporative networks, and also related to the constant monitoring of threats and failures in the whole system. Any potential attack, failure or threat could have a significant impact on any of the different interdependent critical systems (see Chapter 4 for more detail). All of these security issues will be the main focus of this Chapter, where a set of security requirements and solutions including policies, standards, methodologies and software components will be discussed to facilitate the control and automation in SCADA and DCS systems.

The chapter is organized as follows: Section 2 presents the SCADA architecture, its technological advances and its functionality using some existing ICT systems, in addition to discussing interdependencies and their consequences between critical control systems and ICT systems. Section 3 describes secure management needs beyond the ICT of SCADA systems due to their peculiarities as survivable complex systems. Likewise, in Section 4 an exploration of current researches regarding intrusion detection systems and forensic needs for the analysis of incidences is presented. Finally, Section 5 concludes the Chapter and some future lines of work are outlined.

2   Advances in the SCADA Architecture and Security Issues

Since SCADA Systems were first introduced in the 1960s, three main generations have been emerged: *Monolithic, Distributed and Networked*, all of which share a number of characteristics. Firstly, they have adopted the existing ICTs in order to improve the monitoring processes in real-time, as well as the performance and availability of controlled infrastructure (e.g. large industrial lines of oil pipelines). Secondly, they share three types of sub-networks: (i) the central network, (ii) remote substations and (iii) the corporative network. The operations carried out in the central network are related to the control and management of the critical infrastructures. Such operations are managed through specific operator consoles or human-machine interfaces (HMIs), which allow operators to read specific physical parameters (e.g. pressure, electrical signals, temperature, etc) or alarms received from remote substations, or even transmit certain commands (e.g. open/close pumps) to specific field devices localized in remote substations. On the other hand, the operations carried out in the corporative network are directly related to the general supervision of the system whose accesses databases and servers installed in the central network are rather more restricted.

The first SCADA networks were designed in the *Monolithic* generation under a centralized control in a mainframe system. This mainframe was configured as the primary control system; while another mainframe system was configured as the standby in order to cover any functionality of the system in the event of a failure in the main system (see Figure 1, left). Both systems had to register critical data streams, manage and make decisions to efficiently coordinate the monitoring processes developed in the whole system. The architecture of a substation was basically based on one or several special remote terminal units (RTUs), which had limited memory and processing capabilities (e.g. 8-bit microprocessor and 4-16 KB RAM) with output/input (O/I) interfaces to measure/actuate physical signals. These signals had to be retransmitted to the central system via telephone or radio with a low data transmission rate and through property automation protocols such as for instance Modbus serial or IEC-101. Although it meant a great advance in the Industry, the use of property components limited the coexistence with other hardware and software industrial components.

Later, in the second *Distributed* generation of SCADA systems, (see Figure 1, right) new technologies were integrated based on IP addresses so that the monitoring processes were distributed among different network components. The distributed approach significantly substituted the centralized systems whose main components were based on data base servers to register alarms and measurements, master terminal units (MTUs) to establish communication with the substations and HMIs. In addition, the network architecture helped the whole system to improve the primary/standby scheme of the Monolithic generation, as any active device in the network could immediately cover the functionality of another one without having to wait for the change from primary to secondary. The communication with remote substations was established using large (distributed or hierarchical) local-area networks, which were controlled by MTUs installed

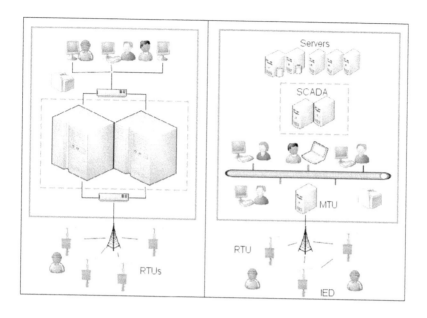

Fig. 1. A centralized and distributed SCADA system

in the central system. The RTUs, configured in such substations, were equipped with advanced serial I/O interfaces with faster microprocessors, memory and math coprocessors to support complex applications, becoming more intelligent and autonomous than previous RTUs. However, both automation protocols and telemetry components continued to be properties.

Finally, the latest advances in SCADA systems are seen in the third generation of *Networked* generation. This generation broke with the isolation concept of the previous generations by including in its network designs open connections using the TCP/IP (Transmission Control Protocol/Internet Protocol). These connections made possible monitoring in real-time, peer-to-peer communication from anywhere at any time, multiple sessions, concurrency, maintenance, redundancy, security services and connectivity. All these technical advances also came to substations, where RTUs were able to provide hierarchical and inter-RTU communication (i.e., interconnectivity among RTUs) under TCP/IP, wired and wireless communication interfaces, Web services, management and forwarding to other remote points. This fact helped RTUs work as data concentrators to store large data streams or as remote access controllers to autonomously and remotely reconfigure/recover parts of the system.

The migration to TCP/IP also involved the standardization and implementation of new SCADA protocols capable of understanding TCP/IP connections. Currently, there are several IP-based SCADA protocols, such as Modbus/TCP, DNP3, IEC-104 and ICCP/TASE2. The three first ones are for the automation,

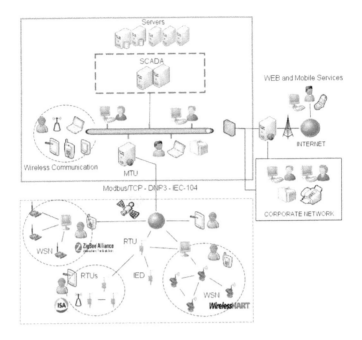

Fig. 2. A current SCADA system

whereas ICCP is specific for the inter-communication between telemetry control systems. However, these protocols lack authentication and data encryption mechanisms at present. For this reason, new standards have been recently specified, such as for example the IEC-62351 or DNP Secure Authentication (SA). Basically, IEC-62351 provides confidentiality with SSL/TLS, authentication and integrity while DNP SA ensures authentication with HMAC and challenge-response.

2.1 The Internet and Wireless Communication in the Networked Generation of SCADA Systems

Following on with the Networked Generation and observing Figure 2, it is possible to note that for a recent future, the control Industry might be one of the main sectors that might be more demanding on the use of wireless technologies and the Internet for the control. Both technologies offer a set of suitable services for control in real-time. Wireless technologies allow operators in the field to locally manage substations, providing mobility and at the same time coexistence with a low installation and maintenance cost. In contrast, the Internet offers remote control of substations, where the SCADA center and operators in the field can interact independently of their geographical location. To understand in detail the advantages of these technologies, an overview is provided below.

The Internet. As was previously commented, the Internet is one of the most demanded technologies by Industry. This special interest is due to the fact that the Internet provides global connectivity independently of the physical locations of components/members of a system. Its public communication infrastructure offers Web solutions, as well as flexibility in the data acquisition and management, data dissemination, maintenance, diagnosis, and interfaces to visualize data streams and resources in real time. In addition, the use of open standards and open Web protocols (e.g. HTML, HTTP or HTTPS) can also significantly reduce costs in terms of hardware and software, time, personnel and field operations [2]. As a result, researchers, engineers and commercial companies are jointly working to study the impact of using the Internet and Web solutions in critical control systems. For instance, Qui et al. proposed in [3] a WSDS (Web-based SCADA Display Systems) system to access the system through the Internet. The same authors also proposed a Web-based SCADA display system based on very-large-scale integration (VSLI) information technologies in [4]. Similarly, Leou et al. proposed in [5] a database management system to centralize the critical data received, providing a Web-based power quality monitoring system. Li et al. presented in [6] a Web-based system for intelligent RTUs with capability for interpreting HTTP. Jain et al. presented in [7] a Web-based expert system for diagnosis and control of power systems. Lastly, several commercial companies, such as for instance Yokogawa [8] or WebSCADA [9], have some Web control solutions already available for the market.

Nevertheless, the use of the Internet could give rise to new security threats and reliability problems in the system. Examples of attacks may be intercepted communication channels, disruption of services, isolation or data alteration. One way of protecting the communication channels could be to use SSL (Secure Sockets Layer)/TLS (Transport Layer Security) services offered by the TCP/IP standard, hard cryptographic primitives, hash functions, key management systems and intelligent mechanisms, such as Intrusion Detection Systems (IDS), Firewalls or Virtual Private Networks (VPNs). This last security mechanism may even be considered a cost-effective high speed communication solution between substations and the SCADA central network over a shared network infrastructure, while simultaneously providing both the functionalities and the benefits of a dedicated private infrastructure [10]. On the other hand, it is also necessary to configure authentication mechanisms to verify the authorized access resources and services in the system, as well as authorization mechanisms to prove an entity's identity and rights in the management of critical data and commands. Data redundancy mechanisms should also be installed to ensure the data availability at any time and from anywhere, as well as registering incidents or anomalous events occurring. Security policies should be put in place and frequent training courses should be available to users to avoid unintentional actions.

Wireless Communication. Another essential technology in automation and control processes is wireless communication, for several important reasons. This technology is able to provide (1) control as a wired infrastructure but with a low installation and maintenance cost, (2) mobility and (3) connectivity with other control components independently of the environmental conditions. To be more precise, many of the critical infrastructures control conditions which are impossible for humans to monitor in person (e.g., high/low temperatures, high/low pressures, noise, underground water/oil pipelines, etc.). These critical conditions force systems to deploy autonomous and intelligent devices in order to cover certain functionalities in these areas (e.g., robots, automation vehicles, sensors, active RFID devices, etc.). In fact, the vast majority of wireless technologies have already been proposed to be included in industrial control networks, such as Bluetooth, WiFi, Mobile technology (UMTS, GPRS or TETRA), Satellite, Global Positioning System (GPS), WiMAX, microwave, Mobile Ad-hoc Networks (MANETs), or Wireless Sensor Networks (WSNs).

Furthermore, a hybrid configuration with different technologies could improve the monitoring processes since each technology could incorporate its own inherent capabilities into the subsystem or the whole system. For instance, WSNs could offer control as an RTU while ensuring prevention of abnormal situations thanks to their sensor nodes, which are equipped with a 4MHz-32MHz microprocessor, 8KB-128KB RAM, and 128KB-192KB ROM, and constantly measure environmental data associated to temperature, pressure, vibration, light intensity, etc. Generally, and depending on the application context, the nodes are linked to an energy supplier or to industrial equipment in order to maximize their lifetime (by between 5 and 10 years). Their sensor nodes, smart and autonomous devices, are capable of processing any information sensed from their sensors and transmitting it to a central system with considerable hardware and software resources, such as for example an RTU working either as a data collection device. Taking advantage of these technical capabilities, field operators may locally access an RTU to manage the real state of substations using for instance a portable device (like a PDA). They can also manage incidences or anomalous events detected by sensor nodes, such as failures (e.g. circuit breaks, leaks) and threats (e.g., environmental changes, strong fluctuations/high voltage in a power line), maximizing the reaction range to prevent a possible effect in cascading. Furthermore, its wireless communication has been recently standardized to ensure the secure control, coexistence with other ICT systems, reliability in the communications and constant performance. Currently, there are three standards: Zigbee PRO, WirelessHART and ISA100.11a, which are depicted in the Figure 2.

However, due to the critical nature of the application context, the nature of wireless networks, which tend to be generally susceptible to attacks, and the vulnerable nature of the technology used, it is necessary to ensure security and reliability in wireless monitoring processes. For example, the security in WSNs is mainly supported by Symmetric Key Cryptography (SKC) primitives because of the high hardware and software constraints of the sensor nodes.

2.2 Interdependencies, Consequences and Security Challenges

So far, we have seen that the vast majority of critical control systems are composed of numerous ICTs for the monitoring and automation. This type of complexity together with the use of TCP/IP connections, wireless communication and open software components have caused a notable increase in weaknesses, vulnerabilities and failures in the system [11]. In particular, a number of logical threats over the last decade have been registered in public databases (e.g. BCIT (British Columbia Institute of Technology), CERT (Carnegie Mellon Software Engineering Institute)), most of which are carried out by malicious insiders (e.g. discontent or malicious members of an organization). Obviously, the consequences can be devastating since a failure or attack could trigger massive deficiencies in essential services which may affect a city, a region, or even a country.

Some examples in the real life have shown the importance of protecting these types of critical systems. For example, in 2003, a slammer worm took over a private computer network, disabling a monitoring system for nearly five hours at the nuclear energy plant Daves-Basse in Ohio [12]. In that same year, numerous blackouts occurred in United States and Canada, and even in Europe (Italy) because of various failures found in the ICT systems [13]. Furthermore, most of these threats are published on the Internet. In February of 2000, an adversary documented and announced how to break into energy company networks and shut down power grids of utility companies in the United States [14]. The Department of Homeland Security (DHS) also presented a video documenting a theoretical cyber-attack on an energy station. The video showed a green diesel generator shaking violently before going into total meltdown. The DHS did not reveal the details of the attack, except that it was an over-the-Internet, man-in-the-middle attack. According to this study, the DHS tried to show that many of our critical infrastructures are subject almost to the same vulnerabilities. In fact, some other studies showed that using wireless technology, an energy system can not only be shut down, but also caused to overload. If this attack had been carried out on a real energy plant, especially at an electrical or nuclear plant, the results could have been catastrophic.

Another of the main security problems related to these threats is the high number of misconceptions in SCADA systems. More specifically, a SCADA system is still considered *an isolated and standalone network* because SCADA systems were built before the advent of the Internet. Thus when the need for the Internet in a SCADA system came about, many system engineers simply integrated the Internet components into the SCADA system without any regard how to expand the network or how an Internet-connected node could affect the security of the system. Also, most of members of the SCADA organization believe that *connections between SCADA systems and corporate networks are secure*. The integration of SCADA systems, which is a decades-old technology, with modern corporate communication networks, poses the problem of compatibility. Thus, access controls that are designed to prevent unauthorized access from outside networks are very minimal, and often inadequate.

It is also assumed that *an extensive knowledge of the SCADA system is required to perform an attack*. In other words, to say that SCADA systems have special safeguards that regular computers do not have is a gross overstatement. In fact, any individual with moderate computer programming knowledge and a computer with network access has the means to break into a SCADA system. Moreover, due to the primitive nature of SCADA systems, it is likely that an average SCADA system is in fact more vulnerable than a state-of-the-art personal computer. Moreover, companies that employ SCADA technologies are also likely targets for cyber terrorists, who are more organized, more motivated and better than a random individual with a computer trying to test out his/her skills as a hacker.

Another security problem is the inherent weaknesses associated to the SCADA network architecture. For instance, SCADA systems and corporate networks of a utility company are often linked. This means that a security failure in the corporate network may lead to significant security failures in the whole system, even if the strongest Firewalls and Intrusion Detection Systems (IDSs) exist. Furthermore, deregulation has led to the rise of open access capabilities, which have led to an equally rapid rise in the potential vulnerabilities in corporate networks [15]. Also, information about the corporate network of a utility company is too easily available on the web, which may be used to initiate a more focused attack on the system [16].

Likewise, members of an organization obtain access to unauthorized areas and email servers, and they use insecure web services and protocols for the remote control. Even worse, the file transfer protocols sometimes provide unnecessary internal corporate network accesses and network connections between corporate partners are often not secured by Firewalls and IDSs. There is also no real-time monitoring of network data, which leads to the oversight of organized attacks over a period of time [17]. Finally, multitude attacks may arise (e.g. eavesdropping or Denial of Service attacks), since most SCADA protocols lack up to date security (see Section 2).

All these vulnerabilities were also detected by the U.S. Government Accountability Office (GAO) in a study done on the Tennessee Valley Authority's (TVA) energy systems [18]. TVA is the biggest public energy company in United States, operating 51 energy plants (including 3 nuclear plants), and it provides energy for over 8.7 million people. With this case study, GAO showed that critical systems can easily be hacked into. The TVA's corporate network was loosely linked to the critical systems that control energy production, thus an adversary could exploit the security weaknesses of the corporate network to easily gain access to the energy production systems. Every Firewall and IDS between the two systems were found to be easily bypassed. As a result, GAO analysts believe a major cause for the lack of security has been the attempts to link SCADA systems to the Internet without any type of protection to this type of public infrastructure. The same analysts had reportedly launched a successful attack on an energy plant outside the United States, causing an energy outage in multiple cities. A major issue in the implementation of security systems has been that there are no federal guidelines regarding such measures, and it would thus not be cost-effective to actually implement them.

Therefore, special attention must be paid to the protection of control systems, where it is necessary to rigorously define security and access control policies, properly configure traditional security mechanisms (in communication servers or Base Data serves, Operative Systems, HMIs, backup systems, etc.), frequently carry out auditing and maintenance processes, authentication, authorization, and provide training. However, this is not enough. It is necessary to configure intelligent management mechanisms to take over alarms and incidences efficiently and at the appropriate moment, as well as to configure status management and anomaly prevention mechanisms, which must be able to recognize SCADA protocols, such as DNP3, Modbus, IEC-104 or ICCP. Furthermore, these preventive or proactive mechanisms could feed Early Warning Systems (EWSs) to help systems to react to an anomalous event appropriately (see the Chapter 6 titled *Early Warning and Attack Detection Mechanisms* for more detail), and in the worst case to feed forensic procedures and recover protocols based on specific methodologies, techniques, policies and standards. All of these security issues and others are the main focus of this chapter and they will be described in detail in the remainder Sections.

3   Security Management in SCADA Systems

SCADA systems are complex systems that can be compared to a living organism. Managing this complexity and their security aspects, interactions and interdependencies is also a complex task which should be broken into parts; starting for their overall architecture [21], [22] that should be in compliance with corporate policies. Initially, the overall architecture should comply with corporate policies.

We should be aware of the differences between ICT and SCADA systems based on their security properties as noted in ANSI/ISA-99.00.01-2007 standard. SCADA system imposed strong real hard real time response, i.e. imposes fixed constrained on the maximum communication time. Moreover, in some situation such constraint should be also very tight with time response of one millisecond range whereas ICT business systems have a permissible time responses of seconds.

We should not forget that these differences have to be taken into account when applying high level control objectives and technical controls (as defined in ISACA CobiT and reviewed in [23], [24].

These studies show that SCADA systems overall management should not be so different from ICT, depending on their, more or less, critical live environment. Apart from the need of creating a novel brand of applicable security standards, policies controls, recommendations and assessments; still there are a great deal of reusable similarities and common applicable security processes to improve their "survivability" capacity to be effective and sustainable for the entire system lifecycle [24].

3.1   Policies, Standards and Organizational Issues: Managing Complexity

Security Management has been intensively studied on ICT systems in relation to cybersecurity, but SCADA Systems have had more physical security concerns due to the isolation and proprietary protocols historically used. Applying the knowledge acquired in managing ICT systems to the protection of SCADA networks and associated CII (Critical Information Infrastructures) is not so straightforward and it requires some integration efforts and particular adaptations to standard security tools and best practices management.

Currently, several standardization initiatives for applying best management and security practices for industrial communication systems are under way. For any system, a security policy must be defined and the security measures must be derived from that security policy.

For example, the ISA99 Committee SP99 has published three guidance documents on introducing ICT security to existing industrial control and automation systems. The first report ANSI/ISA-99.02.01-2009 [25] provides recommendations for a security architecture, and for procedures to achieve and maintain security, including auditing. It describes elements for setting up a cyber security management system and provides guidance on how to meet the requirements for each element. It covers major topics of security management: policies, procedures, practices, and personnel. ICT also serves as the basis for all the standards in the ISA99 series by presenting key concepts, terminology, and models. The second report ANSI/ISA-99.00.01-2007 is a comprehensive survey of the state of the art in security technologies and mechanisms, and it provides comments on their applicability for the plant floor. The third technical report ANSI/ISA-TR99.00.01-2007 provides an updated assessment of various cyber security tools, mitigation counter-measures, and technologies that may be effectively applied to SCADA networks and electronically based industries and critical infrastructures. It describes an overall view of control system-centric cybersecurity technologies: threats, cyber vulnerabilities, and recommendations guidance for using these cybersecurity control objectives.

SCADA security management means the implementation of technical and operational controls coupled with the organization's business model in terms of investment and return of inversion subject to requirements. This means that security governance has to be a continuous effort to keep a system secure in operation and should deal with two major concerns: security architecture design, operational management and effective, survivable and sustainable system lifecycle: design, installation, operation, maintenance, continuous assessment and retirement [26] ISO/IEC TR 17971, [27]. The security issue should be enforced by using a good security policy, together with a security plan and implementation guidelines. All of them can be drawn together by the existing processes interdependencies of the organization and can be structured through common building blocks [28]. This managing tasks means implementing a security policy, knowing the risks and threats, enforcing the principles of least privilege, need to know and segregation of functions; open security design instead of relying on security by obscurity, classifying information, implementing defense-in-depth, using proven cryptographic algorithms, protocols and products; and last but not least, being conscious of human factor needs: behavior, awareness and formation. Without being exhaustive, there are widely accepted standards for security related to ICT systems widely accepted, which in conjunction form the basis for establishing a security control framework. The ISO/IEC families ISO/IEC 13335-X, ISO/IEC 270XX, 27001, 27002; the corporate governance of information technology standards ISACA CoBit and ISO/IEC 38500:2008, ISO/IEC 20000. In addition to U.S. GAO documents "Challenges and Efforts to Secure Control Systems" [29], NIST 800-XX Guides, especially [30] (SP800-82), and its Forum "Process Control Security Requirements Forum" (PCSRF). In the EU CPNI SCADA protection guides [31] and the recompiling effort of ESCoRTS project (European Network for the Security of Control and Real Time Systems) [32].

Security management is a continuous improvement process that for SCADA systems needs a extended and complementary approach beyond traditional ICT security processes. In one hand this implies developing proper metrics based on the existing enterprise risk assessment strategies and other hand developing a comprehensive framework that should allow risk reduction by selecting, applying and assessing an appropriate and integral set of sustainable security control objectives that meet the company's business goals [27]. Furthermore, this may involve modelling a complex system that may have many possible configurations, that even may be inconsistent with the operational system security policies. Such a complex system would offer multiple functions with a complicated internal structure of architectural components that are being part of an overlying CII. However accepting residual risks for these operational systems means evaluating them as a whole, through a well-defined configuration management plan, an auditing program and assessment plan that could make possible acceptance of their certification or/and accreditation [26] ISO/IEC TR 17971. Nevertheless, in part our lack of understanding these systems and cope with their risks arises (in part) from our inability to understand complex systems and modeling them through conceptualizing their component parts and security domains at the required decomposition level in which they can be described, evaluated and assessed [33]. Hence, to provide a complete security perspective for protection of the whole specific system, it should be necessary to establish a certifiable methodology that contributes to the adequate protection, detection and communication mechanisms, based on the current risks, interdependencies and interoperability needs of the whole system.

3.2 Risk Assessment

According to the principle of proportionality, almost all Security Management best practices agree that risk management must be aligned with business goals and used continuously to evaluate the need for protection during the operational system lifecycle, helping in this way to determine the selection, implementation and assessment of security controls in order to mitigate risks and to counter or minimize current existing security risks to a system.

SCADA systems are somewhat special because they can be an essential part
of a Critical Infrastructure (CI), they are not isolated inside the company and
their current threats are slightly different from those of ICT systems [34]. Their
risks can change more frequently than those of ICT systems; which raises three
main points of concern to deal with: the need of an *inventory catalog* that may
identify assets, threats, impacts, attacker potentials, possible applicable controls
and a *clear evaluation criteria* for selecting each of them and a *communication
model*, with a dynamic approach, for risks analysis results, threats and incidents
information exchange in order to improve crisis management and coordinate
response of involved actors.

3.3   Focus on Security Assessment

As stated previously the evaluation and security assessment of operational systems has not been as methodical as expected; but somewhat crafted. This can
be feasible for in house developed components or systems parts; but not for a
system that may have many external or internal dependencies and may be part
of a critical infrastructure. Current security assessment efforts [26] ISO/IEC TR
17971 propose a methodological approach which is an extension of the ISO/IEC
15408-x to enable the security assessment (evaluation) of operational systems.
This approach offers guidance on assessing both the information technology and
the operational aspects of these operational system and can be reinforced by
other methodological specifications (ITSEC, Common Criteria, OWASP, SSE-
CMM/ ISO/IEC 21827).

The currently undergoing eCID project[35] is developing a new certifiable
methodology approach focused on protecting CI and their SCADA systems as a
whole composed of industry sectors security domains. This methodology should
be technologically applied through an underlying architecture of controls based
on current risks that could be evaluated depending on the defined protection
profiles requirements. This project tries to fill some of the gaps for accreditation
and assessment described in the I3P Institute report [33]. Basically, this approach
proposes a framework for protecting SCADA systems jointly with ICT systems
involved. The problem must be tackled from a defense in depth perspective
in which, at least, there are five layers to develop: prevention, protection, alert,
measurement and response coordination within the lifecycle for both; operational
processes and technical control protection measures.

3.4   Technical Controls and Components Security

SCADA systems are important elements of CII and the current safeguards of
ICT can be applied to protect them (technology, policy/practice and people),
but human factor plays an important role in the defense for system survivability.
Examples of selecting applicable controls to SCADA systems can be reviewed
in [36], [37]. They are a not sector specific practices recommended to increase
the security of control systems from both physical and cyber attacks that can
help in the development of a framework for a cyber security program. More

sector specific are the NERC CIP reliability Standards [38] that provide, using reasonable business alignment, a cyber security framework for the identification and protection of critical cyber assets to support reliable operation on an Electric System.

Table 1. Organizational standards control objectives comparison

	Security Policy	Organizational Security	Risk assessment and vulnerabilities	Asset Classification and control	Personnel Security	Physical and environment Security	Communications and operations management	Access control	Systems development and maintenance	Incident management	Business continuity management	Compliance	Certification procedures and Audit
BS 25999											✓		✓
ISO/IEC 27001	✓	✓	✓	✓	✓	✓	✓	✓	✓	✓	✓	✓	✓
ISO/IEC 27002	✓	✓	✓	✓	✓	✓	✓	✓	✓	✓	✓	✓	
ISO/IEC 27005			✓	✓									
ISO/IEC 27006													✓
ISO/IEC 24762											✓		
ISO 19011													✓
MAGERIT			✓	✓									✓
NIST SP800-27									✓				
NIST SP800-30			✓						✓				
NIST SP800-34											✓		
NISP SP800-53	✓	✓										✓	
NIST SP800-61										✓			
NIST SP800-64									✓				
NIST SP800-100	✓	✓	✓		✓		✓		✓	✓	✓	✓	✓
ISO 15408	✓	✓	✓	✓	✓	✓	✓	✓	✓	✓	✓		✓
ISO 19791		✓			✓	✓	✓	✓	✓	✓	✓		✓

The following tables 1 and 2 show a comparative summary of organizational and technical security normative standards applicable to IT and SCADA systems related to their common security control objectives. These standards offer guidance on how to secure SCADA systems and an overview of possible system topologies.Typical threats and vulnerabilities to SCADA systems are identified and security countermeasures are recommended to mitigate the associated risks.

As a conclusion we can deduce the need of a unified subset of SCADA focused standards that comprises both the technical and organizational issues aligned to the overall IT governance and controls. Also, we need to apply dynamic risks changes to measure and evaluate the whole system security and their internal/external needs of "security status" communications to a certain degree of trust. Fortunately, it seems to be a current trend in applying system Protection Profile (PP) [30], [39], [35] referred to Common Criteria, for both the information technology based components and the non-information technology based elements implemented via policies and operating procedures for securing the whole system and their subsystem or security domains.

Table 2. Technical standards control objectives comparison

	Risk assessment	Communications and operations management	Access Control	Systems development and maintenance	Incident management	Business continuity management	Industrial Control Systems (ICS)
ISO/IEC 27005	✓						
MAGERIT	✓						
NIST SP800-30	✓			✓			
NIST SP800-34						✓	
NIST SP800-41		✓					
NISP SP800-53	✓						✓
NIST SP800-54		✓					
NIST SP800-63		✓	✓				
NIST SP800-64				✓			
NIST SP800-82		✓					✓
NIST SP800-83					✓		
NIST SP800-92		✓	✓				
NIST SP800-92		✓					
NIST SPP-ICS	✓						✓
ISA-TR99.00.01-2004 & ISA-TR99.00.02-2004		✓	✓		✓		✓
GAO-04-140T		✓	✓	✓			✓
FIPS Publication 199	✓		✓	✓	✓		
ISO 19791		✓	✓	✓	✓	✓	

Hence, it seems that there are four areas of security controls in which further development is needed to improve its current state of the art. First, the weakest points to consider for securing SCADA are communications that should be improved to reduce costs and increase efficiency. Second, and related to this, is enhancing SCADA protocols and strengthening networks with cryptography using secure-software design principles [40]. Third, monitoring and detection controls through firewalls and intrusion detection systems should be set-up to ensure access policy compliance and detect suspicious behaviors [22], [27]. Finally, a problem that has not been deeply addressed: SCADA information classification. Depending on their levels of classification and range of risks, it should affect the current security classification of their overlying infrastructures as critical.

3.5   Authorization and Access Processes

SCADA networks do not have a usual defined perimeter for proper access control. Improving access control to the networks has to be done firstly, through more tightly, clearly and detailed network access control policies based on the company general access control policy. Secondly, it is necessary to develop proper security mechanisms to ensure authentication, confidentiality, integrity, and privacy of data both in SCADA network components and in the many existing different SCADA protocols. On this regard Network Admission/Access Control (NAC) solutions can help in the task of authenticating distant devices [41]. Thirdly, human factor problems of authenticating humans' users still are of highly importance even in SCADA network.

Who the users are (authentication) and what the users can do (access management) on an operational system depends on the implementation of two intertwined managing concepts: Identity and Access. Access control can include the control of physical access to facilities and computer and electronic systems. Allowing access requires authentication for either a human or a device. They can use a token, that usually says something about whom posses it, to prove that their claimed identity is known, at least, to that system.

The more number of authentication factors the most secure authentication access control is supposed to be. In order to establish a good access policy into a network it is necessary to take into account unauthorized personnel and critical components and, if necessary, to define a perimeter and strong access control policies for both the human and the machine interaction, where it is relevant the bidirectional exchange of credentials among network nodes and devices [31]. Access Control has to be improved from a management point of view with all the existing policies and guidelines like ISO/IEC 27001:2005, ISO/IEC 27002:2005, NIST SP800-82, NIST SP800-53 that addresses some control needs: business requirement for access control, user access management, user responsibilities, network access control, operating system access control, application and information access control, mobile computing and telecommuting. Also, technical solutions should start earlier in the development and support processes and a bunch of evaluable controls be set; as for example the development focused classes (Class FDP: user data protection, access control policy (FDP_ACC), access control functions (FDP_ACF)) specified in ISO/IEC 15408-X:2009 under Common Criteria Methodology.

3.6   Cyber Assessment Methodology

SCADA systems have a high requirement on availability and should be so when performing security vulnerability assessments that identify and resolve vulnerabilities to improve the security of SCADA systems and over/underlying critical infrastructure process [42]. Due to software code complexity it should have a detailed plan that specifies a schedule and budget, targets and goals, expected deliverables, hardware and resource requirements, rules of engagement, and a recovery procedure.

Vulnerabilities assessments performed under the US National SCADA Test Bed (NSTB) [43] had shown the need of categorizing assessment findings and grouping them into general security dimensions and sub-categories according to a settled taxonomy. It seems that there are no clear vulnerability assessment methodologies for SCADA protocols. Currently, there are works on the run that are developing taxonomy of vulnerabilities to provide a framework for the security assessment of these protocols [21], [42]. They are using some of the existing general security assessment methodologies and taxonomies to generate a list of potential vulnerabilities in the target protocols. On the other hand, a good approach to do and define an assessment plan is applying Common Criteria [26] for Securing Operational SCADA systems implies specifying adequate targets of evaluation (TOEs) to be tested for both; products, and security functions of ICT systems. In this case, a TOE usually should be a subset of the SCADA or control system. As an example, a TOE for a SCADA system might be the alarms and commands to and from the field components in response to a man-in-the-middle attack.

Evaluation of operational system requires configuration management that is not usually found in ISO/IEC 15408 product evaluation. As ISO/IEC 15408 treats the life cycle of ICT products from the perspective of a developer, the life cycle only considers operational concerns as they impact the next version of the product. But almost a system has many other process components and manual procedures that need to be taken into account. Extending this capacity the technical report for assessment of operational systems ISO/IEC TR 17971 [26] put a step forward for operational system security assessment because it also expands the security evaluation to the operational processes carried out by personnel.

3.7   Alarm and Incident Management

While policies and mechanisms presented in this Section cover determined security aspects for a control system, it is also necessary to provide intelligent response mechanisms to incidents in order to avoid further increased damage due to an improper collateral impact. A particular case is precisely the alarm management, which is considered to be a field still unexplored. A first approach was proposed by Alcaraz et al. in 2009 [19]. They presented an automated adaptive response mechanism capable of estimating the most suitable operator to effectively respond to incidents and alarms in a control system, and ensure that a critical alert is attended timely. To this end, the mechanism has to make use of a reputation module to store values associated to operators' behaviors and to their reactions when dealing with incidents. The part of decision-making is managed by an incident manager, called as *Adaptive Assignment Manager* (AAM). Both the reputation module and the manager have to be decoupled from the operational activities of the system in order not to affect on the availability and performance of the whole system.

The assignment of alarms is relatively easy. The AMM component takes an alarm as an input, and it determines which operator and supervisor are the most appropriate to provide an early and effective response to the incident, offering all the relevant information to supervisors in a way that they can do their job in an assisted manner. In order to determine which operator or supervisor are the most suitable for taking care of an incident, the AAM considers the following set of four parameters: *Criticality* of the alarm, reputation of the operator and supervisor (member of the organization in charge of monitoring an operator's way to attend an incidence), *Availability* of the operator and supervisor according to their contracts, and *Load of work* of the operator and supervisor, i.e. the overload of critical incidences that an operator/supervisor might be dealing with at a certain period of time. Likewise, the AAM is also in charge of updating the reputation of the operators in the reputation module by using the feedback of the supervisors.

As a result, the alarm management mechanism assures reliability and security. Reliability, identifies the operator that is more suitable for performing a determined activity. Security, provides input information associated to operators and activities to other security mechanisms, such as auditing and forensic mechanisms.

4   Incident Response in SCADA Systems

As part of the security policy to be enforced [49], a procedure must be defined to react when incidences occur. This plan must also include mechanisms to detect attacks, track them and preserve information that can help in the forensic analysis of an incident. Moreover, a restoration process must be specified as well when the functionality of the system is affected by an incident.

As a basis for defining an incident response plan, well-known guidelines proposed by NIST and ISO can be used, expanding the policies and adapting them to the particular circumstances of the scenarios. This is the case with the work presented in [50] where a framework is presented to respond to and manage incidences in a CI. This work introduces a plan for responding to incidents in a Norwegian petroleum industry, focusing on three main phases: (1) prepare a plan for incident response, (2) detect and recover incidents and restore normal operations and (3) learn from the experience of previous incidents handled in the past.

The need for solutions to be applied in phase two is the objective of this section, which will give an overview of the efforts been made to provide an incident response plan with an efficient intrusion detection mechanism and the forensics methodologies to be used. Finally, unresolved issues discovered will be presented as well.

4.1 Detecting Intrusions and Threats

As part of an incident response strategy it is necessary to deploy detection mechanisms that alert security operators when an attack is performed on some of the components of the SCADA network. This type of solution has been used in the industry for early detection of attacks, and it deals with two main aspects of the incident response strategy: awareness of attacker's initial attempts to detect vulnerabilities in the perimeter of a SCADA network, or also to support the forensic process in the analysis of a system failure because of an attack, by gathering evidence of a successful intrusion.

Although there has been increased activity in recent years in the search for new solutions for intrusion detection, few researchers have paid attention to Critical Infrastructures and SCADA systems. Conventional IDS solutions do not fit well into a Critical Infrastructure scenario because its characteristics differ from common ICT systems deployment. In a SCADA network environment it is common to find proprietary protocols and operating systems that make difficult the adoption of current host-based or network-based intrusion detection systems. Besides this, et al. and other terminal nodes that provide information from the surrounding to the control systems are as critical as the equipment used for managing this information, because they affect they final decision that is adopted by an operator.

According to [46] attacks can be performed at different levels:

- RTUs and edge devices: remotely accessing these devices can compromise the overall functionality of the whole SCADA system because this equipment is used as a source of information for the control of the entire infrastructure.
- SCADA protocols: an attacker can exploit vulnerabilities in the protocols employed for obtaining data from RTUs and for the interconnection between SCADA networks. Disclosure of misleading information, spoofed RTUs and system controls are common threats facing any kind of intrusion detection mechanism.
- Network topology: denial of service attacks can saturate information providers causing its disappearance in the global visualization of the status of the SCADA network.

These SCADA specific threats have to be treated as long as other threats that are present in any IT infrastructure. In [51], an analysis of the impact that malware attacks can have on a SCADA system shows how typical operating systems worms (e.g. CodeRed, NIMDA, Slammer and Scalper) can influence on the overall productivity of a control system, causing malfunctioning and disasters in minutes.

Moreover, intrusion detections systems must face other problems which are more specific to this kind of environment. For instance, specific protocol-based network attacks that can harm the infrastructure by employing legacy protocol commands in a misleading way can cause denial of service and other kinds of malfunctioning effects [52]. SCADA systems have another requirement: an IDS must not disturb normal operations by increasing delays in the communication between RTU, control systems and interface applications like HMIs. High-speed traffic analysis is another topic that an intrusion detection solution has to tackle to succeed, as presented in the results of [53].

Therefore, future solutions for the detection of attacks in CIs should be specialized and adapted to the new scenario explained previously, extending their functionality by also monitoring SCADA specific protocols and taking into account the operational context where they are going to be used.

An evolution of the different intrusion detection advances provided by the research community is presented in [54]. In this work, research activity results have been split into two main categories: new distributed detection architectures and advanced detection mechanisms.

Regarding detection mechanisms, three general approaches are present in current IDS solutions to discover attacks or tryouts:

- Signature based: a set of rules of known attacks is used in order to find any suspicious activity in the current traffic of the SCADA network. Previous knowledge of an attack behavior is needed in order to detect it, although some unknown attacks can be detected by searching in the network traffic for traces of commands launched by intruders in compromised systems.
- Anomaly based: normal behavior is the key element of this kind of solutions. Different implementations try to model the normal behavior of the traffic, applications or messages being transmitted. Anomaly based solutions are able to detect unknown attacks and hard to discover intrusion proofs, because of the anomaly of these events with respect to the normal network traffic.
- Protocol or specification based: sometimes attackers employ legitimate protocol commands to exploit a vulnerability in the specification of the protocol used for communicating elements of the SCADA network. These intrusion detection solutions know these deficiencies and validate each command submitted to/from elements of the network in order to detect misbehaviors.

The effectiveness of these techniques depends on many factors. Basically we can find the following requirements for each category: (1) a complete and updated rule set is needed for the signature based implementations together with a scenario that employs protocols known to the IDS, (2) good training and a stable scenario is needed for the anomaly detection of attacks and (3) well-known modelled specification protocol scenario is required for the application of the protocol-based detection approach.

Some signature-based solutions employ a combination of a SCADA specific rule set and pre-processors provided by DigitalBond[55] that inspect protocols widely used in the industry.

Another approach that is commonly used is to adapt an anomaly detection algorithm to better-fit SCADA scenario particularities. This is the case with the work presented in [56] where a neural network schema is used as an anomaly detection mechanism for the intrusion detection. This solution is employed to analyze the traffic between PLCs and control systems, successfully detecting attacks directed to both systems. Although attacks of this kind deployed in the previous work are well known, most of them are not related to the particularities of the communication protocols employed in a SCADA network. Another technique for the anomaly detection work has been adopted in [57], where a SCADA simulator has been used to train a rough classification algorithm that reveals strange values reported by RTUs to the control system.

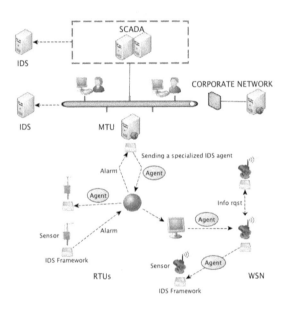

Fig. 3. Sending specialized autonomous IDS agents for solving an incidence or gathering more information

Although in some situations one of the above mechanisms can be successfully used, in many scenarios a mixture of them is commonly used to take advantage of the combined benefits. This is the idea behind the work presented in [58] where a combination of anomaly and signature detection techniques is used. Indeed, because these systems usually have a small set of specific applications, most of them with a long lifetime and with regular and predictable communication protocols, these elements can be easily modelled for detecting anomalies in SCADA components behavior while also using a signature-based algorithm for detecting known attacks. Model-based detection is the technique used for modelling the behavior of the system components in this work. Models were developed for characterizing the normal behavior of applications processes, machines and users in the systems alerting operators when an attack takes place on these models. In particular two protocols were modelled: ModBUS/TCP and DNP3 over TCP/IP analyzing the content of protocol packets, their expected fields content and relationship. This anomaly detection mechanism has been included in a widely used signature-based intrusion detection open source solution named Snort[61].

Regarding the architecture of detection, the benefits of distributed solutions for detecting attacks based on multi-agent systems instead of using host-centralized approaches for a Critical Infrastructure scenario are listed below:

- Autonomous mobile agents are less vulnerable to attacks than architectures employing coordinated or centralized detection,
- They can work even if one component fails or is compromised,
- It is easy to recover a damaged agent and moved it to a safer place in order to be able continue detecting attacks.

Recent distributed IDSs researches are analyzed and compared in [59], concluding that the multi-agent technology increases the performance and accuracy of IDSs. These two characteristics are of great importance in a Critical Infrastructure scenario. An example of a multi-agent IDS for a CI is presented in [60], although this work distributes the operational process into multiple agents, coordinating them by using at least one coordination agent. These multi-agent architectures are not as fault tolerant as the autonomous multi-agent option, because in the case where one of the main operational nodes fails the overall detection system could be disabled.

To date, mobile autonomous multi-agent architectures have not been used so far for defining specialized agents that can monitor SCADA protocols and applications. The SCADA scenario seems to fit perfectly with the benefits provided by distributing the detection work in autonomous and independent agents across the network. Agents can be specialized for analyzing applications or traffic where they reside, minimizing the amount of resources needed for the detection work and also reducing the need for a frequent update of the rule set or experience used for the detection of attacks. Figure 3 shows a scenario where mobile autonomous agents are propagated both for discovering traces of an attack and gathering information from terminal units to be used for analyzing an incident. In case that one of the terminal units is working suspiciously, specialized agents can be propagated to its surrounding for a deep inspection of the network activity.

This combination seems promising, future research should explore how to obtain benefits from the recent advances in the area of new attack detection mechanism, with the use of autonomous multi-agents specialized in the protocols or applications most commonly used in a SCADA network. These agents could be located in many kind of computing environments, from nodes of the SCADA local network to RTUs that have less computing resources available. In fact, mobile autonomous agents have been tested in resource and energy constrained environments such as WSNs ([62] and [63]) where computing efficiency and low energy consumption are normal topics to deal with.

4.2   Analysis of Intrusions

The analysis of intrusions and evidence gathering of malicious activity is another hot topic that requires the attention of the research community. Current forensic methodologies used in the industry need to be adapted for the special requirements that the SCADA systems demand [64]. As reflected in [65] these kinds of systems have the following elements that need to be considered when defining a methodology:

- More than one server in the control system area.
- A human interface (HMI) for the interaction between operators and the system.
- A large number of PLCs deployed in a wide area.
- Numerous remote connections to the central systems.
- A networked intra device environment

Around the middle of 2008 a set of research groups in the digital forensic field met as a working group at the Colloquium for Information Systems Security Education (CISSE 2008), where a list of hot topics in the research agenda of forensic computing for the next few years was compiled. The results of this working group have been gathered together and presented in the work [66]. At the top of this list can be found the need to create forensic methodologies for SCADA systems. Regarding this topic, an overview of open research issues were collected, which includes the need to build new hardware-based capture devices for control system network audit and new IDSs focused on these environments.

In fact, most control systems solutions focus mainly on controlling information while accounting and auditing tasks are not been implemented. As a result, there is a need for research into defining strategies and methodologies that can provide control systems with the forensic capabilities that are needed. To succeed in the application of new forensic methodologies specially adapted to SCADA systems, the following main areas need to be defined: evidence collection, preservation of evidences, analysis of incidents and documentation. But to go forward two of these areas need to be explored by the research community: evidence collection and analysis of incidents. In order to tackle them, new mechanism for analyzing and correlating alerts and intrusion evidences are needed.

Evidence gathering and analysis process imply the adoption of new intrusion detection mechanisms that not only rely on detecting known or common attacks, but also discover attacks to the communication protocols and devices used in a SCADA network. Some results have been presented in the previous section regarding the detection of attacks in control systems, but in order to monitor RTU traffic, new devices have to be used that can be integrated into these components for the analysis and registration of attempts or try outs.

A referential implementation of a RTU Data Logger is presented in [66], together with a denial of service attack that compromises the functionality of the overall system by stopping all communication from the control system RTU to the master node. These data loggers in addition to capturing all RTU network activity, also provide encryption and storing of sensitive data to a hard disk for

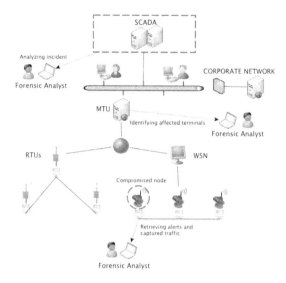

Fig. 4. Analysis of an incident

post incident forensic investigation. Figure 4 shows the different elements of a CI that could take part in the forensic analysis of an incident, from SCADA data servers to terminal units affected by an attack.

The analysis of evidence implies that the information gathered must be correlated and categorized appropriately. Intrusion detection agents, monitoring software, accounting process and information gathered from SCADA terminals (RTUs or WSNs) must be correlated and presented to operators in such a way that different levels of abstraction can be used: from a high level view presenting location of incidences and interdependencies with other components of the SCADA system [67], to a low level analysis of logs and captured traffic that reveals anomalies or attacks in the communication between nodes in the network [58].

5   Study Case: SCADA in Smart Grids

Existing SCADA systems play a role in monitoring emerging renewable energy systems such as Smart Grids. A Smart Grid is a critical infrastructure responsible for distributing and efficiently managing renewable energy to end-users. It is managed by other complex infrastructures (e.g., Advanced Metering Infrastructures (AMIs)), where the Internet and a set of things play a fundamental role in optimizing the whole performance of the system. The integration of things in the Internet is known as the Internet of Things or Internet of Energy (if the application context is developed in an industrial environment).

The first conceptual model of a Smart Grid was introduced by the NIST in 2009 [68], where seven domains were identified: customers, market, service providers, operations, bulk generation, transmission and distribution. Each domain encompasses a set of things, such as: end-users, operators, software and devices (e.g. smart meters, sensors, solar panels, electrical intelligent devices, industrial devices, etc.). The cooperation and information exchange among them helps the development of certain applications, such as for instance solar energy generation, management and storage, whose monitoring is centralized in a SCADA system. Nonetheless, new security risks arise in this new infrastructure, like for example privacy issues since smart metering devices manage the user data automatically, using the Internet as a communication mechanism. [44].

These new elements of an infrastructure need new paradigms to facilitate survivability and resilience. Hence, the grid should be 'self-healing' and capable of anticipating and instantly responding to system problems in order to avoid or mitigate power outages and power quality problems. Therefore, security plays an important role in the deployment of new technology, for both physical and cybersecurity, which will allow proactive identification and response to accidental or intended disruptions [45].

As mentioned previously, management of these new systems and their security need to apply old approaches to security. These approaches are based on prevention combined with response and recovery activities developed in the event of a cyber attack. But the overall cyber security strategy for the Smart Grid also has to take into account interdependencies and interoperability to mitigate risks. Furthermore; a new approach is needed in which the definition and implementation of an overall, technical and organizational cybersecurity risk assessment process should end up in the conformity assessment that should have into account common security evaluation criteria for the overall system and its domains ISO/IEC TR 17971 [26]. As these domains included systems from the IT, telecommunications, and energy sectors, the risk assessment process has to be applied to all these sectors, even home and businesses as they interact in the Smart Grid. This gives rise to potential privacy risks that demand the use of privacy-enhancing technologies (PET) for designing, building and managing these networks [44].

The Smart Grid must be security designed. It is expected to last a long time. It must adapt to changing needs in terms of scalability and functionality, and at the same time it needs to tolerate and survive malicious previously, unknown attacks. Research is clearly needed to develop an advanced dynamic evolving architecture protection that made of survivability and resiliency compulsory design and implementation requirements.

Moreover, detecting attacks directed at these devices is of great importance in order to avoid misuse that can affect their performance, reliability and confidentiality. Clearly new attacks are going to appear that could bring still unknown effects locally or to the surrounding components of a SCADA network. IDSs must be designed that analyze traffic directed to or coming from these devices. Also, host-based intrusion detection systems can take advantage of locally running agents that analyze the behavior of the main software components detecting anomalies that could be a signal of compromised status. Some results are starting to arrive regarding this issue. For instance, in [46] a security solution that employs agents to analyze the behavior of Smart Grid devices is explained. This work reveals the benefits of employing a multi-layer intrusion detection mechanism for detecting known attacks in a power grid environment, although SCADA specific protocol attacks have not been taken into account and should be included in future research works.

6 Conclusions

Nowadays, isolated SCADA networks are converging on standard ICT-based systems bringing new security challenges and a large number of potential risks due to threats, vulnerabilities and failures. Some of these are associated to the TCP/IP standard, the use of open (hardware and software) components and wireless communication technologies.

In order to address some security issues, special attention should be paid to the network management. Critical control networks (SCADA or DCS systems) must supervise, through computational systems, the constant performance of other critical systems, whose services are essential for survivability, like for example electric energy. A failure or threat in the control of a critical system could mean the (total or partial) disruption of its services, and therefore massive chaos among interdependent infrastructures whose impact could be devastating for the well-being of our society and economy.

The main purpose of this Chapter has been to analyze technological advances in the SCADA network architecture and to show how different ICT systems have converged in real-time monitoring processes and also to show how the control system is dependent on these ICT systems. Likewise we have analyzed consequences and their impact over the overall performance of the system in order to identify security mechanisms, (security and access control) policies, standards, recommendations, good practices, methodologies and assessments for a secure network management. In addition, we have reviewed some proactive mechanisms existing in the literature which deal with anomalous events, in order to ensure a timely response and we have considered how to control a possible effect in cascading.

Finally, we would like to highlight that several areas of applicability of evolutionary methods and genetic algorithms on power systems opens up new possibilities for critical control systems and the applicability of bio-inspired systems [47], [48]. In fact, the Immune System (IS) is an example of a highly complex system which evolved to protect the body as such, thus we believe that this concept is a good candidate as the basis for the next generation of bioinformation systems from which we could learn about new protection mechanisms. In addition, as ICT systems provide a distributed control and layered protection with a multiple escalating response to hostile actions and errors as a part of an adaptive mechanism capable of memorizing and learning, they could be implemented in SCADA systems to implement secure future new protocols based on these paradigms.

Acknowledgements This work has been partially supported by the ARES project (CSD2007-00004) and the SPRINT (TIN2009-09237) project, being the last one also co-funded by FEDER. The first author has been funded by the Spanish FPI (Formacion de Personal Investigador) Research Programme.

References

1. IBM Corporation, A Strategic Approach to Protecting SCADA and Process Control Systems (2007), `http://documents.iss.net/whitepapers/SCADA.pdf` (accessed on March 2010)
2. Smith, M.: Web-based Monitoring & Control for OilGas Industry, SCADA's Next Step Forward, Pipeline & Gas Journal (2001)
3. Qiu, B., Gooi, B.: Web-based SCADA display systems (WSDS) for access via Internet. IEEE Transactions on Power Systems 5(2), 681–686 (2000)
4. Qiu, B., Gooi, H., Liu, Y., Chan, E.: Internet-based SCADA display system. Computer Applications in Power 15(1), 14–19 (2002)
5. Leou, R., Chang, Y., Teng, J.: A Web-based power quality monitoring system. IEEE Power Engineering Society Summer Meeting 3, 1504–1508 (2001)
6. Li, D., Serizawa, Y., Kiuchi, M.: Concept design for a Web-based supervisory control and data-acquisition (SCADA) system. In: Transmission and Distribution Conference and Exhibition, Asia Pacific, vol. 1, pp. 32–36. IEEE/PES (2002)
7. Jain, M., Jain, A., Srinivas, M.: A web based expert system shell for fault diagnosis and control of power system equipment. In: Condition Monitoring and Diagnosis, pp. 1310–1313 (2008)
8. Yokogawa, `http://yokogawa.com/scd/fasttools/scd-scada-websuper-en.htm` (accessed on March 2010)
9. WebSCADA, `http://www.webscada.com/` (accessed on March 2010)
10. Gungor, V., Lambert, F.: A survey on communication networks for electric system automation. Computer Networks: The International Journal of Computer and Telecommunications Networking, ACM 50(7), 877–897 (2006)
11. Cardenas, A., Amin, S., Sastry, S.: Research Challenges for the Security of Control Systems. In: 3rd USENIX Workshop on Hot Topics in Security (HotSec 2008), San Jose, USA (2008)
12. Dacey, R.: Critical Infrastructure Protection: Challenges in securing control systems, Information Security Issues. U.S. General Accounting Office (2003)
13. Bialek, J.W.: Critical Interrelations between ICT and Electricity System, Electricity security in the cyber age: Managing the increasing dependence of the electricity infrastructure on ICT (NGInfra), Utrecht, The Netherlands (2009)
14. NERC Power Industry Policies, IEEE Industry Applications Magazine (2004)
15. Choong, S.: Deregulation of the Power Industry in Singapore, IEE Conf. Pub, Vol. 2000, Issue CP478/Vol. 1, pp.11–32, APSCOM (2000)
16. Pollet, J.: Developing a Solid SCADA Security Strategy. In: 2nd ISA/IEEE Sensors for Industry Conference, pp. 148–156 (2002)
17. Riptech, Inc., Understanding SCADA System Security Vulnerabilities, `http://www.zdnet.co.uk/white-papers/riptech/n-1z10rhq/` (accessed on March 2010)
18. Barkakati, N., Wilshusen, G.: Deficient ICT Controls Jeorpardize Systems Supporting the Electricity Grid - A case Study, Securing Electricity Supply in the Cyber Age: Managing the increasing dependence of the electricity infrastructure on ICT (NGInfra), Utrecht, The Netherlands, vol. 15, pp. 129–142 (2009)

19. Alcaraz, C., Agudo, I., Fernandez-Gago, C., Roman, R., Fernandez, G., Lopez, J.: Adaptive Dispatching of Incidences based on Reputation for SCADA Systems. In: Fischer-Hübner, S., Lambrinoudakis, C., Pernul, G. (eds.) TrustBus 2009. LNCS, vol. 5695, pp. 86–94. Springer, Heidelberg (2009)
20. Ronald, L.: Securing SCADA Systems. Wiley Publishing Inc., Indianapolis (2006)
21. Igure, V.M., Laughter, S., Ronald, W.: Security issues in SCADA networks. Computers & Security (25), 498–506 (2006)
22. National Infrastructure Security Coordination Centre (NISCC), Good Practice Guide on Firewall Deployment for SCADA and Process Control Networks, http://www.cpni.gov.uk/docs/re-20050223-00157.pdf (accessed March 2010)
23. Byres, E., Carter, J., Elramly, A., Hoffman, D.: Worlds in collision: Ethernet on the plant floor (2002), http://www.isa.org/fmo/newsweb/pdf/worlds.pdf (accessed March 2010)
24. Philip, L., Campbell, P.: Survivability via Control Objectives. In: 3rd IEEE Information Survivability (ISW 2000), pp. 1–4 (2000)
25. ANSI/ISA-99.02.01-2009 standard, Security for Industrial Automation and Control Systems Part 2: Establishing an Industrial Automation and Control Systems Security Program (2009), http://www.isa.org/MSTemplate.cfm?MicrositeID=988&CommitteeID=6821
26. ISO/IEC TR 19791:2006, Information technology-Security techniques-Security assessment of operational systems, Draft revision ISO/IEC JTC 1/SC 27 Final text for ISO/IEC TR, ITTF (2009)
27. Stamp, J., Campbell, P., Depoy, J., Dillinger, J., Young, W.: Sustainable security for infrastructure SCADA, SAND2003-4670 (2004), http://www.sandia.gov/scada/documents/SustainableSecurity.pdf (accessed March 2010)
28. Alcaraz, C., Fernandez, G., Roman, R., Balastegui, A., Lopez, J.: Secure Management of SCADA Networks. UPGRADE 9(6), 22–28 (2008)
29. GAO, Challenges and Efforts to Secure Control Systems (2004)
30. NIST, SP800-82 Guide to Industrial Control Systems, http://csrc.nist.gov/publications/drafts/800-82/draft_sp800-82-fpd.pdf (accessed March 2010)
31. CPNI, Good practice guide process control and SCADA security guide 7, Establish ongoing governance, http://www.cpni.gov.uk/Docs/Guide_7_Establish_Ongoing_Governance.pdf http://www.cpni.gov.uk/Products/bestpractice/goodpracticearchive.aspx
32. ESCoRTS Security of Controls and Real Time Systems, TD21 (January 2010), http://www.escortsproject.eu/getfile.php?id=316/
33. James, J., Graham, J., Leger, A.: Gap Analysis for Survivable PCS, United States Military Academy Research Report No. 14, www.thei3p.org/publications/ResearchReport14.pdf (accessed March 2010)
34. Kertzner, P., Bodeau, D., Nitschke, R., Watters, J., Young, M., Stoddard, M.: Process Control System Security Technical Risk Assessment, Analysis of Problem Domain, I3P research report No. 3 (2005), http://www.thei3p.org/docs/publications/ResearchReport3.pdf (accessed, March 2010)
35. eCID, enlightened Critical Infrastructures Defense, TSI-020301-2009-18, R&D project co-financed by Spanish Ministry of Tourism and Commerce by Plan Avanza, 2009–2010
36. Evans, R.P.: Control Systems Cyber Security Standards Support Activities (2009), http://www.inl.gov/technicalpublications/Documents/4192219.pdf (accessed March 2010)

37. Department of Homeland Security (DHS), Catalog of Control Systems Security: Recommendations for Standards Developers (2008), http://www.us-cert.gov/control_systems/pdf/Catalog_of_Control_Systems_Security_Recommendations.pdf (accessed March 2010)
38. NERC, Critical Infrastructure Protection (CIP) (2008), http://www.nerc.com/page.php?cid=2|20]
39. NIST, System Protection Profile-Industrial Control Systems, version 1.0 (2004)
40. Sandip, C., Ganesh, D., Graham, H.: Improving the Cyber Security of SCADA Communication Networks. ACM 52(7) (2009)
41. Okhravi, H., Nicol, D.: Applying Trusted Network Technology to Process Control Systems. In: Papa, M., Shenoi, S. (eds.) Critical Infrastructure Protection II. IFIP, vol. 290, pp. 57–70. Springer, Boston (2009)
42. Viking Project (2010), http://www.vikingproject.eu/page3.php (accessed on March 2010)
43. Office of Electricity Delivery and Energy Reliability Common Cyber Security Vulnerabilities Observed in Control, DoE, System Assessments by the INL NSTB Program (2008), http://www.oe.energy.gov/DocumentsandMedia/DOE_SG_Book_Single_Pages.pdf (accessed March 2010)
44. Cavoukian, A., Polonetsky, J., Wolf, C.: SmartPrivacy for the Smart Grid: Embedding Privacy into the Design of Electricity Conservation, Office of the Information and Privacy Commissioner/Ontario (2009), http://www.ipc.on.ca/images/Resources/pbd-smartpriv-smartgrid.pdf (accessed March 2010)
45. Mazza, P.: Smart Grid: Powering Up the Smart Grid-Smart Grid News-Grid Modernization and the Smart Grid (2007), http://www.smartgridnews.com/artman/uploads/1/sgnr_2007_12035.pdf
46. Wei, D., Lu, Y., Jafari, M., Skare, P., Rohde, K.: An integrated security system of protecting Smart Grid against cyber attacks. In: Innovative Smart Grid Technologies (ISGT), pp. 1–7 (2010)
47. Carvajal, F.: Computer Immune System: An overview-creating a cyberimmune operating system. In: Proceedings of the 1st International Workshop on Security in Information Systems, SIS 2002 (2002)
48. IRRIIS Project, Overview on Bio-inspired operation strategies, Deliverable 2.2.3, http://www.irriis.org/File.aspx?lang=2&oiid=9139&pid=572 (accessed on March 2010)
49. Kilman, D., Stamp, J.: Framework for SCADA Security Policy, Sandia National Laboratories report SAND2005-1002C (2005)
50. Jaatun, G., Albrechtsen, E., Line, B., Tondel, I., Longva, O.: A framework for Incident Response Management in the Petroleum Industry. International Journal of Critical Infrastructure Protection 2(1-2), 26–37 (2009)
51. Nai, I., Carcanoa, A., Masera, M., Trombetta, A.: An Experimental Investigation of Malware Attacks on SCADA Systems. International Journal of Critical Infrastructure Protection 2(4), 139–145 (2009)
52. Verba, J., Milvich, M.: Idaho National Laboratory Supervisory Control and Data Acquisition Intrusion Detection System (SCADA IDS). In: IEEE Conference on Technologies for Homeland Security, pp. 469–473 (2008)
53. Cai, N., Wang, J., Yu, X.: SCADA system security: Complexity, history and new developments. In: 6th IEEE International Conference on Industrial Informatics (INDIN 2008), pp. 569–574 (2008)

54. Marhusin, M., Cornforth, D., Larkin, H.: An overview of recent advances in intrusion detection. In: 8th IEEE International Conference on Computer and Information Technology (CIT 2008), pp. 432–437. IEEE Press (2008)
55. DigitalBond, http://www.digitalbond.com (accessed on November 2010)
56. Linda, O., Vollmer, T., Manic, M.: Neural Network based Intrusion Detection System for Critical Infrastructures. In: International Joint Conference on Neural Networks (IJCNN), pp. 1827–1834. IEEE Press (2009)
57. Coutinho, M., Lambert-Torres, G., Silva, L., Martins, H., Lazarek, H., Neto, J.: Anomaly Detection in Power System Control Center Critical Infrastructures using Rough Classification Algorithm. In: DEST 2009, pp. 733–738. IEEE Press (2009)
58. Valdes, A., Cheung, S.: Intrusion Monitoring in Process Control Systems. In: 42nd Hawaii International Conference on System Sciences (HICSS 2009), pp. 1–7. IEEE Press (2009)
59. Patil, N., Das, C., Patankar, S., Pol, K.: Analysis of Distributed Intrusion Detection Systems Using Mobile Agents. In: First International Conference on Emerging Trends in Engineering and Technology (ICETET 2008), pp. 1255–1260. IEEE Press (2008)
60. Tsang, C., Kwong, S.: Multi-agent Intrusion Detection System in Industrial Network using Ant Colony Clustering Approach and Unsupervised Feature Extraction. In: IEEE International Conference on Industrial Technology, ICIT 2005, pp. 51–56 (2005)
61. SNORT, http://www.snort.org (accessed on November 2010)
62. Georgoulas, D., Blow, K.: Intelligent Mobile Agent Middleware for Wireless Sensor Networks: A Real Time Application Case Study. In: Fourth Advanced International Conference on Telecommunications, AICT 2008, pp. 95–100 (2008)
63. Fok, C., Roman, G., Lu, C.: Agilla: A Mobile Agent Middleware for Self-adaptive Wireless Sensor Networks. Transactions on Autonomous and Adaptive Systems (TAAS) 4 (2009)
64. Slay, J., Sitnikova, E., Campbell, P., Daniels, B.: Process Control System Security and Forensics: A Risk Management Simulation. In: Proceedings of SIMTECT 2009, Adelaide (2009)
65. Slay, J., Sitnikova, E.: The Development of a Generic Framework for the Forensic Analysis of SCADA and Process Control Systems, e-Forensics (2009)
66. Morris, T., Srivastava, A., Reaves, B., Pavurapu, K., Abdelwahed, S., Vaughn, R., McGrew, W., Dandass, Y.: Engineering Future Cyber-Physical Energy Systems: Challenges, Research Needs, and Roadmap. In: IEEE North American Power Symposium (October 2009)
67. Tolone, W.: Interactive Visualizations for Critical Infrastructure Analysis. International Journal of Critical Infrastructure Protection 2, 124–134 (2009)
68. NIST, Smart Grid Cyber Security Strategy and Requirements, The Smart Grid Interoperability Panel - Cyber Security Working Group, Draft NISTIR 7628, U.S. Department of Commerce (2010)

SCADA Protocol Vulnerabilities

Julian L. Rrushi

Faculty of Computer Science, University of New Brunswick, 550 Windsor St.,
Fredericton, New Brunswick E3B 5A3, Canada
jrrushi@unb.ca

Abstract. The majority of network traffic in process control networks is generated by industrial communication protocols, whose implementation represents a
considerable part of the code that runs in process control systems. Consequently
a large number of attack techniques that apply to process control systems can
be conducted over industrial communication protocols. In this chapter we provide a technical discussion of possible vulnerabilities in industrial communication protocols, with specific reference to the IEC 61850 and ModBus protocols.
We provide technical background on IEC 61850 and ModBus, and thus proceed
with a description of possible vulnerabilities in those protocols. We also elaborate
on how those vulnerabilities are exploited, and thus describe various techniques
that leverage such exploitations to maximize physical damage to digitally controlled physical infrastructures such as power plants and electrical substations.
The main goal behind this chapter is to provide the reader with technical insight
that is workable in researching and engineering a better cyber defense for process
control systems.

1 Introduction

Ethical cyber security research conducted by the U.S. DoE Idaho National Laboratories (INL) demonstrated the potential of computer network attacks for causing physical
damage to digitally controlled physical infrastructures such as power plants and electrical substations [16]. The INL demonstration, which was referred to as the Aurora
generator test, consisted in attacking the replica of a process control system that is typically used to monitor and control an electrical power generator in a power plant. The
concrete result of the Aurora generator test was a violent physical destruction of the
power generator. Attacks such as the Aurora generator test exploit vulnerabilities in
control applications and their underlying network communication stack that run in process control systems. The majority of network traffic that flows over a typical process
control network is generated by industrial communication protocols.

The implementation of those protocols represents a considerable part of the overall
code that runs in process control systems. Thus, it comes natural that a significant part
of vulnerabilities in a process control system lies in industrial communication protocols, and that a significant part of the computer network attacks that are applicable to
process control systems, including the Aurora generator test, can be conducted over
industrial communication protocols. In this chapter we discuss in technical terms the
various kinds of vulnerabilities in industrial communication protocols. We also elaborate on how those vulnerabilities are exploited and employed to cause physical damage

J. Lopez et al. (Eds.): Critical Information Infrastructure Protection, LNCS 7130, pp. 150–176, 2012.

to a target infrastructure. The main goal behind our chapter is to provide the reader with technical insight that is usable in researching and engineering a better cyber defense for process control systems.

We elaborate on vulnerabilities in industrial communication protocols by referring to IEC 61850 [1] and ModBus TCP [4]. We refer to ModBus as it arguably is a representative of bit-oriented industrial communication protocols in terms of design, and to IEC 61850 as it adopts the emerging paradigm of object-oriented process control communications. The remaining of this chapter is organized as follows. In Section 2 we provide technical background on IEC 61850 and ModBus. In Section 3 we discuss vulnerabilities that regard weak or missing authentication and integrity checks of industrial protocol traffic along with some of the computer network attacks that exploit those vulnerabilities. Section 4 describes memory corruption vulnerabilities as applied to implementations of industrial communication protocols. Section 5 describes various techniques that leverage a computer network attack to cause physical damage via disruption of physical processes and equipment. In section Section 6 we summarize our discussion and conclude the chapter.

2   Industrial Communication Protocols

We now give an overview of the IEC 61850 and ModBus, which serve as reference protocols for this chapter.

2.1   IEC 61850

2.1.1   Historical Development
Byte-oriented protocols such as Modbus and Distributed Network Protocol (DNP) [6] had been optimized to operate over low-bandwidth communication channels. Such an optimization induced lack of interoperability along with configuration costs in terms of both time and complexity. In order to facilitate interoperability between control systems provided to the electric power industry, in 1988 the Electric Power Research Institute (EPRI) and the Institute of Electrical and Electronics Engineers (IEEE) initiated the Utility Communications Architecture (UCA) project under the Integrated Utility Communication (IUC) program. UCA initially was oriented toward communications between control centers, and communications between substations and control centers. EPRI and IEEE carried out the UCA project in collaboration with the Pacific Gas and Electric company and Houston Light and Power company.

The result of such collaboration was a standard communications architecture referred to as UCA version 1.0. This standard architecture was designed to meet a large set of requirements gathered via technical interviews with personnel of electric power companies. UCA version 1.0 provided profiles of protocols suitable for use at various layers of the Open System Interconnect (OSI) communication model. Nevertheless, actual deployment of UCA version 1.0 in the electric power industry was limited. While the specification of UCA version 1.0 was quite rich of functionality, it didn't provide a detailed description of how such a communications architecture is supposed to be practically used in field devices. EPRI and IEEE continued with their efforts to improve UCA by sponsoring a number of research projects such as the substation integrated protection, control, and data acquisition, or the MMS Forum Working Groups.

These efforts led to the specification of UCA version 2.0 which provides thorough object models of field devices such as microprocessor-based intelligent electronic devices (IEDs) commonly found in electrical power utilities. A device object model of a field device such as an IED in the current context is a definition of data and control functions provided by that device. In 1997 EPRI and IEEE combined efforts with the working group 10 (WG10) within the IEC Technical Committee number 57 (TC57) to create a common international standard. These efforts leveraged the fundamental concepts and definitions of UCA into a standard protocol named IEC 61850 especially devised to provide for interoperability, fast communications among field devices, guaranteed data delivery time, configuration support, etc.

2.1.2 Typical Employment

The IEC 61850 standard was devised primarily for electrical substation automation systems, and typical IEC 61850 implementations run in IEDs. Nevertheless, the IEC 61850 standard is also equipped with services and data models for substation to substation communications, substation to control center communications, distributed automation communications, metering, electrical equipment condition monitoring and diagnosis, and for IED to engineering systems communications. Extensions of IEC 61850 were developed also for hydro-electric power plants and wind power plants.

2.1.3 Functional Features

Monitoring and control functions in IEC 61850 are commonly implemented in IEDs. These application functions may be placed in individual IEDs or distributed in several IEDs. IEC 61850 uses the concept of virtualization through which it provides information on aspects of physical devices that are relevant to information exchanges between IEDs. The approach taken in IEC 61850 is to decompose application functions into small entities referred to as logical nodes, which are then used as fundamental entities in IEC 61850 communications. A logical node is a virtual representation of a physical device and its applications. For instance, IEC 61850 defines virtual representations for circuit breakers, circuit switches, current transformers, voltage transformers, etc.

Logical nodes are organized in groups identified by single uppercase letters. The name of each logical node then begins with the letter which represents the group that logical node belongs to. Table 1 provides a list of the logical node groups and their corresponding indicators. As an instance, since the logical node virtually representing circuit breakers belongs to the switchgear logical node group, and the logical node virtually representing current transformers belongs to the instrument transformers logical node group, their names begin with X and T, respectively. IEC 61850 defines some 90 logical nodes for electrical substation automation equipment and their applications.

Further, IEC 61850 provides a set of rules which may be followed to define additional logical nodes in standard extensions such as those developed for hydro-electric power plants and wind power plants. As may be noticed in Table 1, IEC 61850 defines logical nodes for real applications in addition to logical nodes it defines for real equipment.

Table 1. Logical node groups and their respective indicators

Indicator	Logical node groups
A	Automatic control
C	Supervisory control
G	Generic function references
I	Interfacing and archiving
L	System logical nodes
M	Metering and measurement
P	Protection functions
R	Protection related functions
S	Sensors
T	Instrument transformer
X	Switchgear
Y	Power transformer and power transformer related functions
Z	Further power system equipment

Such logical nodes may be distributed over a number of IEDs. Logical nodes in the protection functions logical node group, for example, include logical nodes for differential protection, direction comparison, distance protection, directional overpower protection, directional underpower protection, phase angle measuring, transient earthfault protection, overfrequency protection, overvoltage protection, etc. Similarly, logical nodes in the supervisory control logical node group include logical nodes for alarm handling, equipment cooling control, interlocking functions, etc. Table 2 provides some example logical nodes for each logical node group. A logical node is composed of data objects which in turn are built according to a well defined structure and semantic. Data objects in logical nodes feature status information, settings, measured values, and controls related to real equipment and real applications virtually represented by these logical nodes. Further, it is the data objects that are exchanged between IEDs according to well defined rules. A logical node typically may contain up to 30 data objects. A data object in turn is composed of data attributes. The attributes of data objects are the ultimate carrier of status, settings, measurement, and control information. Each data object typically may contain up to, or in same cases more than, 20 data attributes.

Figure 1 depicts the organization of a logical node that virtually represents a circuit breaker. The information exchange services in IEC 61850, i.e. methods used by IEDs to access data stored in logical nodes, are abstract. Defined groups of logical nodes form logical device models, while defined groups of logical devices form physical device models. Logical devices always reside in individual IEDs, thus they are not distributed. Abstract services in the actual context means that the definition of such services provides a description of what these services provide. Service models along with the data models described earlier in this document exist independently from other protocols. Communication services in IEC 61850 are entirely defined by an Abstract Communication Service Interface (ACSI).

Table 2. Examples of logical nodes along with their description

Indicator	Code	Name
A	ANCR	Neutral current regulator
	ARCO	Reactive power control
C	CALH	Alarm handling
	CCGR	Cooling group control
G	GSAL	Generic security application
	GGIO	Generic process I/O
I	ITCI	Telecontrol interface
	ITMI	Telemonitoring interface
L	LPHD	Physical device information
	LLN0	Logical node zero
M	MDIF	Differential measurements
	MHAI	Harmonics and interharmonics
P	PDIF	Differential protection
	PDIR	Direction comparison
R	RDRE	Disturbance recorder function
	RBRF	Breaker failure
S	SARC	Monitoring and diagnostics for arcs
	SIMG	Insulation medium supervision
T	TCTR	Current transformer
	TVTR	Voltage transformer
X	XCBR	Circuit breaker
	XSWI	Circuit switch
Y	YEFN	Earth fault neutralizer
	YLTC	Tap changer
Z	ZAXN	Auxiliary network
	ZBAT	Battery

ACSI services are organized into two communication models, namely client-server and peer-to-peer. In a client-server communication model a client invokes services to get data from, or set data in, logical nodes of a server. While the peer-to-peer communication model is used for time-critical purposes and is based on fast and reliable exchanges of information between IEDs. The client-server model typically involves one-to-one communications, while the peer-to-peer model involves one-to-one or one-to-many communications depending on the functions being carried out. ACSI defines a set of service models upon which it defines information exchange services.

A server is a service model which represents the externally observable behavior of a given device. There is only one service associated with a server service model, namely GetServerDirectory(). IEC 61850 includes several other service models, each one of which has a number of unicast or multicast services. Let us overview some of these service models. An application association service model is a specification of how two or more IEDs can be connected. It manages the establishment of connections, deliberate interruptions of connections, and unexpectedly interrupted connections. A logical device service model, as described earlier in this document, is a grouping of

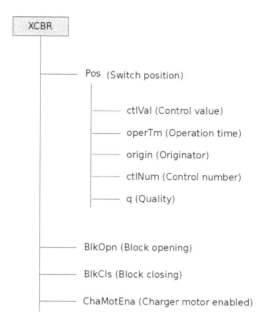

Fig. 1. Excerpt from the hierarchical organization of a XCBR logical node modeling a circuit breaker

logical nodes. A logical node service model is defined similarly as the logical node concept. A data service model is defined similarly as the data object concept. A data set service model represents groups of various data. Data values are grouped in sets for efficient transmission purposes.

Data sets can be manually or automatically created or deleted. A substitution service model represents the possibility that a client for defined reasons may request that a server replaces a data value with a value defined by that client. A setting group control service model specifies how to switch between various sets of setting values, and how to edit such sets. A reporting and logging service model describes the conditions under which reports and logs should be generated. A generic substation events service model represents the capability to provide fast and reliable peer-to-peer exchange of IED binary status data typically for protective relaying. This model defines the Generic Object Oriented Substation Event (GOOSE) and Generic Substation State Event (GSSE), which support the exchange of a variety of data sets and state change information, respectively. A transmission of sampled values service model describes fast and periodic transfer of sample data such as those of current or voltage transformers.

A control service model describes the services to control. A time synchronization service model provides for time synchronization across interconnected IEDs. A file transfer service model specifies the exchange of large blocks of data, such as program code for instance. The information exchanged between logical nodes is referred to as Pieces of Information for Communication (PICOM). PICOMs comprise data items sent from one logical node to another logical node, a specification of the format of these data, and the performance of the information exchange. The IEC 61850 stack is to be mapped to other protocols providing concrete communication means. Such a protocol mapping is carried out by the Specific Communication Service Mapping (SCSM), which associates abstract communication services, data objects and parameters with proper elements of a defined application layer protocol.

2.2 ModBus

ModBus is a simple protocol that enables process control systems to communicate with each other in a client-server configuration within possibly different types of buses and networks [3]. Originally ModBus supported only serial lines, but it was latter extended to support TCP/IP networks [4]. ModBus comprises an application-layer protocol, namely the Modbus Application Protocol [5]. ModBus has a data model that defines four categories of variables which hold I/O values. Discrete input variables are read only single-bit data provided by logical sensors. Coil variables are read and write single-bit data provided by, or destined for, logical sensors and logical actuators, respectively. Input register variables are read only 16-bit data provided by continuous sensors. Holding register variables are read and write 16-bit data provided by, or destined for, continuous sensors and continuous actuators, respectively.

ModBus defines its own addressing model in which each one of the variables of those four categories is assigned an address from 0 to 65535. Modus applications maintain a mapping between addresses of variables as defined by the ModBus addressing model and addresses of locations in random access memory (RAM) variable memory where these variables are stored. The said mapping is vendor specific. A ModBus protocol data unit (PDU), i.e. a network packet payload that conveys information that a sending device wants a receiving device to process, is comprised of two fields, namely a function code and data. Function codes indicate an operation on ModBus variables, such as write single register, read coils, etc. Function codes are encoded in one byte and their valid values lie in the 1 to 255 range in decimal representation. The data field in a PDU that is sent from a client to a server contains additional information such as ModBus addresses, the number of variables that are to be handled, or the number of bytes in the network packet payload.

Server devices need this information to carry out a task specified by the associated function code. Nevertheless, in some specific requests a function code alone is sufficient for a server device to perform the required task, therefore in these requests the data field is of zero length. The data field in a response PDU sent from a server to a client contains the data that the client had preliminarily requested via a request PDU. For example, if a master computer A controlled by human operators needs to acquire the values of four discrete input variables generated by logical sensors and stored contiguously in the RAM variable memory of a programmable logic controller (PLC) B, then A sends B a request PDU in which A specifies a function code of $0x02$, which according to the protocol specification stands for read discrete input, a starting address in the $0x0000$ to $0xFFFF$ range, which in this example will be the address of the first discrete input variable that is being asked to be read, and the number of discrete input variables that A is asking to read, namely four in this example.

In a regular transaction B will derive the action that is to performed from the function code, namely read discrete input, will use the starting address and the number of discrete input variables that A is asking to read for the purpose of determining the address of each one of these discrete input variables, will read their values from RAM variable memory and will place them in the data field of a response PDU, which it then sends device A. In the ModBus addressing model coil variables are addressed starting from zero. Thus, the address of the first coil is *0*, the address of the second coil is 1, and so on. In ModBus the output value *0x0000* requests the coil to be 0 (off), while the output value *0xFF00* requests the coil to be 1 (on).

3   Flawed or Missing Cryptographic Protection of Industrial Protocol Communications

Neither IEC 61850 nor ModBus come with cryptographic protection of their own. With regard to communication confidentiality, these industrial communication protocols may rely on transport layer security (TLS) as several other communication protocols in general purpose networks. IEC 61850, in specific, stipulates that an IEC 61850 implementation should control accesses to logical nodes. In the case of communications between different IEDs, such access control is supposed to be based on identification and authentication of logical nodes. In the case of communications between system operators and IEDs, the access control in question is supposed to be based on identification and authentication of users. Nevertheless, IEC 61850 itself provides no directives as to what cryptographic algorithms to use in order to provide for authentication. It is another standard, namely IEC 62351-6 [2], which provides security specifications for IEC 61850.

More precisely, IEC 62351-6 focuses on the security for the non routable profiles of IEC 61850. IEC 62351-6 allows for minimal computation requirements for these profiles to only digitally sign exchanged messages. Thus, common communications of the profiles in question do not get encrypted. This is mainly due to message delivery requirements, which are typically in the range of 4 milliseconds. ModBus PDUs may be digitally signed and/or encrypted, depending on message delivery requirements imposed by the operation of the digitally controlled physical infrastructure. Cryptographic protection of industrial communication protocols in general may be subject to flaws when implemented and configured in practice. Researchers from the INL have found several of such flaws during assessments of the cyber security of real world process control systems [9]. Weak authentication and poor integrity checks in industrial communication protocols are among the most significant findings of the aforementioned cyber security assessments.

Industrial communication protocols have been found to use weak authentication and weak integrity checks, and in some cases no integrity checks at all, between control servers and field devices such as remote terminal units (RTUs), and between various control system components. We now discuss some of the attacks that are made possible by security drawbacks that regard source and data authentication and integrity checks, and hence flawed or missing access controls.

3.1   Man in the Middle and Spoofing Attacks

Weak authentication in industrial communication protocols opens the way to man in the middle (MITM) attacks in process control networks. A MITM attack in such networks is conducted as in general purpose networks, namely by poisoning the Address Resolution Protocol (ARP) with bogus layer 2 configuration parameters. An attacker launches the attack from a node in the target process control network that he/she controls, such as for example a node that the attacker has compromised. In order for the attacker to interpose the attack node between any two nodes A and B, the attacker sends node A an ARP packet that configures node A to store in its ARP table the attack node's data link layer address as the data link layer address of node B. The attacker sends node B an ARP packet that configures node B to store in its ARP table the attack node's data link layer address as the data link layer address of node A.

As a result of the ARP poisoning, node A and node B send the attack node all network packets, and hence PDUs in ModBus and PICOMs in IEC 61850, that they intend for each-other. The attack node inspects these PDUs or PICOMs, possibly modifies them, and then forwards them to the original destination. As discussed in [9], an attacker through a MITM may modify industrial network communications between control servers and field devices, and industrial network communications between various control system components. These protocol traffic modifications may be conducted on-the-fly, and hence are transparent to target process control systems that communicate over a process control network. In the case of ModBus, the attacker intercepts and possibly modifies commands in PDUs that are sent from a ModBus client device to a ModBus server device along with process status data in PDUs that a ModBus server device sends a ModBus client device.

In the case of IEC 61850, the attacker intercepts and possibly modifies all PICOMs whose source and destination logical nodes lie in logical devices that reside in different physical devices. In addition to being in the conditions of conducting a MITM attack, clearly the attacker may spoof PDUs or PICOMs, and thus gain control over physical processes and equipment while poisoning system operators with bogus information about the state of the digitally controlled physical infrastructure. A taxonomy of the various forms of attack on Modbus based on MITM and spoofing is provided in [29]. Spoofing and misbehavior, i.e. violation of the rules of the industrial communication protocol, conducted by a malicious node in a fieldbus network may also lead to disruption of that fieldbus network as discussed in [7]. Fieldbus networks are industrial communication networks that connect field devices with digital sensors and actuators deployed within a physical infrastructure.

Fieldbus networks such as those that employ the Profibus protocol were developed under the assumption of a totally trustworthy network and mutually trusting nodes. A malicious node in such fieldbus network can send malicious network packets as itself or as any other node in the fieldbus network to corrupt timing parameters that are critically necessary to attain efficient network performance in a fieldbus network [7].

3.2   Protocol Facilitated Upload of Malicious Machine Code

This attack refers to the leverage of specific features in an industrial communication protocol such as IEC 61850 to upload malicious machine code to a target process control system. As written earlier in this chapter, the IEC 61850 protocol has a file transfer service model. This service model allows for exchange of files between IEDs without considering their content as data objects of some logical node. An attacker may use the file transfer service model in a target IEC 61850 application to upload malicious machine code to the IED in which that IEC 61850 application is running. The service of the file transfer service model that the attacker uses to upload malicious machine code is `SetFile()`. An attacker may also attempt to retrieve the code of a target IEC 61850 application, in which case he/she uses the `GetFile()` service of the file transfer service model.

An attacker may attempt to delete the code of a target IEC 61850 application through the `DeleteFile()` service of the file transfer service model. The research in [10] describes another form of loading malicious machine code into a process control system, which may be interesting to the reader. Numerous field devices, i.e. PLCs, Programmable Automation Controllers (PACs), RTUs, and IEDs, are equipped with Ethernet cards that have their own central processing unit (CPU), RAM, and operating system. These Ethernet cards run their own applications for managing connection to local and wide area networks. In most cases, Ethernet card applications consist of firmware. Field device vendors provide the capability to upgrade or replace the firmware in these Ethernet cards over the network through some proprietary protocol.

The security failure is that firmware uploads to Ethernet cards, such as the Rockwell 1756 ENBT Ethernet module and the Koyo H4-ECOM100 Ethernet module studied by the research in [10], may be unauthenticated or authenticated weakly. An attacker who can reach a field device over the network can load malicious firmware into the field device Ethernet card, and thus run arbitrary code in that field device.

3.3   Denial of Service

The overall network communication stack in a typical process control system is built up with layers of protocols. Protocols that lie in higher layers are directly affected by vulnerabilities in lower layer protocols [30]. The research discussed in [30] also revealed that layering may result in unintended interactions between the various protocols, and hence possibly in new vulnerabilities. ModBus TCP and a large part of IEC 61850 employ TCP/IP as carrier of PDUs and PICOMs, respectively. Flawed or missing authentication opens the way to denial of service attacks on the TCP stack, which in turn causes a denial of service on ModBus TCP and IEC 61850. Transmission of a spoofed TCP packet with the FIN flag or the RST flag set tears down a legitimate TCP connection between a ModBus client and a ModBus server [29].

ModBus TCP accommodates two categories of connection pools, namely priority connection pools and non-priority connection pools. Those connection pools in a ModBus device can be exhausted by opening a large number of TCP sessions with that device using spoofed IP addresses. Exhaustion of connection pools causes the ModBus device to reject new connections, and thus deny service to other legitimate ModBus devices [29]. These denial of service attacks cause similar effects on an IEC 61850 application whose communications follow a client-server model. Peer-to-peer communications in IEC 61850 flow directly over a layer 2 protocol such as Ethernet, and thus are not affected by denial of service attacks on the TCP/IP stack.

4   Memory Corruption Vulnerabilities in Protocol Implementations

We now discuss memory corruption vulnerabilities and associated attacks as they apply to a large number of protocol implementations that are actually in production. IEC 61850 implementations are commonly coded in C/C++, and subsequently are deployed in microprocessor-based devices such as IEDs or phasor measurement units (PMUs). ModBus implementations are also commonly coded in C/C++ in addition to languages such as ladder logic, instruction list and other languages of the open international standard IEC 61131. ModBus implementations are generally deployed in microprocessor-based devices such as PLCs and RTUs. Memory corruption vulnerabilities are programming errors that may be exploited by an attacker to corrupt the memory of a computer program such as as a control application that represents an IEC 61850 or ModBus implementation. Examples of memory corruption vulnerabilities in real-world process control systems include a buffer overflow in the ABB's PCU400 process communication unit [12], a bufer overflow in the DATAC's RealWin/FlexView HMI [11], and a buffer overflow in the GE Fanuc's CIMPLICITY HMI [13].

The exploitation of memory corruption vulnerabilities generally takes the form of a control-data attack or a pure-data attack. Control-data attacks corrupt control data, i.e. data that play a role in the memory management of a process during its execution. Examples of such data include saved instruction pointer, saved frame pointer, a function pointer in GOT, etc. Control-data attacks aim at transferring the execution flow of a target process into malicious machine code inserted into the address space of that process, or into existing instructions of that process, which are forced to take arguments that are supplied by the attacker. Pure-data attacks corrupt data that play a role in the actual computation performed by a target process, in our case in the actual computation performed by IEC 61850 or ModBus applications. Examples of such data include the attributes of the Pos data object in the XCBR logical node in an IEC 61850 application, and coil variables and holding register variables in a ModBus application. In this section we focus mostly on control-data attacks. Pure-data attacks are treated later on in this section.

4.1   Protocol Specific Memory Corruptions

Control applications may be subject to exploitations of memory corruption vulnerabilities that are conducted in ways that are specific to them. Examples of these applications include ModBus. ModBus employs an addressing model in which unsigned integer indices in the range [0, 65535] are used to logically refer to ModBus application variables. The ModBus data model maintains a mapping between logical references, i.e. the said indices, which are also known as ModBus addresses, and memory addresses of application objects in a process control system. In general such mapping is vendor device specific. Faulty mappings may possibly lead to memory corruptions on a ModBus application, as discussed in [14]. An instance of a possible faulty mapping is one in which the address of a memory location is calculated by using a logical reference as an offset with respect to a predetermined base address.

In this case a memory corruption attack on a target ModBus application may be conducted through a write request network packet in which the logical reference is such that, when added to the base address, it produces the memory address of control data or the memory address of non-control data other than those non-control data that are normally accessible. An example of an attack network packet, which more precisely in ModBus is referred to as protocol data unit (PDU), is shown in Figure 2. The attack packet in question is structured such as to request a target ModBus application to write two holding register variables, i.e. two 16-bit variables stored in the main memory of a ModBus device, by specifying a specific logical reference. As a result of a possible faulty mapping, that logical reference would produce the address of the memory location where control data are stored. The overwriting value is also specified in the attack packet.

It takes the form of two 16-bit data that are to be written to the said register variables. When joined together, these data form the memory address of malicious machine code preliminarily injected into the address space of the target ModBus application. Thus, the attack packet in question would corrupt control data with the address of malicious machine code injected into the address space of the target ModBus application. This ModBus specific memory corruption is conceptually similar to the attacks on the OLE for Process Control (OPC) [34] that are discussed by Mora in [36]. To the author's knowledge, as of this writing an IEC 61850 application does not have specific ways in which it fails. Nevertheless, a specific characteristic of IEC 61850 is that the manifestation of its possible coding vulnerabilities, including memory corruption vulnerabilities, may depend on the configuration in which the IEC 61850 application is operating.

IEC 61850 configurations are formally described via an XML based Substation Configuration Language (SCL). Each IED is supposed to carry an SCL file that describes its IEC 61850 configuration. Thus, some possible vulnerabilities in an IEC 61850 application appear, and hence are exploitable, when the IEC 61850 is operating in a defined configuration, while other possible vulnerabilities in that IEC 61850 application appear when the IEC 61850 application operates in some other configuration. There is a significant diversity of configurations in which an IEC 61850 application may be operating, each one of which may lead to the emergence of specific vulnerabilities. The security of IEC 61850 objects and services is strongly dependent on proper implementations of associated and underlying protocols which the IEC 61850 stack is mapped to [15]. A commonly deployed protocol which IEC 61850 is mapped to is the standard ISO 9506, i.e. Manufacturing Messaging Specification (MMS).

MMS is an application layer protocol maintained by ISO Technical Committee 184 that provides for reliable transmission in real time of process data between networked devices that carry out data acquisition and control functions. MMS runs over TCP/IP and Ethernet. Thus, IEC 61850 inherits the numerous negotiation techniques and commands with expected responses of MMS, which makes its implementation complex and prone to error [15]. Data structures are encoded according to the Abstract Syntax Notation (ASN.1). ASN.1 data structures are known to be difficult to implement correctly, and hence are easy to exploit [15]. IEC 61850 is also related to time synchronization protocols such as Simple Network Time Protocol (SNTP). SNTP in turn runs over UDP/IP. Since peer-to-peer profiles in IEC 61850 are subject to considerable time constraints, i.e. usually a few milliseconds, they are mapped directly to a layer 2 protocol such as Ethernet.

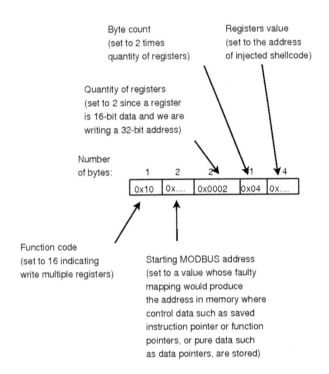

Fig. 2. Organization of an attack packet payload that exploits faulty mappings in a ModBus application

In several deployments IEC 61850 is also mapped to various web service protocols. Although IEC 61850 could be mapped to byte oriented protocols such as DNP, Modbus, Profibus, etc., this is not normally done due to subtleties in mapping object models to bit stream locations. IEC 61850 implementations exhibit lack of robustness in front of specific network packet structures, namely out-of-order network packets that violate the statefulness of IEC 61850, and network packets that are formatted incorrectly [15]. Common consequences of the processing of such network packets by a vulnerable IEC 61850 application include crashes or performance degradation of that application. The set of vulnerabilities in a vulnerable IEC 61850 application that are triggered by out-of-order network packets and incorrectly formatted network packets includes generic memory corruption vulnerabilities, which are discussed in the next subsection.

4.2   Generic Memory Corruptions

4.2.1   Array Overflows
An array overflow allows an attacker to abuse the assignment of a value to an element of an array, and hence attempt to write an arbitrary value to an arbitrary memory location. The conditions that create a possible array overflow are the following:

- An integer that is used to index the array originates directly or indirectly from attacker supplied data
- No checks are performed on the index to ensure that it lies within the array's range
- The value that is supposed to be assigned to an element of the array originates directly or indirectly from attacker supplied data

We now discuss an example of an array overflow in a ModBus application that creates a faulty mapping between ModBus addresses and memory addresses of ModBus application variables. Consider an array of size 65536 whose indices and elements represent ModBus addresses and memory addresses of ModBus application variables, respectively. Thus, the indices are supposed to be in the range [0, 65535], and the corresponding elements are addresses of memory locations actually in use by the ModBus application. In a typical request PDU we can find a ModBus address in the range [0, 65535], which the ModBus application that receives the PDU uses to index the array in question. The memory address found at that index is then used in a read or write operation according to the function code of the PDU.

If no checks are performed to make sure that the ModBus address in a request PDU lies in the range [0, 65535], an attacker could specify in an attack PDU a malicious ModBus address that is higher than 65535. When the ModBus application that processes the attack PDU uses the malicious ModBus address to index the array, it will reach memory locations other than those allocated for the elements of the array. Whatever is stored in those memory locations will be used as the address in a read or write operation conducted by the ModBus application. The attacker will use a malicious ModBus address such that during the array indexing it reaches a memory location where the attacker is able to write a value. This way the attacker will be able to read from or write into a memory address of his/her choice.

4.2.2   Stack and Heap Overflows

A memory corruption vulnerability of the type buffer overflow is a programming error that stores more data on a destination buffer than it can hold. This will cause the destination buffer to overflow, i.e. data will be stored beyond the boundaries of the destination buffer. When the buffer that overflows is allocated on stack, the vulnerability is referred to as stack overflow. Buffer overflows in general may be caused by instructions that do not conduct any checks on the bounds of a destination buffer when storing data into it to ensure that the size of the destination buffer allows for holding all of the data. Functions such as `strncpy()` enable a programmer to explicitly specify the number of bytes that are to be copied into a destination buffer, but they do not null-terminate the destination buffer, i.e. do not store a `0x00` as the last byte stored in the destination buffer.

Such apparently safe functions may lead to the creation of adjacent not null-terminated buffers. This condition may become problematic when it exists in conjunction with a vulnerable function that may cause a buffer overflow. A copy operation on one of these buffers to a destination buffer through that vulnerable function will copy the intended buffer plus one or more adjacent buffers, and hence will overflow of the destination buffer. In one of its very common forms, an attack that exploits a stack overflow is conducted by injecting malicious machine code and corrupting control data like the saved instruction pointer or the saved frame pointer stored on stack such as to transfer the execution flow to the injected malicious code [20]. There might be cases in which no executable memory areas are available to the attacker for injecting the malicious machine code. There might also be cases in which the available buffers are too small to hold the entire malicious machine code.

In these cases, a common attack strategy is to corrupt control data stored on stack such as to transfer the execution flow to existing instructions within the address space of the target application. In the domain of security of general-purpose computer systems this strategy is referred to as return-into-library. The attacks that exploit stack overflows are applicable to control applications which make use of the stack data structure throughout their execution. Not every control application makes use of the stack data structure. When the buffer that overflows is allocated on heap, the buffer overflow vulnerability is referred to as heap overflow. Memory allocator algorithms such as System V in Solaris, Doug Lea's Malloc used by the GNU C Library, RtlHeap in Windows, etc., store heap management data in band on the heap itself.

By overflowing a buffer on heap, an attacker corrupts such heap management data and hence forces the execution of macros making them use attacker supplied data in both sides of various assignment instructions [21,22,23]. Clearly if the attacker controls the data in both sides of an assignment instruction, he/she can write arbitrary values to memory locations of his/her choice. The attacks that exploit stack overflows or heap overflows are commonly applicable to control applications that run on embedded versions of the Windows and Linux operating systems in devices such as HMIs, control servers, PLCs, RTUs, etc. In an IEC 61850 application, one of the possible implementation spots that may be subject to exploitable stack overflows and heap overflows is the implementation of ACSI services that operate on data attributes, especially those that write to data attributes.

For example, referring to the XCBR logical node that models a circuit breaker in Figure 1, if the origin data attribute is allocated on stack or heap, an ACSI service that writes a value to origin and does not conduct any checks on its bounds will create a stack overflow and a heap overflow condition, respectively.

4.2.3 Pointer Corruption

Data or function pointer corruptions are made possible by a preliminary exploitation of a stack overflow or a heap overflow vulnerability. An indirect pointer overwrite [24] takes place when an attacker overflows a buffer such as to reach a memory location where a data pointer is stored. The attacker overwrites the data pointer with a value that points to a memory location that holds control data. Thus, instead of pointing to the original data, the corrupted pointer points to control data. Dereferencing the corrupted data pointer causes the control data in question to be overwritten with attacker supplied data. Similarly to an indirect pointer overwrite, an attacker can leverage a buffer overflow such as to overwrite a function pointer with the address of malicious machine code injected into the address space of a target ModBus or IEC 61850 application.

A dangling pointer vulnerability in a ModBus or IEC 61850 application is created when a pointer that is referenced by that application refers to memory locations that have been already deallocated. A dangling pointer vulnerability may cause the ModBus or IEC 61850 application to conduct an abnormal execution. A double free vulnerability is a specific type of dangling pointer vulnerability. It may lead to a complete program exploitation [28]. A double free vulnerability is created when memory locations on heap that have been deallocated by some memory allocator algorithm get deallocated for a second time by that algorithm. Clearly the memory allocator algorithm does not deliberately deallocate heap memory locations more than once, but is tricked by the attacker into doing so.

4.2.4 Format Bugs

Format bugs [25,26] stem from programming errors that regard format functions. Format functions are conversion functions that are used to represent primitive C/C++ data types in a human readable form. Format functions are used to output data, print error messages, or process strings. A format string, which is stored on stack and may include format directives such as those in Table 3, specifies the types of the parameters that are to be printed by a format function. Thus, the format string along with format directives in a format function determine the behavior of that format function. Parameters are passed to a format function either by value, in which case the value of the parameter is stored on stack, or by reference, in which case the address of the parameter is stored on stack. Thus, in either case the format function works on the stack.

Table 3. Some format directives

Format directive	Its meaning
%d	decimal
%u	unsigned decimal
%x	hexadecimal
%s	string
%n	writes number of bytes printed that far

A format bug vulnerability is created when an attacker can specify the format string to a format function, and thus control the behavior of that function. The format function parses the format string by reading one byte at a time from the stack. If the read byte is not equal to %, the format function copies this byte as is directly to output. If the read byte is %, for the format function the character behind % denotes the type of the parameter that is to be evaluated for display. Thus, in this case a format directive is encountered, and the value of the corresponding parameter is retrieved directly from the stack or from a memory address stored on stack. An exception is considered when the character behind % is an % as well. Two consecutive % are used within a format string to denote the character % itself, which is to be printed as is.

A format function maintains an internal counter and an internal pointer. The internal counter holds the number of printed bytes as the format function scans the format string byte by byte. The internal pointer points to the stack location of the current parameter. In a format bug exploitation, the attacker provides format directives within a format string forcing the format function to conduct its usual routine explained above upon attacker supplied data. For example, the attacker could specify the format directives %x or %s within the format string to display the content of the memory location pointed by internal pointer. The attacker could use several of such format directives to advance the internal pointer and thus read stack content. Similarly, the attacker could specify the format directive %n to write the value of the internal counter at the memory address stored in the memory location that is pointed by the internal pointer.

The attacker specifies the memory address where to write at or read from by including it in the format string. The attacker advances the internal pointer until reaching that address on stack. Recall that the format string itself is stored on stack, therefore the attacker can have the internal pointer point to the address in question within the format string. Once the attacker positions the internal pointer on the memory location on stack that holds the address in question, the attacker can abuse the vulnerable format function through a format directive so that to read from or write at the address in question. %x and %.f are format directives that are commonly used to advance the internal pointer. %x advances the internal pointer by four bytes, while %.f advances the internal pointer by eight bytes. %.f prints only the integer part of the float that would have been printed via %f, and thus avoids division by zero.

Direct parameter access is a technique that allows for referring to a stack parameter directly from within a format string, and thus allows for eliminating the stack climbing sequence from the format string. This technique uses the $ qualifier, which if supported controls direct parameter access. For example, %m$n would access in writing the m-th parameter on the stack. In the case of an aimed write operation, the attacker uses the values of the internal counter as the memory address that he/she aims at writing at the memory address that he/she has specified within the format string. The attacker increases the value of the internal counter by specifying %nu within the format string, where n is a number that the attacker uses to create the memory address that the vulnerable format function will write at the address that the attacker has specified within the format string.

When a format bug vulnerability is in place, an attacker may have the possibility to specify a format string directly, such as for example when a programmer writes printf(buff) rather than printf("%s," buff), with buff being a variable that holds attacker supplied data. The attacker may also specify a format string indirectly, such as in the case attacker supplied data are stored in other variables, possibly in a properly formatted form, before being used by a vulnerable format function. An IEC 61850 has several possible implementation spots that may use format functions that create format bug conditions. An example is represented by the IEC 61850's building blocks for logging, which may make use of families of format functions like err*, verr*, warn*, vwarn*, etc. In an IEC 61850 application, an event monitor inspects power system data in logical nodes.

Upon the occurrence of a specific event, the event monitor informs a log handler. The log handler processes the event, and thereafter possibly generates one ore more log entries, which are stored in a log file or log data base. In order to exploit a format bug vulnerability created by a vulnerable format function in the building blocks for logging of an IEC 61850 application, the attacker sends malicious PICOMs to that IEC 61850 application such as to cause or emulate the occurrence of an event detectable by the event monitor. In some cases the attacker may send the malicious PICOMs to one or more IEC 61850 applications that are related to the target IEC 61850 application. IEDs in the communication network of an electrical substation exchange power data with each-other, therefore forcing the creation of an event at one IED may lead to generation of events at other IEDs. The attacker injects format strings directly or indirectly into the target IEC 61850 also via transmission of malicious PICOMs.

In order to reach the vulnerable format functions in an IEC 61850 application, and thus have them process the format strings carried by the malicious PICOMs, the attacker may have to cause or emulate the occurrence of an event that satisfies specific conditions for generation and storage of log entries. IEC 61850 defines a logging service model that describes the conditions under which logs should be generated. Thus, an IEC 61850 application contains a set of logging trigger conditions that will cause the log handler to generate and store log entries. Such specific conditions are defined on power data change, quality change, etc. Clearly the discussion above holds for an IEC 61850 application in which logging is configured and enabled, which is quite common in real-world IEC 61850 applications. A similar discussion holds with regard to the basic building blocks for reporting in an IEC 61850 application.

4.2.5 Integer Overflows

In a computer science context, an integer is a fixed size region of memory that can store a real number with no fractional part. In an unsigned integer all of the bits are used to hold a value. In a signed integer, the most significant bit is used to represent the sign, which of course can be either positive or negative. If the most significant bit is set to one, the signed integer is negative. If the most significant bit is set to zero, the signed integer is positive. Taking into account that an integer has a fixed size, there is a maximum value that it can store. An integer overflow takes place when an integer is assigned a value that is greater than the maximum value it can store [27]. An integer overflow does not allow for writing beyond the boundaries of the integer. Thus, in most cases an integer overflow is not directly exploitable.

However, an integer overflow may lead to creation of other exploitable vulnerabilities, such as various types of memory corruption, when occurs in conjunction with or in relation to instructions that operate on memory. An integer overflow of type widthness overflow is created when an integer variable of a small size is assigned the value of a variable of a larger size. In a computation that involves operands with differing sizes, the operand with the smaller size is promoted to the size of the operand with a larger size. After the computation in question completes, the operand with the smaller size that was promoted is demoted back to its original size. If the result of the computation is stored in the operand with the smaller size, the demotion of this operand will cause the result to be truncated if it is greater than the maximum value that the operand in question can hold. An example of a situation in which a widthness overflow causes an exploitable stack overflow is the following.

The value of one of the parameters of a procedure is used by a memcpy() function within the body of that procedure as an indication of the number of bytes that are to be copied from a source buffer to a destination buffer. The value of the parameter in question is first copied to a local variable, which in turn is referred to in the memcpy() function. The parameter in question originates from input data, which means that the attacker may be in the position of providing a malicious value for that parameter. Before copying from the source buffer to the destination buffer, the procedure checks that the number of bytes that are to be copied does not exceed the size of the destination buffer. The procedure copies the value that represents the number of bytes that are to be copied, from the aforementioned local variable to another local variable with a smaller size.

In the procedure, the boundary check is performed on the local variable with a smaller size, while the memcpy() function refers to the local variable where the value of the parameter in question was originally copied. If the attacker specifies a large number of bytes as the value of the parameter in question, aiming at causing an overflow of the destination buffer, his/her malicious value will pass the boundary check performed by the procedure but still will overflow the destination buffer. This is because the widthness overflow of the local variable with a smaller size truncates the malicious value, thus passing the test. However, the memcpy() function refers to the malicious value as the number of bytes that is to be copied to the destination buffer, with the consequence being the overflow of that buffer [27]. An arithmetic overflow takes place when the result of an arithmetic operation is stored in an integer and is greater than the maximum value which that integer can hold.

Common consequences of an arithmetic overflow include value truncation and change of sign. Although addition is perhaps the most common arithmetic operation that creates integer overflow conditions, any other arithmetic operation that changes the value of an integer can create an integer overflow condition as well. As the stored result of the arithmetic operation that caused an integer overflow is incorrect, any computation that involves the result in question will be incorrect. One of the most common cases in which an arithmetic overflow creates other exploitable vulnerabilities occurs when the arithmetic operation that causes the integer overflow is conducted to calculate the size of memory that is to be allocated. Another vulnerability condition that may be created in the use of integers is the signedness bug. A signedness bug is not a type of integer overflow, however we discuss it in this section as it stems from integers and the way it can cause other exploitable vulnerabilities is the same as in integer overflows.

A signedness bug takes place when an unsigned integer is interpreted as signed, or vice versa. An example of how a signedness bug causes an exploitable memory overflow is the following. One of the parameters of a procedure is an integer that is used in a memcpy() function to indicate the number of bytes that are to be copied to a destination buffer. The parameter in question originates from input, therefore the procedure checks that the value of such parameter does not exceed the size of the destination buffer. By default, an integer is signed unless it is explicitly declared as unsigned. The parameter in question is declared as integer, and as such it is interpreted to be signed.

If the attacker provides a large negative value as the parameter in question, the bounds check performed by the procedure on that value passes. This is because although the value of the parameter in question is large, i.e. it exceeds the size of the destination buffer, it is negative and hence arithmetically it is less than the size of the destination buffer.

By definition, the memcpy() function expects its parameter that denotes the number of bytes which are to be copied to the destination buffer, to be an unsigned integer. Thus, the memcpy() function interprets the large negative value provided by the attacker as an unsigned integer, with the consequence being the overflow of the destination buffer [27]. A considerable part of process data are represented in a digital form as integers, consequently many IEC 61850 and ModBus implementations make extensive use of integers, and thus may be exposed to integer overflows. In an IEC 61850 application, one of the possible implementation spots that may be subject to arithmetic overflows is the possible code that allocates memory for a number of data objects of a logical node. This code uses arithmetic operations such as addition and multiplication to calculate the size of each data object and hence the size of the logical node.

In IEC 61850, each logical node is an instance of a logical node class. As written earlier in this chapter, a logical node is comprised of data objects. Referring to Figure 1, for example, logical node XCBR comprises the data objects Pos, BlkOpn, BlkCls, ChaMotEna, and other data objects that are not shown in Figure 1 due to space limitations. Each data object is an instance of a data class. Pos for example is an instance of the data class DPC, i.e. controllable double point. Each data class comprises data attributes. Data class DPC, for example, comprises the data attributes ctlVal, operTm, origin, ctlNum, q, etc. Each data attribute belongs to a data attribute type, which has a specific size and hence determines the possible values of that data attribute.

For example, the type of the data attribute ctlNum is INT8U. The INT8U type has a size of one byte, and thus the possible values of the data attribute ctlNum are supposed to be in the [0 - 255] range. It is the size of the type of each data attribute that forms the basis of the calculation of the number of bytes that is to be allocated for storing the data objects of a logical node. The storage of any intermediate or final result of this calculation in an integer, such that the result in question is greater than the maximum value which that integer can hold, creates an arithmetic overflow condition. An example of the creation of a widthness overflow condition consists in the placement of content in a data attribute from an integer with a larger size. For example, the assignment of a value that is greater than 255 to the data attribute ctlNum creates a widthness overflow condition, given that the INT8U data attribute type has a size of one byte.

In IEC 61850 it is the integer data attribute type that determines whether a data attribute of that type is signed or unsigned. IEC 61850 integer data types are given in Table 4. For example, the data attribute ctlNum in Table 1 is unsigned because its integer data attribute type is INT8U. In an IEC 61850 application, a possible signedness bug condition is created when a data attribute defined as unsigned by the corresponding integer data attribute type is interpreted as signed, or vice versa.

In a ModBus application, the attacker creates possible integer overflows and/or signedness bugs through PDUs that write large values to coil variables and holding register variables. Thus, with regard to integer overflows and signedness bugs in a ModBus application, coil variables and holding register variables represent the entry attack point into that target application. The computations conducted by a ModBus application center around the variables that hold I/O values in main memory, therefore most of the software components of a ModBus application are equally exposed to integer overflows and signedness bugs.

Table 4. Integer data attribute types in IEC 61850

Signed	Unsigned
INT8	INT8U
INT16	INT16U
INT32	INT24U
INT128	INT32U

4.3   Pure-Data Attacks on Protocol Implementations

A pure-data attack [18,19] on ModBus or IEC 61850 applications consists in exploiting a memory corruption vulnerability so that to overwrite non-control data in those applications. Recall from the previous subsection that non-control data are data that participate in the actual computation conducted by an application, as opposed to control data whose role is exclusively memory management. An attacker may conduct a pure-data attack to poison or corrupt the execution of control algorithms in a ModBus or IEC 61850 application. Incorrect computations of control algorithms have potential for causing physical damage to physical equipment such as power generators, water pumps, etc. in a power generation station, and power transformers, circuit breakers, etc., in an electrical substation. In IEC 61850, the behavior of each logical node is defined algorithmically.

For example, the PTOC and PDIS logical nodes have algorithms that carry out functions of time overcurrent protection and distance protection, respectively. The corruption through a pure-data attack of those data attributes that are processed by the control algorithms in question causes partial or complete disruption of the time overcurrent protection and the distance protection functions. Let us take the example of a substation situation in which a time overcurrent condition is created. The PTOC logical node uses its algorithm to sense the anomalous condition, and thereafter communicates it to the PTRC (trip conditioning) logical node. The PTRC logical node communicates with the XCBR logical node, which corrects the anomaly by opening a circuit breaker. If a pure-data attack corrupts the computation of the control algorithm of the PTOC logical node, no control signals will be sent to the PTRC logical node, and thus none of the subsequent corrective events will take place.

An attacker causes an incorrect computation of the control algorithm in a ModBus application by corrupting through a pure-data attack the measurement data that are generated by logical and continuous sensors. These measurement data are placed in discrete input variables and input register variables, respectively. The ModBus application processes only PDUs that request to read those variables, and thus rejects PDUs that attempt to write to those variables. However, a pure-data attack writes to the variables in question by exploiting memory corruption vulnerabilities, and thus allows for disrupting the correctness of the control algorithm in the target ModBus application. In addition to poisoning the execution of control algorithms, an attacker may also corrupt measurement data to blind the system operators, i.e. prevent them from creating a correct real-time awareness of the state of the physical infrastructure that is being monitored and controlled digitally.

Another offensive use of a pure-data attack on an IEC 61850 application is to suppress security alerts raised by the IEC 61850's access control. The access control capability in an IEC 61850 application restricts the set of data objects that are accessible to a client IEC 61850 application based on its identity. Such restricted access to logical nodes is referred to as virtual access view. During the initial association with a server IEC 61850 application, a client IEC 61850 application sends authentication parameters, namely a user identifier, a definition of the view that it is seeking to access, and a credential. If the server IEC 61850 application authenticates this client IEC 61850 application successfully, then it provides that client IEC 61850 application with a view on logical nodes and associated services that the client IEC 61850 application in question is authorized to access.

Failed access attempts are detected and recorded by a logical node. More precisely, IEC 61850 has a logical node called the generic security application (GSAL) logical node, which monitors violations regarding authorization, access, service privileges, and inactive associations. The organization of the GSAL logical node is provided in Table 5. The attacker suppresses the security alerts generated by the GSAL logical node in front of other attacks by conducting a pure-data attack to overwrite the data attributes of that logical node, i.e. the data attributes that are presented in Table 5.

Table 5. Description of the GSAL logical node used to monitor security violations regarding access to data objects in logical nodes

GSAL Data	Function
OpCntRs	Resetable Security Violations counter
NumCntRs	Number of counter resets
AuthFail	Authorization failures
AcsCtlFail	Access control failures
SvcViol	Service privilege violations
Ina	Inactive associations

4.4 Detecting Memory Corruption Vulnerabilities in Protocol Implementations

One of the main techniques for finding memory corruption vulnerabilities in an industrial communication protocol such as ModBus was devised by Dutertre [31]. Dutertre uses higher-order logic to model the full specification of the ModBus application protocol. That model defines the format of ModBus requests, and for each type of those requests, it defines the format of valid ModBus responses along with the format of possible ModBus error messages. The model in question is executable, and thus can be used to check whether ModBus responses to malformed ModBus requests are compliant with the specification of the ModBus application protocol. The idea is to send test PDUs to a ModBus device, and thus use the higher-order logic model to verify that the messages generated in response to those test PDUs are valid. Dutertre developed another model of the ModBus application protocol in the Symbolic Analysis Laboratory (SAL) specification language [32], which is more suited for test PDU generation.

The SAL model is a finite state automaton that searches counterexamples to properties postulated in the higher-order logic model. Those counterexamples are then used to generate the test PDUs. The developer environment for automated buffer overflow testing (DEADBOLT) [38] performs a source-to-source transformation in order to insert instrumentation instructions into SCADA code. During automated testing those instrumentation instructions extract memory access data and send those data to a test-run result analyzer, which in turn decides whether any buffer overflows took place and possibly generates suggestions on next to use test cases. Franz in [37] and Mora in [36] employ fuzzing to test implementations of the Inter Control Center Protocol (ICCP) [35] and OPC [34], respectively.

Fuzzing is a simple way of triggering some of the memory corruption vulnerabilities in implementations of industrial communication protocols. Nevertheless, fuzzing is quite limited in terms of state space coverage, and furthermore it may not have the capacity to indicate the location of a triggered vulnerability. blackPeer [33] is an automated testing tool that uses attributed grammars, i.e. grammars whose definition is overloaded with defined attributes, to generate test PDU. blackPeer sends those test PDUs to a ModBus device, and thus automatically interprets the ModBus device behavior that follows the processing of those test PDUS.

5 Protocol Conveyed Attacks on Physical Processes and Equipment

The ultimate objectives of computer network attacks on process control systems are to cause physical damage to physical equipment and sabotage physical processes that those systems monitor and control. It is known in literature that such computer network attacks have potential for causing physical damage [8]. Depending on equipment specifications and the physics behind physical processes, there is a variety of techniques according to which an attacker could manipulate process control systems. Such techniques aim at maximizing physical damage on physical processes and equipment once an attacker has acquired network access to a process control network or process control system. A taxonomy of such techniques that apply to physical equipment is provided by Larsen in [17]. An inertial attack consists of speeding up or slowing down heavy equipment.

An inertial attack has the potential of forcing heavy equipment to fail as in general such equipment is not tolerant to abrupt changes of speed. An exclusion attack takes place when a process control system violates physical dependencies between various equipment, while a wear attack manipulates a process control system so as to consume certain equipment components and hence reduce the life span of the equipment itself. Small variations of continuous process variables such as electric current or fluid flow are recorded by process control systems in the form of a wave. A resonance attack is conducted by repeatedly causing small variations of specific control application variables in order to increase the size of this wave beyond safe limits. A surge attack is mounted by exceeding the limits of specific process parameters beyond maximal values that continuous control systems are capable of handling.

A latent abilities attack exploits latent features in off-the-shelf physical equipment. An example of a latent abilities attack discussed in [17] consists of forcing a servomotor to run in the reverse direction, although such an action may not be part of the servomotor's intended operation in a defined physical infrastructure. There are also various techniques that target physical processes. As of this writing there is no publicly known taxonomy of those techniques. Nevertheless, those techniques generally aim at taking the parameters of a target physical process to abnormal values, which may result in physical destruction if the physical process degradation is not corrected on time. Physical processes within a physical infrastructure are continuously kept under safe conditions by system operators, who use sensor data to monitor their status at any point in time and also generate set points to cause them to evolve in a controlled way.

Thus, the techniques in question generally are supported via an attack technique such as those discussed in Section 4.3 to prevent system operators and/or automatic control applications from becoming aware of the physical process degradation. Let us look at an example of a technique that targets physical processes. Power plants such as those based on the advanced boiling water reactor model employ control rods as one of the primary mechanisms for controlling the rate at which the nuclear fission process take place within the reactor core. If an attacker leverages an attack technique such as those described earlier in this chapter to disable the reactor protection systems, and thereafter to withdraw a large number of control rods, then the power level in the reactor will increase towards abnormal values. If the power level along with related parameters are not brought to normal values on time, the power level will keep increasing beyond the limits of physical safety, with consequences being comparable to those of accidents in power plants.

Some of the techniques in question target physical processes that take place in physical equipment, and hence cause physical destruction of those physical equipment. An example is disruption of the synchronization process during connection of a power generator in a power plant to the power grid. The synchronization process ensures that the connection is established at the exact moment in which the power generator matches the power grid in voltage magnitude, phase angle, and frequency. The synchronization process relies on a circuit breaker to establish the connection when the aforementioned match between the power generator and the power grid is reached. Attacks such as those on IEC 61850 implementations that we discussed earlier in this chapter allow for controlling XCBR logical nodes, and thus the circuit breaker that they model.

By manipulating the Pos data object in the compromised XCBR logical node that models the circuit breaker which the synchronization process relies upon, the attacker can cause a delay in the closure of the circuit breaker in question. Injection of that delay into the synchronization process will connect the power generator to the power grid when the two are totally unsynchronized. That condition is referred to as out-of-step connection, and in most cases results in violent failures in the power generator.

6   Conclusion

In this chapter we provided a technical discussion of vulnerabilities in industrial communication protocols along with associated attacks. Our discussion applied mostly to IEC 61850 and ModBus, which we considered as representatives of the industrial communication protocols currently deployed in digitally controlled physical infrastructures such as power plants and electrical substations. We began the chapter with a technical background of IEC 61850 and ModBus. We then continued with a description of concrete vulnerabilities, some of which are specific to IEC 61850 or ModBus, while others are generic. We also elaborated on how those vulnerabilities are exploited. In the chapter we discussed several techniques that leverage such exploitations to disrupt physical processes and equipment, and thus maximize physical damage to the target infrastructure.

Conducting exploitations of SCADA protocol vulnerabilities such as those that we discussed in this chapter requires the attacker to reach target process control systems over a computer network. An intuitive question that rises from our discussion is clearly why the attacker would need to exploit these vulnerabilities and thus run malicious code in a target process control system, intercept and possibly modify industrial protocol communications, or disrupt fieldbus networks. If the attacker can send network packets to target control systems, the attacker definitely is in the position of issuing commands to those process control systems and hence has direct control over physical processes and equipment. Nevertheless, the control applications that run in a process control system respond automatically to any faults or anomalies in physical processes and equipment monitored and controlled by that system.

Thus, the negative effects of malicious commands issued through network packets get timely and automatically corrected or contained by control applications. This is because control applications perceive the consequences of a computer network attack as faults. For example, an attacker may send a network packet to a PLC to reduce the rate of a water pump for the purpose of reducing the water level within a reactor to a harmful amount. However, normally that condition would not be created as the control applications would sense the "fault", and hence would take corrective actions, perhaps by increasing the rate of the very water pump that the attacker had sabotaged. The reader is referred to [10] for other cases or scenarios in which the attacker would need to run malicious code in a field device.

References

1. International Electrotechnical Commission. IEC 61850: Communication Networks and Systems in Substations, part 1 through 9 (2004)
2. International Electrotechnical Commission. IEC TS 62351: Power Systems Management and Associated Information Exchange - Data and Communications Security (2007)
3. ModBus Organization. ModBus Application Protocol Specification,
   `http://www.modbus.org/docs/Modbus_Application_Protocol_V1_1b.pdf`
4. ModBus Organization. ModBus Messaging on TCP/IP Implementation Guide,
   `http://www.modbus.org/docs/Modbus_Messaging_Implementation_Guide_V1_0b.pdf`

5. ModBus Organization. ModBus Application Protocol Specification,
   `http://www.modbus.org/docs/Modbus_Application`
   `_Protocol_V1_1b.pdf`
6. DNP3 Users Group. DNP3 Protocol, `http://www.dnp.org`
7. Williams, R.D.: Fieldbus Link-Layer Configuration Vulnerabilities with Latent Response.
   Submitted to IEEE Transactions on Industrial Informatics (February 2010)
8. Krutz, R.L.: Securing SCADA Systems. Wiley Publishing (2006)
9. Idaho National Laboratory. Common Cyber Security Vulnerabilities Observed in Control
   System Assessments by the INL NSTB Program. Technical report prepared for the U.S. Department of Energy, Office of Electricity Delivery and Energy Reliability, Under DOE Idaho
   Operations Office (2008), `http://www.oe.energy.gov/DocumentsandMedia/`
   `31-INL_Common_Vulnerabilities_Report.pdf`
10. Peck, D., Peterson, D.: Leveraging Ethernet Card Vulnerabilities in Field Devices. In: Pro-
    ceedings of SCADA Security Scientific Symposium, Miami, USA (2009)
11. Anonymous. DATAC RealWin 2.0 SCADA Software - Remote PreaAuth Exploit,
    `http://www.securityfocus.com/archive/1/archive/1/496759/100/0/`
    `threaded`
12. C4. ABB PCU400 4.4-4.6 Remote Buffer Overflow,
    `http://www.securityfocus.com/archive/1/496739`
13. C4. GE Fanuc Cimplicity 6.1 Heap Overflow,
    `http://www.securityfocus.com/archive/1/archive/487076/100/0/`
    `threaded`
14. Bellettini, C., Rrushi, J.L.: Vulnerability Analysis of SCADA Protocol Binaries through De-
    tection of Memory Access Taintedness. In: Proceedings of the 2007 IEEE Workshop on
    Information Assurance, United States Military Academy, West Point, NY, USA (2007)
15. MuDynamics. IEC 61850 Communications Networks and Systems in Substations,
    `http://www.mudynamics.com/resources/collaterals/`
    `IEC61850-v2a.pdf`
16. Roxey, T.: Nuclear Sector Mitigation Experience - An Aurora Experience. In: Process Con-
    trol Systems Forum Annual Meeting (August 2008)
    `http://csrp.inl.gov/pcsf/2008/d/nuclear_sector_mitigation-`
    `roxey.pdf`
17. Larsen, J.: Breakage. Blackhat Federal (2008),
    `http://www.blackhat.com/presentations/bh-dc-08/Larsen/`
    `Presentation/bh-dc-08-larsen.pdf`
18. Chen, S., Xu, J., Sezer, E.C., Gauriar, P., Iyer, R.K.: Noncontrol-data Attacks Are Realis-
    tic Threats. In: Proceedings of the 14th USENIX Security Symposium, Baltimore, USA,
    pp. 177–192 (2005)
19. Pincus, J., Baker, B.: Mitigations for Low-level Coding Vulnerabilities: Incompara-
    bility and Limitations, `http://research.microsoft.com/users/jpincus/`
    `mitigations.pdf`
20. Aleph. Smashing the Stack for Fun and Profit. Phrack Magazine, 7(49) (1996)
21. Anonymous. Once Upon a free(). Phrack Magazine, 9(57) (2001)
22. Conover, M., w00w00 security team: w00w00 on Heap Overflows,
    `http://www.w00w00.org/files/articles/heaptut.txt`
23. Kaempf, M.: Vudo - An Object Superstitiously Believed to Embody Magical Powers. Phrack
    Magazine 8(57) (2001)
24. Bulba and Kil3r. Bypassing Stackguard and Stackshield. Phrack Magazine 10(56) (2000)
25. Scut and Team Teso. Exploiting Format String Vulnerabilities,
    `http://crypto.stanford.edu/cs155/papers/formatstring-1.2.pdf`

26. Gera and Riq. Advances in Format String Exploitation. Phrack Magazine 11(59) (2002)
27. Blexim. Basic Integer Overflows. Phrack Magazine 11(60) (2002)
28. Dobrovitski, I.: Exploit for CVS Double free() for Linux Pserver,
    http://www.securiteam.com/exploits/5SP0I0095G.html
29. Huitsing, P., Chandia, R., Papa, M., Shenoi, S.: Attack Taxonomies for the Modbus Protocol. International Journal of Critical Infrastructure Protection 1, 37–44 (2008)
30. Edmonds, J., Papa, M., Shenoi, S.: Security Analysis of Multilayer SCADA Protocols: A ModBus TCP Case Study. In: Proceedings of the 2nd Annual IFIP Working Group 11.10 International Conference on Critical Infrastructure Protection, Arlington, Virginia, USA (2008)
31. Dutertre, B.: Formal Modeling and Analysis of the Modbus Protocol. In: Proceedings of the 1st Annual IFIP Working Group 11.10 International Conference on Critical Infrastructure Protection, Hanover, New Hampshire, USA (2007)
32. de Moura, L., Owre, S., Shankar, N.: The SAL Language Manual. Technical Report SRI-CSL-01-02, SRI International, Menlo Park, California, USA (2003)
33. Byres, E.J., Hoffman, D., Kube, N.: On Shaky Ground - A Study of Security Vulnerabilities in Control Protocols. In: 5th American Nuclear Society International Topical Meeting on Nuclear Plant Instrumentation, Controls, and Human Machine Interface Technology. American Nuclear Society, Albuquerque (2006)
34. Iwanitz, F., Lange, J.: OPC - Fundamentals, Implementation and Application. Huthig Fachverlag (2006) ISBN 3-7785-2904-8
35. International Electrotechnical Commission. IEC 60870-6-503 Telecontrol Equipment and Systems, part 6-503, Telecontrol protocols compatible with ISO standards and ITU-T recommendations - TASE.2 Services and Protocols. 2nd edn. (2004)
36. Mora, L.: OPC Server Security Considerations. In: Proceedings of SCADA Security Scientific Symposium, Florida, USA (2007)
37. Franz, M.: ICCP Exposed: Assessing the Attack Surface of the Utility Stack. In: Proceedings of SCADA Security Scientific Symposium, Florida, USA (2007)
38. Zhivich, M.: DEADBOLT: Automated Testing for PCS Software Robustness and Security,
    http://www.thei3p.org/docs/research/deadbolt200904.pdf

Protection of SCADA Communication Channels

Abdelmajid Khelil, Daniel Germanus, and Neeraj Suri

Technische Universität Darmstadt, Computer Science Department,
Hochschulstr. 10 Darmstadt, Germany
{khelil,germanus,suri}@cs.tu-darmstadt.de

Abstract. The modern day e-society inherently depends on Critical Infrastructures (CI) such as power grid, communication, transportation etc. For such CIs to operate efficiently, Supervisory Control and Data Acquisition (SCADA) systems direct their control and monitoring functionality. However, the technological shift is towards commercial-off-the-shelf SCADA systems that are also increasingly interconnected with each other primarily over dedicated network but slowly tending to even Internet level connectivity. This introduces new communication-level threats and vulnerabilities to SCADA systems. Therefore, the disputed concept "security through obscurity" is no longer applicable, and previously unnoticed or ignored security issues might now be exposed. To handle such security challenges, techniques from conventional networked systems are also being adopted to the SCADA domain. This chapter discusses both adopted and newly developed techniques to secure communication in monolithic as well as highly interconnected systems.

1 Introduction

Supervisory Control and Data Acquisition (SCADA) and Distributed Control Systems (DCS) represent a key element of Critical Infrastructures (CI). SCADA and DCS systems still tend to follow a classical electro-mechanical basis lagging behind the development of the information and Internet technologies. This is mainly due to their expected long lifetime (between 7 to 20 years) and their high availability requirements (a very short shutdown must be planned weeks or even months before). Both facts complicate the modernization of these systems. Similarly, the control systems security also lag the current IT security techniques. Furthermore, the differing security requirements and environmental constraints of the control and communication worlds make it challenging to adopt existing security solutions to SCADA and DCS systems.

This chapter is intended as a survey of existing approaches and architectures to enhance the protection of deployed SCADA systems. Primarily focussing on the communication aspects of SCADA, we discuss overall architecture-level aspects (than technology details) to protect a SCADA's core component, i.e., communication channels, from accidental and deliberate disruptions.

Overall, the targeted benefits for the reader are twofold: (a) The existing approaches for SCADA communication protection are comprehensively surveyed and categorized, and (b) upcoming research techniques/technologies on enhancing the protection of SCADA communication are presented. We classify the existing protection mechanisms

J. Lopez et al. (Eds.): Critical Information Infrastructure Protection, LNCS 7130, pp. 177–196, 2012.

into three main categories: (1) Techniques for resilience to network perturbations, (2) cryptographic protection of SCADA communication, (3) trustworthy interconnection of SCADA systems [1]. Besides the adoption of existing techniques [2,3,4,5,6,7,8,9], several new general purpose protection mechanisms have recently been proposed. We focus on middleware techniques as they are have general applicability and also conform with the clear IP trend in SCADA components. We identify two middleware add-on protection techniques in the literature, i.e., the INSPIRE P2P-based middleware [10,11,12,13], and the GridStat middleware [14,15]. Both techniques aim at augmenting the trustworthiness (i.e., security and dependability) of deployed SCADA systems, primarily utilizing the approach of controllable data replication.

While we primarily focus on large-scale interconnected SCADA and on two popular application domains, i.e., powergrid [16,17] and gas distribution [18,19,20], we will provide a wider basis by considering generalized SCADA scenarios. The overall coverage is communication issues in SCADA.

We structure the book chapter as following. In Section 2, SCADA networks trends, requirements and vulnerabilities on security strategies are discussed. Section 3 classifies and presents representatives of each class of existing techniques for SCADA channels protection. In Section 4, we concentrate on middleware based approaches for protection of SCADA communication.

2   SCADA Networks: Architectures, Trends, Requirements and Vulnerabilities

This section briefly describes the communication assets of SCADA systems and their requirements on protection. In addition, we outline the key threats, vulnerabilities and security weaknesses of SCADA systems that may present a danger for the proper operation of SCADA systems.

2.1   Architecture and Trends

The key difference between SCADA and DCS systems is the differing geographic scope of the deployment. SCADA systems usually are wide area and DCS systems are local area distributed control systems. In the remainder of this chapter the term SCADA will span both SCADA and DCS coverage. In the following, we discuss and emphasize key aspects for the communication channel protection. Fig 1 briefly summarizes the terminology and the key communication components of SCADA systems.

Most early and current generation SCADA systems are perceived as stand alone (isolated) systems. However, the trends are changing towards (a) their increasing interconnection among each other or to other networks such as the business and partner networks and directly or indirectly to public networks such as the Internet, and (b) the abundance of proprietary protocols, hardware (HW) and software (SW) to commercial-off-the-shelf (COTS) open standard components. While the drivers of interconnection and openness are enhanced functionalities and lower costs, however, this often comes at the cost of more exposure to the larger interconnected environment.

SCADA communication channels/protocols can be broadly classified into three categories: (i) Protocols based on TCP/IP protocol suite such as MODBUS/TCP and EtherNet/IP, (ii) protocols based on the serial communication model such as IEC 870-5-101 and (iii) protocols that can support both such as DNP3 [21] and IEC 61850. The trend is clearly away from serial towards IP-based open standards. In future, wireless communication is going to play a major role to enable flexible ad hoc communication. Both trends are mainly to reduce costs. Unfortunately, IP and wireless trends lead to increased vulnerability of SCADA channnles/systems to cyber attacks.

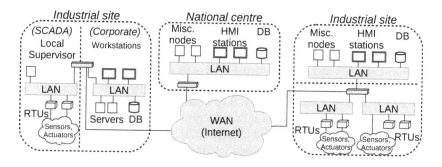

Fig. 1. SCADA Key Architectural Components

The design requirements on the protection techniques are mainly determined by the following specific SCADA constraints [22]:

- SCADA are primarily structured networks mainly due to the fixed network topology and the pre-determined MTU-RTU communication modes and traffic patterns;
- Long node life expectation and evolvable/heterogeneous systems (legacy devices and state-of-the-art ones, heterogenous HW/SW);
- High resilience requirements (availability, safety, security and others);
- Limited resources (resource constrained RTU, low bandwidth and low latency communication among others);
- Responsive Real-Time (RT) communication.

2.2   Requirements on SCADA Channel Protection

Given the specific SCADA constraints, there exist several key differences between the classical IT-security and SCADA security [23][24], namely (1) differing performance requirements, (2) differing reliability requirements, (3) "unusual" SCADA operating systems and applications, (4) differing security architectures, and (5) differing risk management goals. The authors of [23][24] mention the example, that in the classical IT security world patching is common. However, patching an RTU software (a) may be inappropriate as the physical processes are continuous in nature and consequently SCADA are time-critical and often should run for years without shutdown, (b) may require "Return-to-vendor", and (c) may require re-certification of the entire system.

Accordingly, careful adoption/customization of existing IT security techniques to SCADA and appropriate design of new tailored techniques present the main objectives of SCADA security.

In addition, SCADA protection activities also need to consider relevant attacks known from other IT systems as well as attacks specifically designed for SCADA systems such as the Stuxnet worm [25]. The deliberate attacks can be of a physical or cyber type, and may originate either from trusted SCADA operators or externally. For external cyber attacks, also called attackers or intruders, a core activity consists in identifying the *entry points* by which the attackers gain access to the SCADA network.

Considering a representative sample of contemporary and future SCADA networks, the common entry points for SCADA systems are:

- Access of SCADA servers (such as data historian) from (a) trusted enterprise/ business network and (b) less trusted third party operated SCADA networks;
- Remote access to SCADA components (e.g., RTUs) from the outside for the purpose of remote monitoring, testing, diagnosis, or maintenance. These entry points usually manifest in the existence of modems or dial-up connections and are provided for business partners, vendors, regulatory agencies etc;
- Wireless SCADA devices, including satellite links and wireless access on field to RTUs or other SCADA components.

The accessibility to business networks, third party SCADA networks and to partner networks usually means a direct or indirect access to public telephone networks or the Internet. From the point of view extending SCADA functionality and reducing costs, these entry points are valid. However from a security point of view, the entry points of SCADA systems should be as few as possible and well supervised and protected. Accordingly, the operators of SCADA systems should carefully find the appropriate trade-off between the wishes (1) to have higher inter-connection to other systems for enhancing functionality, and (2) to minimize the number of entry points for enhancing protection. This chapter surveys the existing protection techniques for the different possible entry points.

Protection implies the existence of critical assets that need safeguards. The assets of a SCADA system determine the security/dependability/protection objectives concerning the communication channel protection. We identify the following main assets to protect through secure communication:

- Integrity/confidentiality of SCADA data such as RT sensor readings, aggregated information, RT actuator commands, historian data and system configuration data;
- Availability of intra-SCADA communication (within a single system operated by the SCADA operator): Connectivity, Quality-of-Service (QoS) guarantees etc;
- SCADA interconnection to business networks;
- SCADA accessibility to partners, vendors, regulatory agencies and others.

Though the assets appear similar to those in the classical IT world, the requirement and protection objectives of the SCADA assets are specific. In the following we discuss the main security objectives and requirements specific to SCADA:

- Sensor & command and historian data *integrity* is a fundamental security requirement for SCADA communication. This is because of the disastrous consequences of data integrity attacks in SCADA;
- *Authenticity* of communication partners is a second fundamental requirement for secure SCADA communication. This should prohibit malicious sensors to send wrong sensor values to the SCADA servers, and the servers from sending undesired commands to the actuators.
- *Confidentiality* of server data;
- *Availability* of SCADA data to authorized users;
- Eavesdropping of sensor and command data is not a major concern in SCADA systems as long as these can not be used for future attacks against the SCADA system;
- *Non-repudiation* is less important for intra-SCADA communication. However, non-repudiation is crucial for connectivity to third parties or for inter-SCADA communication (i.e., across interconnected SCADA systems that are operated by different operators);
- Transmission of encrypted messages is subject to different national regulations and may be prohibited by law;
- *Privacy* and confidentiality policies for data sharing with other partners are an integral part of SCADA security;

2.3   SCADA Communications Threats, Vulnerabilities and Security Weaknesses

We start by presenting recent significant incidents that show the attackability of SCADA systems. Next, we survey key accidental and potential deliberate perturbations that SCADA systems can likely encounter.

2.3.1   Recent Significant Incidents

According to [24], the category of SCADA incidents clearly started to change in 2001, namely, from accidental/internal ones to more externally-driven deliberate incidents such as intrusions, Denial of Service (DoS) and sabotage. The following contemporary incidents demonstrate the fact that the SCADA network can be penetrated by malicious intruders:

- In 2010, the Stuxnet worm infected thousands of Siemens Programable Logic Control (PLC) systems which are widely deployed in control systems including satellite and nuclear plants [25];
- In 2009, cyber spies penetrated the American electrical grid (Reuters, April 2009, [26]);
- In 2009, the Washington Post declared "Smart Grid Raises Security Concerns" [27];
- In 2009, the Areva company realized that parts of its energy management software are vulnerable as the U.S. Computer Emergency Response Team (US-CERT) found software flaws consisting in a number of buffer overflow and DoS vulnerabilities in the SCADA software;

- In 2007 some researchers launched an experimental cyber attack causing a generator to self-destruct (CNN, September 2007, [28]);
- In 2000, a discontented former employee was able to remotely access the controls of a sewage plant and discharge untreated sewage into the local environment in Maroochy, Australia (National Infrastructure Protection Center Highlights 2002, [29]).

It is often difficult to assess from public reports to what degree a CI industry has been breached. This is because SCADA operators and producers are unwillingly to publicly admit the vulnerabilities of their systems.

2.3.2   Design and Operational Accidental Communication Perturbations

SACDA systems are usually tightly embedded to dangerous physical processes and are deployed in harsh environments. This leads to unexpected node and communications failures and sensor damage. Generally, SCADA design is robust against these accidental failures reducing their occurrence rate. However, if they occur and counter-measures are ineffective, they may harm the SCADA communication and consequently threaten the functionality or safety of the CI.

In addition, modern SCADA systems are increasingly built out of COTS components due to time-to-market and budget pressures. This introduces new challenges regarding dependability of SCADA systems. The main challenge consists in higher rates of communication link/node failures. Usually, the new SW/HW COTS components (routers, protocols, etc) are characterized by lower reliablity/availaibility leading to more frequent communication failures and lower QoS guarantees. These failures degrade the SCADA dependability and require new protection techniques that cope with the introduced perturbations.

2.3.3   Deliberate Communication Perturbations

The North American Electric Reliability Council (NERC) and the US Department of Energy's National SCADA Test Bed (NSTB) issued a list of top 10 SCADA vulnerabilities and proposed mitigations and recommendations for each of them [30]. These vulnerabilities can be classified into three main classes: Insufficient security awareness/qualification, poor security by design and lack of rigorous security assessment. We refer to [31] for a comprehensive discussion of SCADA vulnerabilities.

Subsequently, varied national and international initiatives have been triggered. In US the main driver organizers are DHS, DoE and DoD governmental departments. For example in 2002, the DoE published 21 recommendations to improve SCADA security [32]. In order to increase security awareness, many SCADA vulnerability repositories have been established. The most popular examples include the National Vulnerability Database (NVD) [33], Open Source Vulnerability Database (OSVDB) [34] and Symantec Security Focus. These repositories maintain updated vulnerability information such as attack vectors and severity ratings. In the EU-INSPIRE project [35], an offline tool to automatically discover the vulnerabilities of operational SCADA systems, has been developed. This tool integrates a Bayesian approach and ontologies to support decisions for Critical Infrastructures Protection [36].

Our main interests are to protect the communication channels and well define the electronic security perimeter of SCADA systems. Communication channels are fundamental for the core functionality of SCADA, i.e., the trustworthy transport of sensor and actuator data between RTUs to MTUs. We focus on this functionality and the threats it is exposed to: Message interception, message fabrication, message reply and message alteration. The security perimeter of SCADA is well dependent from its connectivity, i.e., its entry points.

As highlighted in the standards IEC 62351 [37] the following security threats are the most relevant to SCADA communication channels:

- Spoofing: Is an access attack, where the intruder attempts to masquerade as a legitimate SCADA user;
- Modification: This attack involves the deletion or the alteration of SCADA data in an unauthorized manner;
- Replay: An intruder may capture some SCADA real traffic (protocol packets), and later resend that traffic to reach unexpected results. The attack is successful if the target node does not detect duplicate packets;
- Eavesdropping (on key exchange only): When an intruder listens to the encryption keys being exchanged, the intruder can use the keys to acquire knowledge about the SCADA traffic and format which can help conducting further attacks such as replay.

3 Existing Techniques for Protection of SCADA Communication Channels

As discussed earlier in Section 2.2, SCADA channel protection solutions should take the specific properties of these systems into consideration while maximizing the re-use of security techniques from the classical IT world. Accordingly, the contemporary SCADA channel protection techniques mainly consist in customizing well-known security approaches to the SCADA systems. In the remainder of this section we briefly survey these efforts.

We proceed by progressively expanding the considered class of vulnerabilities to comprehensively understand the benefit from the efforts that have been conducted. Thus, four main classes of protection techniques have been distinguished. First, we focus only on accidental failures and present the main techniques for enhancing the resilience of SCADA to network perturbations. Second, we consider isolated SCADA systems and present techniques to mitigate deliberate failures. Here the cryptographic protection of SCADA communication is the key approach. Third, we investigate securing the entry points for a trustworthy interconnection of SCADA systems to other networks. Fourth, and for its importance, we address special considerations for wireless links/entry points.

3.1 Techniques for Resilience to Network Perturbations

Given the increasing number of accidental failures that may disrupt the availability and safe operation of SCADA systems, new counter-measures have to be taken.

Therefore, along with the all-IP trend, Internet architectures for provisioning QoS have been customized for SCADA systems [14,38]. For instance, the Multi-Protocol Label Switching (MPLS) architecture has been modified to cope with routing failures through multi-path enabling. These MPLS optimizations have been shown to improve the resiliency of SCADA systems [39].

An agent-based approach [40,41] has been proposed for fault detection, isolation and service restoration. Mobile agents [42,43,44] are autonomous and decentralized systems used for self-organizational tasks. Their primary target is network or node re-organization in case of perturbations. Mobile agent systems are scalable and flexible. However, the large dependability and security space of mobile agent systems limits their acceptance in the SCADA environments.

In Section 4, we present a P2P-based middleware that provides for basic mechanisms such as replication and multipath to easily deal with node and link failures in heterogeneous large SCADA systems.

3.2   Cryptographic Protection of SCADA Communication

We now discuss techniques needed to protect the SCADA communication channel against physical/insider attackers. For simplicity, we assume the SCADA system is not connected to other networks. There are two main attack patterns of interest: (1) Data integrity attacks such as alteration, and (2) data authenticity attacks such as replay.

The established cryptographic techniques provide for data integrity, confidentiality and authenticity on communication channels and present a powerful protection envelop for SCADA communication. However, due to limited resources on SCADA entities such as RTUs, an adaptation of these techniques is required. We review the existing efforts in this area. In [45], the authors give the big picture on using cryptographic techniques in SCADA systems. [2] presents a suite of security protocols optimized for SCADA/DCS systems which include: Point-to-point secure channels, authenticated broadcast channels, authenticated emergency channels, and revised authenticated emergency channels.

In [8,46], the authors discuss the following authentication concepts to secure communication in a single-operator SCADA system. They are originally proposed for the DNP3 standard [47,48,49,50].

- *Authentication via Digital Signatures*: The sender of a SCADA message (typically the MTU that sends control messages) signs the message so that the receivers (typically the RTUs) can detect messages altered by an intruder. This security model is to protect from replay, spoofing, and modification attacks, but not from eavesdropping.
- *Authentication via On-demand Identity Verification*: This model is designed to verify the identity of the other communication end (MTU or RTU) on a suspicious behavior in order to protect against the man-in-the-middle attack. For instance, an RTU device may initiate the verification of the MTU, when the RTU receives an atypical control value from that MTU. In this case, the RTU sends a nonce to the MTU. The MTU adds a pre-shared secret key to the nonce, calculates a hash digest

(e.g., SHA-1), and sends the digest to the RTU. The RTU calculates a hash digest from the nonce and the shared key and compares it to the digest received from the MTU. In high-criticality SCADA systems, the pre-shared key should be periodically changed.

The above mentioned approach is known as a symmetric key approach. More sophisticated architectures such as those relying on asymmetric keys and those for new SCADA communication patterns (broadcast, RTU-RTU mode etc) have been also proposed for SCADA [51,45,22,52,53,54]. The Cryptographic Modules (CM) discussed above are referred to as SCADA Cryptographic Modules (SCM) as they provide both authentication and encryption capabilities for intra-SCADA channels [19].

3.3 Trustworthy Interconnection of SCADA Systems

Following the discussion on authentication of intra-SCADA communication in the prior subsection, we now focus on securing the SCADA communication with devices and users from the "outside". We structure this subsection depending on the considered entry point.

3.3.1 Protecting Remote Login

Similar to SCM for intra-SCADA channels, the so-called Maintenance Cryptographic Modules (MCM) have been developed [19] in order to provide similar security properties to communication channels from the outside of the SCADA. MCM provide authenticated access to maintenance ports on an Intelligent Electronic Device (IED) or an RTU. In order to provide for secure communication between SCMs and MCMs, The Serial SCADA Protection Protocol (SSPP) is recommended.

3.3.2 Protecting the Interconnection to Other Networks and Devices (Firewall and Demilitarized Zone)

In [55], the UK National Infrastructure Security Co-ordination Centre (NISCC) presented eight DCS/SCADA to enterprise/business networks segregation architectures and approximate ratings of security, manageability and scalability for each of them. We mainly rely on this work to survey the existing architectures for protecting the communication of SCADA with other networks such as the enterprise business network, third party SCADA systems or the Internet.

The basic approach consists in adopting the several traditional Internet-based techniques to protect the interconnection of SCADA systems with external networks. The popularly used techniques are Firewalls [55], Demilitarized Zones (DMZ), Virtual Private Networks (VPN) and Virtual LANs (VLAN).

The eight architectures proposed by NISCC are [55]:

- A1: Network Separation Using Dual-Homed Server without Firewalls
- A2: Network Separation Using Dual-Homed Server with Personal Firewall Installed

- A3: Packet Filtering Router/Layer-3 Switch between DCS/SCADA and Other Network
- A4: Two-Port Firewall between DCS/SCADA and Other Network
- A5: Router/Firewall Combination between DCS/SCADA and Other Network
- A6: Firewall with Demilitarized Zones between DCS/SCADA and Other Network
- A7: Paired Firewalls between DCS/SCADA and Other Network
- A8: Firewall and VLAN-based Process Network Combinations

Fig. 2 illustrates three examples of these architectures, i.e., A5, A6 and A7. Overall, all the eight architectures can be broken down into three general classes:

- Separation using non-firewall devices such as dual-homed workstations, bridges and routers (Architectures A1, A2 and A3)
- Two zone firewall-based designs without a DMZ (Architectures A4 and A5)
- Three zone firewall-based designs with a DMZ (Architectures A6, A7 and A8)

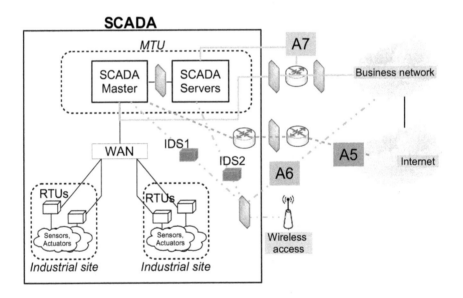

Fig. 2. Illustration of Three Separation Architectures and IDS

Common to all these conventional approaches is to design a protective shield around the SCADA systems. The achieved security is in general "A security by design". This makes all these systems vulnerable to a careless design or implementation flaws that attackers often try to find out and exploit. Therefore, there is a need for complementary techniques that can detect new attacks and provide for "Security by repair". Intrusion detection systems represent an attack detection technique that operates in addition to the protection shields such as firewalls, VPN, and DMZ.

3.3.3   Intrusion Detection System (IDS)

The National Institute of Standards and Technology (NIST) defines intrusion detection as the process of monitoring the events occurring in a computer system or network and analyzing them for signs of intrusions, defined as attempts to compromise the confidentiality, integrity, availability, or to bypass the security mechanisms of a computer or network" [56]. This definition implies that intrusions can be conducted by attackers from inside or outside of the SCADA system. Insider attackers are authorized users that attempt to misuse the assigned access privileges. Outsiders typically operate through the Internet in order to directly (e.g., through the authorized communication channels) or indirectly (e.g., through USB stick infection) to attack the SCADA system.

IDS is a monitoring (mostly software based though often composite software and hardware) tool that can detect abnormal incoming traffic which can point to an intrusion. The key architectural elements of an IDS are: (1) The sensors which collect raw data from the monitored system, (2) the knowledge base which contains experts information about attacks and their signatures, data profiles etc, and (3) the detector which is an engine to process the sensor data and identify intrusions. In Fig. 2, we illustrates the IDS functionality only for Architecture A6. Similarly, the IDS can be easily added for further architectures. The IDS interprets the contents of a log file in a SCADA edge device and the patterns of the incoming traffic. The IDS can be tailored to a network, a host or an application, depending on the system/component to monitor and protect.

There are two main categories of approaches for detector realization [57,58]. The first category relies on an explicit definition of attack patterns. If the current traffic pattern matches the known attack signature, the detector can detect the attack. This category is known as misuse-based. Typically, the misuse-based approaches detect all known attacks with high accuracy. Their main drawback is the failure to detect unknown/new attacks. The misuse-based IDS techniques usually are subclassified into signature based, attack-rules based, state transition analysis based and data mining based techniques [57]. The second category for intrusion detection comprises the techniques which are based on the pre-definition of the system normal behavior (legitimate traffic activities) so that abnormal behavior or anomalies can be detected. This class is referred to by anomaly-based. The key advantage of these approaches is their ability to detect new attacks. Their main limitation relies in the potentially high false alarm rate. The main subclasses of anomaly-based IDS are: Statistical methods, distance based techniques, normal-behavior-rule based systems, profiling methods and model based approaches [57]. A careful combination of both categories is usually recommended and is often used by contemporary commercial products [59,60].

The use of any SCADA-tailored IDS depends on whether we can find any special traffic patterns which is particular to the SCADA system. There exist a few efforts to apply IDS to SCADA systems. Two anomaly-based IDS techniques have been proposed for SCADA systems: A model-based one [61] and a statistical one [62].

3.4   Special Considerations for Wireless Networks

Using wireless links to connect wireless sensors and actuators etc, the emerging wireless SCADA systems are vulnerable to new attacks that are not typical for the traditional wired SCADA systems. Being a broadcast communication medium, wireless technologies offer a simpler forum for physical attacks of SCADA systems. The wireless favored new attacks are easier to conduct in some settings such as the multihop networks where routers use only wireless links. Compared to traditional SCADA attacks, wireless SCADA need to take some special considerations to mitigate the following attacks:

- Communication hijacking: An intruder may capture the wireless channel by connecting an authorized wireless client or posing unauthorized wireless access point that attracts SCADA wireless nodes to connect to it. Unauthorized connected clients can excessively load network resources thus causing DoS to SCADA entities. Also redirecting the SCADA traffic to unauthorized routers limits or disables important SCADA functionalities besides eavesdropping and collection of confidential data (e.g., credentials, encryption keys etc);
- Jamming: An attacker may disturb the wireless communication channel with various frequency domains (cordless phones, microwave ovens) or physical obstacles and limit or even disable communication on that channel.

If no countermeasures have been taken to secure the wireless network then these attacks may provide full access to the wireless network. There are standard security measures that can be used to prohibit an attacker from gaining access to the wireless SCADA. In particular, WiFi Protected Access 2 (WPA2), 802.1X EAP (Extensible Authentication Protocol) can be used for protecting data integrity and confidentiality on wireless communication. For secure authorization, a configurable list of all approved Medium Access Control (MAC) addresses is usually used to grant permitted access to the wireless network. IDS in wireless networks is based on analyzing information about the connections in wireless networks, which is typically collected at wireless access points. For ad hoc wireless communication mode there exist specific efforts for protection [63][64].

4   Middlewares for SCADA Communication Protection

In this section, we show how SCADA communication protection may be realized through a well designed middleware. We mainly focus on two middleware technologies, i.e., Peer-to-Peer (P2P) based and Publish/Subscribe (pub/sub) based middlewares.

SCADA systems underlie the traditional client/server paradigm and are subject to a hierarchical communication organization. Resulting from the interconnection of SCADA systems of different operators, large scale topologies emerge with inter-network communication to facilitate information exchange among different operator domains. The interconnection of different networks may be realized by dedicated or multi-purpose networks. In the latter case, SCADA traffic shares the bandwidth with other networked applications. Since these uninsulated networks may be subject to cyber attacks, resilience mechanisms are strongly recommended. Two important protective goals in the context of SCADA applications are availability and integrity of data.

The two middleware approaches in this section address these protective goals but pursue different architectural and technological trails. An important distinctive feature among these two and also other approaches is the extent of intrusiveness required to add the resilience increasing technology to the SCADA system. Non-intrusive approaches do not require changes to the existing SCADA system, yet this system class requires its own infrastructure, i.e., additional components are appended to the network. Contrary, the intrusive approach requires the modification of existing networked nodes. Modification mainly addresses new software components to be installed which are executed on the existing SCADA system nodes. The non-intrusive approach is beneficial, if the SCADA software can not be adapted. Another reason for the non-intrusive approach are legacy systems whose resource capacities are insufficient for additional software components. Yet, the installation of an additional hardware infrastructure that hosts the middleware is required. Intrusive approaches do not require that additional infrastructure, but sufficient resource capacities on the SCADA nodes and either a customizable SCADA system software or access to the SCADA software source code. Hybrid approaches exist as well and require both, additional infrastructure and access to the SCADA system software.

An example for an intrusive P2P-based middleware to enhance the SCADA resilience is presented in the INSPIRE [10] project. An example for a non-intrusive approach is the GridStat [15] pub/sub middleware. In the following, we present these two different middleware approaches

4.1   The P2P-Based Protection Technique

The P2P-based approach increases the SCADA system's data availability and integrity in the presence of faults or attacks. This is achieved through data replication and path redundancy, which are two basic mechanisms in P2P systems.

P2P systems span so called overlay networks on top of the underlying network topology. The participants of P2P networks are called peers and they take the duties of both, servers and clients. Usually, the service interface of every peer provides very basic functionality, e.g., join, leave, lookup, get, and store operations. The P2P-based protection technique focusses on structured P2P networks [65,66,67] which are adequate for large scale networked applications because of their good scalability and performance properties. Structured P2P networks solely under-perform unstructured P2P networks in terms of maintenance overhead [12]. Peers in structured networks are mapped uniquely into an address space which represents the routing substrate of the overlay network.

Data storage in structured P2P networks is realized by Distributed Hash Tables (DHT). DHTs address their data directly and do not require network search operations, as it is the case in unstructured networks. Addressing mechanisms require a logarithmic number of peer hops until the addressed datum is located. This results in lookup latencies which are adequate for large scale networks.

The architecture of the INSPIRE P2P-based protection technique is middleware driven. It is installed on RTUs, MTUs, and other high level stations and intercepts SCADA communication. The intercepted SCADA data is stored in the DHT and forwarded to its original destination. DHTs replicate data in the network, i.e., more than a single copy is available in the network. This increases the robustness against node failures. Furthermore, communication among peers in the overlay network is sent along redundant and possibly disjoint paths, which improves the overlay's resilience to node or link failures.

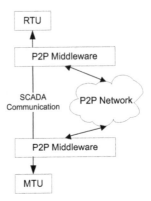

Fig. 3. Architectural Overview of the Peer-to-Peer-based Protection Technique

The protective goals of the P2P-based approach address availability and integrity of data. The approach has been simulated [13] regarding two possible incidents: (i) SCADA data corruption/modification attacks and (ii) router crashes. A data corruption attack occurs somewhere between the source and the destination of data in the SCADA network, e.g., between an RTU and an MTU in case of upward SCADA traffic. Exemplarily, an attacker gains access to the network and then modifies SCADA data in transit. The outcome is incorrect information delivered to SCADA stations which might result in disastrous consequences. A countermeasure for the given incident provided by the P2P-based protection technique is to request at the receiver side each SCADA datum multiple times from the DHT. The received copies are compared with each other and a consensus criterion needs to be fulfilled to accept the original message. Furthermore, it is assumed that an attacker can only take control over a small fraction of nodes in a SCADA network. Also, the network topology must tolerate few node crashes without partitioning, i.e., the network requires an adequate connection degree among its routers.

The second incident is related to router crashes. Many reasons for router crashes exist, e.g., misconfiguration and power outage. Upon a router crash, underlay network routing protocols try to find alternative routes to circumvent the crashed router. Unfortunately, the usual reaction time of SCADA routing protocols often exceeds SCADA timeliness requirements. Accordingly, the P2P protection middleware implements expectancy timers for incoming SCADA messages. If a sensor/actuator datum becomes overdue, then the P2P middleware requests the message via DHT. By virtue of overlay path redundancy and path diversity in the underlay network, the overdue message can be retrieved from the DHT, if the message has been successfully replicated.

To evaluate the performance/quality of designed protection techniques, we use two metrics. First, the effectiveness of the data integrity attack countermeasure is evaluated by the discovery ratio, namely the quotient of detected data integrity violations and the total amount of violations. Secondly, to measure the effectiveness of router crash countermeasures, the recovery ratio is evaluated. It is the quotient number of messages received via DHT and number of overdue messages.

The countermeasures have been experimentally evaluated using simulations and the outcome is quite promising. Simulations were run using Chord [65] and Kademlia [66].

Simulations have shown that Chord's network overhead is one order of magnitude lower than that of Kademlia. Furthermore, Kademlia has better results for the discovery and recovery ratios. For a P2P network with 64 peers, Chord's ratios are above 60%, Kademlia's above 70%. The values improve for increasing peer sets and topologies.

4.2 The GridStat Middleware

We now present the pub/sub based GridStat [15] protection approach. The GridStat scope of application is data dissemination in power grids. The primary protective goal is the availability of data. In comparison to the previously presented P2P-based protection technique GridStat is non-intrusive, i.e., existing SCADA components remain unmodified. Accordingly, GridStat requires a dedicated infrastructure to run its operations which follow the pub/sub paradigm. In a pub/sub system, message publishers are not required to know their subscribers. The dissemination of messages is maintained by message brokers that maintain subscriptions and provide a basis for a m-to-n messaging system, i.e., having m publishers and n subscribers. Therefore, pub/sub systems follow neither a broadcasting nor a multicasting approach in terms of the message source node. Moreover, intermediary nodes in the network decide about multiple forwarding of messages according to subscription lists. The GridStat architecture is two-layered: The management and the data plane. The management plane is hierarchically structured and consists of QoS brokers. Each QoS broker on the lowest level in the management plane maintains subscription lists of data plane status routers (SR) which are part of exactly one cloud. Clouds contain the SRs that are part of a SCADA system on behalf of one operator domain. QoS brokers higher in the hierarchy maintain subscription lists for several leaf QoS brokers, i.e., for more than one cloud. The data plane's main task is to interconnect SCADA nodes and different clouds. SRs dynamically span paths between publishers and subscribers. An overview of the GridStat architecture is given in Fig.4.

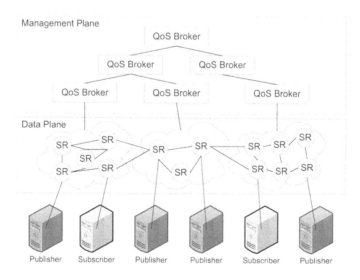

Fig. 4. Architectural Overview of the GridStat Protection Middleware

Besides content selection, a subscription has three more attributes: (i) Subscription interval, (ii) latency request, and (iii) redundancy. According to the given attributes, the management hierarchy tries to set up one or more disjoint paths (according to the redundancy attribute) between publisher and subscriber that meet the latency attribute.

5   Conclusions and Future Research Directions

This chapter summarized basic rules and concepts for securing operating SCADA systems and consequently protecting critical infrastructures that these systems control. First, we carefully discussed the specific requirements on security of SCADA systems. Second, we classified and briefed the key security architectures for securing legacy operating SCADA systems. Next, we presented novel middleware-based approaches that aim to provide for detection of malicious behavior and implement recovery strategies on misbehavior.

It was clear throughout this chapter that the main security strategy for SCADA currently follows the security-by-repair paradigm. Though this is an important effort to secure operational systems, it is costly and lack systematic design. This approach has been followed since the SCADA designers could not foresee the current openness/interconnection trend. However, now as we can not neglect these trends, designers should develop SCADA systems that are to highest extent secure-by-design.

The different initiatives for critical infrastructure protection usually insist in periodic auditing and risk management of deployed systems. However, trustworthiness assessment and evaluation of deployed critical systems demands a comprehensive and powerful set of security metrics that allow for indicator-based quantitative auditing/evaluation/assessment. Unfortunately, the development of trustworthiness metrics is still in its infancy. Consequently, there is an urgent need to develop such metrics that support quantification and assessment of the overall increase of SCADA resilience through a certain protection measure.

Finally, we observe a clear trend in SCADA systems: Away from all-wired SCADA to all-wireless SCADA. This trend is evident if we consider wireless sensor and actuator networks [68] as an all-wireless SCADA system. Sensor nodes are RTUs that self-organize to form a self* network and in order to deliver events. For all-wireless SCADA some nodes will be battery powered and may suffer from energy-drain attacks, i.e., attacks to promptly deplete RTUs batteries making them useless. Since communication in all-wireless SCADA will mainly based on ad-hoc routing there are many attacks to disrupt routes (black-hole attacks etc) or to redirect traffic to an intruder (sink-hole attacks) [69]. Fortunately, there is very active research to protect by-design these future SCADA systems.

Acknowledgement.   Research supported in part by CASED (www.cased.de), EU INSPIRE, and EU CoMiFin.

References

1. Rinaldi, S.M., Peerenboom, J.P., Kelly, T.K.: Identifying, Understanding, and Analyzing Critical Infrastructure Interdependencies. IEEE Control Systems 21(6), 11–25 (2001)
2. Wang, Y., Chu, B.T.: sSCADA: Securing SCADA infrastructure communications. In: Cryptology ePrint Archive, Report 2004/265 (2004),
   `http://eprint.iacr.org/2004/265.pdf`
3. Patel, S.: Secure internet-based communication protocol for SCADA networks. In: PhD Thesis, University of Louisville, Kentucky (2006)
4. Igure, V.M., Laugher, S.A., Williams, R.D.: Security issues in SCADA networks. Elsevier Computers and Security Journal 25(7), 498–506 (2006)
5. Graham, J., Mostafa, S., Arazi, B., Tantawy, A., Hieb, J., Ralston, P., Patel, S.C.: Improvements in SCADA and DCS systems security. In: Proc. of The International Conference on Computers and Their Applications (2007)
6. Hieb, J.L., Graham, J.H., Patel, S.C.: Security Enhancements for Distributed Control Systems. In: Goetz, E., Shenoi, S. (eds.) Critical Infrastructure Protection. IFIP, vol. 253, pp. 133–146. Springer, New York (2007)
7. Lim, I.H., Hong, S., Choi, M.S., Lee, S.J., Lee, S.W., Ha, B.N.: Applying Security Algorithms against Cyber Attacks in the Distribution Automation System. In: IEEE PES (2008)
8. Patel, S.C., Bhatt, G.D., Graham, J.: Improving the cyber security of SCADA communication networks. Communications of ACM 52(7) (July 2009)
9. Chandia, R., Gonzalez, J., Kilpatrick, T., Papa, M., Shenoi, S.: Security Strategies for SCADA Networks. In: Critical Infrastructure Protection (2007) ISBN 978-0-387-75461-1
10. D'Antonio, S., Romano, L., Khelil, A., Suri, N.: INcreasing Security and Protection through Infrastructure rEsilience: The INSPIRE Project. In: Setola, R., Geretshuber, S. (eds.) CRITIS 2008. LNCS, vol. 5508, pp. 109–118. Springer, Heidelberg (2009)
11. D'Antonio, S., Romano, L., Khelil, A., Suri, N.: Increasing Security and Protection of SCADA Systems through Infrastructure Resilience. In: Proc. of The International Journal of System of Systems Engineering (IJSSE). INDERSCIENCE publishers (2009) (to appear)
12. Khelil, A., Jeckel, S., Germanus, D., Suri, N.: Towards Benchmarking of P2P Technologies from a SCADA Systems Protection Perspective. In: Chatzimisios, P., Verikoukis, C., Santamaría, I., Laddomada, M., Hoffmann, O. (eds.) MOBILIGHT 2010. LNICST, vol. 45, pp. 400–414. Springer, Heidelberg (2010)
13. Germanus, D., Khelil, A., Suri, N.: Increasing the Resilience of Critical SCADA Systems Using Peer-to-Peer Overlays. In: Giese, H. (ed.) ISARCS 2010. LNCS, vol. 6150, pp. 161–178. Springer, Heidelberg (2010)
14. Hauser, C.H., Bakken, D.E., Dionysiou, I., Gjermudd, K.K., Irava, V.S., Helkey, J., Bose, A.: Security, Trust, and QoS in Next-Generation Control and Communication for Large Power Systems. International Journal of Critical Infrastructures 4(1/2), 3–16 (2008)
15. Gjermundrod, H., Bakken, D.E., Hauser, C.H., Bose, A.: GridStat: A Flexible QoS-Managed Data Dissemination Framework for the Power Grid. IEEE Transactions on Power Delivery 24(1), 136–143 (2009)
16. Watts, D.: Security and vulnerability in electric power systems. In: Proc. of The 35th North American, Power Symposium (2003)
17. Rrushi, J.L., Campbell, R.H.: Detecting Attacks in Power Plant Interfacing Substations through Probabilistic Validation of Attack-Effect Bindings. In: Proc. of The SCADA Security Scientific Symposium (2008)
18. American Gas Association (AGA). Cryptographic Protection of SCADA Communications, Part 1: Background, Policies and Test Plan. AGA Report No.12, Part 1 (2006)

19. American Gas Association (AGA). Cryptographic Protection of SCADA Communications, Part 2: Retrofit Application. AGA Report No.12, Part 2 (2006)
20. American Gas Association (AGA). Cryptographic Protection of SCADA Communications, Part 3: Protection of Networked Systems. AGA Report No.12, Part 3 (2006)
21. Distributed Network Protocol
22. Dawson, R., Boyd, C., Dawson, E., Nieto, J.M.G.: SKMA-A Key Management Architecture for SCADA Systems. In: Proc. of The Australasian Workshops on Grid Computing and e-Research (2006)
23. Industrial Control System Security Current Trends and Risk Mitigation (2009), http://www.intekras.com/IndustrialControlSystemSecurity.pdf
24. Byres, E.J., Eng, P., Lissimore, D., Kube, N.: Who Turned Out The Lights? Security Testing for SCADA and Control Systems. In: Proc. of The CanSecWest Applied Security Conference (2006)
25. Wikipedia. The stuxnet worm (2010)
26. Cyberspies penetrate electrical grid: report (2009), http://www.reuters.com/article/idUSTRE53729120090408
27. 'Smart Grid' Raises Security Concerns (2009), http://www.washingtonpost.com/wp-dyn/content/article/2009/07/27/AR2009072702988.html?referrer=emailarticle
28. Sources: Staged Cyber Attack Reveals Vulnerability in Power Grid (2007), http://edition.cnn.com/2007/US/09/26/power.at.risk/index.html
29. Slay, J., Miller, M.: Lessons Learned from the Maroochy Water Breach. IFIP, vol. 253. Springer, Boston (2007)
30. Top 10 Vulnerabilities of Control Systems and their Associated Mitigations (2007)
31. Byres, E.J., Hoffman, D., Kube, N.: On Shaky Ground - A Study of Security Vulnerabilities in Control Protocols. In: Proc. of The 5th American Nuclear Society International Topical Meeting on Nuclear Plant Implementation, Controls, and Human Machine Interface Technology (2006)
32. US Department of Energy Office of Independent Oversight The President's Critical Infrastructure Protection Board & the Office of Energy Assurance and Performance Assurance. 21 Steps to Improve Cyber Security of SCADA Networks. U.S. Department of Energy (2002)
33. National Vulnerability Database, NVD (2007)
34. Open Source Vulnerability Database, OSVDB (2007)
35. D'Antonio, S., Romano, L., Khelil, A., Suri, N.: INcreasing Security and Protection through Infrastructure REsilience: The INSPIRE Project. In: Setola, R., Geretshuber, S. (eds.) CRITIS 2008. LNCS, vol. 5508, pp. 109–118. Springer, Heidelberg (2009)
36. Kozik, R., Choraś, M., Hołubowicz, W.: Fusion of Bayesian and Ontology Approach Applied to Decision Support System for Critical Infrastructures Protection. In: Chatzimisios, P., Verikoukis, C., Santamaría, I., Laddomada, M., Hoffmann, O. (eds.) MOBILIGHT 2010. LNICST, vol. 45, pp. 451–463. Springer, Heidelberg (2010)
37. IEC technical committee 57. Data and communications security, part 5: Security for iec 60870-5 and derivatives. IEC 62351-5 Second Committee Draft (2005)
38. Escudero, J.I., Rodrguez, J.A., Romero, M.C.: IDOLO: Multimedia Data Deployment On Scada Systems. In: Proc. of The IEEE PES Power Systems Conference And Exposition (2004)
39. Avallone, S., D'Antonio, S.: Using MPLS in a Wireless Mesh Network to Improve the Resiliency of SCADA Systems. In: Chatzimisios, P., Verikoukis, C., Santamaría, I., Laddomada, M., Hoffmann, O. (eds.) MOBILIGHT 2010. LNICST, vol. 45, pp. 440–450. Springer, Heidelberg (2010)

40. Lim, I.H., Kim, Y.I., Lim, H.T., Choi, M.S., Hong, S., Lee, S.J., Lim, S.I., Lee, S.W., Ha, B.N.: Distributed Restoration System Applying Multi-Agent in Distribution Automation System. In: IEEE PES General Meeting (2008)
41. Lo, Y.L., Wang, C.H., Lu, C.N.: A Multi-agent Based Service Restoration in Distribution Network with Distributed Generations. In: Proc. of The 15th International Conference on Intelligent System Applications to Power Systems, ISAP (2009)
42. Pridgen, A., Julien, C.: A secure modular mobile agent system. In: Proc. of The 2006 International Workshop on Software Engineering for Large-Scale Multi-Agent Systems, SELMAS (2006)
43. Suri, N., Bradshaw, J.M., Breedy, M.R., Groth, P.T., Hill, G.A., Jeffers, R., Mitrovich, T.S., Pouliot, B.R., Smith, D.S.: NOMADS: toward a strong and safe mobile agent system. In: Proc. of The Fourth International Conference on Autonomous Agents, AGENTS (2000)
44. Ketel, M.: A mobile agent based framework for web services. In: Proc. of The 47th Annual Southeast Regional Conference, ACM-SE (2009)
45. Pietre-Cambacedes, L., Sitbon, P.: Cryptographic Key Management for SCADA systems - Issues and Perspectives. In: Proc. of The International Conference on Information Security and Assurance (2008)
46. Patel, S.C., Yu, Y.: Analysis of SCADA Security Models. The International Management Review 3(2), 68–76 (2007)
47. Graham, J.H., Mostafa, S., Arazi, B., Tantawy, A., Hieb, J., Ralston, P., Patel, S.C.: Improvements in SCADA and DCS systems security. In: Proc. of The International Conference on Computers and Their Applications (2007)
48. Graham, J.H., Patel, S.C.: Correctness Proofs for SCADA Communication Protocols. In: Proc. of The 9th World Multi-Conference on Systemics, Cybernetics and Informatics (2005)
49. Hieb, J.L., Graham, J.H., Patel, S.C.: Cyber Security Enhancements for SCADA and DCS Systems. In: Critical Infrastructure Protection: Issues and Solutions. Springer, Heidelberg (2007)
50. Patel, S.C.: Secure Internet-Based Communication Protocol for SCADA Networks. In: Doctoral Dissertation, University of Louisville, Louisville, Kentucky, USA (2006)
51. Lee, S., Choi, D., Park, C., Kim, S.: An Efficient Key Management Scheme for Secure SCADA Communication. In: Proc. of The International Conference on Power Electronics and Power Engineering, ICPEPE (2008)
52. Camtepe, S.A., Yener, B.: Key Distribution Mechanisms for Wireless Sensor Networks: a Survey. TR-05-07, Dept. of Computer Science, Rensselaer Polytechnic Institute (2005)
53. Wright, A.K., Kinast, J.A., McCarty, J.: Low-Latency Cryptographic Protection for SCADA Communications. In: Jakobsson, M., Yung, M., Zhou, J. (eds.) ACNS 2004. LNCS, vol. 3089, pp. 263–277. Springer, Heidelberg (2004)
54. Beaver, C., Gallup, D., Neuman, W., Torgerson, M.: Key management for SCADA. Technical Report, SANDIA (2002)
55. UK National Infrastructure Security Coordination Centre. Good Practice Guide on Firewall Deployment for SCADA and Process Control Networks. TR - British Columbia Institute of Technology (2005)
56. Bace, R., Mell, P.: Nist special publication on intrusion detection systems (2001)
57. Lazarevic, A., Kumar, V., Srivastava, J.: Intrusion detection: A survey (2009)
58. Tucker, C.J., Furnell, S.M., Ghita, B.V., Brooke, P.J.: A new taxonomy for comparing intrusion detection systems. Internet Research 17(1) (2007)
59. Google Directory. Intrusion Detection Systems
60. Dmoz Open Security Project. Intrusion Detection Systems
61. Cheung, S., Dutertre, B., Fong, M., Lindqvist, U., Skinner, K.: Using Model-based Intrusion Detection for SCADA Networks. In: Proc. of The SCADA Security Scientific Symposium (2007)

62. Rrushi, J.L., Campbell, R.H.: Detecting Attacks in Power Plant Interfacing Substations through Probabilistic Validation of Attack-Effect Bindings. In: Proc. of The SCADA Security Scientific Symposium (2008)
63. Yi, P., Tong, T., Liu, N., Wu, Y., Ma, J.: Security in Wireless Mesh Networks: Challenges and Solutions. In: Proc. of The Sixth International Conference on Information Technology: New Generations, ITNG (2009)
64. Patira, R., Saxena, M.: A Survey on Security and Challenges of Ad-Hoc Networks. In: Proc. of Recent Innovations in Software and Computers, RISC (2010)
65. Stoica, I., Morris, R., Karger, D., Kaashoek, F.M., Balakrishnan, H.: Chord: A Scalable Peer-to-Peer Lookup Service for Internet Applications. In: Proc. of The ACM SIGCOMM Conference (2001)
66. Maymounkov, P., Mazières, D.: Kademlia: A Peer-to-Peer Information System Based on the XOR Metric. In: Druschel, P., Kaashoek, M.F., Rowstron, A. (eds.) IPTPS 2002. LNCS, vol. 2429, pp. 53–65. Springer, Heidelberg (2002)
67. Rowstron, A.I.T., Druschel, P.: Pastry: Scalable, Decentralized Object Location, and Routing for Large-Scale Peer-to-Peer Systems. In: Liu, H. (ed.) Middleware 2001. LNCS, vol. 2218, pp. 329–350. Springer, Heidelberg (2001)
68. Akyildiz, I.F., Su, W., Sankarasubramaniam, Y., Cayirci, E.: A Survey on Sensor Networks. IEEE Communications Magazine 40(8), 102–114 (2002)
69. Alzaid, H., Park, D., Nieto, J.G., Boyd, C., Foo, E.: A Forward and Backward Secure Key Management in Wireless Sensor Networks for PCS/SCADA. In: Hailes, S., Sicari, S., Roussos, G. (eds.) S-CUBE 2009. LNICST, vol. 24, pp. 66–82. Springer, Heidelberg (2010)

Cyber Vulnerability in Power
Systems Operation and Control

Ettore Bompard[1], Paolo Cuccia[2], Marcelo Masera[3], and Igor Nai Fovino[4]

[1] Politecnico di Torino, Department of Electrical Engineering – Italy
[2] Terna S.p.A, Department of Dispatching and Grid Operation – Italy
[3] Institute for Energy, Joint Research Center, European Commission
[4] Institute for the Protection and Security of the Citizen,
Joint Research Center, European Commission

1 Introduction

Modern power systems are composed of several interacting national systems synchronously or asynchronously interconnected over large geographic areas, and in the European case on a continental basis. In each country several areas are put under the control of regional centers, connected and coordinated by a national coordination center. Among the various national centers, coordination procedures are made available on an off-line basis.

The lines and substation that represent the physical layers of the system accommodate the power flows. The secure operation of the power systems crucially relies on the reliability of the cyber layers, upon which various types of information are exchanged. From the field, a significant amount of data is derived, in terms of both measured values of electrical parameters and status of the devices. This information is transmitted to the control centers of each area for the state estimation and for undertaking, when needed, the corresponding control actions, through dedicated switching centers; obviously the success of the control actions and the feasibility of the systems rely on the possibility to exchange uncorrupted information promptly.

The reliability of the cyber layer is strictly related to its structure, in terms of architecture, protocols for data interchange, and procedures for the backup and verification of data. The cyber layer is more vulnerable because of the increasing use of networking technologies to interlink the field equipments with the control centers and the control centers with each other; the interconnection of the different actors in the power systems plays a critical role as well. On the one hand the cyber functions are more complex while still using off-the-shelf technologies in many cases; on the other hand they are exposed to malicious actors (insiders such as disgruntled employees, and outsiders such as different types of antagonists).

The reduction of the vulnerability level is strictly related to the implementation of protective strategies (selectivity, in case of the failure of components; coordination between devices, in case of large scale events; coordination among protective and regulation systems...). However, cyber vulnerabilities will not disappear. Information and communication technologies will be employed by power systems in an increasing manner, as they are essential for their efficient control and operation.

J. Lopez et al. (Eds.): Critical Information Infrastructure Protection, LNCS 7130, pp. 197–234, 2012.

When discussing the vulnerability and potential threats to power systems, we will present a synopsis of the most relevant cyber security scenarios and the corresponding countermeasures. The vulnerabilities and potential threats described here should be considered as an indication of the problems in advance, and the effort required for ensuring the robustness of power systems with respect to them.

2   Structure and Operation of Power Systems

Power systems are characterized by a physical layer composed of the bulk transmission system with all the related devices required for its operation, control and protection [1], [2]. This physical layer acts as the support for the electricity transferred from the production sites to the final users. Power flows over a meshed transmission system, from the buses to which the generators are connected to the buses where loads are connected. Both real power (which can be directly exploited) and reactive power (related mainly to the generation of magnetic fields needed in the operation of electric machines and devices) go over the system; real power mainly affects the bus voltage's phases while reactive power its magnitude. The real power injected by the generators needs to be instantaneously matched with the power withdrawn by the loads and lost on the transmission system. This matching is indicated by a constant system frequency (50 Hz in EU and 60 Hz in US); a failure in this respect will possibly result in a black-out. In the meantime, the bus voltages need to be kept close to their rated value through a proper control of reactive power flows and injections/withdrawal over the network.   The lines are operated not to exceed a maximum rated limit for the real and reactive power flows. All those constraints define a region of feasibility for the power transmission grid that must be satisfied though proper control strategies, both human driven and automatic, that are enforced on the physical systems through ICT control and communication centers and devices (cyber layer of the system). In this section we will introduce the basic ideas about the physical layer and its operation requirements while the subsequent section will discuss the cyber layer.

2.1   Architecture and Components for Power Grids

In power systems the physical layers consist of the network hardware, including stations, lines, transformers and circuit breakers [1]. Electricity, in terms of electrical energy, is "produced" or, better, transformed from other energy forms in the power plants that can be of different sizes (from kW to thousands of MW), for the physical transformation principle and for the fuel used. Today we rely mainly on the transformation of kinetic energy (energy of motion) into electricity by steam turbines (sources are coal, natural gas, petroleum or nuclear), combined cycles (gas turbines coupled with steam turbines fed by natural gas) and hydro turbines, with a small amount coming from solar energy, wind generators, and geothermal sources. The power produced is injected into the bulk Extra High Voltage (EHV 220 - 1000 kV) power transmission system (for large size power plants) to reduce the energy lost in the long distance transmission, or locally consumed and distributed at high-medium-low voltage levels in the distribution systems. The bulk transmission system intends to transfer remarkable amount of power (hundreds of MW) over long distances (hundreds of km) while a HV distribution system (132 kV), connected via transformer substations to the transmission system, feeds the MV distribution systems and large customers (>5 MW) as well; the MV distribution system supplies the medium loads (between 100 kW and 5 MW) and feeds the LV distribution system for supplying small loads (lower than 150 kW). The power system structure is depicted in Figure 1.

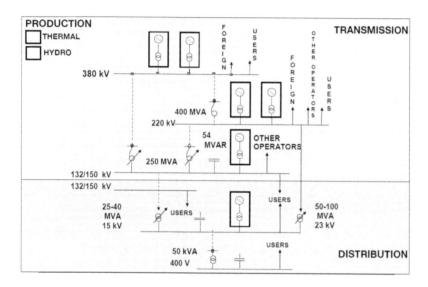

Fig. 1. Typical structure of power systems

The transmission network includes components such as transmission lines, substations, transformers, and control and protection systems. Transmission lines may be of aerial or cable types, AC or DC and they connect the nodes ("buses") of the transmission system that are represented by the EHV substations which can implement, simultaneously or separately, different functions such as production, switching, regulation and control (transformation and/or conversion) of the electric vector. From the topological point of view the substations is characterized by several bus-bar systems at different voltage levels and for each bus-bar the elementary unit is a bay, composed of a group of devices serving to connect a line or a transformer to the bus-bar. The substations may be Air Insulated Station (AIS) or Gas Insulated Station (GIS) and the most important power components are listed as follows:

- *Interconnection transformers EHV/HV*: connection between different levels of the transmission; the two grids that accomplish these functions are both loop-structure grids (meshed).
- *Distribution transformers HV/MV*: connection between transmission function and distribution function, normally accomplished by a radial grid.

- *AC/DC and DC/AC converters*: in case of long distance transmission or transmission over the sea, DC lines are frequently chosen and at both sides of such lines AC/DC or DC/AC conversions are needed.
- *Power capacitors and power reactors*: devices for voltage/reactive power regulation[1].
- *Switchgears*: two kinds of switchgear are employed in HV substations to modify the topology of the grid: a) circuit breakers, being able to terminate normal operation and fault current very quickly (30 ms-150 ms); b) disconnectors, safety devices used to open or close a circuit without current.
- *Measure transformers*: used to feed protection and metering systems at reduced values with respect to the real ones (24 V-220 V, 1 A-5 A).
- *Parallel-resonant circuits*: HV lines are used to transmit information as high frequency signals superimposed to the low frequency power transmission and captured by proper filtering systems.
- *Protection and control system*: the active components of a HV substation are circuit breakers and disconnectors; the operators of the control centers give commands to these devices through the substation control system (maneuver executed in some minutes). In addition circuit breakers are operated by the system relay protection (reaction time of devices 10 ms - 5 s).
- *Communication devices*: the control system of the substations is equipped with a communication system to command and supervise the network remotely.

The transformer substations from HV to MV for feeding the MV distribution (called primary station) system are topologically very simple, with a single bus bar system, two line bays and two transformer bays. HV substations are also used to supply a single large load (delivery station).

The electricity industry has been operated for decades, from the market perspective, as a regulated monopoly of vertical integrated utilities (VIU) that owned and managed the generation, transmission and distribution of power. Starting from the late 1980s competition has been gradually introduced with the consequent unbundling of the previous VIU. This has led to a scenario characterized by a multitude of different production companies, competing to sell the power on the wholesale market, a set of brokers and many retailers selling power to final customers; transmission and distribution systems, managed respectively by one national company and many local franchising companies, remained a natural monopoly due to the impossibility to coexist, on the same territory, of multiple wiring systems and to the need to play a neutral role so that the market outcomes are not affected. Those systems are strictly regulated by the national Regulators. The different national rules are harmonized, for example, at the European level by ENTSO-E, the European network of transmission system operators for electricity

At the physical layer, the network buses may have different roles, in terms of the physical behavior and the ownership. Roughly speaking we can differentiate the buses into four types:

- *Transmission Stations* (TS): buses of the transmission network owned and operated directly by the TSO undertaking its own responsibility.

- *Power Plants* (PP): generation power plants in which energy is transformed from whichever form into electricity. They belong to various competing generation companies. Each company may possess various power plants connected to different buses of the network.
- *Distribution Systems feeders* (DS): buses, equipped with transformers, in which a Medium Voltage (MV) distribution system is originated. Each DSO (Distribution System Operator) owns and operates as a monopolist the distribution system over a certain portion of territory, allowing all retailers to use the distribution network on an un-discriminatory basis. The same distribution company may have multiple feeding buses connected to the transmission network.
- *Large Users* (LU): buses to which the users that demand high power (> 5 MW) are directly connected.

2.2   Functions and States in the Operation of Power Systems

The operation of power systems needs to be undertaken pursuing some attributes, both in the short (the infrastructure is fixed) and long (the infrastructure may be re-enforced) run. The attributes are specified in various definition provided by different authoritative sources [3] [10]. In our perspective we consider the *adequacy* as the ability of the electric system to supply the aggregate electrical demand and energy requirements of the customers; *security* as the ability to withstand a predefined set of perturbations; *reliability* as the general ability to provide service (supply loads). If the system is highly reliable then it is *robust*, if the system is characterized by a low robustness then it is *vulnerable*. In summary, the goal is to have robust power systems, characterized by a high reliability (probability of providing service), which depends on the adequacy (related to the normal operation) and the security (related to abnormal events, ie. natural, accidental or malicious threats) of the system.

In Europe, each national transmission grid is normally under the authority of a Transmission System Operator (TSO) who is in charge of several key-functions related to both the on-line and off-line activities that can be grouped into three main areas:

- *Dispatching and Energy Operation* (on-line control of power grid and related services)
    - o Supervision, control and switching on the national electric system according to quality, security and economy criteria
    - o Operational planning of generation and grid resources (day ahead)
    - o Settlement of energy exchanges
    - o Grid engineering (protection and defense operation).
- *Engineering and infrastructure management* (substations and lines construction and maintenance)
    - o Definition of standards for design, installation and maintenance of the grid
    - o Performance of the activities for control, installation and maintenance of plants based on the development plans.
- *Grid development* (analysis and simulations for network re-enforcement to ensure the efficacy in grid planning, managing the authorization processes for the timely and efficient implementation of plants).

The operational rules, target and the requirement for connecting to the grid are reported in the Grid Code, available for each nation, in which the following aspects are considered:

- *Access to the transmission grid*: general rules for connecting electrical installations (loads, production sites, merchant lines...) to the network.
- *Topology for the connection*: choice of the connection scheme (radial, double, T-derivation...).
- *Performance of the components* (bus bars and bays, transformers...): technical specifications for the physical connection and for the choice of principal components.
- *Performance of generators* (production sites): specifications and standards for generators.
- *Dispatching regulation*: national rules for the set points of power plants.
- *Power quality*: characteristics of the power quality to the users and requirements for the electrical interactions with the network (electrical polluting large size loads).
- *Metering*: requirements for the metering devices.

The system can be operated in various operative states, as represented in Figure 2. The system typically operates in *normal state* for more than 99% of the time [11]. In this state, all the system constraints, including equality constraints in term of power balance and inequality constraints in terms of voltage, frequency, line transmission flows, transient stability, are respected.

The power balance or "Equality" (E) between the demand from load and the supplies available on the network, both in terms of real and reactive power, is a fundamental prerequisite for the system in normal state. "Inequality" (I) constraints define a feasible operation region. In normal state, system is within the feasible region with given security margin, defined by generation spinning reserve, transmission capacity reserve, etc. The occurrence of a disturbance may induce the security level reduction and the system enters the *alert state*. However, all equalities (E) and inequalities (I) are still observed, and the system is still fully synchronized; the system can be kept in feasible for any length of time. Nonetheless, preventive control actions now would be initiated to restore the required system security margin and return the system to its normal state by means of eliminating disturbances, generation shifting, or reserve increase. If preventive control fails or a sufficiently severe disturbance occurs, system will enter the *emergency state*.

From normal state, the system can be driven to the emergency stated in case of severe contingency [12] or transferred from alert state with decreasing security margin. In this state, the power balance is stills satisfied and the system is still synchronized but one or several inequality constraints are violated, some components are overloaded and as these components eventually fail, the system will start to disintegrate. It is most urgent that one should launch emergency control actions to return the system into normal or alert state by means of cutting of faults, rerouting of generation, excitation control, fast-valving generation tripping, generation run-back, HVDC (high voltage DC) modulation or, of last resort, load shedding (curtailment of power to loads).

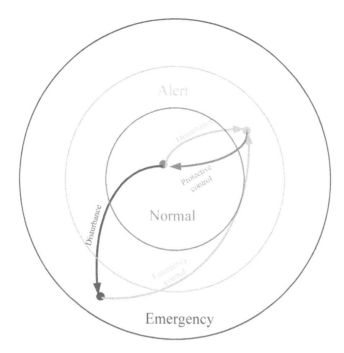

Fig. 2. States for power systems operation and transitions

If emergency control actions fail, the system will go into the *extreme state*: cascading outages and disintegration or islanding. Some of these islands may contain sufficient generation to supply the load. But some of the generators will be constrained by their maximum production capacities. Both E and I are negated in this state. Consequently considerable generator tripping may initiate to eliminate generators' overload, which might lead to overall blackout. To bring it back to normal state, passing through the restorative state, is a time consuming process, typically lasting from hours to days.

2.3   Structure of Interconnected Power Systems

The transmission networks have a meshed structure which makes the grid operation more complex due to the multiple possible paths taken by the power flows; the topology can be changed according to the production dispatching, the weather conditions and the load variations. On the other hand, however, the path redundancy provides higher reliability comparing with the purely radial topology adopted by the networks at lower voltage [12].

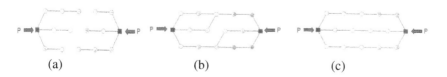

(a)   (b)   (c)

Fig. 3. Radial structure (a) and loop structure (b & c)

The EHV network (the primary transmission network) is managed with all meshes closed by all line breakers at the substations and this state corresponds to the maximum security level. The network is always operated in N-1 security condition meaning that the event of a sudden accidental outage of any component of the system (lines, transformers, generators, groups) does not cause overloads in the other components, and eventually lead to possible cascade failures.

The HV network (the sub-transmission network) is managed with some open loops, i.e., some line breaker are open in the substations. These "operation islands" have different geographical extensions according to the lines available to the TSOs, the power injection points (power plants or EHV/HV transformers), the loads to be supplied. This scheme provides several advantages such as the reduction of short circuit currents, the limitation of the extension of possible severe faults and faster supply restoration, the decrease in the diffusion of disturbance of electric supply (voltage dips, flicker, harmonics...), the simplicity in load flow forecast and in the voltage profile control by the real-time operation, the optimal functioning of protection system.

The rapid growth in electrical energy consumption, combined with the demand for low-cost energy, has gradually led to the development of generation sites remotely located from the load centers. The generation of bulk power at remote locations necessitates the use of transmission lines to connect generation and load sites. The impedance of these lines and the voltages at their terminals determine the flows of active and reactive powers: no way for on line control of the flows exists.

FACTS (Flexible AC Transmission System) and HVDC (High Voltage Direct Current) are controllable devices [13] whose functions are to enhance the security, capacity and flexibility of power transmission systems. Application of these devices in power systems implies an improvement of transient and voltage stability, power oscillation damping and optimal power flow.

MV distribution networks have a radial structure, which is the best solution, in terms of protection simplicity, easiness of operation and control when the energy flow has a predominant direction. The operation in this condition is relatively simple, short circuit currents are contained and technical solutions for system protections are simple, though guaranteeing required selectivity. On the other hand, a fault in the single supply source implies temporary interruption or degradation in the performance of a portion of the network.

2.4   Power Systems Defense and Protection

There are three aspects that define the role of protection systems in power system design and operation: *normal operation, prevention of electrical failure, mitigation of the effects of electrical failure.*

Control actions, such as load shedding and controlled system islanding, are aimed to saving the largest possible portion of the system from blackouts. Each TSO, for monitoring the operation of power system and for assuring normal operation even after a disturbance, adopts and keeps updating a National Defense Plan (NDP) coordinating with those from the other TSOs in its synchronous area. In general, the NDP is based on *4 defense lines* that are realized adopting security procedures, devices and systems related to transmission substations, distribution feeders and power plants.

The *first defense line* focuses on anticipating the electric system operation, by forecasting and programming an operational normal state. Moreover it is permanently supported during normal operation by the regulation of the production systems, which react to the gaps between forecasted and real-time power. This *defense line* is internationally adopted in the interconnected European system [12]. The rules for the TSOs coordination are laid out in the Operation Handbook [14], which defines procedures for co-operation in circumstances where factors outside of the control area can reduce the ability of a TSO to operate its system within the operating limits.

The *second defense line* is the protection system, that has the goal to separate selectively, quickly and reliably the faulted components whilst avoiding further propagation of the fault. It is crucial to maintain proper co-ordination of set values for protection in the grid, particularly for the cases of generators and regulation systems.

The *third defense line* is realized by systems and devices that implement the restorative actions of the interconnection grid, trying to prevent uncontrolled separation. The *fourth defense line* operates in condition of separate networks after the failure of the third line of the defense plan. It is based on automatic devices that have the goal of maintaining the balance between production and demand. With reference to the third and fourth *defense lines*, some examples of actions that can be undertaken are: a) load shedding for under frequency or undervoltage; b) remote generation trip for weak parts of the network; c) manual load shedding on different groups of users; d) intentional islanding; e) automatic voltage regulation (AVR) block (or set point modification) for tap changer of EHV/HV and HV/MV transformers.

Another system to solve the problem of under frequency and undervoltage is to schedule a well-designed set of electrical islands (islanding), by setting conveniently frequency relays at the network buses. This implies to pick out smaller parts of the network so that the frequency will probably become easier to be under controlled when the condition is declining. In case all four defence lines fail, the final step of frequency drop is of course the black out. In this case the restoration of the entire system is required. This extremely hazardous operation is conducted applying preselected strategies, which are thought to identify the most convenient steps to rebuild the systems.

In the normal operation of power systems, an instantaneous balance between generation supply, from one side, and load demand and losses, from the other side, needs to be always assured. A disturbance, in terms of sudden loss of generation or loads, may cause a drop or increase in the system frequency that needs to be compensated by change in the set points of the generators in the control area. In the normal state the voltage profile at all buses of the network should be constrained to a given voltage range (95-105 % of the rated values). The voltage profile is strictly related to the reactive power [15] injections/withdrawal and the related flows over the network. To obtain the desired voltage profile, the TSO can act on various system devices such as generators, static VAR compensators, shunt reactors, synchronous compensators, changing the network topology.

3   Control and Communication in Power Systems

The operation of the power system is managed at the highest level by a decision making layer characterized both by the implementation of automatic control actions and by human decisions. The cyber layer, which is the natural interface to the physical layer, makes possible a bidirectional communication among the physical and decision making layer (data field to the decision making and control actions to the physical).

3.1   Architecture of the Power System Control

The architecture of the control system of the transmission network is based on a clear separation between the function of command and the function of monitoring.
The first one is attributed to the *Switching Centers (SC)* that are in charge of changing the configuration of the network acting on its devices (circuit breakers, disconnectors, tap changers…).

The second one is attributed to *Regional Control Centers (RCC)* that supervise the network status and provide directions to the operator in the SC to act on the network devices.

On top of all that there is a unique *National Control Center (NCC)* that supervises the national electric system and regulate the power flows with other network in according to specific rules.

Figure 4 depicts the architecture of the power system control with its hierarchical organization.

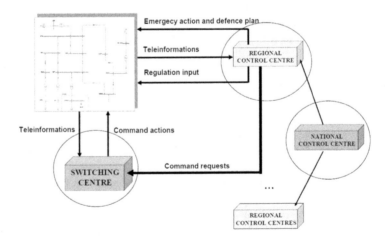

Fig. 4. Control architecture of a transmission network

3.2   Physical-Cyber Layers Interface

Remote Terminal Units (RTU) represent the interface of the network buses in the physical layer with the cyber layers. RTUs are basically devices equipped with a microprocessor and a set of digital and analog input/output channels. Some buses are connected on a "one to one basis" to a dedicated RTU while several others can be grouped under the same RTU resorting to a gateway that simply concentrates the information from many buses in the same location, making them available for a RTU. TS and LU buses are equipped with a dedicated RTU, while, for PP and DS buses, one RTU serves for various generators and feeders belonging to the same production/distribution company (a single PP can manage information of power plants for around 1000 MW). PP are always equipped with a dedicated RTU if a company owns a single PP or in case of large size power plants with a huge number of information (analog/digital signals, alarms, level for load-frequency-control, level for automatic-voltage-regulation…).

RTUs require a bidirectional communications with RCCs and SCs through appropriate communication channels. These channels can be implemented through various physical media (parallel-resonant circuit on power lines, copper telephone wires, optic fiber, radio wave, satellite communications). The communication networks involved in power systems operation and control are mainly:

- TSO network (TSON): is a data network owned and operated directly by the TSO (in the Italian case Terna, the Italian TSO, for its control system, named SCTI, has chosen the international standard protocol IEC 60870-5-104, *its* telecom network has more or less 1150 points of data acquisition; the physical supports are above all optic fibers).
- Public Transmission Networks (PTN): are general-purpose networks, owned and operated by Telecom Companies that can be used for data also from power systems.

RCC, SC and NCC and the TS are connected directly to the TSON by a double circuit. Every private RTU (of LU, PP or DS) is connected by a PTN to two different RCCs. Each communication channel is based on two different and independent media (e.g. [3], [16]).

3.3   Control Strategies

The goal of the control of interconnected bulk power systems is to keep each national system in its *normal state*, regulating the flow interchanges with the neighboring systems; the control actions are focused on the buses of the transmission system, the users plants, and on the devices for the ancillary services [17]. Different types of actions can be undertaken, such as a request of transition to a different grid configuration (switchgear maneuver), an order for the regulation of the set point of a generator, or an emergency or defense command.

The supervision, monitoring and control of power systems, both automatic and human driven, are implemented into dedicated control centers that are equipped with *Energy Management Systems (EMS)* supporting software applications such as power flow computation, state estimation and security analysis. In addition control centers get an extensive set of information related to the power system status (currents, voltages, devices states) through the SCADA (Supervisory Control And Data Acquisition) system.

On the basis of those information, the TSO monitors, in real time, the system's status to keep it in its normal state, considering the economic and security constraints, by adjusting the system control variables (voltage at buses, currents over lines and, consequently, power flows over the lines of the network). At the bottom there is a switching center (SC), responsible for operating several tens of substations, with the connected transmission lines, located nearby. The main task of a SC is to perform actions issued by higher-level control centers through telephone calls. Typical functions of a European SC are the maneuver of the components in the transmission substations, the assurance that the requested maneuvers are carried out correctly and that the activation of inspection procedures on faulted lines. In addition, the SC supervises the devices of the substations.

In the middle there are the *Regional Control Centers (RCC)*. RCCs are in charge of the identification of the line faults and of deciding on actions to recover the functionality of the transmission network. These actions are sent to the SCs through phone calls. Generally RCCs are not able to directly operate the network, except for particular situations (remote load shedding, emergency situations...). The typical functions of a European RCC are:

- Assurance of the optimized management of the ancillary services (Interconnected Operation Services identified as necessary to effect a transfer of electricity between purchasing and selling entities [3], [18]) (spinning reserve, voltage regulation...) on the HV grid control
- Congestion management (a "congestion" i s an operational situation, also potential, of an electrical grid, characterized by deficits in the transport of electrical energy due to grid constraints [3], [19])
- Supervision and control (in cooperation with the National Control Center) of the EHV grid
- Control in real time of the HV grid.

In addition, they contribute to the operation analyses and post disturbances studies, to the updating of the remote data for the control system, the restoration of the system in case of blackout and the design of the HV grid configuration and of the restoration plans. The RCC may undertake a set of possible actions such as the supervision and control of the power flows and security margins, the carrying out the generation programs, the management of the grid topology, the undertaking of emergency actions and restoration procedures.

The highest level is the *National Control Center (NCC)*, which is in charge of the general supervision of the network, of the coordination actions that involve two or more regions, and of the short, medium and long term operation planning. During large disturbances, the NCC also coordinates all the actions in order to restore the normal state. As an example, the Italian TSO receives from the EHV/HV network about 5000 analog measurements and 7000 digital measurements. Typical functions of a European NCC are the control in real time of the EHV grid, the assurance of n-1 security, the management of the ancillary services auctioning to private bidders and the selection, according to a "merit order", of the generation units, the pursue of the economic optimization of the operation, the supervision of the automatic defense plans and the application of the scheduled load shedding, the management of situations close to collapse of the system, the validation of the schedule coming out from the Operational Planning, the post disturbance analyses, the technical specification of IT tools for real-time operation, the definition of the EHV grid configuration and restoration plans.

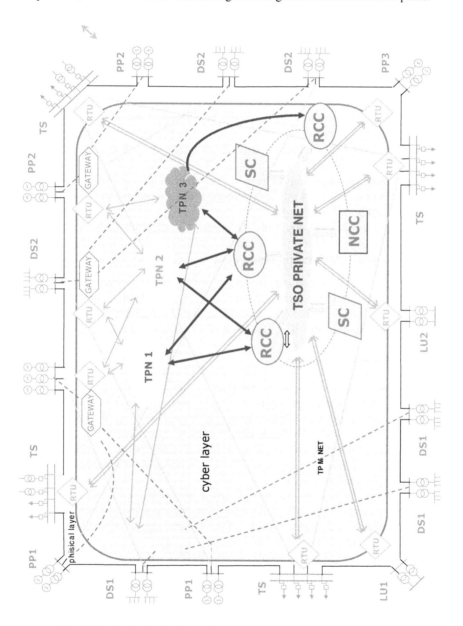

Fig. 5. Physical and cyber layers in power systems operation and control

Both, NCC and RCC, mostly implement the same functions, but the NCC collects the data from all RCC being able to get the overall view of the system and coordinate all the actions from the various RCCs.

The physical and cyber layers of power systems fitted in the control architecture are represented in Figure 5.

4   Information Exchange over Power Grids

A significant quantity of information is exchanged between grid control centers and substations (TS, PP, DS, LU) and between control centers of neighboring TSO. The information can be classified according to various criteria:

- update time (few seconds for the real-time control, some minutes for other controls, hours for commercial items)
- electrical purpose (switchgears status/electric measures on the one hand or commands on the other hand)
- non electrical measurements helping forecast procedures (water level of hydroelectrically lakes or rate of water for hydro-power-plants, speed and direction of wind for wind farms, …)
- links to the regulation loops (Load Frequency Control, Automatic Voltage Regulation, …)
- economic influence (data concerning electrical power and energy)

The information directly managed by control and switching centers is called *real-time information*, which can be internal (national) or external (from neighboring area); the category of the *non-real-time information* concerns a considerable group of technical and administrative data, the most important of which is commercial information.

4.1   Real-Time information

Each electrical infrastructure must integrate in the control processes both real-time and not-real-time information received not only from the TSO but also from all the actors connected to the network (power plants, HV distribution substations and industrial consumers stations). "Real-time data collection" is a collection of data describing a current situation, which can be done periodically, on request or after a change of status or value, in order to support the TSOs in monitoring, coordinating and operating the transmission system.

Operational security is assured by data and information interchange between substations, Control centers of the TSOs, Switching centers and automatic control systems.

To obtain an exhaustive observability of its system, the TSO needs to acquire the information reported in Tab. 1.

The TSOs' technical and operational data required for the operation, planning and analysis of the interconnected ENTSO-E transmission grid, need to be handled under general rules concerning data confidentiality, acquisition, coordination and usage, the back-up procedures, intellectual property and hardship. All parties involved need to comply with the same rights and obligations to support ENTSO-E's internal tasks and external communication policy.

Table 1. Real Time Information

	Real time control			LFC & AVR		Defence plan
	From substations to RCC	From SC to substations	From RCC to NCC	From power plants to RCC	From RCC to power plants	From RCC or NCC to subst.
Voltage from bar VT of every EHV substations and the most important HV substations	X					
Frequency from bar VT of every EHV substations	X					
Active power and Reactive power generated by every relevant generator				X		
Voltage at bars connecting generators with rated power of hundreds of MW				X		
Active power and Reactive power of every HV/MV transformer of distribution system feeders	X					
Position of breakers/disconnectors of every feeder of every bar system of controlled network	X					
Position of tap changers of EHV/HV transformers and Regulation condition of Phase Shifting Transformers	X					
Information (measures and switchgear positions) concerning EHV network			X			
Perturbations signals and alarms	X			X		
State of regulation and parameters, for generators that contributes to load-frequency control and automatic voltage regulation			X	X		
Device intervention signal for substations included in *defense* plan			X	X		
Load-frequency control and automatic voltage regulation set point				X		
In and out of service remote orders for generators included in LFC and AVR				X		
Remote orders for every switchgear of substations bays of controlled network		X				

Table 1. (*continued*)

	Real time control			LFC & AVR		Defense plan
	From substations to RCC	From SC to substations	From RCC to NCC	From power plants to RCC	From RCC to power plants	From RCC or NCC to subst.
Remote orders for tap changers of EHV/HV transformers and PST		X				
In and out of service remote command for power capacitors and power reactors		X				
Load shedding remote command (total or partial)						X
Power generation reduction command (total or partial)						X

4.2   Non-real-Time Information

The non-real-time information exchange among actors in the power system concerns the commercial transactions over the grid. The measurement systems are connected to various points of the grid itself with different purposes. The most important points are:

- Energy input points on the grid where power plants from generation companies are connected
- Energy withdrawal points and interconnection points of the distribution companies with the grid
- Interconnection points of with other countries.

The metering activity is mainly focused on the bidirectional record of the flows over the previous points.

4.3   Format and Communication Standards

The access points to the communication networks of the TSO (TSON) have the following characteristics:

- can be connected to other networks;
- have security systems for verifying the accesses;
- have a centralized control system;
- are protected by firewall systems.

The substations are connected to the communication network in, at least, two different access points in order to assure a redundancy to the systems in terms of communication channels and access points (Figure 6).

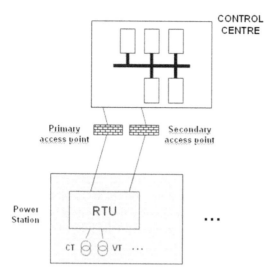

Fig. 6. Access to control system network

4.4   Example Case

The TSO requires that all the actors connected to the grid (power plants, industrial sites that need electrical power connection…) certify the reliability of the information communication system over time. The main features of those systems are briefly described below.

Data Update Time
For the supervision of the installations and correct operation of control, monitoring and defense systems, it is necessary to maintain the update time of information under the following typical values:

- 0.2-1 seconds for switchgear state, protection trips, "out of range" of system control variables included in defense plan (activated by a change in the state of the devices);
- 2-20 seconds for active power, reactive power, current of lines and transformers, voltage and frequency of bus bars (periodically polled by the control system);
- Several minutes for files from perturbations monitoring systems (polled on demand).

Command Execution Time
For the correct function of network control, it is necessary to maintain the regulation command (f/P and V) execution time under the following typical values:

- 0.1-0.2 seconds (transfer on demand) for load shedding commands and generation trips;
- 1-2 seconds (transfer on demand) for circuit breakers, disconnectors and TR tap changers transition command.

Data interchange must be realized using standard communication protocols (see section 4). The RTU devices must respect pre-defined requirements of reliability and availability and can be different according to the importance of the substation. These requirements typically are:

- RTU equipped with redundant CPU;
- RTU dedicate in an exclusive way of data interchange with the TSO grid control system.

When it is relevant for the management of the grid, the RTU device must control two physical connections to 2 points of the TSO grid control, according to the simplified types shown in Figure 7.

The owner of the communication network is responsible for assuring the security against attempts of unauthorized access by the clients working on its assets, in particular when connected through the gateway to the Internet .

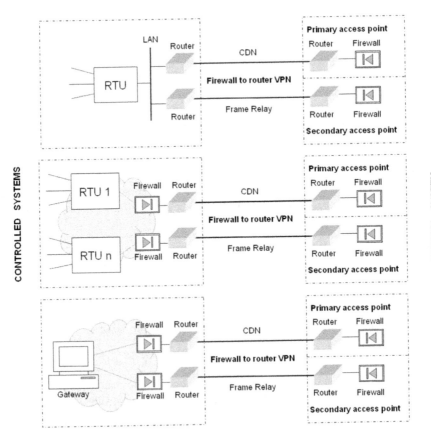

Fig. 7. Types of connections Virtual Private Network

The general requisites for the global security of power systems can be summarized as:

- N-1 security criterion and the activation of defense plans;
- Physical security of substations with burglar-proofing systems of the sites;
- Safety of the personnel by a system of behavior rules and training;
- Security of control systems based on the intrinsic fault tolerance (double scheme computers), and multi-site operation;
- Protection and information back up with duplication of the data on different sites and remote reconfigurable database.

In order to assure the necessary redundancy of systems, communication channels and access points, (in case of Disaster Recovery), the owners of power stations must be connected to the communication grid at least in two different Access Points physically separate, to guarantee the efficacy in case of unavailability of the Primary Access Point [3].

5   Power System Ict Threats

While on the one hand the massive use of use of ICT technologies has made possible a strong integration among the different elements of Power Systems (power plants, substations, transmission grids, business operations, etc.), on the other hand the new interconnections, layers, and communication links have introduced a not negligible set of new threats. Some of them, as showed for example in [15,16], are directly inherited from the traditional ICT world (e.g. generic purpose worms, vulnerabilities of general purpose operating systems etc.) Others are peculiar of the Process Systems controlling power systems. The ICT security of control systems is an open and evolving research field. Adam and Byres [17] presented an interesting high-level analysis of the possible threats to a power plant system, a categorization of the typical hardware devices involved, and some high level discussion about the intrinsic vulnerabilities of common power plant architectures. A Taxonomic approach toward the classification of attacks against energy control systems can be found for example in [19]. A more detailed work on the topic of SCADA security (Supervisory Control and Data Acquisition systems are the core of every industrial installation), is presented by Chandia, Gonzalez, Kilpatrick, Papa and Shenoi [18].

From a purely technical point of view, it is possible to claim that the cyber vulnerabilities affecting Power Systems can be classified as in the traditional ICT world:

- *Software Vulnerabilities*: vulnerabilities due to errors in the implementations of software applications (e.g. buffer overflows etc.);
- *Architectural Vulnerabilities*: vulnerabilities due to weaknesses in the architectural design of the ICT infrastructure;
- *Protocol Design Vulnerabilities*: vulnerabilities due to weaknesses in the design of the communication protocols;
- *Policy Vulnerabilities*: vulnerabilities due to a weak design or a weak implementation of security policies.

The severity of these classes of vulnerabilities (and of the related attacks) is strongly linked with the subsystem they affect. In what follows we provide a description of the main ICT weaknesses of power systems, using as discriminator the subsystems affected. As a result, the vulnerabilities and attack scenarios presented will be grouped according to the following classes:

- SCADA system weaknesses
- Process Network weaknesses
- Control Centre weaknesses
- Network Layer weaknesses

The presented scenarios are generic enough to find application in almost all modern power system architectures.

5.1   SCADA Protocol Weaknesses

SCADA protocols (DNP3, Modbus, Profibus, OPC, IEC 60870-5/6 etc.) are used by field RTUs and PLCs to remotely exchange data and commands with the supervisory system. They constitute the backbone of every industrial system; in particular, the control flows in power systems embedded in the SCADA protocol flows connect the physical components in the field with the overall operational logic of the installation.

SCADA protocols were originally conceived for serial communications, and only later they were ported over TCP/IP and subsequently wireless communication. The porting of SCADA protocols over TCP/IP has obviously introduced new layers of complexity required for reliably managing the delivery of control packets in an environment with strong real-time constraints. In addition, it has opened new possibilities to attackers motivated to cause damage to target industrial systems. However, in this section the focus is not in investigating the vulnerabilities of the communication protocols used to transport the SCADA protocols (see for a discussion of network vulnerabilities section 4.4). We concentrate here our attention on the design weaknesses of the SCADA protocols. In particular, those protocols in their original formulation:

- Do not apply any mechanism for checking the integrity of the command packets sent by a Master to a Slave and vice-versa.
- Do not perform any authentication mechanism between Master and Slaves, i.e. every item could claim to be the Master and send commands to the Slaves.
- Do not apply any anti-repudiation or anti-replay mechanisms.

These security shortcomings can be used by malicious users for attempting to carry out different kinds of attacks:

- *Unauthorized Command Execution*: The lack of authentication between Master and Slave can be used by attackers to forge packets and send them directly to a pool of slaves.
- *SCADA-DOS*: On the basis of the same principle, an attacker can attempt to produce a Denial-of-Service by forging and sending meaningless SCADA packets, always impersonating the Master, and consume the resources of the RTU.

- *Man-in-the-Middle Attacks*: The lack of integrity checks allows attackers to access the production network for implementing typical Man-in-the-Middle (MITM) attacks, modifying the legal packets sent by the master.
- *Replay Attacks*: The lack of anti-replying mechanisms allows attackers to re-use captured legitimate SCADA packets.

Finally, in addition to those classes of attacks, since anti-repudiation mechanisms are not implemented, it is hard to proof the trustworthiness of malicious Masters, which could have been compromised. In depth discussions on these vulnerabilities can be found in [20,21,22].

The impact of the successful exploitation of these weaknesses is immediately apparent: constituting the final, operational part of the entire regulation and control process, any malicious action can directly affect the industrial operation, with cascading effects on the citizens and on the companies owning the power system.

The existence of common vulnerabilities in different components of the power grid can be the cause of extremely dangerous events. In additions, it shows how the protection of the grid should incorporate security mechanisms in the communications network. In a power grid scenario, it will be normal to find the same software and hardware components repeatedly used in many systems. One recurring vulnerability will be exploitable by applying the same mechanism over and over again. This example shows how there is going to be the need for governance mechanisms for the patching and handling of vulnerabilities, linking vendors and users of technologies.

The recent detection of the Stuxnet worm, confirmed what presented in this section. This worm represents the first known example of malware ad-hoc developed for targeting SCADA systems: after infecting SCADA masters of a particular brand and model, it is in fact able to directly interact with the field devices (PLCs) to the point to be able to modify their internal logic. More details on Stuxnet can be found for example in [22].

5.2   SCADA Protocol Possible Attacks

On this basis, the following are possible attack scenarios related to SCADA protocols.

- **SCADA Malware DoS Scenario:** The goal of DoS attacks is to desynchronize (and, when possible, completely disrupt) the communication between Master and Slaves. In light of what presented before, for impairing the control communication stream it would be sufficient to inject a huge amount of SCADA packets against the Master or the set of slaves of the control system. A generic packet generator could be normally identified by Network Intrusion Detection Sensors, or by the anomaly detection engine of firewalls. Ideally, if the packet generator recreates the same traffic shape of some legitimate SCADA protocol traffic, it can circumvent the monitoring systems and interrupt the communication between Master and Slaves.

In the following some infection triggers are listed:

- o   **Email-infection:** the attacker, after gathering information about the hierarchical organization of the ICT security team in an organization, and about the process operators, forges an e-mail identical to the one usually sent for updating purposes (identical not only in the content, but also in terms of its format), with attached malware instead of a normal patch. In that e-mail, the attacker asks the operator to install the attached patch on a target Master, or on a PC in the same network. Once installed, the malware will start delivering massive amounts of well-formed SCADA packets to the slave, until the Master and the Slave are desynchronized.

- o   **Through Phishing Infection:** Phishing attacks are typically mounted in one of the following ways: a) by means of a faked e-mail, displaying a link which seems to point to a legitimate site, but actually linking to a malicious website; or, b) by poisoning the victim's DNS server, thus making it possible to transparently connect to the malicious server. Usually the scope of these attacks is to steal the user credentials. The scenario can be slightly modified: the fake web server can contain a set of malicious scripts that activate the download and execution of the malware on the local machine from which the web page is accessed. The scenario develops as follows:

  1. By social engineering through a fake e-mail, or by poisoning the DNS of the process network, an operator is forced to visit an ad-hoc created web site
  2. A set of scripts on the web-site, using some well known vulnerabilities of web browsers, download and execute of the operator PC the SCADA malware.
  3. The legitimate SCADA traffic is interrupted.

- **SCADA DOS Worm:** the attacker creates a new worm that exploits some known software vulnerability or some zero-day vulnerability. This new worm carries in its payload the code of the SCADA DOS malware. In this way, every time the worm infects a new machine:

  1. It starts to spread itself by using the new host resources.
  2. It executes the SCADA DOS code.

  Below, the step-by-step infection evolution:

  1. From Internet the worm infects the PCs in the company Intranet
  2. If one of the infected PCs in the company Intranet is authorized to access one of the networks hosting the SCADA Servers or hosting any of the control devices, the worm spread itself through such networks.
  3. If the worm discovers SCADA Slaves in the network, it starts to send SCADA packets in order to desynchronize or completely interrupt the Master/slave Command Flow.

- **SCADA Unauthorized Command Execution Scenario:** As SCADA protocols do not provide any security mechanism in order to protect the connections and the data flows, when a master sends a packet containing a command to a slave, this one simply executes it without performing any check on the identity of the master and on the integrity of the packet received. With the porting of SCADA protocols over TCP, this approach has obviously showed all its limits from the security point of view. In fact, since the slave can neither verify the identity of the sender of the commands to be executed nor its integrity, any attacker able to forge ad-hoc packets and having access to the network segment which hosts the slaves could force them to execute un authorized operations, potentially compromising the integrity or stability of the system. If the system is a critical infrastructure like a power plant, the potential damages could be catastrophic.

The list of dangerous commands can be divided into two classes:

o   **Normal Commands:** this class comprises all the commands normally used in the communication between Master and Slaves, like "open a valve, close the switch etc."; when used in the wrong context, they might cause damages (e.g. the attacker sends a "close valve command" which, due to the particular architecture of the system under attack, will have as result the increase of the pressure in a certain pipe.)

o   **Maintenance Commands:** the attacker uses commands designed for maintenance use.

In the following, taking as example the DNP3 SCADA protocol, we provide some examples of licit commands that be used for malicious objectives.

o   The command *Reset Link* re-synchronizes the communication between a Master and a PLC. It is useful when a PLC restarts, but if sent during a regular transmission, it could introduce an inconvenient delay in the network.

o   In the same way the functions *Reset User Process* and *Request Link Status* require an acknowledgement *ACK* from the PLC, which can easily flood a network if there are too many.

o   The function code *Write (0x02)* linked with the object *Current Time (0x50)* allows to control the Master command delivery. By manipulating this function, an attacker can control the time synchronization of the PLC and potentially isolate it from the others.

o   The functions code *Freeze and Clear (0x09)* and *Freeze and Clear no Ack (0x10)* store an object in a separate memory, and erase it from the on-time configuration of the PLC. With this command, an attacker forces a PLC, for example, to hide the evolution of the temperature in a power plant.

These examples are applicable to almost all the SCADA protocols such as IEC 60870-5 (which is under several aspects quite similar to DNP3).

Several can be the triggers of these attack scenarios; here we list two of them:

1.   **Direct Access:** the attacker is an insider (e.g. disgruntled operator), or in any case an actor that has physical access to the process/control networks. In that

case: (a) he inspects the network in search of PLCs/RTUs; (b) he guesses the best sequence of commands to be sent in order to create a certain damage; (c) he writes a software able to send SCADA protocol packets; (d) he sends those packets to the PLCs/RTUs.

2. **SCADA Virus:** As in the previous DOS attack scenarios, the attacker creates a malware able to send commands to the field devices. In that case, the malware, once it has reached the industrial process network will be able to substitute itself for the SCADA server, and to virtually take the control of the SCADA system. The infection triggers in this case could be the same presented in the case of the DOS worm. Nai et. al. demonstrated the feasibility of this kind of attack in [14]

- **SCADA System Data Poisoning:** as a direct result of the intrinsic vulnerabilities of the SCADA protocol, attackers having access to the process network can easy impersonate a set of PLCs and provide false information to the SCADA server. The effect of this attack has a significant chain effect. In fact, since the information provided by the PLCs to the Master is aggregated and provided to the operational databases, and then used by the diagnostic systems and by the high level control centers, a similar attack could drive the operators in a completely wrong direction, with potentially catastrophic effects. A possible implementation of that attack scenario could be the following:

  1. The attacker (or the malware written by the attacker), perform a DOS against a set of PLCs in order to block the data flow between them and the SCADA Master.
  2. The attacker (or the malware) impersonates the blocked PLCs
  3. The attacker (or the malware) provides false data to the Master

As in the previous case, in order to implement such an attack, the attacker needs an access to the process network, which can be physical, or obtained through a malware infection. This attack scenario, as well as the *OPC corruption scenario* presented in the next section, can be easily classified also as *state estimation attacks*, in the sense that their aim is to make the upper level control system fail in estimating the correct state of the field system.

- **Coordinated Worm Based SCADA Attack:** This attack scenario is based on the same concepts presented in the previous examples. To make it realistic, although the vulnerabilities related to the different SCADA protocols are quite similar, we assume in this scenario that the field network uses Modbus. Moreover in this scenario, the attacker wants to hit the power grid simultaneously in different points. In the following we provide the description of the attack:

  1. The attacker collects as much information as possible about the ICT network structure of the power grid he wants to attack. Key information is the set of public IP addresses of the systems that provide the interface between the internal network of each control station and the external corporate network of the

transmission system operators. This information will be used to improve the effectiveness of the attack by better identifying the targets. Nevertheless, the attack would work also without this kind of information.

2. As in the previous scenario, the attacker, after having reverse-engineered Slammer, selects from the obtained code only the infection engine.

3. The attacker builds a new function that forges Modbus packets containing the function code "write discrete output register" (which basically sends a command to a field device like a switch, or a digital instrument). The payload of this function will tell the PLC to write the specified value into all the output discrete registers available.

4. On the basis of the information gathered by the attacker in the previous phase, the value to be written in the register should be the one that, if written on a register that corresponds to a field device that controls the "node connection", causes its disconnection.

5. The new malicious code will have a delayed activation after the infection of the target machines: it will launch the malicious packets after a certain data, by checking the local clock. This will enable a coordinated attack by all copies of the malware.

6. The attacker merges together the infection engine of Slammer and the new code, obtaining a completely different virus for which there is no signature yet.

7. The attacker creates two versions of the malware: one will target the IP addresses retrieved during the first phase of the attack, and another will use a random address generator. In this way, also systems of which the attacker was unaware will possibly be infected.

8. The attacker releases the two versions of the malware "in the wild" (meaning in the corporate network for a targeted attack against a company – on the condition that the attacker has access to it -, or in the Internet, in a general attack against operators using that technology).

9. The malware will start to spread until reaching a target machine. Every time it reaches a new system, it starts to infect other systems in the neighborhood, and then silently puts itself in a dormant situation.

10. When the pre-defined data occurs, each piece of the malware resident in different machines or systems will wake-up and start to send the malicious Modbus packets against every possible IP address, starting from the ones in the same subnets, then proceeding with the ones in the nearest subnets and so on.

11. In a few minutes, entire lines of the grid will start to be disconnected by the PLCs executing the command received by the malware, and causing a coordinated loss of power cuts.

5.3   Process Network Weaknesses

The process network hosts the SCADA servers, the OPC servers (where used), the Builder servers (used to program the field devices) and the HMI. Compromising this level will enable the attacker to potentially take full control of one (or more) portions of the Power System. In what follows we describe some attack scenarios aiming at causing damages to the industrial installation.

- **OPC DOS:** the OPC servers (where used) act as a bridge between the SCADA server and the Control Network. A denial of service against them has the effect of completely separating the two networks, interrupting then command flow between Master and Slaves. It can be implemented in several ways:

  o   **Network DOS:** the attacker sends a huge amount of meaningless packets to the network cards of the OPC server, which will not be able to deliver in time the SCADA traffic. This scenario can be implemented in different ways: (a) the attacker has direct access to the process network, and is able to run a traffic generator. In order to accelerate the effects, it could use for example a UDP packet generator (as it is easier to generate a huge amount of traffic using UDP instead of TCP); (b) the attacker can use some malware which by infection is able to reach the process network and perform a DOS against the OPC server

  o   **Application Based DOS:** in this case the attacker might take advantage of one of the typical vulnerabilities of windows systems in order to take down the server.

- **OPC Corruption and Poisoning:** the OPC server is typically a MS-Windows machine, with the typical vulnerabilities of that kind of system. An attacker might be able to take advantage of those vulnerabilities and corrupt the OPC server. In that case, it would be able to:

  o   Send unauthorized commands to the PLCs;
  o   Send false data to the Master (poisoning the data provided to the operators);
  o   Interrupt the communication flow between Master and Slaves.

- **OPC Protocol Corruption:** the OPC communication protocol is far from being completely secure. Authentication and integrity mechanisms exist, but they are not always applied. For that reason an attacker (or a malware) having access to the process network, might be able to directly interfere with the communication channel between the SCADA master and the OPC server. In this way, an attacker can violate the integrity of the packets, modifying the command flow or poison the data flow. In both cases the net effect may be extremely dangerous. An attack scenario in that case might involve a DOS against the OPC server (to stop it from answering to Master requests) and impersonation (the attacker inject fake OPC traffic spoofing the identity of the OPC server). The effects of those attacks can, again involve data falsification and unauthorized command execution.

- **SCADA Server DOS:** A denial of service against the SCADA Master is extremely dangerous. This server controls directly the PLCs and more generally the process driving the industrial installation. If an attacker would be able to block it, the whole industrial system might run into a critical state. Moreover, the information flow between the process network and the higher level of the system (up to the operators and other decision makers) will be interrupted. As in the case of the OPC server, this malicious scenario can be generated either through a classical network

DoS (the attacker in that case needs to have direct access to the process network, or needs to use some malware able to reach that network), or by taking advantage of some software vulnerabilities.

- **SCADA Server Corruption:** the effects of a SCADA server corruption can be extremely negative. If an attacker can take control of this system, he will be able to perform many kinds of malicious operations: (a) unauthorized command execution, (b) data poisoning, (c) system halt, etc. Several studies (see for example "ICT Security Assessment of a Power Plant, a Case Study", Nai, Masera and Leszczyna, Second Annual International Conference on Critical Infrastructure Protection, 2008) showed how computer systems in industrial process networks have usually a low patching speed. This directly implies that the window of opportunity opened by the vulnerability of these systems in relation to new threats is always large enough to permit a well-determined attacker with sufficient resources to take advantage of it. In this scenario, we can assume that one of the installed software in the SCADA server would be vulnerable to one or more attacks (e.g. buffer overflow, format string attacks etc.) allowing the attacker to gain control of the system. The scenario, as usual, is based on the precondition that the attacker has access to the server, or to the network used by the server.

- **SCADA Server Data Flow Corruption:** the communication protocols used by the SCADA systems are usually not protected via authentication and integrity mechanisms. An attacker might be able to interfere with those data flows (the flows between the SCADA server and the HMI, or with the related databases and other servers). In these cases the possible damages can be caused in the following ways:

  o   An attacker can provide false information to the HMI, in order to hide some other malicious operation in act in the control network.
  o   An attacker can modify the content of the command flow, making the PLCs to execute unauthorized or dangerous operations.
  o   An attacker can modify the content of the data flow between the SCADA server and the databases, poisoning the information flow from the field to the operators and other decision makers.

The scenario can be easily implemented if the attacker has access to the process network (he can for example perform a DoS against the SCADA Server and then send in its name unauthorized commands or data). In addition, this scenario can be implemented by creating an ad-hoc virus, which, once reached the process network, performs the same kind of operations.

- **HMI Corruption:** the HMI provides the local interface to the operator. Its corruption can affect the operability of the system, but the impact would always be limited, since the operators will always be able to directly operate the SCADA server, bypassing in this way the HMI. The kind of attack scenarios against this system are basically the same described for the SCADA server.

5.4   Control Centre Network Attacks

The control centre network hosts normal PCs which might act as HMI, in order to enable the operators and the decision makers to access to the industrial installation (i.e. to access to the databases). Those systems are usually also connected, directly or indirectly, to the Internet. This implies that they are easily accessible to attackers. However, these PCs usually have stricter patching and security policies. However, virus infections, or other classical attacks, are always possible. Once an attacker is able to gain control of one of these systems, he will have to obtain the credential of one of the users authorized to access the remote system. This can be done in different ways (e.g. by using key loggers etc.). If in possession of the authorized credential, the attacker will then be able to perform a large number of malicious operations:

- Injection of malicious software in the remote process network
- Poisoning of the databases
- Infection of the diagnostic systems
- Network DoS against the exchange server switch (to block the traffic coming from the process network)
- Access to the process network
- Injection of malicious SCADA packets into the process network

5.5   Network Layer Attacks

Power Systems rely heavily on the underlying ICT network layer. Attacks against switches, routers, and networks might have serious impact on the efficiency and on the control functionalities of the power system. It is possible to classify those attacks in:

1. **Network Interference/Noise:** injection of ah-hoc crafted streams of packets aiming at creating noise on the network (e.g. Packet Flooding Attacks, Short Burst DOS and more sophisticated). The level of exposure of the different subnets of the Power System to this threat is quite different. The field networks are usually less exposed (but more susceptible), since they constitute the deeper and farthest from external interferences part of the network. The network devices interconnecting the different subnets are instead the more exposed. The potential effects of attacks depend on the local target: if the field devices are the target, the net effect will be the disconnection of a local portion of the network. On the other hand if the attack takes as target the interconnections between the different subnets, the impact might be more extended.

2. **Single Implementation Vulnerability Attacks:** they aim at exploiting a vulnerability peculiar of a particular model of network devices, due to implementation errors. Those vulnerabilities usually have as main results: to turn-off / slow down the network device, to modify the network device configuration. Depending on the type of vulnerability exploited, an attacker might be able to re-route packets, crash the network devices, and inject new ad-hoc crafted packets.

3. **Protocol Related Vulnerabilities:** aiming at taking advantages of some design/implementation weaknesses of the network protocols used. Power Systems employ other communication protocols, e.g. the TCP/IP suite is widely used. In the following a list of the possible classes of attacks related to TCP/IP is provided:

    o   TCP SYN attacks
    o   IP Spoofing
    o   Routing attacks (Routing Information Protocol (RIP) based)
    o   ICMP attacks
    o   DNS attacks

All these classes of attacks can be used as bricks to mount more complex scenarios for carrying out DOS, to inject fake packets, or to re-route the traffic.

As described in Section 3, the communication among different parts of the Power System WAN, when using communication lines provided by third parties (i.e. ISPs) relies on the use of MPLS. The Multi Protocol Label Switching provides a mechanism for routing the network traffic in a more efficient way, providing at the same time segregation functionalities. It is largely used by the ISP providers to guarantee high quality of service to the network traffic of some customers. The devices involved in communications using MPLS can be classified in two classes: the devices that are part of the MPLS Core Architecture, and the devices outside the core. If an attacker has access to devices outside the core, it might be successful in performing the following attacks:

- Rogue Path Switching
- Rogue Destination Switching
- Enumeration of Label Paths
- Enumeration of Targets
- Label Information Base Poisoning

All these attacks can be used in the specific case Power System to interfere with the legitimate control traffic. In particular, the last one can be used to perform an extensive Denial of Service. If an attacker has access to devices inside the MPLS core all the previous scenario remain valid but their impact assumes a higher magnitude. More details about MPLS and its vulnerabilities can be found in [24].

6   Countermeasures

In light of what presented in the previous section, it is evident that Power Systems need to be protected against potential cyberattacks. In this section we identified a set of security countermeasures for each class of vulnerabilities described in the previous section.

6.1   Communications Protocols Countermeasures

Communication protocols are the core of every ICT infrastructure. They are the means for providing distributed services, remote management services, data sharing etc. Unfortunately, as describe in the previous section, can be, and indeed are, used as target of attacks or as vehicle put under attack a third target. Several of the traditional ICT countermeasures involve the enforcement of the communication protocols. Taking as example the attacks presented in section 4, several of them would be seriously limited by introducing in the used protocols some "integrity, confidentiality and authentication" mechanisms. Unfortunately in the context of Power Systems and especially for process networks/SCADA systems, these mechanisms are not always easy to be deployed for several reasons:

- *Real-Time constraints*: the use of encryption mechanisms introduces delays in the communication channel; such delays, in strong real-time environments might not be well tolerated
- *Computational Constraints*: signature/verification operations are usually computationally demanding. Devices as PLCs traditionally have low power computation, making hardly feasible the use of traditional encryption schemas such us RSA.*Key management*: the management of the encryption keys (from the distribution to the revocation), and the use of Key Management Systems not trivial in a fully distributed infrastructure as the network of PLCs of an Energy Grid. Again here also the computational constraints play a relevant role.
- *Integration in the existing infrastructure*: the integration of these new mechanisms into the existing infrastructure is not trivial, implying systems stops, reconfigurations etc. impacting heavily on the economical aspects of the management of the Energy System.

In the following we present an overview of the different countermeasures related to the communication protocol vulnerabilities

6.1.1   TCP/IP Countermeasures

TCP/IP protocols are quite vulnerable to classic attacks, such as man-in-the-middle, replay etc. This is due to the intrinsic lack of authentication mechanisms embedded into the protocol itself. These vulnerabilities are obviously not acceptable in SCADA systems, which need to be secure. Luckily there exists a huge scientific and technical literature about the protection of TCP/IP flows from these vulnerabilities. These protection techniques are part of the encryption tunneling family. In other words, in order to protect a network flow, it is sufficient to insert it into an encryption tunnel between the sender and the receiver. In this way: (a) only the receiver will be able to understand the contents of the flow, (b) nobody will be able to modify the packets sent, and (c) nobody will be able to reuse packets (is the encrypted tunnel include also timestamp mechanisms).

In the case of a typical energy system architecture, as will be showed in the following section on Filtering, this kind of solution is usually applied in order to create secure channels between the PC of operators located in the intranet and the process network firewall, and between a remote site and the local intranet of a plant hosting a SCADA system.

These secure channels are also known as point-to-point (or Site-to-Site) Virtual Private Networks. They can be built adopting several techniques. IPv6 supports these mechanisms, but the same performance can be used adopting IPsec (an extension of IPv4). Alternatively a cheaper, but less efficient (in terms of performance) solution could be built creating a VPN based on SSL/TSL [26, 27] channels. For a full reference about the TCP/IP cryptographic based enforcing mechanisms, we point the reader to [28].

The use of secure mechanisms for protecting TCP/IP flows is a quite well established practice; however, as claimed in the introduction of this section, these mechanisms are conceived for general purpose ICT systems. In other words, while they are normally applied in the upper ICT layers of the Power Energy Infrastructure, they can be hardly used, as they are, in the lower layers (e.g. the SCADA network and the field network).

6.1.2   SCADA Protocol Countermeasures

In the last years the scientific community finally acknowledged the need for more secure SCADA protocols. Several variations of the classical SCADA protocols embedding security features have been recently proposed:

- Secure DNP3 [6]
- DNP3Sec [7]
- AGA12 [8]
- Secure Modbus [9]

As described in the introduction of this section, a not negligible problem is related to the key management system (KMS)

Some initiatives related to the KMS infrastructures exist in the Energy Field:

- Working Group 15 of Technical Committee 57 of the International Electrotechnical Commission (IEC) presented a standard for the cyber-security of the electric system [24]. The document do not indicates explicitly a KMS architecture, but defines some key design aspect related with it.
- The IEEE PESS Committee presented a draft for the "Trial Use Standard for Retrofit Cyber Security of Serial SCADA Links and IED Remote Access". The document describes some KMS functional requirements [25].

The use of these secure protocols would make harder the successful attack of SCADA systems, i.e. the lower e most vulnerable levels of the Power System. However, it has to be remarked that the integration of the new secure protocols into existing architectures is not painless and in several cases would not be possible at all, requiring a complete re-engineering of the process system. Challenges in this field might be identified in the development of light-weight secure mechanisms limiting as much as possible the impact of the additional cryptographic layer on the performances of the SCADA system.

6.2   Filtering Countermeasures

A quite common security arrangement for ICT based industrial systems is to isolate the different logical area by means for dedicated firewalls. This approach is not effective for the industrial part of power systems, since modern firewalls are not able at the moment to analyze in deep SCADA protocols.

Thus, from a theoretical point of view, a SCADA system should be a closed system controlled only by trusted elements. Unfortunately, as described in [10] for maintenance purposes the process network might need to be accessed from external elements (e.g. remote operators, vendor support services etc.). That means that the process network and the external network are in some way connected, i.e. there exists, even if limited, a communication channel between the SCADA system and a potentially hostile environment. A firewall, or a firewalling architecture, is then needed to create filtering between the external network and the process network. In the literature some guidelines for configuring firewall in SCADA environments have been released in the past, for example the *NISCC Good Practice Guide on Firewall Deployment for SCADA and Process Control Networks* [29] and the *NIST Guide to Industrial Control Systems (ICS) Security* [30]. Both documents provide overviews of the typical infrastructures of a Process Control Network, presenting a set of traditional firewall best practices adapted to those particular infrastructures.

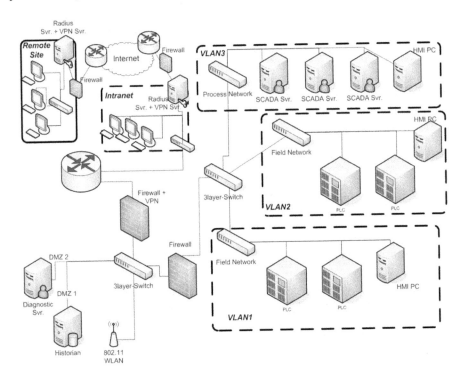

Fig. 8. Example of Firewalling Architecture

Figure 6 shows and example of firewalling architecture for Industrial Systems. As it is possible to see, operators hosted in a remote site can connect to the local Intranet through a site-to-site VPN, showing their credentials to a Radius authentication server. Moreover, also in order to access the plant networks (DMZs, process and field networks), the operators hosted in the Intranet, will need to authenticate themselves to the VPN-firewall, which will also permit the creation of a host-to site VPN connection between the PC of the operator and the firewall. In this way the access to the plant networks is indeed extremely hardened.

While modern firewalls are extremely advanced when analyzing traditional ICT traffic, they are not able to analyze in depth SCADA protocols. In this field Byres proposed a solution [11] aiming at enforcing the SCADA architecture by filtering at low level each single packet sent to a target PLC/RTU. This approach can provide a good low-level of protection; however, still an open issue remains related to more complex and subtle attacks. In order to better understand the problem, let's consider the following example: we have a system with a pipe in which flows high-pressure steam. Two valves (1 and 2) regulate the pressure. An attacker connected to the process network sends a DNP3 packet to the PLC controlling valve 1 in order to force its complete closure and a command to the PLC controlling valve 2 in order to maximize the incoming steam. It is evident how such commands, when considered locally, will result perfectly legitimate, while jointly will bring the system to a critical state. In order to mitigate this risk, it is necessary to provide the firewall with a detailed, explicit knowledge of the SCADA system under analysis (components, commands and critical states). The area of industrial processes, although extremely complex from an architectural point of view, has the advantage to be extremely structured and well defined. Nai et al [12], present an innovative filtering technique for industrial protocols based on the state analysis of the system being monitored. Since this approach focus its attention on the system behavior rather than on modeling the behavior of the possible attackers, this approach enables the detection of previously unknown attacks This kind of approach seems to promise good results in fighting against SCADA ICT attacks.

6.3   Monitoring

Firewalls are powerful security protections, but the way in which they work is quite invasive (they have to stay physically in the middle of a communication channel in order to be effective). In some places, for example in the field network, and in some particular situations, the delays introduced by the presence of firewalls, especially in real-time networks, might create unwanted problems. For that reason in the last ten years firewall architectures have been combined with Intrusion Detection Architectures (IDS).

IDS techniques have as main characteristic that of being passive, i.e. they analyze the behavior of networks or of PCs in a silent way, without excessively interfering with the environment under control.

Traditionally, IDS techniques can be classified in two families on the basis of the source of information to be analyzed:

- Network IDS: sensors analyzing network flows in search of attack proofs
- Host IDS: sensors installed on a target server, which analyze the operation it performs in search of malicious behaviors.

Unfortunately, host based IDS are quite invasive since they need to be hosted by the same system being monitored. For that reason, for SCADA systems, one should prefer to use NIDS (with obviously exceptions in particular cases).
IDS can be also classified according to the techniques used to identify the threats:

- Signature based IDS, which compare the information gathered with signatures which characterize the target attacks
- Anomaly based IDS, which compare the actual behavior of the system with a "behavioral template" in search of deviations from the normal profile, i.e. in search of anomalies.

Both techniques can be used in power systems, the first in order to quickly identify known attacks, limiting the risk of false positives; the second in order to identify unknown attacks.

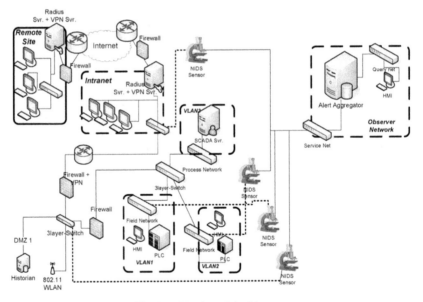

Fig. 9.   Monitored Architecture

Figure 7 "Monitored Architecture" shows a networked architecture for SCADA systems integrating Intrusion Detection Sensors.

Ideally, the Observer Network interconnects the different sub-networks of the system with the sensors and with the Alert Aggregator. Roughly speaking, that means to connect the switches, the sensors, and the database.

Modern Intrusion Detection systems are quite mature regarding the detection of traditional ICT threats and attacks; unfortunately, they are generally unable to analyze

SCADA protocols (e.g. Modbus, Profibus, DNP3 etc.). For that reason some attack profiles, properly crafted in order to take advantage of the vulnerabilities of those industrial communication protocols, cannot be easily detected. For example, if a malicious user, able in some way to have access to the process network, starts sending legitimate Modbus packets to a pool of slaves (i.e. PLCs) attempting to change the state of the system, a traditional IDS will not be able to detect it since the Modbus packets, (contained into the payload of a TCP packet) are just "meaningless payload" for that IDS.

Only recently some extensions, for example for Snort (a well known IDS), have been developed in order to allow IDSs to analyze single packets [31]. However, also in this case, more complex and articulated attacks, will not be understandable for those IDS, that cannot decipher that a chain of legitimate commands would drive the system into a critical state. In other words, not knowing what is the current state of the monitored system, and IDS will hardly able to understand if an apparently licit command can, indeed, be considered, under particular system conditions, dangerous. In order to solve this problem, Nai et al. have developed a State Based Intrusion Detection System for SCADA systems, which can identify, by analyzing chains of SCADA commands, whether a system is maliciously evolving from a safe state to a critical state. This approach permits to detect new and unknown attacks, since the attention is given not to the way in which the attack is conducted but to the state in which the system is evolving [13].

As described in the previous sections, Energy Systems are quite complex, distributed and composed by a huge amount of heterogeneous elements. Traditionally all these properties are also those considered the most undesirable from an IDS perspective. In fact, the more the system is huge and heterogeneous, the higher is generally the probability of making the IDS generate false positives and generally speaking "alert noise". In order to make IDSs effective in protecting this kind of systems, it is then needed a set of multilayer aggregation features to correlate events generated from different sources (e.g. correlating events coming from the process network of a remote transmission substation with events coming from the office network of a control center) in order to detect large scale complex attacks. This probably represents the next research challenge in this field.

6.4 Software Management and Update Mechanisms

Several attacks exploit known vulnerabilities and bugs of software. For this reason, software management and update procedures are necessary to avoid or recover from security problems. The proactive management of vulnerabilities and related patches aimed at reducing or preventing their exploitation. This management should be more effective, requiring less time and effort than recovering the system and responding after some exploitation has been performed.

Organizations should provide documentation providing the software patching and hardening policy for theirs systems. The policy should be reviewed every year in order to address new threats and discovered vulnerabilities. The policy has to be consistent, for example software patching cannot reinstall software removed for hardening the system, or change security setting, and so on.

A typical model of systematic software patching is based on a pattern cycling through four phases:

- Assessment and Inventory, aimed at identifying, classifying and assessing the software components of the system, possible security threats and vulnerabilities, and determining the most appropriate policy the organization can apply for software update and vulnerabilities discovery.
- Patch Identification, for identifying software updates available, understanding their relevancy and effectiveness, and determining the urgency of updates (i.e. response to security emergency or normal software update).
- Evaluation, Planning and Testing, aimed at i) deciding which patches are to be deployed in the operational environment, ii) planning when and how to perform software updates, and ensuring that the software update fulfills the system requirements, without compromising its business and operational aspects; and finally iii) testing the proposed patches in a realistic setting for verifying the potential negative effects onto the system.
- Development, aimed at actually carrying out the software updates in the operational environment, minimizing the impact on the system.

A rigorous qualification of the software used, as well as its security conformity certification (performed by third party certification laboratories and authorities) might also be considered a way for enforcing the security of the Power System. In the same way, the adoption of an Information Security Management System (ISMS) such as the standard ISO 21001, can help in adopting a systematic approach to the management of the cyber security of Energy Systems.

7   Conclusions

Power systems deployed over long distances and covering large areas are one of the most crucial infrastructures of our society. They are managed and operated by several companies that have to coordinate their policies and procedures, and can cross national borders and therefore deal with various authorities. In this context, Information and Communication Technologies (ICT) are the single most important enabling constituent: without them it would be impossible to the required control, communication, sensing, monitoring, protection and defense functions.

In this paper we presented and discussed how the cyber layer is normally implemented nowadays, with emphasis on the structure and interconnections between the different actors of the power infrastructure. Among them, the link between Transmission System Operators and Distribution System Operators has an obvious preeminence.

The central position of ICT is discussed in detail in the paper, together with the main consequence of this role: currently cyber vulnerabilities represent an extremely weak point that should be seriously taken into consideration by industry and authorities. The thorough discussion of the threats and the relative potential attacks clearly shows that the present situation demands an urgent and significant action.

The solutions to this condition of vulnerability extend over different fields: they are not only technical. The countermeasures discussed in Chapter 6 should be understood as a first, unavoidably partial, account of the actions that can be promptly taken by all interested stakeholders if they want to confront this issue.

However, it is evident that some of the countermeasures, mainly due to the interconnectedness of the power systems, can only be effective if implemented in a coordinated way by all the actors. The most critical cyber threats are those menacing the system as a whole, more than the single installation. For this reason, industry-wide actions, supported by adequate governmental policies, appear to be needed. Security in general, and cybersecurity in particular, should be taken as the joint responsibility of the stakeholders taken part in the power infrastructure.

References

[1] Sarma, J.D., Sarma, M., Overby, T.: Power System Analysis & Design. Thompson (2008)
[2] Grainger, J.J., Stevenson, W.D.: Power System Analysis. McGraw-Hill, New York
[3] Codice di trasmissione, dispacciamento, sviluppo e sicurezza della rete (04/01/10) – TERNA (Italian TSO)
[4] IEC International Electrotechnical Vocabulary - IEV number 191-21-03
[5] Definition and Classification of Power System Stability. IEEE Transactions on Power Systems 19(2) (May 2004)
[6] IEC International Electrotechnical Vocabulary - IEV number 191-12-01
[7] IEC International Electrotechnical Vocabulary - IEV number 191-02-06
[8] IEC International Electrotechnical Vocabulary - IEV number 603-05-02
[9] IEC International Electrotechnical Vocabulary - IEV number 191-02-05
[10] NERC Glossary of Terms Used in Reliability Standards
[11] Policy 3: Operational Security (19/03/09), from Operation Handbook – ENTSO-E
[12] http://www.tofinosecurity.com (Last access, June 1 2010)
[13] Fovino, I.N., Carcano, A., Masera, M., Trombetta, A., Delacheze-Murel, T.: Modbus/DNP3 State-based Intrusion Detection System. In: Proceedings of the 24th International Conference on Advanced Information Networking and Applications, Perth, Australia, April 20-23 (2010)
[14] Policy 1: Load – Frequency Control and Performance (19/03/09), from Operation Handbook – ENTSO-E
[15] Sivanagaraju, S., Sreenivasan, G.: Power System Operation and Control. Pearson
[16] Policy 6: Communication infrastructure v0.9 (03/053/069), from Operation Handbook – ENTSO-E
[17] Policy 7: Data Exchanges (03/05/06), from Operation Handbook – ENTSO-E
[18] Kirschen, D., Strbac, G.: Power System Economics. J. Wiley and sons (2004)
[19] Trasmission Code (16/08/08) – Swissgrid (Swiss TSO)
[20] UCTE Glossary v2.2 (20.07.04), from Operation Handbook – – ENTSO-E
[21] Secure DNP3,
    http://www.digitalbond.com/wiki/index.php/Secure_DNP3
    (last access June 1, 2010)
[22] Majdalawieh, M.: DNPSec: Distributed Network Protocol Version 3 (DNP3) Security Framework. In: Proceedings of ACSAC 2005 Tech-Blitz (2005)
[23] Cryptographic Protection of SCADA Communications, AGA Report N. 12

[24] Nai Fovino, I., Carcano, A., Masera, M.: Secure Modbus Protocol, a proof of concept. In: Proc. of the 3rd IFIP Int. Conf. on Critical Infrastructure Protection, Hanover, NH, USA (2009)

[25] Nai Fovino, I., Masera, M., Leszczyna, R.: ICT Security Assessment of a Power Plant, a Case Study. In: Proceeding of the 2nd Int. Conference on Critical Infrastructure Protection, Arlington, USA (March 2008)

[26] Carcano, A., Nai Fovino, I., Masera, M.: Modbus/DNP3 State-based Filtering System. In: Proceedings of the IEEE International Symposium on Industrial Electronics, Bari, Italy, July 4-7 (2010)

[27] Nai Fovino, I., Carcano, A., Masera, M., Trombetta, A.: Experimental Proof of Malware Attacks on SCADA Systems. In: Shenoi, S. (ed.) International Journal of Critical Infrastructure Protection, vol. 2(4), pp. 135–144. Elsevier (2009)

[28] Mohan Mathur, R., Varma, R.K.: Thyristor-based FACTS controllers for electrical transmission systems. IEEE Press Series on Power Engineering (2002)

[29] Philipson, L., Willis, H.L.: Understanding Electric Utilities and De-Regulation. M. Dekker, New York (1999)

[30] Murty, P.S.: Operation and Control in Power Systems. CRC Press,

[31] Miller, R.H., Malinowsky, J.H.: Power System Operation. Mc-Graw-Hill

[32] Rothwell, G., Gomez, T.: Electricity Economics, Regulation and Deregulation. IEEE, Wiley-Interscience (2003)

[33] Stoft, S.: Power System Economics, Designing Markets for Electricity. IEEE, Wiley-Interscience (2002)

[34] Ilic, M., Galliana, F., Fink, L.: Power Systems Restructuring, Engineering and Economic. Kluwer Academic Publishers (1998)

Sector-Specific Information Infrastructure Issues in the Oil, Gas, and Petrochemical Sector

Stig O. Johnsen[1], Andreas Aas[1], and Ying Qian[2]

[1] Norwegian University of Science and Technology and SINTEF
[2] Shanghai University
Stig.O.Johnsen@gmail.com

Abstract. In this chapter we have discussed vulnerabilities and mitigating actions to improve safety, security and continuity of the information and process infrastructure used in the oil, gas and petrochemical sector. An accident in the oil and gas industry can become a major disaster, and the suggested steps should help mitigate some of these hazards. This chapter consist of four parts, described in the following:

1. Background and Introduction – the Oil, Gas and Petrochemical Sector
2. Accidents, Threats and Resilience in the Oil, Gas and Petrochemical Sector
3. Risk Mitigation and Improvement of Resilience in the Sector
4. Conclusion and Suggestions for Further Exploration and Research

The introduction describes the general challenges to explore oil and gas reserves in difficult areas. The regulation philosophy and regulation strategy of the oil and gas sector is discussed. A description of process control systems (i.e. supervisory control and data acquisition - SCADA systems) and information and communication technology (ICT) is given. Challenges posed by integration of SCADA and ICT systems are discussed. Challenges raised by new technology used in the oilfields of the future are mentioned.

In the next section we are giving a theoretical description of how accidents are analysed and structured. Then we have described major accidents in the oil and gas sector. Next we have described specific vulnerabilities of integration of ICT and SCADA systems, based on an empirical survey. This is followed by a discussion of technical risks related to integration of ICT and SCADA systems.

In the third section we have described how the challenges and risks identified can be mitigated through rule compliance and risk management. We are suggesting a set of "best practices" to mitigate the risks, explored with success in Norway. Our perspective has been to include technology, organization and human factors in risk management. Due to the increased complexity and uncertainty in the sector we have suggested an improved risk assessment including resilience as a strategy. To expand the field of learning we are suggesting exploring successful recoveries in addition to accidents and incidents. Action research has been suggested as a method to improve safety based on a participatory and reflective discourse during risk assessment.

In the last section we have listed our conclusion and are suggesting areas of further exploration and research. The main conclusion is to design for resilience and safety and to establish common risk perceptions through scenario analysis.

J. Lopez et al. (Eds.): Critical Information Infrastructure Protection, LNCS 7130, pp. 235–279, 2012.
© Springer-Verlag Berlin Heidelberg 2012

1   Background and Introduction – The Oil, Gas and Petrochemical Sector

In this section we have given an introduction to the oil, gas and petrochemical sector and the general challenges when exploring oil and gas reserves in difficult areas. The regulation philosophy and regulation strategy of the oil and gas sector is discussed shortly. A description of process control systems and information and communication technology (ICT) is given. Differences and challenges posed by the increased integration of process control systems and ICT systems are discussed. Challenges raised by new technology used in the oilfields of the future are mentioned. In the next section, a description of accidents, threats and risks in the sector is given.

The oil, gas and petrochemical sector is of key importance in a modern society. The use and consumption of oil, gas and petrochemicals has been increasing in the last decades, see Figure-1. In the figure, "liquids" are crude oil, gasoline, heating oil, diesel, propane, biofuels, natural gas liquids and other relevant liquids.

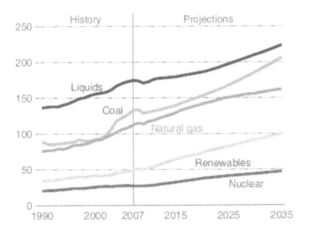

Fig. 1. Use of Energy in Quadrillion Btu by Type, from [1]

The reserves of oil and gas are limited; we are consuming more and more of existing and proven reserves. Thus the existing oil and gas reserves are being depleted at an increasing rate. The oil and gas reserves that are easily extracted have been prioritized in production so far. There is focus on improving ability to extract more oil and gas from existing fields, but this is technically and operationally challenging.

In the future more complex and challenging oil and gas fields are planned to be explored, see [2]; examples are fields under deep water, deep wells, fields having high pressure and/or high temperature, fields with difficult conditions in the well or fields in vulnerable areas such as in the arctic.

In addition, there is "unconventional oil and gas reserves" i.e. extra heavy oil, natural bitumen and oil shale deposits. The total amount of unconventional oil resources in the world considerably exceeds the amount of conventional oil reserves, but the resources are more difficult and more expensive to develop and produce.

There is a need to improve safety and to improve the ability to recover when the industry has to explore more challenging fields, even if the probabilities of accidents or incidents are very low. Due to the possibility of large consequences and the difficulties when we have to handle incidents at great depths, high pressure or in vulnerable areas, there must be an increased focus to mitigate or handle these low probability events. To avoid accidents, the variability or unwanted incidents must be dealt with in such a manner that the system recovers or goes to a safe state – i.e. the system should have an ability to "bounce back" or be resilient.

In this article we have considered accidents, threats and defences in the perspective of MTO (Man-Technology-Organization), i.e. a broad socio-technical approach. The MTO perspective explores knowledge from many different areas, such as psychology, human factors and organizational sciences. A further exploration of the MTO perspective is given in [3] and [4]. Safety is defined as: *"freedom from unacceptable risks"*, from [5]. Resilience is defined as *"the intrinsic ability of a system to adjust its functioning prior to or following changes and disturbances, so that it can sustain operations even after a major mishap or in the presence of continuous stress"*, from [6]. Risk has been defined as *"Combination of the probability of occurrences of harm and the severity of that harm"* see [5].

Oil and gas production is a complex and technology intensive process, and our intention is not to give a comprehensive description of that process. However, to discuss infrastructure issues in the oil and gas industry, we must give a simplified description of the key steps in order to define the scope of our exploration. Some of the key steps or processes in oil and gas production are:

1. Reach the oil and gas reservoirs through drilling and exploration – as an example done by specialized drilling platforms offshore.
2. Perform production/extraction from the reservoirs through pumping and treatment of the oil and gas – as for example done by production platforms offshore that are retrieving and processing oil and gas from several wells.
3. Distribute the oil and gas to process plant via different transportations means such as pipelines, ships, train or car.
4. Refine oil and gas at a process plant, usually a large complex installation onshore.
5. Distribute refined oil and gas products to the consumer through gas pipeline, trucks, railroads or other transportation.

These processes are further described and explored in [7].

Process control systems (PCS) and information and communication technology (ICT) are key supporting systems in all these processes. The PCS are used to manage the different steps in the oil and gas production, giving status from production, control the production and identify deviations. The ICT systems are integrated with the PCS systems. If unexpected conditions are identified in the production process, process shut down (PSD) or emergency shut down (ESD) can perform controlled halt of the production. These automated shut down systems are designed to bring the production system to a safe state. The control systems are further described in the following section. The collection of systems needed to control these processes, and PCS/ PSD/ ESD, are in this section called supervisory control and data acquisition systems (SCADA). The systems are integrated and distributed, and can be accessed by different user groups. Due to the large consequences of vulnerabilities or malfunctions in the SCADA systems, the systems must support both safety and security. Security has been seen in the context of health, safety and environment (HSE) since a key issue in production has been to avoid large-scale accidents. Thus we have focused on activities to maintain safety in the production process. In this section we have not focused on protection of critical infrastructure at the National level, as described in [93].

1.1   Regulation Philosophy

The regulatory regime of oil and gas production is usually described by existing health, safety, security and environment regulations, in addition to industry specific and national regulations.

There are differences in the general regulatory regimes across the industry. Specific regulations and practice related to security is also variable between different countries. In [8], the regimes and regulation in US were seen as a model for cyber security.

In the oil and gas industry, there has been a development from strict rule based regulatory regime, towards more industry self-regulation regime, however with a greater belief in using both approaches under one regulating context. There has been a development in regulatory strategy from prescriptive requirements, inspections and specific instructions towards more focus on goal setting, audits/verification and dialogue. This demands more knowledge based collaboration and trust between the different stakeholders. There has also been a trend towards more extensive use of common norms or international standards across borders.

However there are some issues that we would like to explore by looking at the differences between the regulation regime in US and Norway, where the regime in the US is more prescriptive based and the regime in Norway are more based on goal setting and self-regulation. The differences are explored in detail in [9].

The main differences between the regulation regime in US and Norway, related to oil and gas industry, are:

- In Norway, the regulations are mainly performance based and with supplementary prescriptive requirements. In U.S. the regulations are primary prescriptive.
- In Norway the regulations are risk-based while in the U.S. there are no general requirements to systematically identify and mitigate risks.
- In Norway there is a strong focus on having at least two barriers in operations of critical activities. Barriers is defined in [10], as a "measure which reduces the probability of realizing a hazard's potential for harm and which reduces its consequence". In the U.S. there are no requirements to systematically establish barriers.
- In Norway the operator has overall responsibility to ensure that all subcontractors comply with the regulatory health, safety end environment requirements. There is no similar requirement in the U.S. Responsibility is thus clearly placed on the operator in the Norwegian regime, while responsibility may be fragmented in the US.

The interaction between subcontractors and operator is challenging when we are working with safety and security. As an example we can mention an ICT security issue mentioned in [11]. The ZOTOB.E worm was introduced from a subcontractor, crossed organizational and regional boundaries and impacted several key systems of the oil and gas operator. As a result of this incident, the operator now mandates that all the subcontractors connecting to their network must test and certify that equipment has been checked for virus and worms. Thus, awareness, knowledge and mitigation of vulnerabilities in key systems such as the process control systems are an important issue for all involved, such as subcontractors.

Awareness, knowledge, acceptance and understanding of procedures, rules, regulations and risks are important factors when working with safety and security. The process used to establish regulation, rules and procedures are thus important, because it can be used to improve the quality, understanding and thus adherence of procedures. Involvement and participation in the process from key stakeholders such as authorities, industry, management and the workforce are important. This kind of collaboration has been a key factor in establishing regulations in Norway. "Forum for best practice" has been established as a common arena between authorities, management and the workforce. The result of this collaboration has been common best practices, and these are documented in "Working together for Safety" at www.samarbeidforsikkerhet.no.

In [8], an international survey of critical infrastructure in the oil and gas sector is documented and analysed. The survey is based on answers from around 60 key informants from the oil and gas sector. The survey suggested that the SCADA systems operated in a high threat environment, facing a range of risks. The increased interconnection and use of Internet, could lead to a wide range of risks. Increased regulation was seen as a way to improve security.

It seems that many SCADA systems seldom are properly secured. As an example, in [12], there is a description of an audit of the SCADA systems used in water and transport services. The result of the audit was that the operators are not properly securing their infrastructure control systems, and that they do not comply with relevant industry standards or suggestions such as [13] or [14]. The similar weaknesses have been identified in the ICT/SCADA systems used in the oil and gas industry on the Norwegian Continental Shelf as described in [15].

1.2   Control Systems Used in the Oil, Gas and Petrochemical Sector

The collection of systems needed to control these physical processes is here called supervisory control and data acquisition system (SCADA). Such a system consist of three main parts – 1) the control centre, 2) the communication link and 3) field equipment/sensors used to gather data. This is further described in [16] and below:

1. Control centre, consisting of:
   - Human-Machine Interface (HMI) – the software and hardware that enables the human operator to monitor the production process, modify control settings and manage the operations.
   - Data historian – a centralized database for logging all process data.
   - Connection to other networks, such as local area networks (LAN) used to connect to ICT systems or other support systems.
   - Safety Instrumented Systems (SIS) used to perform emergency shutdown, i.e. go to a safe state, and used to perform necessary actions such as deluge or shut down when there is fire or gas emissions.

2. Communication links, such as:
   - Radio link, network fibre, satellite or switched telephone lines.

3. Field equipment and sensors, such as:
   - Programmable Logic Controllers (PLC) – industrial computers used to perform the logic functions executed by hardware, Remote terminal Units (RTU) – a special purpose data acquisition and control unit to support remote stations, Intelligent Electronic Devices (IED) – a smart sensor or actuator used to acquire data, process data and communicate with other units. The use of sensors are increasing, both in the wells, in the pipelines and in machinery. Sensors in machinery can be used to monitor performance and improve maintenance.

In Figure-2, we have illustrated the general layout of a typical SCADA system.

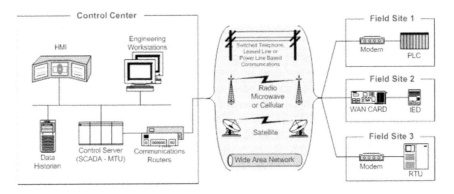

Fig. 2. General layout of SCADA system – from [16]

Based on interviews and expert discussions the increased networking and communication between these systems are usually implemented gradually. In addition there has been a gradual involvement of subcontractors in these systems. A risk assessment of these gradual changes is seldom done. This development indicates the need for increased focus on periodic risk assessment, information security and improved resilience to avoid unwanted incidents and accidents.

The term *"information security"* is defined as *"protecting information and information systems from unauthorized access, use, disclosure, disruption, modification, or destruction in order to provide: integrity, confidentiality and availability"*, from [17]. An incident in an ICT/SCADA system is understood as an incident that could imply loss of availability, loss of integrity or loss of confidentiality related to the ICT or SCADA systems in production systems and thus influencing the production process (leading to a halt or deviation) or leading to an unwanted HSSE (Health, Safety, Security, or Environment) incident or accident.

Due to differences in technology and standards, the technical systems used in operations can be divided into three main architectures; the ICT infrastructure, the process control systems (PCS) and the safety-instrumented systems (SIS), Figure-3.

The ICT solutions consists of network, supporting systems used in the production such as SAP (Systems, Applications and Products in Data Processing) i.e. an enterprise resource planning system, maintenance systems, infrastructure such as telephone support systems, radar and closed-circuit television (CCTV).

Process control systems (PCS) are used during production and include sensors and process shut down systems (PSD). The safety-instrumented systems (SIS) are used during emergency shutdowns (ESD) and to prevent fire & gas emissions (F&G). The PCS and SIS systems together are usually called safety and automation systems (SAS) or SCADA system. The systems are connected through data networks and usually have power supplies with UPS (Uninterruptible Power Supply).

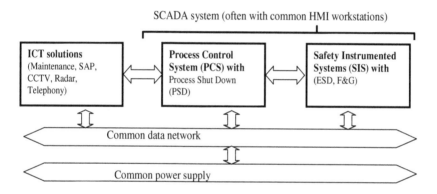

Fig. 3. SCADA system with common components

We have performed a local survey of existing SCADA and ICT systems used in the oil and gas industry, documented in the next section. We found that data networks and power supply often were shared between ICT, PCS and SIS systems. Often PCS and SIS shared the same HMI (Human Machine Interface) through the workstations. When PCS and SIS were from the same supplier, the systems were more tightly integrated and had more common elements. All these shared and common elements are increasing the risks of common cause failures.

1.3   Comparison of ICT and SCADA Systems

SCADA and ICT systems are used to manage oil and gas production. The integration between SCADA and ICT systems are increasing, and ICT technology are more used in the SCADA systems. In this section we have compared the ICT and SCADA systems based on organizational, knowledge and technical issues. In Table-1, we have listed some of the organizational challenges, in Table-2 we have listed factors related to human factors and in Table-3 we have listed technical differences.

Table 1. Organizational differences between SCADA and ICT systems

Organizational issues	SCADA	ICT systems
Responsibility/ Knowledge	Local. Special solutions are often not well documented and rely on key personnel expertise.	Centrally managed and standardized.
Outsourcing	Rarely used – Low experience and knowledge in the general market.	Often used – High experience and knowledge in the general market.
Risk Management	Explicit safety risk and hazard analysis are performed. Emergency Shutdown System (ESD) is essential. Information security has seldom been an issue.	Safety is rarely an issue. Shutdown is not critical. Contingency plans exist for business critical systems. Information security is an issue in many systems.
Cooperation	SCADA and ICT are organized in different organizational silos and have different meeting arenas. Cooperation between SCADA and ICT departments is not well established.	
Changes	Changes in organization, guidelines or processes may be a challenge, due to differences in organization, terminology, and basic knowledge,	

The key issues related to differences in organization and knowledge seems to be structural differences impacting both knowledge sharing and ability to establish organizational collaboration. There are basic differences in standards and knowledge that can lead to misunderstandings, wrong perceptions, poor communication, and mistakes that could escalate to an incident. In addition, collaboration, communication and knowledge sharing must be done different due to the locally managed SCADA systems vs. a centrally managed ICT system.

Due to these structural differences it may be a challenge to establish cooperation between the SCADA and ICT departments. These differences and challenges should not be underestimated. Key mitigation factors related to these challenges could be to focus on increased training, increased awareness, cooperation and as well as the establishment of common goals and an understanding of common risks between the relevant stakeholders.

Table 2. Differences in knowledge between SCADA and ICT environments

Knowledge	SCADA	ICT systems
Widely used technical standards related to safety and security	IEC 61508 *Functional safety of electrical/ electronic/ programm-able electronic safety-related systems*, [18]. IEC 62443 *Security for industrial process measurement and control, [19].* ANSI/ISA-99.02.01 *- Security for Industrial Automation and Control System, [20].*	*ISO/IEC 27001 Information Technology -Security Tech-niques - Information Securi-ty Management Systems - Requirements, [13].* *ISO/IEC 27002 Information Technology - Code of Prac-tice for Information Security Management, [14]*
ICT threats and vulnera-bilities	Low	Moderate to high
ICT skills	Low	Moderate to high
Human Factors	Using standards such as ISO 11064, [21] and EEMUA 191, [22].	ISO 9241 Ergonomics of Human System Interaction, [23]
Production and real-time issues	High	Low
Risk Impact	Loss of control. Loss of produc-tion. Loss of Life.	Loss of data. Loss of reve-nue

The technical differences when integrating SCADA systems and ICT systems are well known; some of the key factors are documented in Table-3.

These technical differences imply that one of the key challenges in integrating SCADA systems and ICT systems are the complexities of the systems to be integrated – thus the integration effort should not be underestimated. A checklist based on *ISO/IEC 27001* [13] named "Information Security Baseline Requirements for Process Control, Safety, and Support ICT Systems", has been developed by the Norwegian Oil Industry Association (OLF) to help identify key challenges when integrating ICT and SCADA systems, see [24].

In addition, the SCADA systems should be certified to be able to be integrated with ICT systems. Testing should be done to ensure resilience against DoS (Denial of Service) attacks and protection from viruses, worms and other malicious code. New threats and vulnerabilities due to increased integration must be identified. A hazard analysis such as HAZOP (Hazard and Operability Study), as described in [38], should be performed. The risk should be developed in close collaboration between management, ICT personnel, personnel from (SCADA) operations, and human factors experts to ensure common risk perceptions across the different organizational silos.

Table 3. Technical differences between SCADA and ICT system

Technical issues	SCADA.	ICT systems
Architecture	Individually/local design. Complex.	Usually standardized. Centrally managed.
Lifecycle	5-25 years	3-5 years
Change	Seldom, local, and informal. Use of work orders is infrequent.	Usually frequent. Centrally managed.
Information Security (IS) focus areas	Most important is the availability of the systems, (key processes must be managed in real-time) followed by integrity of the data. Confidentiality is usually ensured by physical means.	Confidentiality and integrity are important. Availability focuses on system up time. Response-times are typically measured in seconds and delays of 10-20 seconds are generally not business critical.
Antivirus	Difficult to deploy. Manually updated. Local specialties.	Standardized. Centrally managed.
Patches	Long delays, complex testing, and certification from vendor.	Standardized. Centrally managed.
Automated Tools	Limited. Used carefully. Local use.	Widely used. Centrally managed.
Testing of integration	Systematic testing of integration between SCADA and ICT system is not always done. At a SCADA facility - 16% to 34% of SCADA components broke down when exposed to a high load of ICT traffic, see [25] Luders (2006).	

1.4 New Technology - Integrated Operations and the Oilfields of the Future

The exploration of SCADA and ICT systems is changing and creates the need for improved collaboration. One example of increased exploration of new technology is the implementation of integrated operations (IO) in the oil and gas industry on the Norwegian Continental shelf. Integrated operations (IO) are a major initiative to increase oil recovery, reduce production cost and increase safety. The benefits of IO are estimated to be in the order of 25 000 Mill. USD from 2005 to 2015, see [26]. In a white paper [27], integrated operations were defined as: *"use of Information and Communication Technology (ICT) to change work processes, to improve decisions, to enable remote operations of equipment and processes and to move functions and people onshore."* Two key issues enabling the exploration of new technology have been the implementation of high capacity fibre networking between the oil and gas installations in addition to strong collaboration between management, workforce and authorities regarding implementation of new technology.

The implementation of IO is a large scale change process; on the technical side integrating ICT and SCADA systems, sharing real time production data. On the organizational side the implementation of IO is leading to changes and implementation of new work processes onshore and offshore. One key issue is the consequences of moving parts of the operations to virtual organizations, e.g. to a geographical distributed network where the stakeholders are residing in different organizations but interconnected by ICT.

The technologies used to manage production are changing from proprietary stand-alone systems to standardized PC-based ICT systems integrated in networks, which may be connected to the Internet. The standardization and increased networking between the production systems, SCADA systems, and the general ICT infrastructure leads to tighter couplings and higher complexity; and this may increase the possibilities of unwanted incidents, as described in the normal accident scenario in [28]. The costs of production stops on the Norwegian Continental Shelf vary greatly, but a one day halt of a production platform could lead to losses of 2 to 3 Million USD, see [29].

The operating organization is changing; IO enables better utilization of expertise independent of geographical location, leading to more interaction between different professionals placed at different sites. Several tasks in operations and maintenance have been outsourced and this trend is likely to increase. The increased connectivity is illustrated in Figure 4.

Stakeholders are the Central Control Room (CCR) offshore, the operators' onshore operation centre, the vendor's onshore operation centre and external experts. All these stakeholders are influencing safety and security in IO.

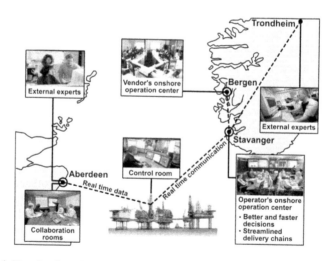

Fig. 4. Key distributed stakeholders involved in integrated operations- from [26]

The increased connectivity, geographical distances and outsourcing leads to a network of stakeholders, which by accident, misunderstanding or purpose can inflict unforeseen incidents or accidents causing economic loss; and in the worst case, loss of lives. *In one example, maintenance of the process control system was outsourced.*

The supplier wanted to test a change from onshore. By accident, the test was performed in production and a pump was halted. The incident was discovered by the offshore control room operator, which managed to start the pump again, and avoided an incident.

As described, we are moving from teams close to the operational environment i.e. close to people offshore; to remote operations when IO is implemented. In remote operations more of the team is isolated from the operations i.e. other people offshore, environment such as weather (storm or calm), sound (does the sound of the mechanical equipment indicate need for maintenance) or smell (such as the smell of leaking gas). This is a challenge when operational knowledge and situational awareness must be shared to improve operations and avoid incidents or accidents.

The main benefits of IO so far, have been improved recovery of oil and gas, and improved planning of tasks offshore.   The impact on maintenance and general organization of operations has not been significant so far – due to the early stages of implementation and due to organizational challenges between management and workforce. It is assumed that IO may improve maintenance significantly by exploring sensors to signal needed maintenance "just-in-time" where there is need. In addition, the implementation of IO is going to impact the onshore organization in many ways due to improved need for collaboration and new work processes.

2   Accidents, Threats and Resilience in the Oil, Gas and Petrochemical Sector

In this section we are starting with a theoretical description of how accidents are analysed and structured via different accident models. Then we have listed some major accidents in the oil and gas sector and key vulnerabilities. Next, we have described more specific vulnerabilities related to the integration of ICT and SCADA systems. This is followed by a risk assessment describing key risks related to the integration of ICT and SCADA systems. Lastly we have suggested a proactive investment in incident response capability. In the following next section we are describing how these risks can be mitigated through rule-compliance and risk management, exploring resilience and action research in the hazard analysis.

2.1   Accident Models and Accident Avoidance

In this section we are considering both accidents and accident avoidance by means of positive recoveries. Different accident models help us to get insight into the mechanisms behind accidents and incidents. The models may suggest causal chains, root causes, and barriers to reduce probability of incident or consequences of incidents. The underlying causes behind positive recoveries (i.e. accident avoidance) can also be part of such models.

There are mainly three kinds of models, described in [6]:

- *Sequential models*, assuming simple linear dependences in accidents, explaining accidents as malfunctions or failures, using models such as fault trees.
- *Epidemiological models*, assuming more complex linear dependencies in accidents, explaining accidents as unsafe acts in combination with weak defences. Using

barrier models, accidents are caused by missing barriers or "holes" in barriers. In this context resilience can be discussed based on improvement of barriers or better management of barriers by using proactive indicators to signal the status of a barrier. Examples of these models can be found in [30] and [31].

- *Systemic models,* assuming non-linear dependencies, explaining accidents as a result of complexity and tight couplings or performance variability. Examples of a systemic model based on complexity and tight couplings are described in [28]. When interactions are complex and couplings are tight, it is proposed in [28] that the outcome is a normal accident. An alternative point of view is mentioned in [32] and [33], describing complex organizations with tight couplings and few accidents as High Reliability Organizations (HRO). It is proposed to explore resilience and HRO in this context as a mechanism to avoid normal accidents.

When safety is explored, the positive ability to avoid accidents and recover should also be analysed and modelled. Thus we have explored models and theories that have been used to describe positive characteristics of organizations and complex systems – such as resilience, safety culture and high reliable organizations (HRO):

- Resilience is described in [6]. We have suggested exploring resilient principles, enabling us to foresee and avoid incidents, but also to increase resilience in general i.e. to be able to recover from something bad happening or reducing the consequences.
- The concept of safety culture seems useful to explain accidents and accident avoidance. In [30], it is argued that safety culture could explain some of the differences in safety in airlines. The probability of becoming involved in an airline accident varies by a factor of 42 across the world air carriers, regardless of the substantial standardization of technology, organization and human competence in the airline industry. There are many different definitions and descriptions of safety culture, see [34]. There is a disagreement on the possibility of improving or changing culture. We have focused on the ability to improve safety by exploring safety culture as an element during change, helping to identify areas of concern. We have based our approach on methods used in the oil and gas sector as described in [35].
- High Reliability Organization (HRO) is described in [32], [33] and [36]. The description of HRO is an important source of positive and resilient properties that should be explored when trying to build positive ability to avoid accidents and reduce the consequences of accidents.

2.2   General Incidents and Accidents in the Oil, Gas and Petrochemical Sector

In this section we have listed examples of some major accidents in the oil and gas industry from 1980. We have done this to show possible consequences of accidents in the oil, gas and petrochemical sector. The accidents have some relation to missing control or missing management of the SCADA systems. The areas selected are:

- Offshore drilling – i.e. "blowout" on drilling rigs, on production platforms, accident in risers and pipelines and process accidents.
- Process plants – i.e. fire or explosion during process treatment of oil and gas.

- Transport – i.e. in this case ruptures and explosions related to pipelines. (Pipelines are usually conveying flammable or explosive material, such as natural gas or oil and pose special safety concerns.)

Incidents and accidents related to vessel collisions or structural failures have not been listed. In [38] there is a discussion of the chemical process industry and their approach to safety – and discussion of safety issues related to more major accidents such as in Bhopal, see [39] for a further exploration. More areas could have been included such as transhipment terminals or Liquefied Natural Gas (LNG) facilities, but due to limitation of scope, these areas are not included.

OFFSHORE DRILLING

1988 – The Piper Alpha platform exploded and sank while drilling in the North Sea in a field operated by Occidental Petroleum, killing 167 workers. The handover between shifts did not identify that a backup pump was under maintenance and could not be used. However, the backup pump was used due to a failure in the operational pump, and started leaking gas, leading to an explosion and fire. The operator had inadequate maintenance and safety procedures and when the control room was destroyed, no (backup) emergency control room was available. Poor situational awareness and poor emergency routines made the nearby connected platforms Tartan and Claymore continue to pump gas and oil to the burning Piper Alpha platform until its pipeline ruptured, and increased the consequences of the accident, see [40]. Among several issues raised after the accident, it was also concluded that it was a conflict of interest to have both production and safety overseen by the same regulatory agency.

2010 – The Deepwater Horizon blowout. On 20 April 2010, while drilling the Macondo well, an explosion on the rig caused by a blowout killed 11 crewmen. Deepwater Horizon sank on 22 April 2010, leaving the well gushing at the sea floor and causing the largest offshore oil spill in United States history, see [41]. There were eight key primary issues identified by BP in their accident report, see [42], indicating that best practices were not followed, human errors were made, warning signs were overlooked on the rig and there may have been some failure of equipment. Causal analysis to identify root causes has not yet been performed. The accident seems to be based on a complex set of factors including technical failures, organizational shortcomings and human factors. Causal analyses of the accident is on going at the present time, and further reports are going to be published in late 2010, 2011 and 2012.

PROCESS PLANTS

1998 – Esso Longford gas explosion. On 25 September 1998, an explosion took place at the Esso natural gas plant at Longford in Australia, killing two workers and injuring eight people. Gas supplies to the state of Victoria were severely affected for two weeks. Some of the causes of the accident were that the Longford plant had excessive alarm and warning systems. Too many alarms had caused workers to become desensitized to possible hazardous occurrences. In addition, the relocation of plant engineers to Melbourne had reduced the quality of supervision at the plant, and situational awareness, see [43]. The company had neglected to commission a HAZOP

(HAZard and OPerability) analysis of the heat exchange system, which would have highlighted the risk of tank rupture caused by sudden temperature change, see [44].

2003 – Davis-Besse nuclear power plant worm incident. The Nuclear Regulatory Commission confirmed that in January 2003, the Microsoft SQL Server worm known as Slammer infected a private computer network at the idled Davis-Besse nuclear power plant in Oak harbour, Ohio, disabling a safety monitoring system for nearly five hours. The plant's process computer failed, and it took about six hours for it to become available again. Slammer reportedly also affected communications on the control networks of at least five other utilities by propagating so quickly that control system traffic was blocked, see [45]. This incident is highly relevant to process plants in the oil and gas industry, since the degree of Internet connectivity is increasing in the oil and gas industry.

2005 – BP Texas City Refinery explosion. In March 2005, BP's Texas City, Texas refinery, one of its largest refineries, exploded causing 15 deaths, injuring 180 people. A large column filled with hydrocarbon overflowed to form a vapour cloud, which was ignited by a pickup truck when it was started. The explosion caused all the casualties and substantial damage to the rest of the plant. There was no lagging or leading indicators related to process upsets and fires on the area – key performance indicators did not indicate possibility of major process upset. The incident came as the culmination of a series of less serious accidents at the refinery, and the engineering problems were not addressed. Alarms and signals from the SCADA systems were not explored, and there was poor safety culture, see [46].

2005 – The Zotob Worm impacting production in oil and gas and manufacturing. The worm attacked Statoil, a major Norwegian oil and gas company. 157 PCs were infected; many of these were located on offshore networks. The probable cause of the attack was a portable PC that had been connected to the network by a third party supplier. One of the challenges facing the production company was poor understanding of the security consequences on safety critical production issues. The ICT staff had to explain the consequences at some length before suitable and adequate mitigating actions were taken - in one case patching and restarting PCs used in safety critical operations. Fortunately no accidents happened as a consequence of the infected systems.

In other industries, Zotob knocked 13 of DaimlerChrysler's U.S. automobile manufacturing plants offline for almost an hour; stranding workers as infected Microsoft Windows systems were patched. Symptoms include the repeated shutdown and rebooting of a computer. Zotob and its variations caused computer outages at heavy-equipment maker Caterpillar Inc., aircraft-maker Boeing, and several large U.S. news organizations. See [11] and [16].

PIPELINES

1982 – Explosion in the trans-Siberian Pipeline in USSR (Targeted attack). One of the largest non-nuclear explosions in history occurred along the Trans-Siberian Pipeline in the former Soviet Union. It has been alleged that the explosion was the result of CIA sabotage and hacking of the SCADA control systems of the Pipeline. This is an example of a planned attack, which can be coordinated against key infrastructure, see [47]; however this example may be a hoax. Reliable and confirmed information is difficult to get in these circumstances.

A targeted attack was discussed in 2009. Between 2009 and 2010 the Stuxnet computer worm created a great deal of interest, since it also seemed to be an example of a targeted attack. Stuxnet was designed to take advantage of a number of vulnerabilities in the Windows operating system and Siemens SIMATIC WinCC, PCS7 and S7 product lines. Stuxnet was designed to target industrial systems that use Siemens PLCs with the apparent objective of sabotaging industrial processes, see [48]. At present we do not know the goal of the Stuxnet attack or the consequences. It has been suggested that process equipment in the nuclear industry in Iran was the target, but this is difficult to confirm, see [94]. However, these kind of targeted attacks should be a part of the risk management in the oil and gas industry, especially related to operation and protection of SCADA and ICT systems.

1999 – June 10, a pipeline rupture in Bellingham, Washington led to the release of 277,200 gallons of gasoline. The gasoline was ignited; causing an explosion that caused 3 deaths, 8 injuries, and extensive property damage. The pipeline failure was exacerbated by control systems not able to perform control and monitoring functions. Immediately prior to and during the incident, the SCADA system exhibited poor performance that inhibited the pipeline controllers from seeing and reacting to the development of an abnormal pipeline operation. One recommendation from the National Transportation Safety Board, report issued October 2002, [49], was to utilize an off-line development, testing and certification of changes to the SCADA system.

2005 – Safety Study – Supervisory Control and Data Acquisition in Liquid Pipelines.
In 2005, the National Transportation Safety Board (NTSB) examined 13 pipeline mishaps involving various liquids from 1992 to 2004. They found that "*in ten of these accidents, some aspect of the SCADA system contributed to the severity of the accident.*" In many cases, the problems were aggravated when workers monitoring the systems failed to quickly recognize and respond to leaks. Key issues in the report were related to Human Factors aspects of the SCADA systems, such as: leak detection systems, display graphics, alarm management, controller training and controller fatigue, see [50].

2008 – Utility was not able to send gas through its pipelines for four hours. A natural gas utility hired an ICT consulting organization to conduct penetration testing on its ICT network. The consultants carelessly ventured into a part of the network that was directly connected to the SCADA system. The penetration test locked up the SCADA system and the utility was not able to send gas through pipelines for four hours, [16].

2009 – Tampering with SCADA systems controlling pipelines connecting company derricks to the shore. In [8] there is an example of an ICT-consultant that was tampering with the SCADA systems after a dispute with the firm about future employment and payment. He tried to interfere with the SCADA system used to control leaks and pressure in the pipelines connecting company derricks to the shore.

2.3   Vulnerabilities of Integrated ICT and SCADA Systems

We have performed a survey of the integrated SCADA and ICT systems used offshore, on 46 different installations on the Norwegian Continental Shelf. A short version of this survey is presented in [51]. A structured questionnaire was distributed to the installations and was mostly completed by local operators in close collaboration with the suppliers of the SCADA systems.

The survey was performed among many different international companies, but was focused on installations in one country. However, the results seem applicable to other countries, since the key issues have been identified in other relevant publications, such as [16].

All 46 questionnaires were completed and returned. However, only a qualitative assessment of the results can be provided because "Yes"/"No" answers were rarely given; in most cases, the respondents provided comments along with qualifying statements. Additional information was solicited from the respondents after the survey to clarify issues during analyses. In retrospect, the questionnaire and terminology could have been more precise.

However, the survey and the subsequent discussions yielded several key results:

- *Possibility of common failures in the network used to control production and emergency response:* SCADA systems and safety instrumented systems (SIS) often had common power supplies, operator stations and network components, which significantly increased the probability of common failures. Furthermore, systems from the same vendor were closely related and had many common components. While no critical failures of SIS have been reported in the oil and gas industry, from the Industrial Security Incident Database (ISID) [16], stress tests have uncovered vulnerabilities that can influence SIS operation, i.e. the SIS systems may have a problem to go to a safe state. The identified problems with the SIS have been prioritized for mitigation by vendors, but there may be vulnerabilities yet not identified making it difficult to go to a safe state.
- *Lack of testing or certification of interconnection between SCADA and ICT systems:* Poor ability to handle ICT network loads in SCADA systems has been identified as a possible vulnerability in operations, see [25]. The SCADA systems were not certified as being resistant to large volumes of ICT network traffic or denial of service (DoS) attacks. At seventeen installations, a limited surveillance and testing of network traffic was conducted. A certification process is in development. Industry collaboration, such as The ISA Security Compliance Institute, manages the ISASecure™ program, which recognizes and promotes cyber-secure products and practices for industrial automation suppliers and operational sites, see [87]. Proprietary certification solutions have also been established, such as Achilles from Wurldtech Security.
- *Poor risk analysis and risk awareness:* Only five of the 46 installations had performed risk analyses related to the integration of ICT and SCADA systems. ICT professionals and SCADA professionals collaborated on risk analysis efforts at only eight of the 46 installations. ICT and SCADA professionals used different standards and procedures to assess risk. In particular, ICT professionals employed security standards such as [14] while SCADA professionals used safety standards such as [18].

- *Absence of systematic knowledge sharing and awareness training:* Information about undesirable ICT/SCADA incidents had not been shared among the relevant stakeholders. Two installations had no procedures for reporting ICT/SCADA incidents. One organization used three different reporting systems. Systematic awareness training related to ICT security and SCADA security had not been performed.
- *Poor scenario training and emergency preparedness:* A set of undesirable incidents that could be explored as the basis for emergency training had not been identified; examples could be loss of communication to critical systems or loss of telecommunication facilities. Emergency preparedness plans to handle ICT/SCADA infrastructure failures had not been developed nor had scenario-based training been performed.
- *Lack of consistent safety/security guidelines:* Three installations did not apply safety and/or security guidelines of ICT/SCADA systems. In twenty cases, various guidelines were referenced; however, we were unable to find even one concise guideline that contained all the relevant material. A consistent safety/security guideline of SCADA/ICT systems was missing. This is also a key issue on the national level as described in [93].
- *Poor standardization:* Standardization across companies was lacking and many different solutions had been established within the same company, see [51].This created a more demanding operational environment because remote support was more complex. At the same time, different solutions can enhance resilience in the industry because the same vulnerability is not necessarily present in all the solutions. However, most of the installations used Windows platforms with Ethernet (TCP/IP) for communications.
- *Lack of barriers in the network between SCADA and SIS:* Few barriers existed between SCADA systems and SIS such as firewalls or network segmentation. Furthermore, network design "best practices", as suggested in ANSI/ISA-99.02.01 (2009), was not employed. Poor network design can affect resilience. Malfunctions and DoS attacks can impact SCADA systems and SIS.
- *Inadequate review of firewall logs:* In general, firewall logs were not reviewed and analysed. There were several cases where logs were not inspected due to high workload or other factors, see [51].
- *Inadequate deployment of patches to mitigate vulnerabilities:* In general, the ICT infrastructure and applications were centrally administered and patched. However, the SCADA systems were administered and patched locally. Patches should be deployed immediately after they are made available to address vulnerabilities, to protect against attacks and to enhance resilience. The deployment of patches in SCADA systems varied widely: some SCADA systems were patched systematically while some systems were not patched at all.

The key issues above indicate a complex environment, needing collaboration between different organizational silos such as telecommunication, process and ICT to create understanding, collaboration and ability to prioritize critical issues. There are many possibilities to create unwanted incidents by normal variability, errors or attacks. Some of the key issues that are identified are interrelated, i.e. lack of safety/security guidelines based on "best practice" may lead to poor risk analysis. Poor awareness of risks can lead to poor design of systems. In addition, poor awareness of existing and new risks can lead to vulnerabilities that can be exploited or uncovered later as use of the systems are changing. Due to poor risk analysis and poor risk awareness, scenario training and emergency preparedness can be missing – leading to poor management of unwanted incidents.

These findings should be mitigated by several actions – our suggestions are to establish a learning and improvement loop, as listed in the following:

1. Perform risk analysis among stakeholders in all the organizational silos – and identify key proactive indicators to be able to "be on top" of the development. At the same time, improve knowledge and awareness of vulnerabilities and unwanted incidents related to ICT/SCADA systems among the relevant stakeholders though the reporting and sharing of incidents.
2. Discuss and prioritize mitigating actions to reduce risks and avoid incidents.
3. Establish safety and security guidelines and rules that are going to be followed in the future.
4. Measure safety results trough the indicators. Improve awareness and understanding of safety through the discussion of proactive indicators. Share unwanted incidents between key stakeholders, in order to improve risk analysis, knowledge and awareness.

Based on these key vulnerabilities, we have tried to establish a simple risk matrix, documenting some of the key risks in SCADA/ICT systems used in oil and gas production and to be able to reflect on risks, awareness and mitigating actions.

A risk matrix is commonly used to discuss risks and prioritize mitigating actions. We have used the risk matrix as an example on how we should prioritize risks and identify mitigating actions as shown in Figure-5. At the end of this section, several incidents have been analysed and placed in the risk matrix to help us focus on the major risks.

- Ideally all risks should have low consequences and low probability, and be in the quadrant marked ①.
- In the real world however, some of the risks will have high probability and high consequence and be in the quadrant marked ②. These risks are not acceptable to the organizations, and by implementing security controls and measures the organization will seek to reduce the probability or the consequence – or even better; both, i.e. move the risk in the direction of the arrow, into the acceptable zone.
- Some risks have a high probability of happening, but do not necessarily cause any serious harm ③. For these risks security measures should be implemented based on cost/benefit-analysis.
- In the other end of the matrix, we find the unwanted events that fortunately rarely happen ④. Typically these are incidents where it would be too costly or even impossible to implement measures to prevent them from happening. However, these types of accidents could fundamentally change our way of thinking, se [90]. For these risks the organizations will have to explore resilience as a way to reduce probability of an incident and reduce consequences in addition to developing contingency/catastrophe plans.

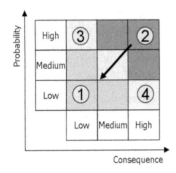

Example on a Probability (Frequency) scale:
P1-Low: 10 years and upward
P2-Medium: Between 1 to 10 years
P3-High: Several times a year

Example on a Consequence Scale:
C1 Low: Up to USD 1,000
C2 Medium: USD 1,000 – USD 100,000
C3 High: USD 100,000 and upward.

Fig. 5. Risk Matrix used to discuss risks and mitigation; [11]

Based on interviews and discussions with representatives from the oil and gas industry we have documented some generic or common risks as well as some actual security incidents in the following.

2.4   Key Risks Related to Integration of PCS/SCADA and ICT

In the following we have suggested four risks, all with high consequences and medium probability, based on assessment from the industry. Behind these risks, there may be different causal chains as suggested in the previous chapter, such as poor risk analysis, poor collaboration, poor knowledge and poor awareness. The suggested risks are examples; there are usually combinations of normal variability and/or unanticipated incidents that also are combined, to create an accident. The suggested risks are:

- Poor or incorrect situational awareness.
- Loss of critical communication in distributed network.
- SCADA and/or SIS system halts due to high network load.
- Virus or worm attack impacts critical SCADA/ICT systems.

These risks are described in the following:

Poor or Incorrect Situational Awareness: (C3 High, P2 Medium)
The system, organizational responsibilities or perceptions does not give a comprehensive overview of the situation, creating poor situational awareness among the involved stakeholders, leading to communication problems, misunderstandings, and unwanted events that can lead to an incident or accident. As examples:

- During the Piper Alpha incident, the operators at nearby sites were pumping oil and gas to the burning platform, due to poor situational awareness.
- An offshore PC server had to be restarted every 30 minutes, due to poor stability. This was done for a week, and then the poor stability was mentioned to the ICT department. The ICT department found that a virus had infected the server. However the server was not connected to the SCADA network at this point in time, and hence the virus was not spread to the SCADA system.

In general, issues related to incorrect situational awareness in critical areas should be identified and should be an area of exploration and training. Scenario analysis could be explored in order to improve situational awareness. Proactive indicators should be developed in order to avoid missing or wrong situational awareness. Challenges related to remote operations are further explored in [84].

Loss of Critical Communication in Distributed Network: (C3 High, P2 Medium)
At a test at CERN, it was discovered that 30% of the SCADA components stopped, if they were subject to high ICT traffic/network load due to denial-of-service attack (DoS) or erroneous traffic, see [25]. Thus, if a component malfunctions and continually sends out error packets, this may impact the stability of the SCADA system, in addition to degradation of communication capability in the network. Communications may be lost to key stakeholders such as control room operators or to key systems.

SCADA and/or SIS System Halts due to Network Load: (C3 High, P2 Medium)
The process control system is jammed or stopped because of unplanned, unexpected, or unauthorized traffic from the ICT systems attached to the PCS system. This may be due to the vulnerability and poor testing of most SCADA networks. Some sort of alarm should be given in the case of high network load or DoS attack. All relevant process/ICT personnel should have knowledge of such incidents, the symptoms and the mitigating actions required. The method CheckIT, [79], could aid in the awareness process, where as [24] could aid in establishing resilient technical solutions.

Virus or Worm Impacts Critical SCADA/ICT Systems: (C3 High, P2 Medium)
A virus is being spread, causing unpredictable behaviour or closing down key SCADA components, disturbing the production process. This can happen if a portable PC, memory stick or other ICT equipment is connected to the network. This was the case mentioned earlier with the ZOTOB.E worm. The organization should train on handling virus and worm attacks in the production systems, to test the resilience of the technical solutions and in the work processes. Some sort of alarm should be given in the case of a virus or worm attack. All relevant employees should be informed about the threats and consequences from viruses and worms, and mitigating actions to prevent these types of attacks from happening. Some examples are:

- The slammer worm attacked a drilling rig. The ICT department discovered the attack and consequently wanted to shut down all the systems and thereby stopping the drilling operation. The cost of a shutdown was estimated between USD 2 Million and USD 4 Million. Due to the consequences, a more robust solution had to be found, and in this case it was possible to find a satisfactory solution based on collaboration between ICT and SCADA professionals.
- A pornographic picture was downloaded from the Internet to the PC server containing the SAP system offshore. The SAP system contained maintenance information of safety critical equipment used in production, such as safety valves. The pornographic picture could contain a virus that could destroy safety critical information in the SAP system, but luckily no virus was present this time.

One approach to build resilience and prepare the organization for these kinds of unwanted events could be to conduct scenario training on a regular basis.

2.5   Reactive or Proactive Investment in Incident Response Capability

Today companies are facing increasing information security risks, as their daily operations are more and more dependent on ICT system. Computer and Internet have greatly improved productivity, yet they also create a rich environment for breeding vulnerabilities and risks. Most organizations view security control as an overhead and adopt a reactive security management approach, i.e., they address security concerns only when security incidents are discovered. Not all incidents are discovered. Some stay latent in the system. Such a reactive approach could be represented as the following model.

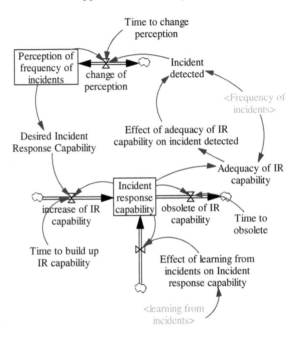

System Dynamics Model - Investment in Incident Response, [37]

The lower part of the model represents the change of incident response (IR) capability. The IR capability measures how many incidents could be handled per month. The increase in IR capability is mainly from the management's investment, which is based on the desired IR capability. The management invests to adjust the IR capability to the desired level. Note that this adjustment takes time. If the desired IR capability level is lower than the real IR capability, no further investment will be made. IR capability obsoletes over time. The desired IR capability is based on the perception of the frequency of incidents. The upper part of the model focuses on the perception of the frequency of incident. It is related to detected incidents. People can only perceive detected incidents. How many incidents (percentage) that can be detected depend on the adequacy of the IR capability. With a low IR capability, fewer incidents will be detected, and the perception of frequency of incidents will be low, as well as the desired IR capability, As a result, investment in IR capability will not be enough, which might cause severe incidents in the future. This is a capability trap that might eventually lead to disaster.

If the company's data shows a nice picture of few incidents and low risk, it could be that the company has managed its information security risk very well and that it is resilient to threats. However, it could also be that people are not aware of the incidents happening, or they are not reporting the incidents. More detailed analysis of the situation is needed before jumping to a conclusion; an audit program for information security would be worthwhile to investigate the real picture of information security risks. This is also discussed in [37]. In the following we are suggesting to work proactively to avoid incidents, through the exploration of "best practice" rules and through proactive risk management.

3   Risk Mitigation and Improvement of Resilience in the Sector

In this section we have described how the challenges and risks identified in the previous sections can be mitigated through rule compliance and risk management. We are suggesting a set of "best practices" to mitigate the risks. Our perspective has been to include technology, organization and human factors in risk management. We have suggested an improved risk assessment to be used due to the increased complexity and uncertainty in the oil and gas sector. We are suggesting using resilience as a strategy during the risk assessment. In addition, action research has been suggested as an approach to improve participatory and reflective discourse during risk assessment. We have suggested an approach and activities to be explored in an extended preliminary hazard analysis, which is suggested to be used to mitigate the risks in the oil and gas industry.

The ICT/SCADA system with SIS is an important barrier to avoid major accidents or reduce consequences of incidents. Based on earlier incidents we have seen that there are several vulnerabilities in the SCADA and ICT systems, but so far there have been few reported major accidents caused directly by SCADA/ICT systems, however some of the risks may have low probability but high consequences.

Operations are becoming more complex, involving different stakeholders from different organizational units. Due to the complexity and new technology - all the risk may not be known. Since more stakeholders with key expertise are collaborating in design and operation – a key issue is awareness and common risk perceptions. Thus we see the need for open processes discussing risks, involving stakeholders from different organizations. Action research as an approach seems to be well suited to these challenges, and is described later in this section. Action research is an established method for implementing changes based on reflection and participatory problem solving in team settings. Action research varies in form, but it usually involves technological, organizational and human issues in a change process. The philosophy is that complex changes can be best understood and influenced by action as described in [62].

Our point of view is that action research can improve safety, security and resilience. The argument is that the process of action research, together with the involved stakeholders, sometimes called the community of practice, helps us to identify relevant issues in design and operations, and also identify mitigating actions. The involvement of a community that includes management, ICT and SCADA professionals and workforce members increases the likelihood that the mitigating actions will be implemented successfully. Action research is especially useful in complex settings such as when multiple entities collaborate on safety-critical oil and gas operations. In [91] Westrum suggests that an organization whose workforce is aligned, aware and empowered is better at rooting out underlying problems. Action research can assist this endeavour by enabling "hidden" problems to be identified and highlighted. At the same time, action research can involve different stakeholders (or communities of practice) in a meaningful and positive dialog, fostering understanding and lasting collaboration. All this can ensure that issues related to safety, security and resilience are handled in a sensible matter. Although the work processes are fragmented, the "entire picture" can be analysed due to the involvement of all the relevant participants.

Our scope has been to explore safety and security both in breadth and height/depth. By breadth we mean exploring issues related to man, technology and organization:

- Issues related to man, should include knowledge and awareness. Knowledge is a broad area related to tasks, responsibility and what is necessary; but issues such as team collaboration could be a part of necessary knowledge. Team collaboration and team effectiveness in distributed and complex organization may be an important issue, as explored in [89].
- Issues related to technology should in addition to technology include tasks to ensure that technology could operate as planned, i.e. such as testing and certification.
- Issues related to organization should include responsibility, incident handling and reporting.

By height/depth we mean to focus on one specific area from top to bottom. Initially there should be possible to get advance warning of an incident through proactive indicators and resilience should be explored. Resilience should also be explored to reduce consequences, such as by having working barriers to mitigate or reduce consequences of an incident. Proactive indicators related to barriers are described in [70]. An exploration of the effect of proactive security work is also given in [37] – suggesting that a proactive approach can reduce the level of incidents.

Based on the preceding material and discussions we have in the following:

1. Documented a set of best practices that can be explored in design and operation of ICT/SCADA systems based on man, technology and organization.
2. Exploring resilience as a part of the risk analysis, in order to mitigate incidents of high consequences and low probability.
3. Used action research as a part of the risk analysis to improve risk analysis and risk communication across different organizational silos.
4. Giving an example of how accidents or scenarios can be analyzed in a risk analysis in order to ensure understanding and involvement across different organizational silos.

3.1   Suggested Good Practice

In the following we have described good practice from technical guidelines, human factors verification and validation, and safety/security culture.

3.1.1 Suggested Good Practice - Relevant Technical Standards and Guidelines
Several standards and good practice have been established within ICT and SCADA security. In this section we are trying to document some of the key documents covering both areas – ICT and SCADA.

Awareness of risk is of key interest, a best practice document can be found in [71]. In [72], a list of cyber threats can be found, this document is continually updated.

National Institute of Standards and Technology in USA has documented a broad based guidance to establish security in industrial control systems such as SCADA systems, see [16]. The two fundamental technical standards within each area, SCADA and ICT, are:

- From the SCADA environment: IEC 61508 "Functional safety of electrical/electronic/programmable electronic safety-related systems", [18].
- From the ICT environment: ISO/IEC 27002 – "Information Technology - Code of practice for information security management", [14].

These standards are established within their respective community, and are so far not integrated. Some recent SCADA/ICT security standards have however been established, such as:

- IEC 62443 "Security for industrial process measurement and control", ISO/IEC 2008, see [19].
- ANSI/ISA-99.02.01 (2009) - International Society for Automation, "Security for Industrial Automation and Control Systems: Establishing an Industrial Automation and Control Systems Security Program", ANSI/ISA-99.02.01-2009, Research TrianglePark, North Carolina, see [22].

The specific interdependencies between local ICT and SCADA systems have been a key issue in this paper, but we have not focused at interdependencies "at large" in this paper. This is however discussed and elaborated in [92].

A technical risk assessment methodology for the oil and gas industry, see [73], has been developed at The Institute for Information Infrastructure Protection (I3P). I3P is a consortium of universities, national laboratories and non-profit institutions dedicated to strengthening the cyber infrastructure of the US, see www.thei3p.org.

In the Norwegian oil and gas sector, a good practice guideline related to safety and security of SCADA systems has been established; see [24] and [11]. We have selected seven key issues from [24] based on identified vulnerabilities:

- **1. An Information Security Policy for process control, safety, and support ICT systems environments shall be documented.** An Information Security Policy is an overall management document that lays down the foundations for information security in the production environment. The policy describes the management intent and direction for information security.
- **2. Risk assessments shall be performed for process control, safety, and support ICT systems and networks.** The risk assessments shall identify probabilities and consequences of security incidents, taking into account the security activities and actions that have been undertaken to mitigate potential risks.
- **3. Infrastructure shall be able to provide segregated networks and all communication paths shall be controlled**. The ICT infrastructure must be able to provide segregated networks, so that ICT systems with different levels of security, real-time systems that require a guaranteed network throughput, or especially sensitive systems can be installed in separately divided networks.

- **4. Users of process control, safety, and support ICT systems shall be educated in the information security requirements and acceptable use of the ICT systems.**
- **5. Disaster recovery plans shall be documented and tested for critical process control, safety, and support ICT systems.** The requirements should as a minimum include the information security baseline described in this document. The vendors, suppliers, and contractors shall document their degree of compliance.
- **6. Process control, safety, and support ICT systems shall have adequate, updated, and active protection against malicious software.** The protection software should be configured to automatically update itself, when available and approved. Systems that are part of critical real-time operations may be excluded from this requirement if protected by other security measures.
- **7. Procedures for reporting of security events and incidents shall be documented and implemented in the organization.** The organizational responsibilities for handling and managing information security events and incidents shall be clearly specified and documented.

This good practice guideline has been established as a standard in the oil and gas industry in Norway from 2006, it is included in guiding documents, it is used during commission and procurement; and it has been referenced by the authorities in audits.

3.1.2 Suggested Good Practice - Human Factors Design of Control Centres – Validation and Verification Using the CRIOP Methodology

Human Factors in the control room (CR) are of key importance when safety is at stake: this have been documented in several of the accidents that have been mentioned earlier, see [49]. In [21], the ergonomic design of the central control room (CCR) is specified. A verification and validation methodology of control rooms, called CRIOP, see [74], has been developed based on [21] and other best practice standards. The CRIOP method contains checklists containing "best practice" related to the CCR such as: layout, working environment, control and safety systems (including alarms), e-operations (integrated operations, eField, field of the future), job organization, procedures and training. In addition CRIOP contains tools to perform a scenario analysis to validate that the CCR can handle unwanted incidents in a safe and secure manner.

CRIOP can help to identify critical areas related to man, technology or organization when the use of the SCADA/ICT system is verified or validated. CRIOP has been accepted in the Norwegian and international industry, and is increasingly used, see [75].

3.1.3 Suggested Good Practice - Assessment and Improvement of Culture

Personnel involved in the oil and gas industry have a tendency to focus on technology, often at the expense of organizational and cultural issues. This technical focus can be negative related to safety, as documented in [46]. The reliance on outsourcing and collaboration between dispersed sites create the need for common risk perceptions and a common security and safety culture among the involved organizations in order to reduce risks of unwanted incidents. A focus on "soft issues" such as culture among these different groups can ensure that different professions and organizations share a common understanding of the new risks and can cooperate to improve communication and resolve incidents. Our definition of security and safety culture is: *"The security and safety culture of an organization is the product of individual and group values, attitudes, perceptions, competencies, and patterns of behaviour that determine commitment to, and the style and proficiency of, an organization's security and safety management"*, based on [76].

In some instances there is a positive correlation between safety culture and safety; see [77]. We suggest that improvement of safety culture could be an important step to reduce the risk in oil and gas exploration and production. Our assumption is that culture can be measured, managed, and manipulated as assumed from the functionalistic tradition, [78]. Thus, developing a tool for the improvement of security and safety culture has been done. CheckIT is such a tool, see [79], available from www.checkit.sintef.no.

The basic package of CheckIT comprises of 31 questions. Each question is presented and three alternative main answers are presented in a table next to the question. The aim is to develop a rating of the organization on a numerical scale from 1 to 5, where levels one, three and five are textually described. The described alternatives correspond to the cultural taxonomy described in [80]:

- Denial culture   (Level 1)
- Rule based culture   (Level 3)
- Learning/generative culture   (Level 5)

The utilization of a five-point "Likert" scale provides a basis for a normalized score throughout the organization and makes it possible to reflect on results over time or between organizations.

The implementation and use of CheckIT could be a challenge in a technology driven industry. To ensure positive change to improve safety, we suggest following the practices related to leading change, see [81]:

- Establish a sense of urgency among the participants in the organization and in the cooperating organizations.
- Creating a coalition, involving management, key stakeholders and employees.
- Developing a motivating vision that is relevant to the actual business and communicating the change vision to empower broad-based actions.
- Generating short-term improvements, document the improvements, consolidating the gains and producing more change and anchoring new approach in the culture.

3.2   Resilience to Be Used in Risk Assessment

In the oil and gas industry, there is an environment with high consequences but some times with low probability. The consequences can be major as seen by the "Deepwater Horizon" disaster, [41]. Thus, the ability to build and sustain resilience should be of key importance in the oil and gas industry.

We have tried to identify key issues in resilience, in order to be able to explore resilience in risk assessment. We have explored resilience based on review of theory, in [51] and review of actual accidents and incidents in the oil and gas industry from [52]. Our approach has been to explore chain of events both in successful recoveries and in accidents. In combination with a survey of relevant theory we have suggested a set of resilient principles i.e. "root causes" assisting resilience.

Based on our review we have suggested seven resilient principles, described in the following: *redundancy; the ability to graceful and controlled degradation; the ability to "rebound" from a degraded system state; flexibility in systems and organization; ability to manage margins close to performance boundaries; establishment and exploration of common mental models; reduction of complexity; and reduction of couplings.* The suggestions are listed in the following:

1. One of the key issues from HRO, [32], is the ability to handle deviations or unexpected chain of events by redundant solutions either by redundant organizations, redundant personnel or redundant technology. The ability to handle an incident by alternate functions is also mentioned, see [53], thus we suggest *redundancy* as a resilient principle.
   - *Redundancy* is defined as having several alternate and independent ways of performing a function. The function can be performed by different organizations, by different technical systems or by different procedures. Redundancy could support the ability to degrade gracefully. Redundancy may be achieved by standby spares or by concurrent use of multiple devices. Redundancy may introduce complexity and it may be vulnerable to common cause failures. An alternative to redundancy is diversity (but this is placed in the category flexibility.). The use of redundancy should be assessed and the improvement in safety should be evaluated against features including costs, increased complexity and common cause failures.
2. In [53] there is an example of improvisation using manual system and organizational crosschecking to avoid medical misadministration during the "MAR-knockout". This is suggested to be an example of *graceful degradation*, which can be used as a principle in addition to the *ability to rebound*, as described in the following.
   - The ability to *graceful and controlled degradation (A)*, when system functions or barriers are failing. Proactive impact analysis must be performed and risky behaviour is identified and mitigated. There is an ability to perform a partial shutdown of functions. This should be designed in the system, ensuring safety in intermediate states, including shutdown. The complementary principle is *(B) the ability to "rebound or recover"* and achieves normal operation from a degraded system. The ability to recover is based on knowledge of the state of the system. Human intervention may aid in the recovery. Effective recovery is both based on timely impact analysis and competent mobilization. The use of competence in the whole organization can be used in collaboration with technical systems as a contributor to resilience. This ability to "controlled degradation and rebound" is seen as one of the key elements in resilience, and is explored in [55].
3. In HRO there is a focus on flexibility in combination with resources, and in [56], brittle systems are characterized by no flexibility related to changes or the unexpected. *Flexibility* can be used as a principle, described in the following.
   - *Flexibility* in systems and organizations or diversity – having different ways of performing a function within a specific system. Flexibility related to resilience should include error tolerance – errors should be immediately observable and reversible. Flexibility can also be demonstrated by improvisation, going "outside the box" in order to achieve goals such as "safety" in a stressful situation. However the systems must be designed to be flexible, accept improvisations and error tolerance.

4. In HRO, the organization is alert and can foresee unwanted performance based on efficient handling of local cues and local interactions. The organization has the ability to detect drift to boundaries or danger zones. In [57], a brittle organization is not able to accept signals or cues and is not able to foresee and avoid something bad happening. *Management of margins* is suggested as a principle, also in accordance with [58] and focuses on the boundaries of acceptable safety performance, as described in the following.

   • *Managing margins* – ensure that performance boundaries are not crossed. This can be managed by using proactive indicators of margins - reporting status related to performance boundaries. An important principle should be to design for controllability – i.e. using principles as incremental control, decision aids and the ability to monitor. It is important to be able to explore the ability of the system to manage margins through testing and exploration of scenarios. The approach should be to perform testing based on several "worst case" scenarios, and perform repeated testing at performance boundaries. Testing must also include scenarios involving humans that can simulate decisions in a stressful environment. Sacrificial decisions, i.e. decisions balancing productivity versus safety must be a part of the scenarios. Management of margins should include both the slow erosion of margins and the more dynamic sacrificial decisions, leading to crossing of boundaries. When an optimum stress level is reached, and this can be formulated as a function, the derivate of the optimum is zero – that means that we must try to identify changes in the function or states, in signals or indicators changing, as from positive to negative. The management of margins can be realized by surveillance of trends, such as traffic and congestion of networks, or reporting of due maintenance – exploring proactive indicators as measurements of closeness to margins or indicators pace of change. When error rates decreases and reliability increases – the risk may be increasing due to reduced safety focus from people. It is important to measure and manage such drift. A measurement of "the participants' awareness of risk" may provide a good measure of the actual risks from [59]. The ability to manage margins can be done by exploring proactive indicators to avoid crossing boundaries of safety performance as discussed by [58]. This ability to manage margins is seen as a key element in resilience.

5. In HRO there is a strong focus on shared beliefs and values ensuring good collaboration, supporting organizational crosschecking as a contributor to system resilience. In addition there is a strong focus on extensive system insight. In [57] there is a strong focus on common information and information flow across the organization to ensure resilience. Use of *common mental models* is suggested as a principle, and described in the following.

   • Establishment of *common mental models* – ensuring that communication and collaboration across organizations and systems are flowing freely. Some of the factors to establish common mental models could be extensive system insight, and organizational knowledge and readiness, ensuring that the systems could be explored to their full extent and ensuring that the competence in the organization is utilized when needed. Mental models play an important role in handling deviations and in recovery; but they also play an important role in understanding and describing the causes of accidents as described in [38], in addition to creating a framework of learning from accidents. The process to create models and the selected different mental models are important in order to improve resilience, but need careful reflection and work. Key stakeholders and management should participate in the process, since management participation and involvement across organizational silos are key issues in creating a common understanding and reducing accidents.

6. and 7. In [28] there is a focus on "normal accidents" as the consequence of complexity and tight couplings. *Reduction of complexity* and *reduction of tight couplings* are suggested as principles, and are described in the following.

- *Reduce complexity:* As described in [28] this can be achieved by going from proximity to segregation, from common mode connection to dedicated connections, from interconnected systems to segregated systems, from limited substitution to easy substitution, from several feedback loops to few or none feedback loops, from multiple and interacting controls to single purpose and segregated controls, from indirect information to direct information and from limited understanding to extensive understanding. This approach can also be used on organizations to reduce probabilities of accidents. Inefficient organizational structures such as multi-layered hierarchies with diffuse responsibilities and poor communication appears to be related to accidents.

- *Reduce tight couplings* as described in [28] by enable processing delays, enable flexibility in order of sequencing, enable flexibility in methods used to reach the goal, allow flexibility and slack in resources, design in buffers and redundancies and assure availability of substitutions.

3.3   Action Research and Resilient Risk Assessment

We have extended the risk assessment as suggested in Figure-6. Usually a risk assessment is focusing on past accidents and poor ability to react and recover and identifying mitigating actions to reduce risks. We have in addition tried to learn from the positive ability to react and recover, and to sustain and improve resilience through resilience engineering and improving safety culture. We are analysing risk influencing factors, and resilient factors in our approach called resilient risk assessment.

Strong ability to react and recover	1. Learning from resilient practice, HRO, Safety Culture.	2. Build resilience and safety culture
Weak ability to react and recover	3. Learning from incidents and accidents	4. Mitigate risk of accidents
	Learning from past	*Future risk analysis*

Fig. 6. Factors used in resilient risk assessment

Risk influencing factors can be based on factors from the literature, from [60]: *Design, hardware, maintenance, housekeeping, error enforcing conditions, procedures, training, communication, incompatible goals, organization and defences.*

Resilient factors, such as: *redundancy, flexibility* has been described earlier.

These two classes of factors, risk influencing factors and resilient factors, are explored when we are performing a resilient risk assessment, as suggested in Figure-7. The result of the risk assessment is both a process, creating understanding and awareness of risks among the involved stakeholders, but also a set of risk mitigating actions and a set of proactive indicators to be explored in future operations.

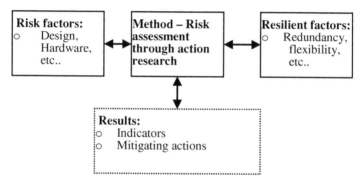

Fig. 7. Exploration of both risks and resilience in risk assessment

Suggested Use of Action Research

In [61] action research is described as *"the touchstone of most good organizational development practices."* The iterative method of action research has been formalized in [62] as an iterative process model with five canonical action research principles: (i) Researcher client agreement; (ii) Cyclical process model; (iii) Theory; (iv) Change through action; and (v) Learning through reflection.

Our survey of the action research literature reveals that it contributes to safety and security improvements. Our survey findings are based on a limited data set and, therefore, may be somewhat biased. However, the key issue in our survey has been to identify causal relationships between the change process used in action research and the development of safety, security and resilience. In the survey we are especially interested in identifying:

- Action research activities that influence safety, security and resilience,
- The stakeholders involvement in the action research process and
- The application domains exploring action research.

In the following, the result of our survey is documented, in order to describe activities that should be performed during a risk assessment based on action research.

The involvement of stakeholders and the commitment from the "client" are important in relation to ownership, process, results, learning and reflection. Action research is an approach that is well-suited to complex problems. The relevant stakeholders should be involved in the process because development and improvement may involve many stakeholders outside the organization (e.g., suppliers and service providers). Action research has been used to improve safety and security in complex organizations. In [63], there is a description on how an action research program conducted across the entire New South Wales (Australia) Government contributed to better compliance, increased understanding and knowledge, improved policies, and effective business continuity plans. Similar results have been obtained in the Australian health care industry; described in [64]. These results have also been achieved in the oil and gas industry, as described below.

In [65] there is a documentation of the improvements in safety and productivity from an action research project conducted at an offshore oil rig. The number of injuries at the rig decreased and the productivity (drill meters per day) increased. Moreover, the number of incidents involving injuries dropped to one-third of the previous number. Some key issues are highlighted in [65]:

- Building on communities of practice by involving people who formed working communities at the platform, regardless of the company for which they worked; and
- Implementing a "bottom-up" process involving first-line workers to ensure ownership by all the relevant employees regardless of line position.
- Focus on issues and challenges that the involved personnel deem to be most important, and
- Using search conferences, see [66], as a tool to create understanding and participation among the workforce.

In [67], similar improvements in safety (and efficiency) are documented related to the use of service vessels in the oil and gas industry. The initiative realized dramatic reductions in injuries and collisions. Injuries on service vessels (per million working hours) were reduced from 13.8 in 2001 to 2.6 in 2006. Service vessel collisions were reduced from twelve in 2000 to an average of one per year from 2001 through 2005.

The key issues highlighted in [67] are:

- Building on communities of practice whose safety is at stake (e.g., crews on service vessels and offshore installations) and using workgroup meetings (search conferences) as a tool for fostering workforce understanding and participation; generating enthusiasm;
- Developing a unified approach to safety in the logistic chain;
- Focusing on an interpretive bottom-up process in addition to "top-down" support of activities and mitigating actions; increasing worker understanding and ownership of challenges and solutions; basing the work on practical experience from the workforce; and implementing safety improvements without having to wait for an accident, which contributes to mitigating actions being perceived as more legitimate by workers.
- Shifting from a "blame-oriented" to a "learning-oriented" culture with regard to incidents; and focusing on dialog and reflection (i.e., "two-way" communication).

In [68] it is documented that action research on accident prevention caused accident rates at two Danish enterprises to drop to about 25% of the average of the preceding five years. She observed that safety could be improved by:

- Building on communities of practice;
- Focusing on an interpretive bottom-up process in addition to top-down support of activities and mitigating actions;

- Increasing worker understanding and ownership of challenges and solutions; and using search conferences as a tool to create understanding and participation by the workforce.

These results could be a manifestation of the so-called "Hawthorne effect", see [69], where increased attention to the principal issues is the real reason for safety and productivity improvements. However, the results appear to have a prolonged effect, lasting more than six months. The thesis that "structured" attention has a positive effect on safety and productivity clearly deserves further investigation, and has been used as a basis to suggest using action research when performing risk analysis.

Based on the above discussion, we are suggesting including the following steps to structure the hazard analysis, as illustrated in Figure-8:

1. Perform a risk assessment – different techniques can be explored such as HAZOP or FMECA, as described in [38].
2. Discuss and prioritize risks and mitigating actions in an open search conference, involving key stakeholders as described above.
3. Implement mitigating actions together with indicators that can give status of the mitigating actions.
4. Measure (results of) mitigating actions and reflect on effect of the actions in collaboration with key stakeholders – the next step is then again 1)

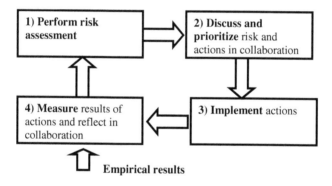

Fig. 8. Risk assessment supported by action research

In the risk assessment, we have to identify key safety and security processes in order to develop a unified approach to safety in the process chain. We have to focus on bottom-up process in addition to "top-down" support of activities and mitigating actions; to increase worker understanding and ownership of challenges and solutions. We have to focus on dialog and reflection (i.e., "two-way" communication), trying to establish a proactive learning culture avoiding "scapegoats" and blame.

We are suggesting exploring risk assessment methods and techniques described in [38], such as Preliminary Hazard Analysis (PHA), hazard and operability study (HAZOP) and Failure Modes Effects and Criticality Analysis (FMECA). In addition we are suggesting exploring resilience as a strategy. This is suggested in Figure-7 and embedded in the action research approach as described. In the following we mainly describe how a resilient PHA process can be performed, supported by a short description of a resilient version of HAZOP and FMECA.

3.4   Use of Preliminary Hazard Analysis (PHA)

The PHA usually consists of the following main steps:

1. PHA - Context and scope – define the goal, process and object to be analysed
2. PHA - Hazard Identification and Identification of resilient principles
3. PHA - Consequence and frequency estimation, risk ranking and follow-up

The PHA should focus both on human, technical and organizational factors, as mentioned initially.

1) PHA - Context and Scope – Define the Goal, Process and Object to be Analysed

We are suggesting using an "action research" process, when working with safety, security and resilience in the oil, gas and petrochemical industry – since different stakeholders from several organizational silos must be involved, and different perspectives and knowledge must be explored.

The object to be analysed should be precisely described, and the objectives of safety, control and resilience should be documented. The "object" should be extended, in the sense that man, technology and organization should be included as a part of the "object" to be analysed, both individually and as a whole. Of special interest are boundary conditions, when we are testing the boundaries of acceptable performance. In addition, indicators should be explored when we are close to boundaries.

Experiences from past accidents should be used to identify hazards and risks, but experiences from past successes should also be used to ensure that resilience is propagated in future design.

The main results from PHA context and scope should be:

- Document stating the objectives of safety, control and resilience
- Document a list of functions with appropriate hazards and resilient principles
- Document the object to be analysed – man, technology and organization
- Document a list of main boundary conditions to be controlled and a set of proactive indicators to document closeness to boundaries

2) PHA – Hazard Identification and Identification of Resilient Principles

Hazards and resilient principles must be identified and explored. Hazard should be controlled and consequences of variability or incidents should be reduced or contained.

Hazards related to boundary conditions should be described and high-level information needs related to boundary conditions should be identified together with necessary (areas of) proactive indicators. The ability to "manage margins" should be made more specific related to the identified performance boundaries and "sacrificial judgments". If the system is planned with the ability to be flexible, to have redundancy or to have "degraded" states, these states must be explored and state transitions must be tested and checked. To simplify, there should be at least one safe shut down state when the technical system is turned off. When the system has gone to a safe state, the ability to use the organization and manual procedures as a "degraded" system should be explored.

One of the key issues in resilience is the ability to perform continuous monitoring of the system and to follow indicators to identify boundary conditions or slow drift towards boundaries as early as possible, see [70]. An updated list of major hazards and relevant indicators should be available to increase risk perceptions and risk understanding. There are clearly two types of indicators:

- Dynamic indicators, showing performance related to boundaries – such as network load, stress of people in key positions, the level of alarms, the level of gas emissions or small fires.
- Drift indicators, showing more long-range slow drift Technical or organizational drift may impact safety. The daily minor modifications or small changes in technical equipment could accumulate and create a more risky environment. Such small changes should be assessed periodically. Organizational drift could be the gradual change of risk perceptions in the workplace that may lead to complacency and later serious incidents due to the erosion or ignorance of several barriers. Tools to evaluate this kind of slow drift could be worker perception of safety (i.e. safety climate questionnaire) as mentioned in [82].

Exploration of HAZOP to Build Resilience

HAZOP has been developed by the process industry and is appropriate in the oil and gas industry. The analysis is process oriented. HAZOP has also been adapted to software development; see [88]. HAZOP is based on a system theory model, assuming that accidents are caused by deviations. Due to the flexibility and broad based approach of HAZOP it should be appropriate to include resilience as a part of a HAZOP. Some of the benefits of HAZOP are:

- The team approach – ensuring different perspectives from different participants
- Broad based, trying to establish top down and complete picture
- Can be used in both operations and in design

The HAZOP analysis consists of five main steps

    I. Documenting and elaboration of the design intention
    II. Discussing potential deviations from the design intentions (using guideword such as No, More, Less, As well as, Reverse…)
    III. Discussing causes of the deviations from the design
    IV. Exploring consequences of the deviations
    V. Exploring how the deviations or consequences could be prevented, avoided or reduced

Keywords are used as guidewords to discuss causes and effects. The principles in resilience could be explored as the part of the discussion both in (II) potential deviations and in (IV) consequences and (V) prevent, avoid or reduce deviations or consequences. Resilience should be explored in (II), by using key words such as "flexibility" or "redundant". Margins and resonance should be explored using keywords "at limit", "weak signals" or "resonance". When discussing prevention, in (V) – issues from resilience should be explored such as redundancy, graceful degradation, flexibility or management of margins. Could redundancy, graceful degradation, flexibility or management of margins prevent the deviation; make it less likely; or protect against the consequences?

The result from the HAZOP should be a report documenting the guidewords used, the deviation, possible causes, possible consequences and mitigating actions including resilience.

Exploration of FMECA to Build Resilience

FMECA is a failure mode, effects, and criticality analysis, see [85]. After performing FMECA, recommendations are made to design to reduce the consequences of critical failures. This may include selecting components with higher reliability, reducing the stress level at which a critical item operates, or adding redundancy or monitoring to the system when it is close to performance boundaries. Thus, discussion of resilience is well suited to suggest recommendations based on a FMECA.

FMECA is appropriate in a design phase but it can be very time consuming, and should focus on key issues. The goal of the analysis is to establish probability of operation without failure. A FMECA of a subsystem, consist of analysis of the following entities: 1) Item (component of subsystem); 2) Failure modes; 3) Cause of failure; 4) Possible effects; 5) Frequency/probability; 6) Consequence; 7) Possible action to reduce cause/ frequency/ consequence.

In 7) Possible action – the list of resilience principles should be elaborated in order to discuss the possibility to reduce cause, frequency or consequence. The principles should be implemented by technical, organizational or human factors issues.

The main results from activity should be:

- List of major hazards in the system
- List of major resilient principles in the system
- Documentation of critical margins and the relevant proactive indicators

3) PHA - Consequence and Frequency Estimation, Risk Ranking and Follow-Up

Consequences and frequency estimation of unwanted incidents must be assessed, based on existing data, expert judgment, or modeling. Many different models are available to perform these types of estimation. One technique is Fault Three Analysis as mentioned in [86].

Based on consequences and frequency estimation, or subjective assessment we must identify a set of unwanted incidents. These incidents must be analyzed and mitigating actions must be prioritized, based on an assessment of risk and/or cost of mitigating actions.

When looking at technical, organizational and human factors, scenario analysis should be performed on prioritized unwanted incidents and mitigating actions. It is suggested that the scenarios are explored in a step diagram, as described in Figure-9. A set of key critical scenarios should be identified, and they could be tested and explored both in design and as a part of operations. A set of key scenarios could be used in training to increase risk perceptions and risk understanding.

Having a system approach to safety and resilience, it is important to measure and follow the development of resilience in the organization in addition to the resilience in the systems. Management plays a key role, especially related to prioritizing of safety vs. production. In [82], scenario analyses are used to discuss the management prioritizing of safety vs. production, in upward appraisals or managerial scripts. The use of scenario analyses should be used to explore the emergency preparedness in the organization.

Periodic audit and assessment of risk and resilience should be performed based on unwanted incidents and successful recoveries.

The main results from the activities should be:

- List of major hazards in the system (and if possible a risk matrix)
- Documentation of mitigating actions
- Documentation of critical margins and the relevant proactive indicators to survey status of all relevant margins (Example of one important indicator is subjective assessment of risk – see [59], in addition to systematic audit of risks and resilience.)
- Critical scenarios to be explored to increase safety and resilience, and to create appropriate risk perceptions

4) Illustration of Scenario Analysis Using the STEP Methodology

We have made a scenario, see Figure-9, which could be used as a starting point to explore what could happen in an actual production system where ICT and SCADA systems are integrated. We have used the STEP methodology, see [83], to describe the scenario, documenting:

- **Actors:** The actors who are involved in the incident are identified, i.e. leading up to the accident and afterwards by their own actions, decisions or omissions. The actors are drawn under each other on the left side of the STEP diagram.
- **Events:** Identify the incidents and events that influenced the accident and how the incident was handled. The events are described by "whom", "what" and "how", and are placed in the diagram according to the order in which they occurred.
- **Sequence:** Place events in the correct place on the time-actor sheet, attempts should be made to identify the correct order of events.
- **Causal links:** Identify the relationship between the events, their causes, and show this in the diagram by drawing arrows to illustrate the causal links. For each event the previous events leading to this event should be assessed by the use of a logic test. The logic tests checks if the event is sufficient to "cause" the following event. If it is not sufficient, then the other events that are necessary in order to "cause" the events must be identified.

When the STEP diagram has been drawn, it can be analysed to identify the weak points, that may be mitigated by barriers or resilience. In Figure-9 the triangle represents the weak point. The threats, which can lead to a weak point, can be identified, and the underlying root causes leading to the threat can be found. Barriers can both be used to reduce probability of an event and barriers can be used to reduce negative consequences and impacts of an event.

This scenario was discussed in a meeting with several stakeholders. The scenario is based on a possible incident where a supplier connected a portable PC with virus to an actual production network. The virus jams the network; the SIS system does not manage to stop production due to a SIS vulnerability, and does not manage to shut down the system to a defined safe state. In addition, there is uncontrollable release of hydrocarbons, that are ignited and an explosion takes place. The scenario is drawn in Figure-9. The STEP analysis helps to create understanding among the stakeholders and also helps in discussing resilience in the scenario.

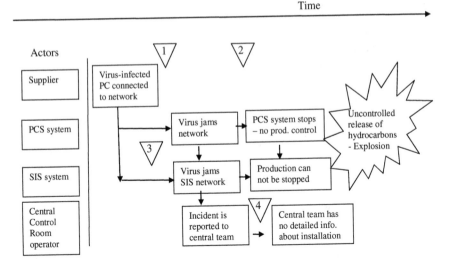

Fig. 9. SCADA Scenario with weak points and safety barrier analysis

Weak Points as indicated by triangles:

1. No scanning of PC prior to connection to network (see B1).
2. Latest patches not deployed to network and systems connected to network, making a successful virus attack more probable (see B2).
3. SIS network integrated in PCS system, the SIS/PCS network are common, making it possible to jam the SIS through the PCS system (see B3).
4. The technical central team has not sufficient detailed knowledge of the local complex SCADA system and does not manage to stop or shut down production (see B4).

Suggested barriers (B) to be attached at the weak points:

- B1-1) Supplier must guarantee that all PC's to be connected to the network should be scanned prior to connection.
- B1-2) Use a staging facility to scan PC prior to connection to the network.
- B1-3) Awareness training of supplier (PC owner) – ensuring that no virus are established at the PC.

- B2-1) All components attached to the network have latest patches, ensuring that the virus attack is not successful.

- B3-1) Firewall between PCS system and SIS.
- B3-2) Separate networks for SIS and PCS systems.
- B3-3) Redundant components available to manage operations.

- B4-1) Better documentation of SCADA systems or more standardized solutions.
- B4-2) Expert onshore with high competence, manage to stop release of hydrocarbons.

4   Conclusion and Suggestions for Further Exploration and Research

The sustained need for oil and gas drives the need for exploration and operations of new technology and new challenging oil and gas fields. The exploration and operations in new and demanding environments seem to create the need for new and advanced technological solutions that must be managed through ICT and SCADA systems. The ICT and SCADA systems are operating in an environment where they have to focus both on safety and security. The HSE consequences of an incident may be huge. The ICT and SCADA systems are also vulnerable, and may be a tempting target.

Safety, security and resilience in a Human Factors perspective must be a key issue in order to avoid accident or incidents with huge impacts, such as the Deepwater Horizon incident, see [41]. The scope of work must include technical issues in the ICT, SCADA and process environments, organizational factors and human factor related to awareness and knowledge of risks.

The key issues we have identified are:

1. **Design for resilience, safety and security in an extended environment.** The earlier independent ICT, SCADA systems and organizations must now be designed to be integrated. The individual SCADA and ICT components must be able to handle network load and demands across the different environments, based on a certification scheme. The network integrating SCADA and ICT should be segmented and designed to ensure safety, security and resilience between key components such as PCS and SIS. Human Factors should be included in the design, in order to utilize the benefits of human operator assistance. Virtual organizations is increasing, involving personnel from onshore and offshore. Knowledge and skills to improve collaboration in a distributed organization must be improved, especially related to handling of unwanted incidents.

2. **Establish common risk perception through a risk and vulnerability assessment** of the integration of ICT and SCADA systems. Resilience should be a part of the assessment in order to explore the positive ability of recovery. The assessment must include technical, organizational and human issues. This demands collaboration across different organizational silos and between different professionals such as ICT and SCADA professionals in addition to Human Factors expertise. We have suggested using action research to achieve this. We have suggested a set of methods with different perspectives that could be explored such as a HAZOP including resilience; an assessment of safety and security culture through the method CheckIT and exploration of good practice in the industry through methods such as CRIOP.

3. **Perform systematic scenario analysis and testing of the technical integrated system**, i.e. the ICT and SCADA systems. The system should be tested extensively, both related to internal incidents and external incidents such as simulated attack through "red team" testing, exploring vulnerabilities from the point of a remote attacker. The testing should cover technical, organizational and human factors issues, such as the ability of the organization and the system to handle loss of communication or loss of critical parts of the systems or other key incidents. Testing should include the ability to be resilient.

4. **Focus on resilience in operations, and focus on proactive indicators.** Exploration of indicators and incidents should be an area of learning and knowledge management in the organization. Indicators should be explored in order to avoid incidents.

The systems used in the oil and gas industry are complex and they can have a huge impact on HSE. Designing, developing, testing and exploring these systems under different conditions are difficult. To improve our knowledge and abilities to design safe, secure and resilient SCADA/ICT systems in distributed environments with high consequences, we are suggesting the following areas of further exploration and research:

- There is a great need to improve understanding and documentation of resilience in the industry. The first step should be to improve methodologies and techniques used to assess both risk and resilience in complex organizations, using SCADA/ICT. The result of resilience analyses should be evaluated, in order to assess the effect of an analysis including resilience.
- Systematic documentation of risk perceptions, unwanted incidents and successful recoveries from the SCADA/ICT systems used in the oil and gas industry should be performed. Data should be gathered, shared and analysed among industry and researchers, in order to survey trends impacting safe operations of the systems. As a part of these activities, proactive indicators should be evaluated in order to understand the relationship between indicators and the actual operational risks and resilience in SCADA/ICT systems. Analysis of successful recoveries should be an area of interest, in order to study and understand mechanism behind recoveries.
- Establishment of an ICT/SCADA test-bed of technology used in oil and gas industry. This "test-bed" should be available to do research of safety, security and resilience of integrated SCADA and ICT systems that are distributed, to systematically assess vulnerabilities and resilience. Improvement of methodologies and techniques used in development and testing of SCADA/ICT systems should be done. This should be done together with the industry in order to improve resilience, safety and security of the critical SCADA/ICT systems.

The SCADA/ICT systems used in the oil and gas industry are a part of the critical infrastructure. The industry, technology and threats are rapidly evolving and could have severe impact on HSE. Safety, security and resilience of SCADA/ICT systems should be an important area of concern both to avoid HSE incidents but also as a possibility to improve the quality and operations of this critical infrastructure.

References

1. EIA, U.S. Energy Information Administration "International Energy Outlook", report DOE/EIA-0484 (2010), http://www.eia.gov/oiaf/ieo/index.html (retrieved at August 01, 2010)
2. Holditch, S.A., Chianelli, R.R.: Factors That Will Influence Oil and Gas Supply and Demand in the 21st Century. MRS Bulletin 33 (April 2008), http://www.mrs.org/bulletin (retrieved at May 08, 2010)
3. Rollenhagen, C., Evenéus, P.: Development of a systemic MTO perspective on dam safety management. In: International Symposium on Modern Technology of Dams. The 4th EADAC Symposium, Chengdu, China, October 13-18 (2007)

4. Aas, A.L., Johnsen, S.O., Skramstad, T.: Experiences with Human Factors in Norwegian petroleum Control Centre Design and suggestions to handle an increasingly complex future. In: Reliability, Risk and Safety – Theory and Applications (Esrel 2009), pp. 285–291. CRC Press (2009) ISBN 978-0415555098
5. ISO/IEC Guide 51, Safety Aspects – Guidelines for their Inclusion in Standards (1999)
6. Hollnagel, E., Woods, D., Leveson, N.: Resilience Enginering. Ashgate (2006) ISBN 0-7546-4641-6
7. Hyne, J.N.: Nontechnical guide to petroleum geology, exploration, drilling and production, PenWell, Oklahoma, USA (2001)
8. Baker, S., Waterman, S., Ivanov, G.: In the crossfire – Critical Infrastructure in the Age of Cyber War (2010), `http://csis.org/event/crossfire-critical-infrastructure-age-cyber-war` (retrieved at July 01, 2010)
9. DNV, Det Norske Veritas - "OLF/NOFO – Summary of Differences Between Offshore Drilling Regulations in Norway and U.S. Gulf of Mexico" (2010), `http://www.olf.no/news/dnv-report-solid-petroleum-regulations-in-norway-article19670-291.html` (retrieved at September 01, 2010)
10. ISO 17776, Petroleum and natural gas industries — Offshore production installations — Guidelines on tools and techniques for hazard identification and risk assessment (2002)
11. Johnsen, S., Ask, R., Røisli, R.: Reducing Risk in Oil and Gas production. In: Goetz, E., Shenoi, S. (eds.) Critical Infrastructure Protection, ch. 7. Springer, Heidelberg (2008)
12. Victorian Auditor-General, Security of Infrastructure Control Systems for Water and transport (2010), `http://download.audit.vic.gov.au/files/20100610_ICT_report.pdf` (retrieved at October 01, 2010)
13. ISO/IEC 27001, Information technology – Security techniques – Information security management systems – Requirements, ISO (2005)
14. ISO/IEC 27002, former ISO/IEC 17799 – Information Technology - Code of practice for information security managemen, ISO (2005)
15. Johnsen, S.O., Skramstad, T., Hagen, J.: Enhancing the Safety, Security and Resilience of ICT and SCADA systems Using Action Research. In: Palmer, C., Shenoi, S. (eds.) Critical Infrastructure Protection III, pp. 113–123. Springer, Berlin (2009)
16. Stoufer, K., Falco, J., Kent, K.: Guide to Supervisory Control and Data Acquisition (SCADA) and Industrial Control Systems Security. NIST Special Publication 800-82, National Institute of Standards and Technology, Maryland, USA (2008)
17. US. Code Title 44, ch. 35, Subchapter III, § 3542, `http://Uscode.House.Gov/Download/Pls/44c35.Txt` (retrieved at December 31, 2010)
18. IEC 61508, Functional safety of electrical/electronic/programmable electronic safety-related systems, IEC (2010)
19. IEC 62443, Security for industrial process measurement and control - Network and system security. ISO/IEC 2008 (2008)
20. ANSI/ISA-99.02.01, International Society for Automation, Security for Industrial Automation and Control Systems: Establishing an Industrial Automation and Control Systems Security Program, ANSI/ISA, Research Triangle Park, North Carolina (2009)
21. ISO 11064, Ergonomic design of control centres, ISO (2000)
22. EEMUA Publication No.191, Alarm systems: A guide to Design, Management and Procurement (2007)

23. ISO 9241, Ergonomics of Human System Interaction
24. Ask, R., Røisli, R., Johnsen, S., Line, M., Ueland, A., Hovland, B., Groteide, L., Birkel-
    and, B., Steinbakk, A., Hagelsteen, E., Rong, C., Losnedahl, T.: Information Security
    Baseline Requirements for Process Control, Safety and Support ICT Systems. ISBR,
    OLF104 (2006),
    http://www.olf.no/en/Publica/Guidelines/Integrerte-
    operasjonerIntegrated-operations/104/ (retrieved at January 01, 2010)
25. Luders S.: CERN tests reveal security flaws with industrial networked devices. The Indus-
    trial Ethernet Book, GGH Marketing Communications, Titchfield, United Kingdom, pp.
    12–23 (November 2006), http://www.iebmedia.com (retrieved on December 05,
    2009)
26. Oljeindustriens Landsforening (OLF - Norwegian Oil Industry Association). Integrated
    Work Processes (2005),
    http://www.olf.no/getfile.php/zKonvertert/www.olf.no/Rapporter/
    Dokumen-
    ter/051101%20Integrerte%20arbeidsprosesser%2C%20rapport.pdf
    (retrieved at February 01, 2010)
27. Stortingsmelding 38 (2004),
    http://www.regjeringen.no/nb/dep/oed/dok/regpubl/stmeld/200320
    04/Stmeld-nr-38-2003-2004-.html?id=404848
    (retrieved at December 03, 2009)
28. Perrow, C.: Normal Accidents: Living with High-Risk Technologies. Basic Books, NY (1984)
29. Jaatun, M.G., Johnsen, S.O., Line, M.B., Longva, O.H., Tøndel, I.A., Albrechtsen, E.,
    Wærø, I.: Incident Response Management in the oil and gas industry – SINTEF report
    A4086 (2007)
30. Reason, J.: Managing the risks of Organizational Accidents. Ashgate, Aldershot (1997)
31. Hollnagel, E.: Barriers and Accident Prevention. Ashgate, Aldershot (2004)
32. Roberts, K.H.: Some characteristics of one type of high reliability in organization. Organi-
    zation Science 1(2), 160–176 (1990)
33. Roberts, K.H.: New challenges in Organizational research: high reliability organizations.
    Industrial Crisis Quarterly 3, 111–125 (1989)
34. Yule, S.: Safety culture and safety climate: a review of the literature, pp. 1 – 26. Industrial
    Psychology Research Centre (2003)
35. Hudson, P., van der Graaf, G.C.: Hearts and Minds: The status after 15 years Research. In:
    Society of Petroleum Engineers (SPE 73941) International Conference on HSE in Oil and
    Gas Exploration and production, Kuala Lumpur (2002)
36. LaPorte, Consolini: Working in Practice But Not in Theory: Theoretical Challenges of
    "High-Reliability organizations". J. Public Adm. Res. Theory 1, 19–48 (1991)
37. Qian, Y., Fang, Y., Jaatun, M.G., Johnsen, S.O., Gonzalez, J.J.: Managing emerging informa-
    tion security risks during transitions to Integrated Operations. In: 43rd Hawaii International
    Conference on System Sciences, Koloa, Kauai, Hawaii (2010) ISBN: 978-0-7695-3869-3
38. Leveson, N.: Safeware – system safety. Addison-Wesley (1995)
39. Bogart, W.: The Bhopal Tragedy. Westview Press, Boulder (1989)
40. Cullen, W.D.: The Public Inquiry into the Piper Alpha Disaster. Stationery Office Books (1990)
41. Dept of the Interior (DOI), Increased safety measure for energy development on the Outer
    Continental Shelf', Salazar report (2010),
    http://www.doi.gov/deepwaterhorizon/loader.cfm?csModule=security/
    getfile&PageID=33598 (retrieved at July 31, 2010)

42. BP Deepwater Horizon Accident Investigation Report (September 8, 2010),
    `http://www.bp.com/sectiongenericarticle.do?categoryId=9034902` `&contentId=7064891` (retrieved at September 15, 2010)
43. Hopkins, A.: Lessons from Longford – The Esso Gas Plant Explosion, CCH Australia (2000)
44. Victorian Coroner's Report into the Longford Gas Explosion (1998),
    `http://web.archive.org/web/20070622023036/coron`
    (retrieved at June 03, 2010)
45. NRC, Nuclear Regulatory Commission, "The effects of Ethernet-based, nonsafety-related controls on the safe and continued operation of nuclear power stations", NRC Information Notice 2007-15, Washington, DC (2007),
    `http://www.nrc.gov/reading-rm/doc-collections/gen-comm/info-notices/2007/in200715.pdf` (retrieved on January 01, 2010)
46. Baker, et al.: The BP U.S. Refineries Independent Safety Review Panel (2007),
    `http://www.csb.gov/assets/document/Baker_panel_report1.pdf`
    (retrieved at January 01, 2010)
47. Reed, T.: At the Abyss: An Insider's History of the Cold War (2004) ISBN 0891418210
48. Byres, E., Howard, S.: White Paper - Analysis of the Siemens WinCC / PCS7 "Stuxnet" (October 14, 2010),
    `http://www.tofinosecurity.com/professional/siemens-pcs7-wincc-malware` (retrieved at October 20, 2010)
49. NTSB, National Transportation Safety Board, "Pipeline Rupture and Subsequent Fire in Bellingham, Washington (June 10, 1999)". Pipeline Accident Report NTSB/PAR-02/02, Washington, DC (2002)
50. NTSB, National Transportation Safety Board, "Safety Study – Supervisory Control and Data Acquisition (SCADA) in Liquid Pipelines". Report NTSB/SS-05/02, Washington, DC (2005)
51. Johnsen, S.O.: Resilience in Risk Analysis and Risk Assessment. In: Moore, T., Shenoi, S. (eds.) Critical Infrastructure Protection IV. Springer, Berlin (2010) ISBN 978-3642168055
52. Johnsen, S.O., Okstad, E., Aas, A.L., Skramstad, T.: Proactive indicators of risk in remote operations of oil and gas fields. Presented at SPE International Conference on Health, Safety and Environment in Oil and Gas Exploration and Production (2010), doi:10.2118/126560-MS
53. Jackson, S., Madni, A.M.: A Practical Framework for the Architecting of Resilient Enterprises. In: Hollnagel, E., Pieri, F., Rigaud, E. (eds.) Proceedings of the third Resilience Engineering Symposium. Ecole des mines de Paris (2008)
54. Woods, D., Cook, R.: Incidents – Markers of Resilience or Brittleness. In: Hollnagel, E., et al. (eds.) Resilience Engineering. Ashgate (2006)
55. Sundstrøm, G.: Learning How to Create Resilience in Business Systems. In: Hollnagel, E., et al. (eds.) Resilience Engineering. Ashgate (2006)
56. Hale, A.: Defining resilience. In: Hollnagel, E., et al. (eds.) Resilience Engineering. Ashgate (2006)
57. Westrum, R.: A Typology of Resilience Situations. In: Hollnagel, E., et al. (eds.) Resilience Engineering. Ashgate (2006)
58. Rasmussen, J.: Risk Management in a Dynamic Society. Safety Science 27, 183–213 (1997)
59. Fleming, M., Flin, R., Mearns, K., Gordon, R.: Offshore workers perceptions of risk: Comparisons with quantitative data. Risk Analysis 18(1), 103–110 (1998)
60. Tripod, Ref Tripod Beta Foundation (2006). Incident Analysis Primer (2010), Source: `http://www.tripodsolutions.net` (retrieved at January 15, 2010)

61. Van Eynde, D., Bledsoe, J.: The changing practice of organizational development. Leadership and Organizational Development Journal 11(2), 25–30 (1999)
62. Davison, R., Martinsons, M., Kock, N.: Principles of canonical action research. Information Systems Journal 14(1), 65–86 (2004)
63. Smith, S., Jamieson, R., Winchester, D.: An action research program to improve information systems security compliance across government agencies. In: Proceedings of the Fortieth Annual Hawaii International Conference on System Sciences, p. 99 (2007)
64. Armstrong, H.: Managing information security in healthcare - An action research experience. In: Qing, S., Elo, J. (eds.) Information Security for Global Information Infrastructures, pp. 19–28. Kluwer, Boston (2000)
65. Alteren, B., Sveen, J., Guttormsen, G., Madsen, B.E., Klev, R., Helgesen.: Smarter together in offshore drilling - A successful action research project? In: Proceedings of the Seventh International Conference on Probabilistic Safety Assessment and Management, pp. 1302–1308 (2004)
66. Greenwood, D., Levin, M.: Introduction to Action Research: Social Research for Social Change. Sage Publications, Thousand Oaks (2007)
67. Antonsen, S., Ramstad, L., Kongsvik, T.: Unlocking the organization: Action research as a means of improving organizational safety. Safety Science Monitor 11(1) (2007)
68. Richter, A.: New ways of managing prevention: A cultural and participative approach. Safety Science Monitor 7(1) (2003)
69. Mayo, E.: The Human Problems of an Industrial Civilization. Macmillan, New York (1933)
70. HSE, Developing process safety indicators (2006),
    http://www.hse.gov.uk/pubns/books/hsg254.html
    (retrieved at January 01, 2010), ISBN 0 7176 6180 6
71. ENISA, Measuring information security awareness - current practices (2008),
    http://enisa.europa.eu/doc/pdf/deliverables/enisa_
    measuring_awareness.pdf (retrieved at January 01, 2010)
72. SANS, The 2009 Top Cyber Risks Report (2009),
    http://www.sans.org/top-cyber-security-risks/
73. RiskMap (2008),
    http://www.thei3p.org/docs/research/riskmap200904.pdf
    (retrieved at January 01, 2010)
74. Johnsen, S.O., Bjørkli, C., Steiro, T., Fartum, H., Haukenes, H., Ramberg, J., Skriver, J.: CRIOP – A scenario method for Crisis Intervention and Operability analysis. SINTEF (2011), http://www.criop.sintef.no (retrieved at December 05, 2011)
75. Aas, A.L., Johnsen, S.O., Skramstad, T.: CRIOP: A Human Factors Verification and Validation Methodology that Works in an Industrial Setting. In: Buth, B., Rabe, G., Seyfarth, T. (eds.) SAFECOMP 2009. LNCS, vol. 5775, pp. 243–256. Springer, Heidelberg (2009)
76. ACSN, Third report of the Advisory Committee on the Safety of Nuclear Installations - Organizing for Safety - Health and Safety Commission (1993) ISBN 0-11-882104-0
77. Itoh, Andersen, Seki: Track maintenance train operators' attitudes to job, organisation and management and their correlation with accident/incident rate. Cognition, Technology and Work 6(2), 63–78 (2004)
78. Schein, E.H.: Organisational Culture and Leadership. Jossey-Bass (1992)
79. Johnsen, S.O., Hansen, C.W., Line, M.B., Nordby, Y., Rich, E., Qian, Y.: CheckIT – A program to measure and improve information security and safety culture. International Journal of Performability Engineering 3(1 Part II), 174–186 (2007)

80. Westrum, R.J.: Cultures with Requisite Imagination. In: Wise, Stager, Hopkin (eds.) Verification and Validation of Complex Systems: Human Factors Issues. Springer, Heidelberg (1993)
81. Kotter, J.P.: Leading Change. Harvard Business School Press (1996)
82. Flin, R.: Erosion of Managerial Resilience: From Vasa to NASA. In: Hollnagel, E., et al. (eds.) Resilience Engineering. Ashgate (2006)
83. Hendrick, K., Brenner, L.: Investigating Accidents with STEP. Marcel Dekker, New York (1986)
84. Henderson, J., Wright, K., Brazier, A.: Human factors aspect of remote operation in process plants. Prepared by Human Reliability Associates for the Health and Safety Executive (2002), http://www.hse.gov.uk/research/crr_pdf/2002/crr02432.pdf (retrieved at March 01, 2008)
85. IEC 60812, Analysis techniques for system reliability – Procedure for failure mode and effects analysis (FMEA) (2006)
86. IEC 61025, Fault Three Analysis, IEC (1990)
87. IsaSecure - International Society for Automation, ISA Security Compliance Institute, Research Triangle Park, North Carolina (2010), http://www.isasecure.org/ (retrieved at February 01, 2010)
88. Redmill, F., Chudleigh, M., Catmur, J.: System Safety: HAZOP and Software HAZOP. Wiley (1999)
89. Salas, E., Goodwin, G.F., Burke, C.S.: Team Effectiveness in Complex Organizations: Cross-Disciplinary Perspectives and Approaches. Routledge (2009) ISBN-13: 978-0805858815
90. Taleb, N.: The Black Swan: The Impact of the Highly Improbable. Random House, New York (2007)
91. Westrum, R.J.: Removing latent pathogens. Presented at the Sixth International Australian Aviation Psychology Conference (2003)
92. Utne, I.B., Hokstad, P., Vatn, J.: A structured approach to modelling interdependencies in risk analysis of critical infrastructures. In: ESREL 2009, Prague - Czech Republic, September 7-10 (2009)
93. Nystuen, K.O., Hagen, J.M.: Critical Information Infrastructure Protection in Norway. In: The Critical Infrastructure Protection (CIP) Workshop (2003)
94. Keizer, G.: Stuxnet researchers cautious about Iran's admission of centrifuge issues. Computerworld (November 30, 2010)

Telecommunications

Stuart Goldman[1] and Huseyin Uzunalioglu[2]

[1] 5531 E. Kelton LN, Scottsdale, AZ 85254, USA
familygoldman@gmail.com
[2] Alcatel-Lucent, 600 Mountain Avenue, Murray Hill, NJ 07974, USA
huseyin.uzunalioglu@alcatel-lucent.com

Abstract. The telecommunication network is a key critical infrastructure in any modern society. Any protracted loss of the ability for key personnel to communicate will inevitably lead to the complete collapse of that society. This chapter discusses many security and reliability concerns associated with the operation and maintenance of the telecommunications infrastructure. Telecommunications is a unique infrastructure in that other critical infrastructures are increasingly dependent on telecommunications as well as telecommunications itself being a critical infrastructure that serves many crucial needs such as Public Safety, communications for restoral of critical services, and informing the public regarding emergency situations. In this chapter we define the architecture of the next generation telecommunications network, and describe types of infrastructure failures that need to be prevented or at least minimized. In terms of protection schemes, we explain the different mechanisms that operate at different layers within the network. Particular emphasis is placed on the ability of the network to detect, isolate and resolve service impacting abnormalities. Thus, the network can restore itself to some level of operation and to maintain critical services for specified users, even when the network is degraded owing to internal or external failures or overload conditions.

Keywords: priority, critical, essential, network, information, Infrastructure, services.

1   Introduction

Telecommunications infrastructure plays a unique role in the set of critical infrastructures as it is not only a critical infrastructure in isolation but also a key component of other critical infrastructures or essential services such as power, financial services, transportation, and public safety[1]. In fact the interdependence of other critical infrastructures on the telecommunications infrastructure is increasing as the use of the Internet Protocol (IP) networking is becoming widespread, and due to the advances in Internet and web technologies. For example, telecommunication infrastructure is the

---

[1] In most countries a short code (example: 911 in US, 112 in the European Union countries) is used by the public when requesting urgent emergency assistance such as police, fire or ambulance.

J. Lopez et al. (Eds.): Critical Information Infrastructure Protection, LNCS 7130, pp. 280–300, 2012.
© Springer-Verlag Berlin Heidelberg 2012

core and the main enabler of the upcoming Smart Grids [19]. The legacy Public Switched Telephone Network (PSTN) is no longer growing and is expected to not so slowly contract until it become extinct. Ubiquitous access to the IP networks by any application makes it easy for the application users to depend on the telecommunications infrastructure as the key component of these other critical infrastructures. As IP networks are rapidly becoming the technology of choice for "future" network deployments, we focus this chapter on these networks, and the applications and services running over them as we investigate the ability of the telecommunication network to detect and defend itself against service impacting anomalies, whether these would be arising from failures caused by natural or man-made incidents.

Packet networks, such as IP networks, are designed in a layered fashion. At the lowest layer, there is a physical network, which is responsible for the physical transport of the information between the network nodes. At the highest layer, there are applications that utilize the transport services provided by the lower layers. Many layers exist between these two layers as traditionally defined by the OSI's 7-layer architecture. The appropriate defenses against network anomalies are implemented in each of the various layers. In this chapter, we first introduce the reference telecommunications network architecture as the framework to be used in the investigation of the telecommunication infrastructure protections. For this purpose, we use the International Telecommunication Union-Telecommunication Standardization Sector's Next Generation Network (ITU-T NGN) architecture, and we present the major layers and components of this architecture as it will then be referenced in the rest of the chapter. In Section 3, taxonomy of telecommunications failures are introduced. In Section 4, protection techniques that apply to the underlying transport technologies are provided. Section 5 focuses on the protection techniques implemented at the Services layer. These techniques include the application of the user's prioritization to provide services to a subset of users during incidents where the telecommunications infrastructure has lost all or some fraction of its capacity because of anomalies. Furthermore, defense schemes that can be used by the network applications such as overlay routing are also addressed. Such mechanisms provide additional protection independent of whatever the network is already providing regarding reliability and resiliency. Although the focus of the chapter is the IP NGN, it should not be forgotten that legacy, non-IP, networks will be in use for many years (decades?). Thus, in Section 6, we present the issues relating to the interoperability of the NGN with the legacy network. In Section 7, we discuss the importance of quantifying the impact of cascading failures affecting telecommunications and other infrastructures and critical services. In Section 8, we present our concluding remarks.

2   Next Generation Network Architecture

ITU-T defines the Next Generation Network (NGN) as "a packet-based network able to provide services including Telecommunication Services and able to make use of multiple broadband, QoS-enabled transport technologies and in which service-related functions are independent from underlying transport-related technologies." [1]. Based on this definition, NGN is a packet network, which can be implemented currently or in the future as an all-IP network, although this IP network may interconnect with legacy networks at gateways. Broadband and QoS-enabled transport are also seen as defining features. Finally, there is a clear separation between service-layer functions and transport-related technologies. ITU-T further defines the main characteristics of the NGN network in [1]. The service and transport layers replace the 7-layers of the traditional OSI architecture. While the full details can be found at [2], the fundamental need for this simplified 2-layer model is really due to the observation that the OSI architecture was very rigid with the individual layers and their functionalities. Such rigidity can result in greater design effort along with reduced capacity because of the "handling" of the components between each layer. In practical implementations, an NGN system can use less than the 7 layers, and the functions of individual layers chosen may not correspond to classic layers in the OSI model. Thus, ITU-T defined NGN architecture simplifies the layered architecture, and provides greater efficiency and flexibility. Clear separation of services from the transport allows both layers to evolve independently from each other. In this Section, we provide details of the NGN layers as we present the telecommunications infrastructure protection schemes in reference to these layers in the following sections.

In the NGN architecture, transport functions reside in the transport stratum and the service functions related to applications reside in the service stratum. The transport stratum is responsible for the transport of the information between any two geographically separate points. The transport stratum roughly encompasses the lower 3 layers of the OSI architecture which are the physical, link, and network layers. Regarding the technologies being deployed today, this covers wireless and wireline physical transmission technologies such as cellular, optical, and electrical at the physical layer, and Ethernet, IP, and Multi Protocol Label Switching (MPLS) technologies at the link and network layers.

In the NGN architecture, the services functions reside in the Service stratum as the name suggests. This stratum may include a set of services platforms to support communication services such as voice, video, and data. Communication applications access to these services provided by the NGN network. As an example to these service functions, IP Multimedia Subsystem (IMS) [13] provides a support infrastructure such as call control and signaling, subscriber databases, and policy control and management to multimedia communication applications. A next generation IMS application such as video telephony and Presence-enabled group communication may utilize these functions without implementing them from scratch. Calls to 911 from mobile devices now include the current location of the caller as derived from the built in GPS capability, and increasingly there is a desire to be able to include real-time pictures or video from the built in camera to more clearly convey the emergency situation.

Protection of the Telecommunications infrastructure needs to be addressed at both stratums of the NGN architecture. Each layer and each underlying technology has its own protection scheme. For example, the transport stratum can be implemented to be resilient against connectivity problems through the use of re-routing techniques which can be implemented for different technologies independently. In Section 4, we present protection techniques that can be implemented in the transport stratum and describe IP/MPLS networks as an implementation example. Even though the transport stratum can be designed to handle connectivity problems and deliver highly available connectivity functions to the communications applications and the services stratum, this is no guarantee that it will be completely successful in handling all types of possible network anomalies. There will be configuration errors in the deployment of even the best protection schemes, attacks on the network by people with the knowledge of the network internals, and overload problems related to natural or man-made events. The applications and the services stratum also needs to implement defenses against the anomalies that can impact the capacity and functioning of the underlying transport stratum. In Section 5, we review two of these defenses, namely the subscriber prioritization that provides uninterrupted communication services to a subset of users even when the transport stratum lost an important fraction of its capacity, and application overlay routing, which utilizes intelligence within the application to find alternate paths between server locations to circumvent connectivity problems. However, before we go into describing these network defenses, types of infrastructure failures are explained first in the following section.

3   Types of Telecommunications Infrastructure Failures

In this section we discuss various types of telecommunication infrastructure failures and the degree to which they are "isolated to a single node" or can cascade through multiple nodes in the network. Furthermore we focus on how these failures impact not only the telecommunication critical infrastructure but also the end users and applications accessing to it. The impairment of the applications can in turn adversely impact the proper operation and restoration of other critical infrastructures beyond telecommunication since there is a strong interdependence between the various critical infrastructures which should be apparent simply because they are so critical to the operation of society. Upcoming Smart Grids will make this interdependence very clear even to consumers who are not experts in the technology areas.

3.1   Power

The loss of power is not exactly a telecommunications infrastructure issue in of itself, but is nevertheless devastating to the telecommunication functions. While we like to think the populous is well aware of the technical limitations of their user equipment that is largely not the case. If we picture a typical house, we see that the user may have cordless phones scattered around the premises and may not have even a single hardwired phone. With the loss of AC power, the user has lost his phone service simply because the end instruments no longer have power. Moving onto the Internet side of the home we find that the cable modem also plugs into the AC and ceases to function. The router (wireless or wireline) also stops. And finally, the desktop computer is also without power except for those very few users who have purchased an uninterruptable power supply. Even the laptops will quickly deplete their batteries. The cell phones in the home will continue to work, but their batteries will soon exhaust. Few users have supplemental batteries or solar bases as chargers. (The authors of course do have such devices but we represent an infinitesimal section of the populous). Thus we see that while the telecommunication infrastructure may still be fully functional, access to it will be severely limited as a result of user power outages. Such was the case in Italy during the black-out of 2003 when there was a considerable delay in the power industry restart process because, due to an insufficient dimensioning of the power reserves in some telecommunication nodes, it was not possible to tele-control some of the power plants. [15]

A typical business environment will prove to have the same fundamental characteristics as the home described above but magnified by the size of the business and the immediacy of the impact due to the loss. We have all experienced attempting to buy something with a credit card at a store only to be told that the power is out or the computer system is down and they cannot process the credit card. (Memory is short and they have forgotten the use of the now "old fashioned" card machines that make a physical imprint of the card and the transaction along with pen and ink signature for manual input later on.)

Expanding this exercise further, we discuss the prolonged loss of power to the actual Telecommunication infrastructure. Most of the local access and backbone infrastructure nodes do have some form of limited backup power in case of loss of the commercial power, but a sustained absence of such power will soon cause the batteries to drain and the diesel generators to exhaust. In the past some telephone offices had connections to the natural gas lines and their generators would be able to run indefinably based on that accessibility. Alternatively some telephone offices had large pools of fuel to extend the time they could remain in service. Some even had two separate leads to AC from different substations.

As we were writing this chapter, we saw a news article that is a clear example of successful" thinking out of the box." An aging transmission line built in 1948 is the only link between the U.S. power grid and the city of Presidio in West Texas. So Presidio has invested in a single huge battery that can power the entire town and serve as emergency backup for the frequent outages caused by the line going down. The huge battery can store up to four megawatts of power. [2] While this addresses the town's backup for power generation/reception, it does not address the possibility of more localized transmission failures within the town. Critical telecommunication applications are still vulnerable and need to have localized power backup plans in place.

Indeed there are situations showing the strong cross dependency between the power infrastructure and that of telecommunications. Restoration of power requires telecommunications between key personnel and systems, which can be hampered if the telecommunication infrastructure fails because it has been deprived of power for too long.

3.2   Hardware Failures

The telecommunication infrastructure contains a multitude of nodes. In the IP (Internet Protocol) network, these nodes are massively interconnected in a strong mesh architecture which contrasts the traditional hierarchal architecture of the legacy PSTN. The hardware at any given node is subject to a spontaneous failure, just like any other hardware box. This is of course a weakness in the network to the extent that

---

[2] Heard on National Public Radio.

the same or similar component is used in a large majority of the nodes, even when manufactured by different vendors. A systemic weakness in such a component can result in a higher than acceptable failure rate across the nodes, but the likelihood of the component failing simultaneously in a collection of the nodes is miniscule. Thus the network is likely to stay up (based on the massive mesh routing capabilities) even though the operators may face higher maintenance costs than expected as well as the need for a program to replace the defective component in the nodes. Furthermore, such failures may result in loss of functionality for a period of time until a backup becomes operational. The length of this recovery time is a function of the type of the failure and implemented recovery technology.

Failures in the local environment surrounding a node can cause the node to fail. An example happened in Italy in 2004 where the failure of the air-conditioning system in an important Telco node created very large impact. [18] Following the 9-11 event in New York the dust in the air caused numerous air filters to clog and critical air conditioning failed leading to subsequent equipment outages.

3.3   Software Failures

Software failures can be more insidious than the aforementioned hardware failure because there is a somewhat greater possibility that an undiscovered software error can adversely affect all of the nodes, especially when upgraded to a new release. Such a risk can be minimized by the operators following a conscious, well paced rollout of new releases rather than a "flash deployment". Such an approach is recommended even in light of known problems with the current load that the vendor promises will be fixed in the new release. (Remember the Microsoft Vista release promises and its reality.)

Another example of a software error that can spontaneously manifest itself in all the nodes is a date or other event driven logic error. We all remember the great fear that our society would come to a sudden halt as we entered the year 2000. The fear was that planes would fall from the sky, elevators would freeze up, hospital operating rooms would shut down in the middle of operations and computers everywhere would fail and erase all of our financial records. Of course none of this actually happened but the fear that should something have happen, it would be replicated in all of the devices with that software load across the planet. Thus, it would not just be one wayward elevator but all of the elevators in the building (same model) and elevators across the planet made by the vendors with the faulty software.

3.4   Unexpected Overload

Each year there are numerous unanticipated focused overloads on some portion of the network which can overwhelm the capacity to correctly handle the offered traffic. Special events, call- ins, weather events, etc. can cause a surge in traffic that is both unexpected and beyond the capacity of the network to handle. Natural disasters such as earthquakes or man-made events such as the one experienced on 9/11 often result in an unprecedented amount of communications load instantaneously coming into affected areas as people try to reach friends and family, at the same time as the outgoing traffic also spikes. Such levels of traffic loads are, in general, an order of magnitude larger than the telecommunications infrastructure in the area can handle. If the equipment is simply left to its own, the overload can make it useless as most of the computing resources would be spent by processing messages unsuccessfully, i.e. the throughput of the system goes down. Traditional telecommunication networks such as PSTN have solved this problem by blocking the remote traffic at the origination nodes using controls such as manual or automated controls such as Code Gapping, where the originating node blocks certain amount of traffic destined to the affected area. Although some telecommunications operators are already implementing such controls in their next generation networks, not all are convinced that similar controls are needed in the NGN network. Furthermore, as the PSTN networks are still in use, the impact of overloads in IP networks is not well-tested in the deployed networks.

3.5   Cascading Failures

Cascading failures are the most troubling in that the collapse of the entire network is possible, and the network may even fail to come back from a cold restart. Without proper protection such a massive failure could reach global proportions. The impact on commerce and national security can be significant.

When a node no longer functions as designed, the traffic spills over to other nodes in the network based on the massive mesh based architecture. Normally this works well as the sessions are able to continue with the node excluded. However if a number of nodes are affected at the same time, the resulting redistribution of traffic results in other nodes going into congestion and attempting to spill over traffic to yet other nodes. Very shortly one can imagine that the situation becomes intolerable with more and more nodes shutting down. We have seen a similar situation with the power grid where a minor problem at one substation was able to escalate, resulting in more and more portions of the power network going offline. A shutdown and restart of the network was required to bring it back to an operational status.

If there is a software problem, data error or an attack on the network, the degree of cascading and the speed of the network collapse can be quite rapid. Rumor has it that a new virus attack can spread across the globe in seven seconds. Wither true or not, this does establish the order of magnitude with which a cascading event can occur. In fact, to exemplify, in 2003, SQL Slammer infected 90 percent of vulnerable hosts, around 75,000 Microsoft SQL Servers, within 10 minutes [14].

3.6   Deliberate Attacks

Sadly, in our current society we must consider that the above errors may not only occur naturally, but there may (will) be cases of deliberate attack by people wishing to cause havoc for whatever misguided reasons. The reasons are far outside the scope of this chapter but may be interesting reading in the psychological, social and political writings of others. We describe some of the possibilities but purposely not giving a recipe of exactly how to do it for obvious reasons.

Without effective control of the supply chain from third party vendors as well as internal manufacturing controls, one disgruntled person can effectively sabotage a critical hardware component. Since components are tested in various stages of equipment assembly, it would be much more effective not to "break" the component outright but rather to adversely affect its expected life, operating temperature range, etc.

In a similar vein, the addition of a "backdoor" in the software can then give the perpetrator the ability to cause the software in all the nodes to execute the malicious code at the will of the attacker. An example happened in 2000 in Maroochy Shire (Australia) where an ex-employer inserted some backdoors in a SCADA systems of a sewage plant and were able to remotely penetrate into the system causing several problems. Even more troubling is the recent Stuxnet worm attacking a nuclear plant.[17] Denial of Service (DoS) attacks can either bring down a site or so congest it that service is denied for the legitimate users. The perpetrator may enlist an "army" of contaminated computers (botnets [10]) to form the attack as a distributed denial of service. As one might imagine this form of attack is harder to combat since it comes from a multitude of addresses.

Viruses and worms can easily be released on the IP network and if not immediately detected and neutralized, they can make the entire network unusable in minutes. This can have severe worldwide consequences.

Perpetrators may not be content to simply attack the network from afar, but may physically attack vulnerable elements. Cable cuts, destruction of hubs and other nodes are a possibility that should be considered in planning alternatives.

3.7   The Unimaginable Happens

Let's envision a telecommunication infrastructure that has been designed following all the best practices and no money has been spared in procuring the finest parts and most comprehensively designed and tested software. One might imagine that such a well crafted network would be immune to the vectors discussed above. It would be unstoppable and "unsinkable".

We must remember that the forces of nature often can destroy even the best of our creations. For every Titanic designed, there may be a bigger iceberg waiting to strike.

We learnt on 9-11 that the massive increase in communication attempts overwhelmed the legacy telecommunications network for hours and hours. Calls failed to complete even between points far away from New York City.

We learnt from New Orleans that a massive widespread flood can disrupt the telecommunication network by destroying facilities and interrupting power to remaining facilities. This was compounded by the inability to replenish fuel for generators at undamaged sites.

We learnt from Haiti that massive destruction can literally destroy the wireline communication in a whole city. Diversifying the Public Safety Answering Points (PSAP)[3] is a best practice that had been instantly made ineffective when both sites were destroyed simultaneously by the earthquake.

---

[3] PSAPs are the special purpose call centers to which public requests for emergency assistance (911, 112, etc.) are routed. The call takers at the PSAP are trained to quickly identify the nature of the emergency and dispatch assistance, be it police, ambulance, or fire trucks. The PSAP call takers can provide reassurance to the often panicked caller that help is on the way.

4   Transport Stratum Protection Techniques

The goal of the transport stratum in the NGN architecture is to provide connectivity between two geographically dispersed locations to allow the transfer of information of any kind, packed into IP packets. In this section, we introduce the basic concepts of protecting transport stratum in a generic way and then introduce Multi Protocol Label Switching (MPLS) technology as an implementation example of these concepts. In Figure 1, an abstraction of a transport stratum of the communication network is presented. The network consists of a number of nodes (N) and links (L) connecting them. Users of the network are exemplified by U_A and U_B. The goal of the network is to transfer information from the U_A to U_B, or vice versa. Information transfer follows the many possible paths possible, some of which are shown in the figure. Exact path to follow and processing occurring in intermediate nodes depend of the technology of use. In fact, the network in Figure 1 can depict an optical network, an Ethernet network, an IP network, or an MPLS network.

   In a network, such as the one shown in Figure 1, the two modes of communication are defined as connection-oriented and connectionless. In a connection-oriented communication mode, the path from a network node such as N_A in Figure 1 to another node such as N_B is well defined, pre-established, and persistent for the duration of session. When an end user, such as U_A, sends packets to another end user, such as U_B, these packets are identified as being assigned to the path from N_A to N_B. The intermediate nodes dynamically decide on how to forward the packets based on this identification. As examples of the connection-oriented technologies, circuit-switched networks such as PSTN[4], ATM, and MPLS[5] can be given. In Section 4.1 we provide a brief description of the MPLS technology.

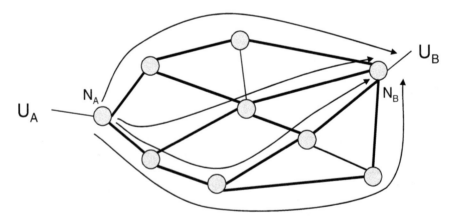

Fig. 1. An abstraction of a communication network

---

[4] The PSTN SS7 protocol supports both connectionless and connection orientated messages.
[5] Multiprotocol Label Switching (MPLS) is a technology in telecommunications networks which directs and carries data from one network node to the next along a pre-established network path.

Connectionless networks, on the other hand, have no concept of a persistent transport connection between the end nodes. Instead, individual nodes dynamically decide how to route a given packet based on the destination address information contained in the packet header. Since the decision is made for each packet, the route for any given packet may differ from the proceeding or subsequent packets between same two endpoints. The best example of this mode is the IP networking technology. IP routers rely on routing protocols such as Intermediate system-to-Intermediate System (IS-IS) [7] or Open Shortest Path First (OSPF) [8] to create a routing table that maps the destination addresses to an outgoing interface at a given router.

In terms of protecting the transport stratum, the architect's goal is to protect the network from singular failures, accidents, and attacks rendering a node or link out of service. However, there can be no complete protection scheme that can eliminate the failure scenarios completely when multiple nodes and links are compromised. The protection scheme relies on redundancy and this strategy is overwhelmed when a multitude of the elements are compromised simultaneously. Therefore, in addition to physical protection of the elements, networks are architected to be resilient against failures through protocol and network design. Protocol design for resilience involves providing intelligence and capabilities to the underlying transport technology. As an example, a common resiliency method is to do rerouting when there is a failure in the network. A number of re-routing mechanisms can be defined:

– Active/Standby Paths: This scheme is applicable to connection-oriented networks. Between different network nodes there are at least two paths. One of them carries traffic, hence referred to as the active or the primary path, while the secondary path, although pre-established, does not carry any traffic as long as the primary path is fully functional, this is referred to as the standby path. If the primary path fails, the standby path becomes operational and starts to carry traffic. A key performance metric for a re-routing mechanism is the restoration time, which is the time it takes to move the traffic in the failed path into a new path to re-establish the connectivity. With the active/standby arrangement, as the standby path is pre-established, the switchover occurs very fast once the primary path failure is detected by the originating node of both paths. The failure detection time is a function of the size of the network and the discovery method implemented in the technology. In one such method, path originator node sends periodic messages to the path termination node, which echoes back these messages to the origination. If the origination does not hear this "heartbeat" for a predefined period, the primary path is declared to be down and the traffic is switched over to the secondary path. In a different failure detection method, the node closest to the failure detects the failure and informs the path origination. This latter method results in faster discovery as local failure detection relies on information from the physical layer, which detects the connectivity problem almost instantly. During the network design, routing of the active and standby paths are optimized such that during a path switchover, the standby path has the necessary resources to support the traffic to be carried.

– Path Re-route after failure: This method is similar to the active/standby as defined above except that the standby path is not pre-established. Once the path originator detects the path failure, a new path is established through signaling. This method results in longer recovery delays as the path establishment causes additional delay. Furthermore, the network designer should make sure that the network has sufficient bandwidth resources to establish the new path. Otherwise, the path may not be established or if it can be established, the lack of sufficient bandwidth results in congestion in the network impacting the quality of the existing and new communication sessions.

–   Local Path Re-route: With this method, when a failure occurs, neighboring nodes detect the failure and the communication path is recovered by the remaining network nodes re-routing the failed section of the path around the fault. This technique can work quite fast as it benefits from the local failure detection and re-routing, although the resulting new path is longer than optimal. To switch to a better path, this method is used in addition to the active/standby or path re-route after failure methods as defined above. Upon a failure, Local Path Re-route recovers the connectivity very quickly. The resulting path is replaced by an optimal one, established by the origination node following the active/standby or path reroute after failure schemes.

In connectionless networks, such as pure IP networks, when a link or node fails, the failure information is distributed to all over the network through the OSPF [8] or the IS-IS [7] routing protocols. Upon receiving the link failure information, each router re-computes its routing table. As IS-IS and OSPF are distributed routing protocols, it takes some time for all the network nodes to converge into the same network topology and routing plan. Although, in recent years, there have been some work in new protocols for fast re-routing, network operators today generally prefer connection-oriented networks and protocols such as Multiprotocol Label Switching (MPLS) [3].

In terms of resilient network design, the following principles are commonly used when networks are deployed:

–   Physical Diversity: The network should provide diverse paths between a given node pair such that it is possible to have a working path when the primary path fails. For example, in the active/standby method, if the active and the standby paths have common physical nodes and/or links, the protection scheme is insufficient as the failure of these shared resources takes down both the active and the standby paths, possibly resulting in disconnected nodes after failure. Thus, in industry, special attention is given to designing networks with path and node physical diversity, and network operators make sure that primary and secondary paths are link and node disjoint, although due to economical reasons, some operators would prefer to go with a lesser degree of protection than this by taking risks.

–   Hardware Redundancy: Of course a hardware failure can take a communication node out of service. Communication nodes are built with this vulnerability and protection in mind. Active/Standby arrangement in the concept of communication paths is also applied to the hardware elements. At its best, each hardware card in a node is protected by a redundant card so that if the primary card fails, the standby card takes over and the node remains in service unless there are multiple, simultaneous failures within the node[6]. This way, it is possible to limit the hardware downtime to a few minutes a year. Still, the quality of protection depends on the economics where some operators may prefer to do less than the 1+1 protection, such as N+K protection, where N cards are protected by K cards where K is less than N. If the underlying hardware is highly reliable, even the N+K protection may result in highly-available networks.[7]

- Redundant Capacity: As mentioned in the above discussion of the path protection methods, when a secondary path is activated, the network operator needs to ensure that the links used by this path have sufficient resources to support the traffic switched over to the path as well as the traffic already being carried on these links. It does not help if the traffic put onto the new path congests a link, resulting in unacceptable communication quality. This failure to properly engineer the traffic capacity in the case of a switchover during peak traffic can result in a growing, cascading of failed routes until the entire network has been compromised.[8] Capacity issues can be addressed during the design phase where the architect confirms the failure scenarios to determine the new resource requirements after failures. If each link and node supports these requirements, in operation, capacity requirements are met. Another method is to limit the utilization of the network links to well below 50% of the engineering limit of the link[9]. This way, if the traffic on a link is failed over to another link, the resulting traffic is still utilized under the engineering limits.

- Geographical Redundancy of Servers: Most Internet technologies use client/server architectures where many clients access a server, such as a web server, database server, an IPTV server, etc. As these servers would be providing services for critical infrastructures, they have to be designed to be highly available with respect to failures, which may result from natural events such as earthquakes and fires to man-made events such as terrorist attacks. A common way of protecting these resources against such disasters is to provide a replica of the server in a different location[10], far away from the serving node following the active/standby concept. Both locations are kept in sync of each other and hence when the active site fails, the standby can take over very quickly without loss of information. Another approach to the redundancy is load sharing where both nodes are active and share the load. Should a node go out of service the mate assumes the entire load, so again the engineering must be conservative with the load factor being well below half of the peak traffic.

---

[6] Loss of power, fire, loss of air conditioning, water damage, physical destruction are a few examples of damage to a node that overwhelms the concept of simple redundancy.

[7] This scheme is also overwhelmed by the mechanisms previous cited in the prior footnote.

[8] In such cases it may be necessary to shutdown the whole network and perform a managed restart of the network in order to restore the traffic to the engineered paths.

[9] Because traffic is not uniform, it may be the case that because of spikes in traffic, the capacity limit may be closer to 35-40% of engineered capacity to allow for a graceful processing of the spikes in offered traffic.

[10] Geographic diversity. This includes the node as well as the paths to the node.

4.1   Technology Example: Path Protection in MPLS Networks

MPLS [3] was first introduced as a technology to create virtual paths, known as Label Switched Paths (LSPs), over an IP network, although it was later expanded to work over Ethernet and optical networks. As explained above, IP routers decide how to forward the packets based on the destination IP address and the routing table that was built using a routing protocol. In MPLS, routers rely on the so called "label" to decide on which output interface to send the packets. At the ingress to the IP/MPLS network, the first router, also referred to as the Label Edge Router (LER), inserts an MPLS header into the IP packet. The header has fields such as the label and traffic class. Specific label to insert is decided upon the rules configured in the LER. As an example, the rule can be based on the destination IP address only, or the combination of the destination address and application type that the packet belongs to. In the example depicted in Figure 2, the LER R1 relies on the destination IP address to insert a label "4" and send the packet on its output port "2". Based on this, the packet reaches the Label Switch Router (LSR) R3 at its input port "1". R3 relies on its label switching table to replace the label to "6" and then sends the packet out at the output port 3. The packet reaches LER R4, which serves the destination address 135.17.1.2. The router R4 pops the label and forwards the IP packet to its destination. As the example shows, MPLS creates paths over a connectionless network such as IP. These paths can be assigned certain quality of service. For example, if the path is carrying voice traffic, it can be given higher priority at each router in comparison to best-effort Internet packets. Similarly, based on the protection requirements of the traffic, path recovery methods as explained above can be implemented.

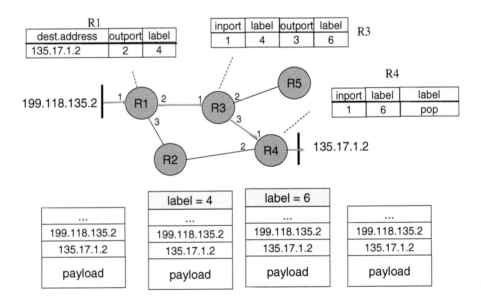

Fig. 2. Packet forwarding in MPLS networks

The LSPs in an MPLS network are pre-configured by the network operator using a configuration management system, which generally instructs the LERs in the network to signal the set up of the LSPs to terminating LERs. An origination LER, also referred to as the head-end LER, issues a Resource Reservation Protocol-Traffic Engineering (RSVP-TE) [5] message towards the terminating LER, also referred to as the tail-end LER. All routers along the path of the RSVP-TE message configure their label switching tables to create the LSP, which becomes the primary path to carry traffic between the head-end and the tail-end LERs. Based on the protection scheme [4], network operator can also create a secondary LSP as the standby LSP for a given primary LSP. What is common to both LSPs are the head-end and tail-end LERs. Under normal operations, the head-end LER matches IP packets into individual primary LSPs and inserts them into these paths as described above. A path failure is detected by the MPLS routers through the use of link probing techniques or path continuity tests. Link probing used by neighbor LSRs to detect the failure of the link between them. Upon the detection of the failure, these LSRs would try to fix the problem by locally re-routing [6] the path around the failed link, if configured that way by the network operator, and by informing the head-end LER simultaneously of the failure. With the path continuity test, head-end LER sends probing messages to the tail-end LER, which echoes back these messages to the head-end LER. When the failure of the primary path is detected by the head-end LER, traffic is diverted into the standby LSP. When there is no standby LSP configured, the originating LER can try to signal a new LSP to carry the traffic. MPLS technology allows configuration of LSPs into paths that are optimized to achieve network performance objectives in an economical way, and is very common in new IP network deployments.

4.2 Effect of Network Topology

The major legacy telecommunication nodes are generally placed into buildings that are owned or leased by the network provider. These buildings have special AC power and security arrangements. Furthermore they are located on fiber optics cable routes. Thus it is not an easy job to introduce new locations with the same level of security and protection into the network. As a result, when transforming existing telecommunication infrastructures into Next Generation Networks, the new architecture inherits some features of the existing networks, such as the location of the nodes and their physical connectivity. Not all locations are same regarding the degree of connectivity. Some nodes are located on major fiber optics hubs and are connected to many other nodes via several links. Some other nodes have limited number of connectivity options, and thus they have fewer neighbor nodes and links to these nodes.

There is a growing trend to use "hoteling" as a means of distributing equipment into common closets that are shared by a number of service providers. While this approach has considerable cost savings as well as the issue of availability, the downside is that security is reduced to that of the least sophisticated provider with access to the common area. Damage can result from neglect, human error, and sadly from willful attack. To compound matters, the diversity being relied upon for reliability may not be present if the "redundant" equipment from another service provider is in the same location and can be compromised by an action or event common to both equipment elements.

The nodes that have higher connectivity carry higher aggregate traffic compared to the nodes that have lesser connectivity. This makes these nodes even more critical for the network's resilience. Compare two example networks shown in Figure 3. Both networks have the same number of nodes and link. The graph on the left has more homogenous nodes with regard to connectivity. All the nodes except one have three neighbors while the remaining node has four neighbors. A random node failure will have limited impact on this network, and failure of any node would result in similar impact. Network on the right in figure 3 has one node with five neighbors and two nodes with four neighbors. *Node A* (N_A) is a hub for many connections. If node A fails, the impact will be much worse than the failure of any of the other nodes. Removing the randomness out of the picture, a terrorist attack on *node A* would cripple the network. Thus, it is vey important to keep the network connectivity information and node locations confidential although today some of this information is publicly known or can be purchased legitimately. Perhaps a best practice would be to avoid creating such points of concentration and vulnerability in the first place. The initial design and deployment of complex networks, or networks that are likely to become more complex over time, should address intentional and unintentional conditions. [16]

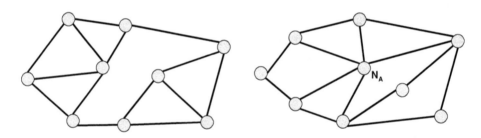

Fig. 3. Network topologies with different vulnerability levels

5   Service Stratum Protection

Service stratum, as described in Section 2, provides common service infrastructure functions to applications accessing the NGN network. Different applications rely on these functions to signal connection set-ups and to request specific quality of service. Thus, if these common service functions support protection schemes, the applications can take advantage of these without the application developers spending a lot of time to design and to implement common protection schemes. In this section we describe two such solutions as subscriber prioritization and overlay routing. Note that the later solution can also be implemented by the application instead of or in addition to the service stratum

5.1   Subscriber Prioritization

In 1988 the T1X1 committee in North America created the High Probability of Call Completion standard, which is the Standards basis for the US Government

Emergency Telecommunication Service (GETS) for voice calls from government authorized users in times of congestion. GETS was widely deployed in the United States starting in 1995 for wireline originated calls. In 2002 a similar program, Wireless Priority Access (WPS), was developed and deployed to provide a similar level of priority for wireless calls.

Multilevel precedence and preemption (MLPP) [11]: "In military communications, a priority scheme (a) for assigning one of several precedence levels to specific calls or messages so that the system handles them in a predetermined order and time frame, (b) for gaining controlled access to network resources in which calls and messages can be preempted only by higher priority calls and messages, (c) that is recognized only within a predefined domain, and (d) in which the precedence level of a call outside the predefined domain is usually not recognized. The International Telecommunications Union approved the MLPP recommendation in March 1993."

The Internet Engineering Task Force (IETF)[11] has added the optional Resource Priority Header (RPH) to the SIP Invite message [9] to allow for priority on IP session requests. Detailed procedures are under development at the time of writing this chapter which will provide a framework for ensuring a high degree of certainty that such critical sessions can be established and maintained with an acceptable quality of service even when the IP network is severely damaged or in massive overload. It is envisioned that this mechanism can be used for government authorized users during periods of congestion, communications from PSAPS responding to emergency calls from the public, and agencies such as the US Defense Information Systems Agency (DISA). This mechanism can be used for various types of sessions including voice, data, and video. It is applicable to any session type invoked with a SIP invite message.

Standards are being developed at 3rd Generation Partnership Project (3GPP)[12] for Enhanced Multi-level Precedence and Preemption (traffic) for wireless session prioritization.

It should be noted that there has been a misconception regarding these mechanisms giving faster session establishment for the users. Generally that is not the case and sessions may even take a bit longer to establish because of the additional authentication processes invoked, as well as the queuing for resources. These mechanisms should be viewed as giving the user a much greater probability of establishing a session when others are failing to do so because of a massively congested network.

5.2 Overlay Routing

As explained in Section 4, the function of the transport stratum is to carry information from a starting point to an end point using a network of transport nodes. These nodes and the links connecting them are protected to achieve resilience, and path re-routing schemes are in place to restore connectivity after failures. However, this type of

---

[11] http://www.ietf.org/
[12] http://www.3gpp.org/

failure protection generally does not address drastic, widespread failures caused by disasters and man-made events. To complicate the matter further, the communication between two end points may travel through the infrastructure of multiple network providers with different resilience and restoration plans. To increase the reliability of the communication further, it is possible to utilize protection techniques at the service stratum and in the application, both of which are above the transport stratum. One useful technique is the use of overlay routing, where nodes in the services stratum or application servers act as routing nodes for the network application. Figure 4 explains the concept using a simple example communication from Host 1 to Host 2 (shown as unidirectional for simplicity). The figure shows four separate networks, potentially representing different network providers. The intermediate node connected to network C can be implemented in the service stratum or at the application layer (part of the application running between the two hosts). The direct path between the hosts goes through the networks A, B, and D, and is governed by the transport stratum topologies and technologies. Without overlay routing, a disaster impacting network B would lead to communication problems for the hosts. In such a case, the traffic can be routed through the intermediate node going over the networks A, C, and D. Note that it is possible to preferentially use the overlay path when its performance is better than the direct path. Thus, the overlay routing provides a means to achieve both reliability as well as better performance especially when the end hosts are served by different networks.

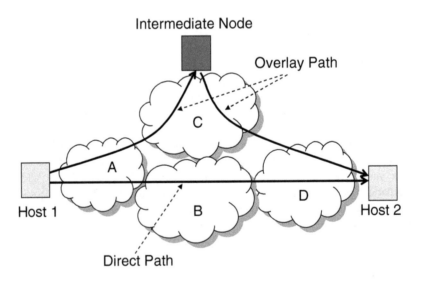

Fig. 4. Example of the use of Overlay Routing for Resilience

6   Interoperability with Legacy Systems

The legacy TDM network will coexist for at least the next decade or two with the new NGN. Some people will continue to have service from legacy providers for the foreseeable future while others will be served exclusively by NGN providers. It is a given that the populations demands full ubiquitous access from any user to any other user. A "phone number" is a phone number and people will expect and demand they can place such calls and the appropriate magic happens to make the connection. The call is not aware of the network type used to provide service for the terminating party. Today the caller does not generally know if he is calling a land line or a mobile phone; he simply wishes to reach the desired person without further explicit action on the part of the caller. The same model will apply to service provided over twisted pairs of copper wire, wireless, or NGN packet technologies. The interworking at the gateway nodes between the networks must be transparent for the caller. The gateway node is tasked with providing security between the two networks such that an attack cannot easily cross the barrier. The gateway needs to "speak" both protocols[13] and correctly format the information into appropriate messages as the session crosses between the two networks. Procedures must be defined to address those informational elements that are not supported in both networks or have differences that must be addressed by default procedures in the gateway.

The need for, and the functionality of, such gateway nodes make them key vulnerability points when connecting to the legacy networks. A deliberate attack on these gateways may isolate the networks from each other. Since the gateways act as a point of presence, there is a natural tendency to concentrate the traffic through a small number of such gateways. Thus, it is very critical to utilize multiple, geographically separated, interconnection points between networks. Another issue, although not directly an interoperability one, is that when transitioning to the NGN network, improper sizing of the new and the legacy networks during the transition period can make the telecommunications infrastructure more vulnerable to capacity problems and overloads.

7   Critical Infrastructure Interdependency Modeling

As telecommunications is a key infrastructure, it is of the utmost important to understand the interdependence of telecommunications with the other critical infrastructures. Knowing how this interdependence plays out when the unexpected happens is the first step needed to be taken when designing proper mitigation scenarios. Another constraint when designing mitigation scenarios is how to best effectively use the always scarce resources, monetary and otherwise, to minimize the impacts of an outage and shorten the recovery time. Towards this end, quantification of the critical infrastructure interdependencies through modeling plays a key role. Only with this quantification, one can know the highest risks areas that will require urgent investment towards mitigation. As an example of how to quantify critical infrastructure interdependencies, a suite of simulation tools [12] to study the effect of telecom outages has been developed. The simulation suite covers telecommunications networks ranging from the PSTN to packet data networks. These tools [12] were used in conjunction with

---

[13] Such as SS7 and SIP.

a system-level simulation of power and emergency services to quantify the interdependencies between power, telecommunications, and emergency services. The particular scenario studied was such that power blackouts cause loss of telephone service for those without power back-up, which then impacts the ability of people to call 911 in emergency service situations. The impact of the scenario was quantified as the inability to call the emergency services results in moderate injuries becoming major injuries, and major injuries becoming fatal. At the core of this scenario, there is the increasing dependency of the people over communication devices that fully depend on AC power as explained in Section 3.1 earlier. Namely, these devices include cordless phones, wireless phones, and voice over VoIP phones. The modeled scenario included a period of 34 hours of a complete blackout followed by four hours of recovery. Under this power failure scenario, network telecom efficiency falls to around 65% in several hours.. (A 100% telecom efficiency means that everyone is able to make telephone call in general, and 911 calls in particular.) Emergency services consist of police, fire, and medical. In the model developed in [12], when the calls to medical services fail, some of the minor injuries become major, and some of the major injuries become fatal, resulting in an incremental monetary cost to the society. Based on the simulation results, for a metropolitan area of five million people, a 34 hour power outage results in an incremental cost of $36M taking into account only the cascading effect induced on telecommunication infrastructures
. Sensitivity analysis shows that the incremental cost increases as function of the outage duration, fraction of the population with AC-power dependent communication devices, and whether or not the incident also causes damage to the telecommunication infrastructure other than loss of power. As this example shows, the impact of a failure scenario that touches on multiple infrastructures and critical services can be quantified in monetary terms and the results can be used to decide on whether the risk is acceptable and what the mitigations methods are, if not.

8   Conclusions

In this chapter, we presented a general telecommunications architecture, and laid out potential vulnerabilities and protection schemes. We have discussed the concept of protection of individual nodes and paths at the various layers, and pointed out that however robust these protection mechanisms can be made, they can be overwhelmed by multiple failures. These mechanisms are needed in the normal, everyday operation of the network and we do not intend to denigrate their essential value. However, if there are failures in both the active and standby sides of a node, then the node may well be out of service. We also have suggested a best practice of avoiding the creation of high concentration points needlessly in order to reduce the impact on the rest of the network during a failure of these nodes.

If you now believe that the Telecommunication Infrastructure is at risk of temporary wide spread outages and no defense will be completely preventative, then we have succeeded in our task to spread the warning. One of the authors was out of the US on 9-11 and learnt that ATM's cannot be relied upon to provide the currency needed to buy dinner if the telecommunication network (used to validate credit cards) is in massive overload.

The following lists our recommendation to protect the telecommunications infrastructure against large-scale problems, and to restore service after failures resulting from un-predictable and unavoidable incidents.

- Telecommunications vendors should police the supply chains for both hardware and software.
- Each user needs to have a continuance plan should the telecommunication infrastructure becomes unavailable, either for a short period of time or for a sustained period.
- Providers need to realize that the speed of a collapse is very short. There is no time for manual detection, confirmation and action. To survive, there must be pre-approved automated plans in place which will execute without human intervention.
- Each governmental authority needs to have a priority communication scheme in place, not just planned. The scheme must be periodically tested and the authorized users must have the necessary familiarity with the scheme to use it effectively. The priority service must not need manual intervention to activate.
- Each user of telecommunications needs to develop plans to address continuity of business during such unavoidable outages. While we can hope that such outages will be very rare and short lived, the critical applications of the user need to have a "plan B" in order to prevent coming to a grinding halt.
- A careful evaluation by each user is in order. While users expect the electric lights to function against darkness, most businesses have emergency battery powered lights and homes have candles and flashlights, just in case. In a similar vein the users need to ask the question if the Telecommunications were to fail at this end or at the destination end, "how could I continue to perform my critical functions," "Do I have backup "off network" procedures in place that will let me continue to function at some level?" and similar.
- Each government, each business and each citizen needs to have fallback plans on how to survive when the unimaginable happens, because it can.
- Modeling of critical infrastructure interdependencies is very important to quantify the risks associated with a particular vulnerability. Only through this quantification, investment resources can be used where the highest vulnerability exist.

References

1. International Telecommunications Union (ITU),
   http://www.itu.int/ITU-T/studygroups/com13/ngn2004/
   working_definition.html
2. General principles and general reference model for Next Generation Networks, ITU-T
   Y.2011 (2004)

3. Multiprotocol Label Switching Architecture, RFC 3031, Internet Engineering Task Force (2001)
4. Framework for Multi-Protocol Label Switching (MPLS)-based Recovery, RFC 3469, Internet Engineering Task Force (2003)
5. RSVP-TE: Extensions to RSVP for LSP Tunnels, RFC 3209, Internet Engineering Task Force (2001)
6. Fast Reroute Extensions to RSVP-TE for LSP Tunnels, RFC 4090, Internet Engineering Task Force (2005)
7. OSI IS-IS Intra-domain Routing Protocol, RFC 1142, Internet Engineering Task Force (1990)
8. OSPF Version 2, RFC 2178, Internet Engineering Task Force (1998)
9. Internet Engineering Task Force (IETF) RFC 5478,
   `http://bgp.potaroo.net/ietf/idref/rfc5478/index.html`
10. Botnets and Hackers and Spam, Federal Trade Commission (FTC),
    `http://www.ftc.gov/bcp/edu/pubs/consumer/alerts/alt132.pdf`
11. MLPP (Multi-Level Precedence and Preemption) for US Government,
    `http://jitc.fhu.disa.mil/tssi/configurations/siemens/`
    `mlpp_fue.pdf`
12. Conrad, S.H., LeClaire, R.J., O'Reilly, G.P., Uzunalioglu, H.: Critical National Infrastructure Reliability Modeling and Analysis. Bell Labs Technical Journal 11(3), 57–71 (2006)
13. Technical Specification Group Services and System Aspects (2006), IP Multimedia Subsystem (IMS), Stage 2, TS 23.228, 3rd Generation Partnership Project (2006)
14. Chen, T.M., Robert, J.-M.: Worm Epidemics in High-Speed Networks. ACM Computer 37(6), 48–53 (2004)
15. Bologna, S., Setola, R.: The Need to Improve Local Self-Awareness in CIP/CIIP. In: Proc. of First IEEE International Workshop on Critical Infrastructure Protection (IWCIP 2005), Darmstadt, Germany, November 3-4, pp. 84–89 (2005)
16. Albert, R., Jeong, H., Barabasi, A.: Error and attack tolerance of complex networks. Nature 406, 378–382 (2000)
17. `http://www.switched.com/2010/09/27/`
    `stuxnet-worm-strikes-nuclear-plant-in-iran/`
18. Panzieri, S., Setola, R.: Failures Propagation in Critical Interdependent Infrastructures. Int. J. Modelling, Identification and Control (IJMIC) 3(1), 69–78
19. Budka, K.C., Deshpande, J.G., Doumi, T.L., Madden, M., Mew, T.: Communication Network Architecture and Design Principles for Smart Grids. Bell Labs Technical Journal 15(2), 205–227 (2010)

Financial Services Industry

Bernhard Hämmerli

Norwegian Information Security Laboratory,
Department of Computer Science,
Gjøvik University Collage, Norway
bmhaemmerli@acris.ch, Bernhard.Hammerli@hig.no

Abstract. Critical infrastructure and services in financial industry are important for our society and the financial industry starts to understand the topic beyond the normal and well maintained Business Continuity Management and Disaster Recovery Plans (BCM & DRP). Today, the international backbone financial infrastructures operate pretty well, but in the infrastructure towards clients, two issues are utmost critical for the banks: Drive By Download and Phishing; both are related to steeling identity and money via e-banking. This is one of the results achieved by the EU project **Parsifal** (**P**rotection and Tru**st** in **F**inancial Infrastructure (Parsifal-Team, 2010), for compositing a research agenda for the cyber security of the financial industry.

Keywords: Critical Information Infrastructure Protection, Financial Industry, Resilience and Robustness, CIP, CIIP.

1 Overview

The financial sector is vital to the economy to keep key processes up and running. Key processes are cash for the population, providing liquidity and core processes as payments, credit, clearing, securities trade, settlement and foreign exchange. The international infrastructure is based mainly on SWIFT communications and messages, the national payment systems are very divers and many states have even more than one system. The financial sector was very early aware on information risks and provided according business continuity plans.

First we describe the financial service and market infrastructure (section 2), then about the regulation and standards (section 3) and we elude on technical risks (section 4). As in every new trans-disciplinary topic, a glossary and an ontology (how the terms relate to each other) accepted for all parties has to be developed (section 5). Some aspects of actual status and trends of the financial infrastructure are presented in section 6. The Parsifal project's findings and its recommendation (section 7) give an introduction in the pending research challenges as it is in 2010, including the view of the experts and their priority.

J. Lopez et al. (Eds.): Critical Information Infrastructure Protection, LNCS 7130, pp. 301–329, 2012.
© Springer-Verlag Berlin Heidelberg 2012

2   Financial Services and Market Infrastructure

2.1   Services of the Financial Sector

The Banking and Finance Sector, the backbone of the world economy, is a large and diverse sector primarily owned and operated by private entities. This Sector consists of many fine grained and a few worldwide operating financial institutions, including:

- depository financial institutions
    - banks
    - thrifts
    - credit unions
- insurers
- securities brokers/dealers
- investment companies
- certain financial utilities

Financial industry provides a broad array of products to their customers. These products:

- allow customers to deposit funds and make payments to other parties, nationally and internationally;
- provide credit and liquidity to customers;
- allow customers to invest funds for both the long and short term;
- transfer financial risks between customers (trade finance business);
- access to stock exchange; and
- currencies, equity shares, bonds, derivatives as well as loans.

The financial institutions that provide these services are all somewhat different, each within a specific part or parts of the financial services marketplace. Financial institutions operate to provide customers the financial products they want, ensure the institution's financial integrity, protect customers' assets, and guarantee the integrity of the financial system. As such, financial institutions and the financial market manage a wide variety of financial and certain non-financial risks.

2.2   Financial Market Infrastructure

Today, financial institutions deal primary with financial information and risks. The money itself (coins and bills) is less and less important, since most accounts are kept and transfers are executed on the electronic money, hence all within the cyber infrastructure. The computing systems and its inter-networking is therefore an essential infrastructure for the financial sector. The banks are mostly interlinked with the Society for Worldwide Interbank Financial Telecommunication (SWIFT) network.

SIWFT means three things for the financial institutions:

1. a secure network for transmitting messages between financial institutions;
2. a set of syntax standards and market practices for financial messages (for transmission over SWIFTNet or any other network)
3. a set of connection software and services, allowing financial institutions to transmit messages over SWIFT network.

The SWIFT messages are today transmitted with the IP protocol in a secure way (with VPN) often in dedicated high secure and high reliable networks. The most important interbank systems are depicted in (Figure1).

| Market Infrastructures | | | | Client Side | |
Market Infrastructure	Data Format	Commu- nication	Back Office Systems	Commu- nication	Data Format
T2 Nat. Clearing e.g. SIC	SWIFT or nat. Formats	SWIFT or nat. Exchange protocols	Payment	SWIFT	SWIFT	→ Whole Sale
				National od. EBICS	National	→ Others
T2S ICSD CSD	SWIFT	SWIFT	Securities	SWIFT	SWIFT	→ Whole Sale
				National od. EBICS	National	→ Others
CLS bilateral	SWIFT	SWIFT	Foreign Exchange	SWIFT	SWIFT	→ Whole Sale
			Credit		

Specifically the main elements of such interbank system are (see Figure 1):

Details in Figure 1:

- CLS (Continuous Link Settlement) Market infrastructure for multi-currency settlement of western currencies (USD, EUR, JPY, CHF, etc.)
- CSD (Central Securities Depository) Market infrastructure for settlement of Securities
- ICSD (International Central Securities Depository) Market infrastructure for cross border settlement of securities transfers
- SIC: Swiss Interbank Clearing as an example for national clearing and formats
- T2 (TARGET2): Market infrastructure for settlement of payments (in Euro)
- T2S (TARGET2SECURITIES) Market infrastructure for settlement of payments and securities (delivery versus payment). Operations planned for 2014.

SWIFT uses own message types, developed in the last 30 years (named MT), the ISO15022-standard in the securities business and since a few years also ISO 20022 standard for financial services messaging. ISO20022 describes a metadata repository containing descriptions of messages and business processes, and a maintenance process for the repository content.

The **Electronic Banking Internet Communication Standard** (short **EBICS**) is a transmission protocol between banks and clients for orders and getting information. It's a secure channel over internet with a client-driven authentication and used in Germany and France. Switzerland and Austria are in the discussion to use also this standard for here customers. So the "E" in EBICS is changing from "Electronic" to "European".

Additionally, strong identification and authentication systems are systems every network participant has to trust and to rely on SWIFT uses (IdenTrust) Public Key Infrastructure Identities.

It is evident that banks are heavily dependent on high reliable and secure communication infrastructures; towards customers the public internet with VPN is predominant, amongst the institutions itself the internet protocol is used often on rented "private communication links". However, those links are in shared Telco infrastructure by today. In the data processing centre message queues are used to store orders and task. The messages are structured and standardized, and as description language more and more XML is used.

In respect to financial infrastructures, the focus of the following considerations will be on the financial ICT infrastructure, and how to increase its protection in the framework of the critical information infrastructure protection (CIIP)

3   Regulation and Standards

3.1   Regulation of the Financial Sector

In addition to the actions of financial institutions, direct financial regulation applies to many, but not all, financial services providers. The regulation of the financial sector is fragmented and reaches form worldwide institutions (World Bank, Bank for International Settlements BIS) to large scale regional regulation e.g. EU, US down to single national state regulation. In general, financial regulation is complex; it manages and regulates various forms of risk and guard against prohibited practices.

3.1.1   Regulations from Bank for International Settlement

BIS (Wikipedia on Bank for International Settlements) takes care for regulation as follows:

- to make monetary policy more predictable and transparent among its 57 member central banks
- to regulate capital adequacy and make reserve requirements transparent.
  Role in banking supervision: The BIS provides the Basel Committee on Banking Supervision with its twelve-member secretariat, and with it has played a central role in establishing the Basel Capital Accords of 1988 and 2004. There remain significant differences between US, EU and UN officials regarding the degree of capital adequacy and reserve controls that global banking now requires. Put extremely simply, the US as of 2006 favoured strong strict central controls in the spirit of the original 1988 accords, the EU was more inclined to a distributed system managed collectively with a committee able to approve some exceptions. The UN agencies especially ICLEI are firmly committed to fundamental risk measures: the so-called triple bottom line and were becoming critical of central banking as an institutional structure for ignoring fundamental risks in favour of technical risk management.

3.1.2 Basel II Regulations

The financial sector holds many risks which could endanger a financial institution. As in every business, the first risk priority is focused on the essential market risks, which are according Basel II regulation categorized in three prioritized main pillars (Wikipedia on Basel II):

1. The first pillar deals with maintenance of regulatory capital calculated for three major components of risk that a bank faces: **credit risk, operational risk,** and **market risk**. Other risks are not considered fully quantifiable at this stage.

    ➢ The credit risk component can be calculated in three different ways of varying degree of sophistication, namely standardized approach, Foundation IRB and Advanced IRB. IRB stands for "Internal Rating-Based Approach".

    ➢ For operational risk, there are three different approaches - basic indicator approach or BIA, standardized approach or TSA, and the internal measurement approach (an advanced form of which is the advanced measurement approach or AMA).

    ➢ For market risk the preferred approach is VaR (value at risk).

2. The second pillar deals with the regulatory response to the first pillar, giving regulators much improved 'tools' over those available to them under Basel II. It also provides a framework for dealing with all the other risks a bank may face, such as **systemic risk, pension risk, concentration risk, strategic risk, reputational risk, liquidity risk** and **legal risk**, which the accord combines under the title of residual risk. It gives banks a power to review their risk management system.

3. The pillar aims to promote greater stability in the financial system by allowing market discipline to operate by requiring lenders to publicly provide details of their risk management activities, risk rating processes and risk distributions.
    Market discipline supplements regulation as sharing of information facilitates assessment of the bank by others including investors, analysts, customers, other banks and rating agencies. It leads to good corporate governance. When marketplace participants have a sufficient understanding of a bank's activities and the controls it has in place to manage its exposures, they are better able to distinguish between banking organizations so that they can reward those that manage their risks prudently and penalize those that do not.

On the operational side the activities against money laundering and terrorism are an example, introduced from the government side and resulting in a deep impact for the operational business, even on a daily base.

As shown, the financial sector has many risks inside the business part of the sector, which are by far more important than the infrastructure risks but also influenced by technical risks. A clear confirmation of this fact was the financial turmoil in 2008 (Dick K. Nanto, 2009) which caused the financial institutions to focus on their core business and neglected for a period the infrastructure risks.

However, the infrastructure, mainly the ICT infrastructure and its security, remains essential for the financial services operation. This means a technical risk which influence from a basic level mostly of other risks. Therefore, the next subchapter will elaborate on ICT.

3.2   Characteristics of EU Financial Services

As a strategic goal EU regulators act for customer interests to push financial services towards an adoption of increased open market competition and the provision of harmonized services across national boundaries in all EU member states.

As stated in section 1, the financial services industry is heavily dependent on ICT technology and its providers. Therefore, competitiveness in the financial services sector depends on the cost of accessing and processing data and hence on the technological solutions that allow such data access and processing. Furthermore, market advantage means accessing better financial data (including background data) and accessing it faster. Even more advantage get the biggest banks with whole sale conditions (the larger the dealt volume is, the better are interest rates, conditions and direct access to central systems of the financial sector. In this context the evolution of data standards and data exchange rules define positions for market competitiveness. Because of the importance of these positions, rules are strongly controlled by the financial services community itself. And last but not least, only a certain parts of financial data are really sensitive. But if so, confidentiality of these data is essential for activities in the financial services sector.

3.2.1 Single European Payment Area (SEPA)

The European Commission has established the legal foundation through the Payments Services Directive (PSD) which was translated by the European Payments Council (EPC) into operation, in more than 30 European Countries. By the end of 2010 SEPA had a cross border market share of 14%, meanwhile the political will was to be predominant by at this point in time. The European Commission took measures to foster SEPA.

The EPC is committed to delivering three pan-European payment instruments:

- For credit transfers: *SCT – SEPA Credit Transfer,* operational January 2008
- For direct debits: *SDD – SEPA Direct Debit*, operational November 2009
- For cards: *SEPA Cards Framework,* operational, 2011

The Euro system however urges more efforts in the area of card payments and the urgent resolution of issues with the third type of payment instrument, SEPA Direct Debit (SDD).

The fast introduction of SEPA to user should not suppress that in the national domains still specialists and often manifold payment systems are operational. To be effective, harmonization of payment services is still an important objective such that national entities are directly applying SPEA standards as ISO 20022 (XML message transfer format), IBAN and BIC to gain full benefit in local and EU processing. SEPA is not just a business project, but is also closely linked to the political ambition to move towards a more integrated, competitive and innovative Europe and therefore today and even more in future a critical financial infrastructure.

3.2.2 Markets in Financial Instruments Directive (MiFID)

The goal of MiFID[1] (introduced Nov.1, 2007) is to protect investors, increase transparency of the financial markets and integrity of the financial service provider and provides standards for the following key aspects:

1. **Authorisation, regulation and passporting:** Firms covered by MiFID will be authorised and regulated in their "home state" (broadly, the country in which they have their registered office). Once a firm has been authorised, it will be able to use the MiFID passport to provide services to customers in other EU member states. These services will be regulated by the member state in their "home state" (whereas currently under ISD, a service is regulated by the member state in which the service takes place).

2. **Client categorisation:** MiFID requires firms to categorise clients as "eligible counterparties", professional clients or retail clients (these have increasing levels of protection). Clear procedures must be in place to categorise clients and assess their suitability for each type of investment product. That said, the appropriateness of any investment advice or suggested financial transaction must still be verified before being given.

3. **Client order handling:** MiFID has requirements relating to the information that needs to be captured when accepting client orders, ensuring that a firm is acting in a client's best interests and as to how orders from different clients may be aggregated.

4. **Pre-trade transparency:** MiFID will require that operators of continuous order-matching systems must make aggregated order information on "liquid shares" available at the five best price levels on the buy and sell side; for quote-driven markets, the best bids and offers of market makers must be made available

5. **Post-trade transparency:** MiFID will require firms to publish the price, volume and time of all trades in listed shares, even if executed outside of a regulated market, unless certain requirements are met to allow for deferred publication.

6. **Best execution:** MiFID will require that firms take all reasonable steps to obtain the best possible result in the execution of an order for a client. The best possible result is not limited to execution price but also includes cost, speed, likelihood of execution and likelihood of settlement and any other factors deemed relevant.

7. **Systematic Internaliser:** a Systematic Internaliser is a firm that executes orders from its clients against its own book or against orders from other clients. MiFID will treat Systematic Internalisers as mini-exchanges hence, for example, they will be subject to pre-trade and post-trade transparency requirements.

In infrastructure terms, MiFID compliance means best execution in respect to technical performance, e.g. order of execution, speed and overhead costs. Especially in degraded infrastructures are MiFID requirements difficult to perform.

---

[1] These requirements tend to be applied in future to other financial instruments.

3.3   Standards in the Finance Sector

In the financial markets in the nineties, the desire to automate the electronic execution of equity transactions and their related derivative products led to the emergence of Financial Information eXchange FIX (FIX-Group F. S.)   and Financial products Markup Language FpML (FIX-Group), based on eXtended Markup Language XML, as open standards that were pushed by the major fund managers and traders such as Fidelity Investments and JPMorgan. Further standards efforts are:

1. The Expert Group on e-Invoicing triggered in 2008 a harmonization between CEFACT, NES and ISO on supply chain standards.
2. Pan European Public Procurement Online (Peppol-Team), an EU FP7 project is pushing efforts to align company identifiers and product identifiers in multiple EU countries. Collaboration between distinct players around open standards is evolving at the same time.
3. The adoption of Microsoft Advanced Message Queuing Protocol AMQP[2] has brought a close collaboration between Microsoft and the open source community in the further development of cloud computing
4. The collaboration between the European Payment Council EPC and GSMA – the mobile operators association - around open standards for mobile payment processing brings two industries together that previously were fighting for the same customers of these mobile payment services.

4   Technical Risks

4.1   Technical Infrastructure Overview

Analysing the technical infrastructure, we have to be aware on the dependability aspects: It is really important to now that the public internet and Telco system has to work, that the power provider must deliver electricity (of course sever have uninterruptable power supplies UPS, but not all (network)-infrastructure and certainly not the end user PC, even so laptops have battery for a few hours) in order to operate the bank owned infrastructure. In some case, where water is used for cooling, also the water supply must be available to avoid damage at the electronic components (yellow infrastructure in Figure 2).

Furthermore the operating systems, then various tiers of middleware and the applications must be up and running such that a bank can operate. The red arrow in figure 2 just shows one element in the chain of dependability considerations. In reality all chains involved into critical services must be analysed in equal way to get a profound analysis of the service availability.

With software oriented architecture SOA the application landscape changes, and will be for more distributed on different systems, internally, but partly also depending externally in case that data or service element of external services (e.g. stock prices,

---

[2] http://www.amqp.org/

exchange rates etc.) are used. This trend – together with the virtualization and introduction of could services, leads to deeper and more specialized production chains in informatics, in analogy to the one, which Taylor[3] (1856-1915) has introduced in mechanical production in the late 19th century. Details are discussed in the next subchapter.

The overall complexity and robustness is obvious in Figure 2:

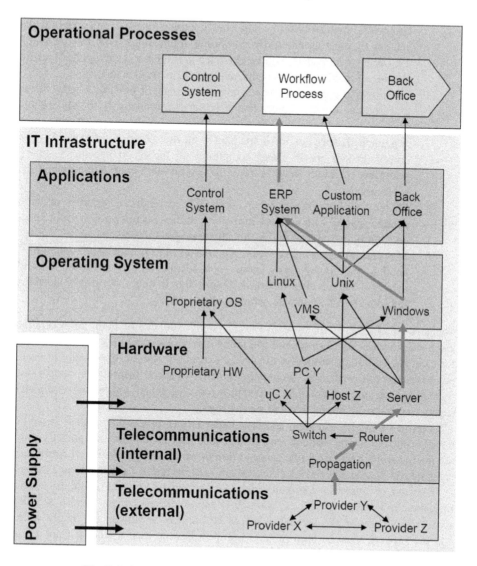

Fig. 2. Robustness of a single process (red: dependability chain)

---

[3] http://en.wikipedia.org/wiki/Scientific_management

4.2   Risks of Mechanism for Distributed Processing

The following trend in IT-architecture has been observed in vast discussion and in many related literature, e.g. (Financial-Services-Club, 2009):

1. Decoupling of data storage from data processing and the further growing capacity and performance improvement of data processing.
2. Proliferation of data processing is the use of "Mashups", a means to create composite applications to share and combine internal and external data sources by creating enterprise composite applications: with this technique, the value creation chain will be extended in respect to geographical location, number of involved components, number of involved actors.
3. Use of cloud computing, which promise to make it possible for the sharing of resources on an unprecedented scale. Additionally is to add the cost pressure towards cloud computing: economy of scale allows offering severs at a much cheaper rate in comparison to on site server production. Also, the corporate data are in cloud computing on the cloud provider's servers: according measures must be taken to comply with confidentiality and data protection law.
4. Shared infrastructure services with this centralized security operation centres dealing with network intrusions, threats; security policy enforcement and configuration lead to dynamically managed infrastructures.
5. The delocalisation of services (e.g. storage in one country, computing in another one) is by today more an academic option; however, it would increases the number of attack points, but it might be also a chance to improve overall resilience, when applied properly.

The security challenges of the above trends apply can become both, point of attack and a step towards better structured and maintained process: additional point of attack for example with the distribution of service execution, and an opportunity to ensure processes are followed more accurately and that financial institutions comply with regulations because of detailed formulation of contractual issues and completely separation of service production and service audit.

In terms of C(I)IP very long and distributed service production chains, as well as outsourcing and the movements into clouds adds many additional components which are internetworked and might be cause to turn down the overall system. It needs more accurate risk assessment and specific evaluation of overall resilience and robustness.

In terms of business continuity, the distribution of services could be even a measure for robustness, if every service is ran at different places and a seamless switch over between the service instances is foreseen. Assuming this really works, still the network must be high reliable and must have at least a second if not a third channel for emergencies. Given this architecture, the positive effect on resilience and robustness will happen.

Finally, banking secrecy law prohibits in some countries outsourcing of banking. Encrypted data would enable in spite of privacy concerns outsourcing. Processing of encrypted data is a research field by today, but still in its infancy.

4.3   Facilitating Customer Access to Financial Data and Cash

4.3.1   Developments in Online Banking

The accessibility of financial data by customers of banking services is emerging: e.g. in US on-line banking grew in 2008 nearly 30%. And in September 2008 SWIFT launched a product that enables SMEs to connect directly to this bank-owned network for the instruction of payments and collection of bank account information. To make this happen, the bottlenecks of middleware in the secure distribution and processing must be removed, especially for very high volumes of financial information between multiple applications. Advanced Messaging Queuing Protocol AMQP, which has been implemented by Microsoft, is one solution to the challenge.

The acceptance of online banking including online banking security was researched in depth (Detecon Consulting, 2001) in four EU countries. Customer acceptance and willingness to secure end device vary through the researched countries. However, acceptance and according customer end protection are essential prerequisites.

4.3.2   Banking Moving into Mobile Space

Small devices basically split up in tow technologies: GSM based systems and Internet protocol driven Systems. For both the European Payments Council (EPC) has accelerated the deployment of services that enable consumers to pay for goods and services in shops, restaurants and other locations using their mobile phones. Initially, it was about defining a contractual framework document detailing the minimum set of requirements for a so-called Trusted Service Manager to interface with banks and mobile operators. Mobile banking is mainly delivered by technologies like SMS or Unstructured Supplementary Service Data USSD (value added GSM service), Mobile Internet Browsers or downloadable applications (typically Java). In numbers, 25% of transactions will be in 2011 from mobile internet and around 10 % from native mobile telephone protocol, such as SMS or USSD.

Meanwhile in the beginning only very few mobile services were offered, today already quite sophisticated applications are available, e.g. the EPC (European Payment Council) has enabled SEPA payments across 31 countries via cell phone. Furthermore, some production chains include mobile technology as part of the native or the security process. E.g. mobile transaction number as security for home banking or Hal-Cash, which uses SMS for ATM withdrawal without plastic card: Persons in need (e.g. lost bourse) can just type in a secret code received by SMS and they receive the money signed off by a friend at any ATM in Europe (Wilcox, 2009) (Flatraaker).

4.3.3   Identity Management in Financial Services

As a key issue of electronic financial data the control over customer accesses requires a resilient identity management system IdM (e.g., reduced sign-on, provisioning and access-management) constantly progressing in accordance to the overall internet developments. IdM is one of the key critical financial infrastructures without it any reliable and secure transaction can take place. The market offers dozens of IdM technologies —including biometrics, smart cards, tokens, radio frequency identification (RFID), public key infrastructure (PKI), and Bluetooth-based devices—in the field of credential issuance, authentication, and verification, but none of these technologies has emerged as a universal standard.

In the modern world steeling identity means at the end steeling money. Especially in the view of e-banking, secure processing of sensitive data is essential to avoid significant losses and attacks on customer information and assets. Some of the currently available digital identity methods of verifying transactions in e-banking services are:

- **Biometric ID:** This verification method linked to human trait has the major advantage of being secure against faking. However, if biometric Id is not processed on a second channel, the application can still be intercepted with the effect that the higher degree of security becomes useless.
- **Federated ID:** At present, each bank establishes its own electronic ID. The setting up of multi-part IDs would result in important saving to companies admitting such identities, as e.g. the BankID in Norway already does.
- **Mobile Transaction Authentication Numbers (mTAN):** These and similar forms identify identities on a separate channel such as special hardware devices which are already able today to discover attacks produced by "drive-by downloads" or e-mail attachments. However, the automation of the process is weak and therefore this method serves for private individuals only. Furthermore, with the next generation of mobile users, there will be no assurance, that the mobile IP connection and the mTAN are on different channels.

Again, the value and urgency of secure and cost optimized identities is absolutely critical and crucial for secure banking, without any workaround we know of by today!

In respect to financial C(I)IP the trend to mobility adds an additional component, which is significant for the society and therefore critical. Certain processes, as e.g. mobile TAN require a robust and reliable mobile infrastructure: another element added which must be up and running to complete processes. But also in the general online access, secure and cost optimized identities are a prerequisite to operate B2B and B2C. A failure of IdM would cause equal effect as a blackout of the whole infrastructure.

4.4   Technical Risks: The Sectors View

In a discussion with financial experts working in the business continuity and critical infrastructure field some challenges were depicted in an interview which demonstrate the broadness of the topic expanding the infrastructure issue by personnel and localisation issues:

1. Non predictable message volumes: The institution can handle normal everyday volumes of electronic orders. To stress test infrastructures up to 2005 one believed, that a factor 3-5 of the normal everyday volume would be sufficient. However, a few extraordinary situations in recent years let the

volume increase to factor 20. Meanwhile everyday statistics can be handled well institutions have to be prepared for an unknown increase, which might appear again, but very rarely. Options to act are – both additional and longer delays in processing the message queues - or a black out for the time of too intense processing requests.

2. Every institution can prepare itself, however, whether in the inter-institution communication, the counterparty is able to operate messages in the back office is not predictable, even so, contract are designed such they it should be able.

3. Larger institutions have back up sites and are able to transfer while operating the business form one data centre to another. Within a national state this has no legal obstacles, internationally, there are rules partly prohibiting a swap over.

4. Another major concern is operations with human interactions: First the human interactions are not scalable. Extra work force needs time to build and cannot be increased by factors within hours. Second, diseases such as bird's flue, SARS and new virus combinations may lower the operational workforce within hour to days, e.g. in two days the workforce could shrink by 80%. To counter fight such scenario, isolation of people, home working places, additional hygienic measures are foreseen, as well as reassigning displaceable work to other sites, where the disease is not active.

5. The cash process must be organized in a crises resistant way, such that without power and telco the population can provided with cash or according other payment options.

6. Liquidity processes are essential to banks and allow operating the business. Especially centralized settlement (like TARGET2, CLS) was introduced at large – after the Herstatt case in 74 (Wikipedia, 2010) - to avoid unnecessary counter party risks.

Elaborating on the challenges, there are three backup pillars which must be kept in mind:

1. IT: IT involved in critical processes must have according backup infrastructures, often direct backup sites as well as swap over to processing centres of other locations in case of worldwide institutions.

2. Personnel: Epidemics must be prepared, crises scenarios trained and shifting work or personnel to other non-epidemic sites of the world, if available.

3. Localities: is the third element in the strategy which allows lots of flexibility as shown in the first two points. Important is to realize that all three together lead in a pre-prepared optimized interaction to best results.

Furthermore, the interests in CIIP have to be elaborated:

1. Legal compliance must be kept with regulatory frameworks of the international regulators as well as national and local regulators. This is a prerequisite to get the license to run the business and to get access to the according provider (e.g. SWIFT).

2. The single institution has interest to protect itself in a way that economic prosperity of the institution is maintained: Business Continuity Management BCM and Disaster and Recovery Planning DRP are used to keep the institution alive and operational for economic purposes. Most institutions are good at this.

3. National economic supply: National states are usually not interest in a single institution, but in keeping critical sectors alive. Even single institutions are in general not in the focus of national states, very large single institution with a "Too big to fail" challenge are very much in the focus. Both, the collection of many average sized institutions and very large one, offer critical services to the citizen and companies, which could damage if not available – social life or have a long lasting negative impact as e.g. economic problems, poverty etc. The usual approach to identify challenges and actions to be taken is starting with public private partnership round tables (facilitating government experts, sector delegates and specific suppliers, delivering core infrastructures). The work is defining vulnerabilities of the sector and according risks, discussions of counter measures and incidents, such that best common effort can be taken to counter fight incidents - either in advance or if already happened – with concentrated common effort.

4.5   Incidents: The Motivation to Act

Security in general, information- and IT-security, military and CIIP follow all the line, that the primary trigger to act on improving security, resilience and/or reconstruction /crisis preparation are incidents. No incidents is often translated in a yearly budget decrease a round 10%. Unfortunately, this is not the case of the financial sector that suffered for several incidents in the last years. In the follow we report some of them to stress, further to the urgency to improve the protection of the IT components, the need to learn on past event in order to design more efficiently robust solutions.

4.5.1 Swiss Telekurs Payment System

Telekurs (today SIX group) operates on behalf of all Swiss banks the Point of Sales POS electronic payments and the network of automatic teller machines ATM for withdrawing cash. It is an essential infrastructure for all Swiss citizens. Saturday, December 23, 2000 a tape was falling into the central tape robot and blocking this device (Neumann). As a consequence, at the day of most turn over in the year – the day before Christmas – the complete system, i.e. all POS and ATM were blocked and did not allow the customers to pay!

This incident triggered to a redesign of the POS/ATM system, increasing offline capabilities and business continuity. Switzerland had – because of this incident – much earlier realized robustness in POS/ATM compared to other countries.

4.5.2 Swiss Post Finance

Slammer malware was discovered and – after billions of US $ damage – remediated with virus control in Jan 2003. However, October 8 2003, Swiss Post Finance had a major incident, with Slammer. In a closed server farm – not connected to the outside world, and therefore not performing all updates and protection measure – was Slammer introduced by a maintenance computer. For hours one of the very core financial systems of Switzerland was unusable.

This incident lead to completely new awareness levels, in respect to counter measure and updates.

4.5.3 Mariposa

In 2009/2010 the Defence Intelligence group31 discovered a botnet with one of the most extensive networks ever observed. A sinkholing conducted between December 2009 and February 2010 made it possible to detect 11 million unique IP addresses. The network was called "Mariposa" (Spanish for "butterfly") (MELANI, 2010-1), since the botnet was created using the Butterfly malware kit. The Spanish name is due to the fact that the botnet operators were Spaniards.

The main purpose of the botnet was to steal sensitive data from infected computers. This included information about accounts, names of users, passwords, and details concerning online bank accounts. Part of the infected computers also included malware to launch DDoS (distributed denial of service) attacks. Clients of the 40 largest banks worldwide as well as computers of at least half of all Fortune 1000 companies were victims of this botnet. The victims came from 190 countries.

The Butterfly malware kit was developed by a hacker named Iserdo. The 23-year-old was recently arrested in the Slovenian city of Maribor. The botnet operators were arrested in Spain the beginning of the year. The operation conducted by the Guardia Civil led to the arrest of three Spanish citizens. These were identified by the pseudonyms they used on the Internet and their ages: Netkairo, 31, Johnny Loleante, 30, and Ostiator, 25.

However, the Spanish justice authorities had to follow their own country's criminal code. According to statements by Major Cesar Lorenzana, the deputy director of the technological crimes unit of the Guardia Civil, it is not a crime in Spain to operate a botnet or to disseminate malicious code. The only possible indictment is data theft.

4.5.4 ZeuS and SpyEye – Merger of Largest E-banking Trojans?

The Trojan "ZeuS" is probably the most widespread e-banking malware currently in circulation. There are numerous reports, articles and activities on this topic (MEALNI, 2010-2). From early 2010, another e-banking malware called "SpyEye" made a name for itself. SpyEye integrates a function with the name "ZeuS Killer Code". This function seeks to determine whether an infected computer already contains ZeuS. If it does, the rival is eliminated. This effectively led to a war between the two trojans. The author of recently became famous in the underground scene when he announced in July that the author of "ZeuS" had given him the code of the malware and delegated administration of its customers to him. In various subsequent messages, Harderman publically announced that version 2 of ZeuS would no longer be further developed. The community would be able to count on a new malware, however, which would be developed from the merger between SpyEye and ZeuS.

4.5.5 Waddell and Reed Financial Inc. Impact of Erroneous Human Input on Algorithmic Trading

May 6, 2010 around 14.45 a trader made an erroneous input for a deal and sold 75000 E-mini Futures (actual value ca. 4 billion USD) for very little money, because the decimal dot in the number was set wrong (Westbrook, 2010).   Figure 3a demonstrates the impact on the E-mini future, 3b shows Dow Jones impact, 3c shows the impact on the Waddell & Reed Inc. stock and 3d demonstrates influence on other stocks, went to pennies within minutes: Accenture, shown at left, fell from above $40 at 2:47 to $0.01 at 2:48, but then within 90 seconds, the Dow was back up 543 points and ended up closing out down only 3.2% overall.

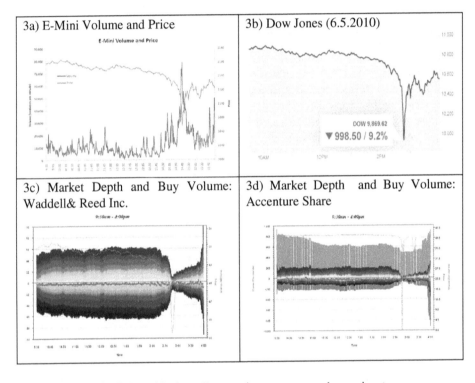

Fig. 3. Algorithmic trading reaction on erroneous human input

Concluding this case nothing really went wrong in infrastructure, it was just a human error. However, there have been no controls on plausibility when this deal was made. Such a control could avoid the very short break down of the market and the unjustifiable losses and win's which occurred. The danger stemmed from the fact, that – after erroneous human input - finally algorithm versus algorithm followed to trade without any human interaction.

4.5.6 Asking for Realistic Countermeasures in a Given Context

These fundamental different attacks represent some danger for the financial sector. However, all these attacks had no long lasting bottlenecks in large regions for the broad publicity, as the criticality definition of CIP would require. Considering the criticality, we have indicator what could happen, when we do not react carefully; but as in most other sectors, the real CIP incident did not happen yet. This fact – in spite of all excitement for C(I)IP – is very important to recognize, such that the community can position itself correctly in a given context and is not over demanding measures.

4.6 Relationship between Technical Risks and Business: Alignment Countermeasure to Threats

The common power of around 80 financial ICT experts was used to generate mini cases / scenarios for which security or criticality is important. The 160 mini cases or scenarios were analysed in tow aspects: Firstly, distribution from local to global (horizontal) and secondly, fragmentation of the service creation chain (from all concentrated to fine grained fragmentation) (Susan Morrow, 2009) :

- Vertical: longer and longer value chains lead naturally to fragmentation between players, everyone contributing to separated or integrated services. At the same time there is a concentrated move which may result from several factors: It may be standardization across borders (e.g. Single European Payment Area SEPA) or single – shop local or regional trade platforms.
- Horizontal: this naturally reflects the concerns of transactions extending across borders between states, across regions or across continents.

The fascinating insights received from this analysis, was a misalignment of today's countermeasures in respect to the basic threat properties along the two axes. Even so, experts already know that the arms race of computer defence and computer attacks is very asymmetric in the favour of the attackers, this view opens aspects with a big potential to identify new countermeasures facing the arms race challenge.

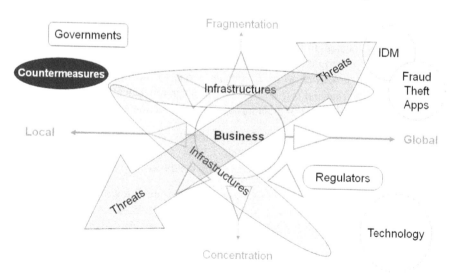

Fig. 4. Positioning threats in the global IT infrastructure

Explanation of the Identified Elements

- **Business blob:** it simply illustrates that nowadays there is no firm trend regarding financial business. In all areas financers and bankers are opportunistic risk takers, while financial markets and mathematical trading exacerbates short terms views to the level of the second!

- **Technology:** is dominated by world-wide providers, with a strong appetite to offer more than just tech services world-wide.

- **Infrastructures:** from being mostly local and fragmented they evolve. Not exactly like business. There is a trend towards regionalization or globalization but as the stakeholders describe it along two separate paths, one is along fragmented infrastructures – this may mean of different banking institutions with a global reach or of connected systems. For example from a technical infrastructure perspective CLS (Continuous Link Settlement) is one platform while it is interconnected with many other systems- the other one is towards concentrated market places or interbank systems (see e.g. the NYSE, or TARGET2).

- **Threats:** One could say that threats may arise from anywhere e.g. hackers are very opportunistic too. However stakeholders expressed their concerns somewhat differently. They see them concentrating along one axis from local/concentrated (see e.g. 9/11, identity thefts by the millions) to global/fragmented (see simultaneous flash attacks coordinated across borders, for which there is currently no adequate response).

- **Governments** are by nature local and fragmented. This is somewhat counterbalanced by mostly regulatory institution e.g. the Bank of International Settlement (BIS), the European Central Bank (ECB). Overseeing systemically important infrastructures is a joint effort in a few instances. For example, for the oversight of SWIFT the National Bank of Belgium acts as the lead overseer as SWIFT is located in Belgium. However, they are supported by G-10 central banks. The oversight focuses primarily on ensuring that SWIFT has effective controls and processes to avoid posing a risk to the financial stability and the soundness of financial infrastructures. Similar arrangements are in place for CLS. This seems to fall short of a comprehensive view/action capability.

- **Countermeasures** may be defined regionally or less often globally. They are always acted and controlled locally. This state of affairs seems in strong contradiction with the challenges posed by the threats.

- **IDM, Fraud, Theft and Apps:** however there are a few areas where solutions seem to be at hand or close to it. They are fragmented. Some complain: there are already too many possibilities. There is a call for standardization, interoperability or even uniqueness. The latter seems to be justified for concentrated infrastructures only.

4.7   CoMiFin Communication Middleware for Monitoring Financial Critical Infrastructure to Enhance Cyber Defence

CoMiFin (Communication Middleware for Monitoring Financial Critical Infrastructure) (Comifin-Team, 2008) is an EU project funded by the Seventh Framework Programme (FP7), started in September 2008 and continuing for 30 months. The research area is Critical Infrastructure Protection (CIP), focussing on the Critical Financial Infrastructure (CFI).

An increasing amount of sensitive traffic is being carried over open communication media, such as the Internet. This trend exposes services and the supporting infrastructure to massive, coordinated attacks and frauds that are not being effectively countered by any single organisation. In order to identify threats against critical infrastructures and business continuity, CoMiFin aims to facilitate information exchange and distributed event processing among a subset of participants grouped in federations. Federations are regulated by contracts and they are enabled through the Semantic Room abstraction: this abstraction facilitates the secure sharing and processing of information by providing a trusted environment for the participants to contribute and analyse data. Input data can be real time security events, historical attack data, logs, and other sources of information that concern other Semantic Room participants. Semantic Rooms can be deployed on top of an IP network allowing adaptable configurations from peer-to-peer to cloud-centric configurations, according to the needs and the requirements of the Semantic Room participants.

A key objective of CoMiFin is to prove the advantages of having a cooperative approach in the rapid detection of threats. Specifically, CoMiFin demonstrates the effectiveness of its approach by addressing the problem of protecting financial critical infrastructure. This allows groups of financial actors to take advantage of the Semantic Room abstraction for exchanging and processing information, thereby allowing them to take proactive steps in protecting their business continuity, for example, through generating fast and accurate intruder blacklists.

5   The Need for Glossaries and Ontologies

Glossaries and ontologies (SLTTGCC, 2005), (Gresser, Draft Ontology Of Financial Risks & Dependencies, 2009), (Gresser, Ontology of Financial Risks & Dependencies: Vol 2 Glossary, 2009) are very useful when scientifically approaching a new domain as it is the critical financial services. Many organizations made home grown and national language based terms which are of limited use in pan European discussions of the sector. In (Gresser, Draft Ontology Of Financial Risks & Dependencies, 2009) a comprehensive set of ontology graphs were developed: Figure 5 is intuitively understandable and describes the basic financial services and system.

To approach the CIP component of the financial services, the single graph must be expanded in mind to many corporate entities, delivering the service, in many different states, also exchanging information worldwide. Such a heavy secure and worldwide distributed and interconnected system is provided by the Society for Worldwide Interbank Financial Telecommunication, SWIFT, for financial messaging, containing payment information in the message body. Beside of the technical challenge to design and operate such systems, there are also legal challenges concerning regulations which are different in cross-border situations.

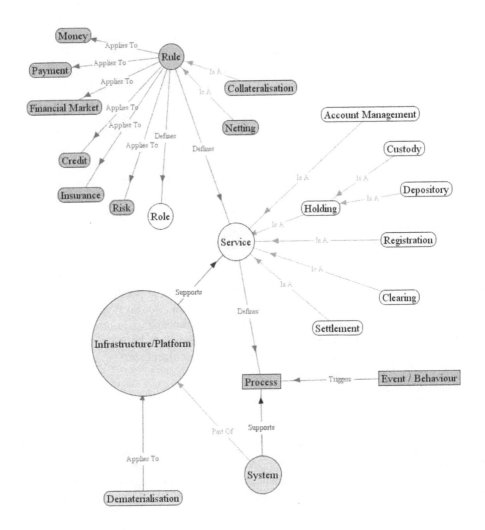

Fig. 5. Top Level Financial Industry Ontology

And finally, CIP is about understanding of the dependencies and vulnerabilities in local, cross-border and international dimensions and converting the respective analysis in measures before, during and after the crises.

6   Financial Infrastructure: Status and Trends

6.1   Today's Status of Open and Harmonized EU Financial Market

The financial market has a rapid emergence of open infrastructures, with a widespread sharing of data. On the upside, this is perceived as a real opportunity in enabling new forms of performing financial business or to introduce new value added services. On the downside, the gradual replacement of physical boundaries with logical boundaries was regarded to be a major challenge for the financial services sector and their critical infrastructures. The reality of a situation where information is shared rapidly with third party companies such as suppliers and partners could compromise the privacy of customers and harm competitiveness by putting intellectual property and commercially sensitive information at risk. Increased openness of infrastructures is perceived to create risk for the owners of the Critical Financial Infrastructures (CFI) but also for the users of data processed by these infrastructures.

6.1.1   Markets Access of Non-banks
These regulations have indeed facilitated the ability of non-banks to offer traditional banking services. As an example of the changing landscape for financial infrastructures, VocaLink made public in 2008 that its bank shareholders are looking to sell a stake in the firm to non-bank investors.

In the investment banking arena, many experienced traders have in recent years established hedge funds that have become key trading partners of the traditional investment banks and independent technology providers have established electronic trading platforms that increasingly gain market share from the traditional exchanges.

A growing number of service providers have started to offer information processing services to the customers of banks (fund managers, companies and even consumers) that directly compete with the existing financial services. These offerings also cover increasingly the value added services that the banks were intending to include in their services portfolio (such as e-invoicing and identity management).

Non-banks are less regulated and therefore more flexible in service creation. The market share of non-banks has been increased and is also a threat to the stability of the financial market. Also, non-banks IT systems perform often better and through technological performance business advantages are attempted.

6.2   Accelerated Dematerialization of Supply Chains in the EU

The application of new web technology and its improved integration techniques began in 2008 leading to substitution of paper by electronics means. This substitution is called dematerialization of the supply chain.

SEPA and e-invoicing are expected to contribute to the Lisbon agenda by making Europe the most competitive and dynamic knowledge-based economy in the world by the end of 2010. E-invoicing does not form a part of SEPA, but is a value added services are built on top of SEPA, which relies on the clearing and settlement infrastructures.

Furthermore, 10 public administrations in Europe started in the fall of 2008 to execute on the Pan European Public Procurement Online (Peppol project www.Peppol.eu) on cross border e-procurement, e-ordering and e-invoicing which has today less than 20% of EU's GDP, but as strategic target is more than 50% coverage.

The trend to electronic processing increases the dependability on the according infrastructure and its criticality. Robustness and resilience are therefore central design criteria.

6.3   Growing Complexity, Volume and Transaction Speed

The discussion what could be different in financial IT systems from others, the resulted in the combination of complexity, volume and speed of executing financial transactions meanwhile maintaining reliability, confidentiality and integrity.

The speed of transaction processing was given a further boost by the introduction in 2008 of faster payments by the UK banking community. Previously cleared funds arrived with the beneficiary after passing through a three-day clearing cycle. But pressurized by the UK government, payees are able to receive cleared funds rapidly and payers have the certainty that their funds have been debited immediately. Similar developments in the EU by establishing the TARGET2-system offer the same near-time settlement for the Euro. Further developments in the TARGET2SECURITIES system (T2S) will allow customers to settle not only the payments in near time, also reduce the settlement time for securities. This will cause enormous efforts in changing the way how clearing works by today.

Growing Complexity in Foreign Exchange Markets.
Historically, currency trading has been a "closed" market, reserved primarily for central banks. However, with the advent of web-based trading applications and overall advances in technology, small retail traders and even individuals can now participate from their desktops directly in the forex markets on equal footing with these large institutions. Examples for electronic trading technology are electronic trading platforms such as OANDA[4] or Swissquote[5]. These platforms use innovative computer and financial technology to provide Internet-based forex trading and currency information services to everyone and is rapidly becoming more attractive as an alternative investment opportunity.

New Complexity: Adaption to New Internet Ipv6.
Ipv6 will enable Internet to reach almost any object on the planet. This will inevitably extend the number of contact points for financial transactions by several orders of magnitude, likely not to its final reach but still very significantly. IPv6 will bring first enormous efforts for switching the infrastructure to the new protocol. Many devices

---

[4] http://www.oanda.com/
[5] www.swissquote.ch

must be changed because upgrades will not be available. Additionally, new opportunities for banks as well as new "transaction" operators, e.g. robots, may be generated as well as the complexity of infrastructure (number of nodes) will increase dramatically.

6.4   Conclusion on Current Situation in Financial Sector

It is important to recognize that we take a dynamic view of the situation with regard to key decisive factors while classical risk analysis tends to be more static. The fact that EVOLUTION IN ITSELF IS A RISK FACTOR is often minimized by classical approaches of risk assessment. They tend to be static and do reflect reality to a limited degree only.

Nowadays the finance and the defence communities may not perceive risks in the same way:

- Finance top managers tend to perceive IT infrastructures, as an amplifier of financial moves see the current crisis. This has been known for some time. Is it permanent or can something dampen the effect? "Fuses" are already in place for stock markets;
- Finance people tend to prioritize the threats on their infrastructure less than other issues like (financial) risk management. Do they actually take them as something for IT specialists or do they give sufficient consideration to the consequences? The current trend is probably closer to the first option, which has proven by the financial turmoil 2008/2009.

Finance top managers are likely to act on two factors: first the consequences which may result from threat scenarios especially when compliance is not met, and second what they can actually do when such a scenario occurs. With respect to infrastructures these factors play in opposite directions: the more IT will take over services, the fewer financiers can act on infrastructure and will therefore not feel in command. This latter trend is very hard to reverse and deserves a more detailed analysis, respectively, the causality of unfortunate incidents and how business or management attitudes may trigger or facilitate these incidents and identifies lessons from it. Another issue is threat & risk assessment. Said bluntly, some of the threats might not interest bankers because their customers will bear all consequences.

7   Challenges in the Future: Results of Parsifal

Parsifal: Protection And tRuSt In FinanciAL infrastructures (Parsifal-Team, 2010) project was launched in September 2009 and targeting the ambitious objective concerning coordination activities between the stakeholders necessary to protect CFI and information infrastructures, both today and tomorrow, and specifically those areas which span beyond a single bank or a single country. Parsifal goals are:

1. Bringing together Financial industry and R&D stakeholders from ICT Security areas;

2. Contributing to the understanding of CFI challenges in the next five years;
3. Developing longer term visions, research roadmaps, CFI scenarios and best practice guides;
4. Coordinating the relevant research work, knowledge and experiences.

The Parsifal project had 6 Partners and was running for 18 month.

7.1 Parsifal Methodology

The PARSIFAL objective is to provide input to future research programmes and further strengthen the engagement between the European Commission and the financial Services industry in terms of trust, security and dependability of these critical financial ICT infrastructures.

The main tool to achieve the project's ambitious objectives has been the setting up of an expert stakeholder group (ESG), comprising stakeholders from the industry and research communities. This group included representatives of several key actors in critical financial service industry CFI protection. Among them were high level representatives and decision makers that have the power to decide where to invest in research in the upcoming years.

To get a comprehensive and high quality input from the stakeholders, two workshops were organized. The first workshop included presentations from relevant experts to stimulate the discussion and identify the main issues in CFI protection: This set the ground for the working groups in three main streams:

1. Controlling Instant On Demand Business in CFI: Authentication, Identity Management, Resilience and Denial of Service.

2. Entitlement Management and Securing Content in the Perimeterless Financial Environment: Identity, Policy, Privacy and Audit.

3. Business Continuity and Control in an Interconnected and Interdependent Service Landscape: Cross Border and Cross Organisations.

The three stakeholder working groups used written exercises and discussion to define future scenarios and challenges in CFI protection. The final result was a set of eight recommendations for research.

The next step was to prioritize these recommendations. The second workshop was used to present the recommendations to the stakeholders and ask them about their priorities. Using an online survey (*via* web and email), a wider group of stakeholders was contacted to include their priorities and recommendations.

7.2 Parsifal Recommendation and Research Directions

In table 1 the eight recommendations are explained with reflection of the streams in which they were elaborated.

Table 1. Work streams and Recommendations

Stream 1: Instant on Demand Business	1. Classification of identity attributes for on-line and mobile users of financial services should be defined and well understood by providers of these services and their customers.
	2. Trust indicators need to be developed, which allow for the various gradients of trust any entity might achieve when using specific financial services.
	3. Support platforms are needed for the management of multiple identities to allow consumers to authenticate themselves with various professional and private identity attributes.
Stream 2: Entitlement Management	4. Digital identities are required that are highly standardised across the financial services sector, with the introduction of mandatory IDs for all financial institutions, cross border interoperability and a "single/global" identity issuing authority.
	5. Data Security measures are required, such that a digital identity links directly with a security policy to a data object, that data is secured as encapsulated entities, and with flexible security policies that are based on individual access rights plus Digital Rights Management (DRM) for enterprise content to allow for flexible security policies and geographic boundary control.
	6. New Computing Paradigms need to be analysed, which allow for de-perimeterization of the organisation, e.g. Cloud Computing, supported by any new security focus. Predictive models need to be created to understand security risks. Cross border legal issues need to be resolved.
Stream 3: Business Continuity	7. Design and implementation of secure platforms and applications, which should include an alternative and secure communication system/infrastructure, to be overseen by adequate coordination response team(s) at a national and international level.
	8. Testing, design and implementation of such secure platforms, applications and infrastructures through trustworthy exercises between CIP-sectors and governments. Models for business continuity need to be extended to (1) sharing risks and (2) end-to-end communication between trade participants, as well as to (3) the volume and the complexity of specific financial markets. These models should be "crash" tested, regularly evaluated and updated.

7.3   Prioritisation of the Eight Parsifal Recommendation

Experts were invited to vote on the eight recommendations. The following options were available for voting: Absolutely urgent, urgent, must be addressed, not urgent. Although the results are apart from each other, the results points clearly out, that the recommendations and priorities have found agreement in the community.

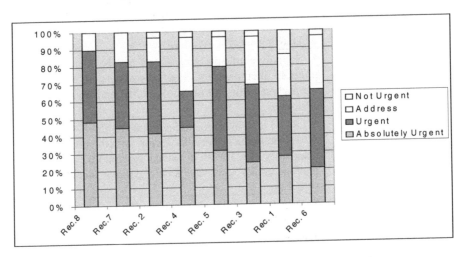

Fig. 6. Voting results of the experts on the eight recommendations

In a complex process with consideration of the stream and sense of urgency figure 6 was developed showing the timeline (starting with recommendation eight), the dependencies and interrelation of the eight recommendations. The timeline is important when considering the sequence in which recommendation are dealt with.

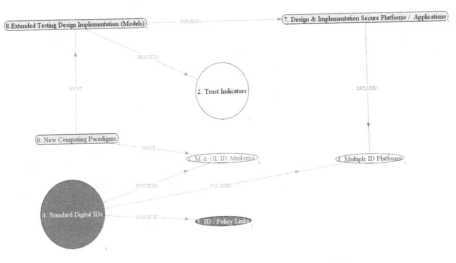

Fig. 7. Dependencies between the eight recommendations

7.4   Conclusions on Future Challenges in Financial ICT

The very first and important statement we have to make is the excellence the financial sector has reached. Form all infrastructure failure we have experience by now are only very on a recognizable level. And even those were not really long-lasting and impacting essentially economy or society. Vice versa the business failure have tradition and occur periodically form 1929 to 2009 again and again. Obviously the infrastructure risks were easier to handle and sector handled those better than their business. However, the ICT has a very unpredictable side, and this needs attention.

From the Parsifal project stakeholder group we know what the future focus should be (table 1). We observe from the eight main challenges that there are many challenges related to identity management (1,3,4,5), two are related to business continuity management BCM and are rated as the most important one (7,8) and the last two (cloud computing risks stemming from new technologies and trust indicators enabling clients to estimate trust-level for inter-acting with banks when connected with different infrastructures (home, office, public wireless etc.).

Meanwhile the BCM and new technological risks are well known to the community, the identity and cloud challenge might be often underestimated in both, the critical meaning for the sector and the cost saving potential. Especially identities are essential for interacting in the virtual rooms. In research secure cross-border identities an identity economics are often discussed, but seldom the risks beyond the corporate relevance, such as the criticality for the sector.

Acknowledgment. Parsifal project team are indirect co-authors and kindly permitted to use the projects documents to write this chapter: Rafael Llarena & Aljosa Pasic ATOS Origin Spain, Susan Morrow & Sandy Porter Avoco Secure, Henning Arendt Arent Business Consultant,   Jean-Yves Gresser and Tom Buschman Edge international BV, James Clarke and Kieran Sullivan Waterford Institute of Technology Ireland.

Furthermore, Christian Kleine UBS AG, Rolf Prantl (especially for figure 1, he was contributing) and Pius Steiner deserve my thanks for review and content enhancement.

Specific References

Comifin-Team. Communication Middleware for Monitoring Financial Critical Infrastructure (2008) Von, http://www.comifin.eu/abgerufen

Detecon Consulting. Study - The Value of Information Security to European Banking Institutions. Zürich, Detecon (2001)

Dick K., Nanto, C. S.: The Global Financial Crisis: Analysis and Policy Implications. Abgerufen am 26. 4 2011 (October 2, 2009) von,
http://www.fas.org/sgp/crs/misc/RL34742.pdf

Financial-Services-Club (October 2009) Von,
http://thefinanser.co.uk/fsclub/2009/10/cloud-computing-needs-better-definition-to-succeed.htmlabgerufen

FIX-Group. (kein Datum). Abgerufen am 2011. 7 31 von Request for Participation: FIX-FpML Collaboration Working Group,
http://www.fixprotocol.org/discuss/read/5341e8a6

FIX-Group, F. S. (kein Datum). FIX Protocol. Abgerufen am 2011. 7 31 von
http://www.fixprotocol.org/what-is-fix.shtml

Flatraaker, D.-I.: Sepa Standards – Sepa goes mobile. EPC Newsletter (January 2009)

Gresser, J. Y.: Draft Ontology Of Financial Risks & Dependencies. Abgerufen am 26. 4 2011 von parsifal-project.eu (2009),
http://www.parsifal-project.eu/images/PublicDeliverables/
PARSIFAL%20D2.1%20Draft%20Ontology%20of%20Financial%20Ris
ks%20Dependencies%20Within%20and%20outside%20the%20Financ
ial%20Sector%20V3.0%20(Glossary).pdf

Gresser, J. Y.: Ontology of Financial Risks & Dependencies: Vol 2 Glossary.Abgerufen am 26. 4 2011 von parsifal-project.eu (2009),
http://www.parsifal-project.eu/images/PublicDeliverables/
parsifal%20d2.1%20draft%20ontology%20of%20financial%20ris
ks%20and%20dependencies%20within%20and%20outside%20the%20
financial%20sector.pdf

IdenTrust. (kein Datum). IdenTrust. Abgerufen am 31. 7 2011 von
http://www.identrust.com/pdf/IdenTrust_Privacy_WhitePaper
.pdf

MEALNI. (31. 12 2010-2). Semi-annual report 2010/2. Abgerufen am 27. 04 2011 von,
http://www.melani.admin.ch/dokumentation/00123/00124/0112
2/index.html?lang=en

MELANI. (30. 6 2010-1). Semi-annual report 1/2010. Abgerufen am 27. 4 2011 von,
http://www.melani.admin.ch/dokumentation/00123/00124/0111
9/index.html?lang=en

Neumann, P. G. (kein Datum). ACM Digital Library. Abgerufen am 31. 7 2011 von,
http://portal.acm.org/citation.cfm?id=505778&dl=ACM&coll=
DL&CFID=37083720&CFTOKEN=98694083

Parsifal-Team. Protection and Trust in Financial Infrastructures. Abgerufen am 2011. 7 31 von (2010), http://www.parsifal-project.eu

Peppol-Team. (kein Datum). eProcurement without Bbroders in Europe. Abgerufen am 2011. 7 31 von http://www.peppol.eu

SLTTGCC. Critical Infrastructure Data Taxonomy: Common Terminology for Describing Critical Infrastructure. Abgerufen am 26. 4 2011 von US Departement of Homeland Security (2005),
http://www.dhs.gov/files/publications/gc_1226595934574
.shtm

Susan Morrow, G. J.-Y.: D3.4 Mapping of Research Challenges to CFI Scenarios.Abgerufen am 29. 4 2011 (October 13, 2009) von,
http://www.parsifal-project.eu/index.php?option=com_
content&view=article&id=73&Itemid=59

Westbrook, N. M.: Bloomber Business Week. Abgerufen am 31. 7 2011 (2010) von,
http://www.businessweek.com/news/2010-10-01/waddell-reed-
trades-said-to-help-spur-may-6-crash.html

Wikipedia on Bank for International Settlements. (kein Datum). Abgerufen am 26. 4 2011 von,
http://en.wikipedia.org/wiki/Bank_for_International_Settl
ements

Wikipedia on Basel II. (kein Datum). Abgerufen am 4 2011 von,
        http://en.wikipedia.org/wiki/Basel_II
Wikipedia, S. r. Settlement risk. Abgerufen am 6. 5 2011 (August 26, 2010) von,
        http://en.wikipedia.org/wiki/Herstatt_Risk
Wilcox, H.: Banking on the mobile - Mobile Banking, Strategies, Applications & Markets
        2008-2013. Juniper Research White Paper, Basingstoke (January 2009)

General References

[1] European Payment Council: Towards our single payment area (February 25, 2009),
    http://www.europeanpaymentscouncil.eu/index.cfm
[2] COSO - Enterprise Risk Management - Integrated Framework , Executive Summary
    (September 2004),
    http://www.coso.org/Publications/ERM/COSO_ERM_
    ExecutiveSummary.pdf
[3] Research and Development Committee, Financial Services Sector Coordinating Council
    for Critical Infrastructure Protection and Homeland Security (FSSCC), Research Agenda
    for the Banking and Finance Sector (September 2008)
[4] International Telecommunication Union, Information Society Statistical Profiles, 2009 –
    Africa, http://www.itu.int/dms_pub/itu-d/opb/ind/D-IND-RPM.AF-
    2009-PDF-E.pdf
[5] Committee on Payment and Settlement Systems (CPSS - Bank of International
    Settlement), The interdependencies of payment and settlement systems (June 2008)
[6] European Central Bank (ECB), Public consultation on glossary of terms related to
    payment, clearing and settlement systems (September 30, 2008)
[7] Federal Office for Information Security, BSI – Standard- 100-4, Business Continuity
    Management, version 1.0 (2009) http://www.bsi.bund.de/grundschutz
[8] British standard Institute, Information technology — Security techniques — Information
    security management systems — Code of practice for information security management,
    BS ISO/IEC 27001:2005, BS 7799-1:2005 (July 2007)

Transportation*

Mark Hartong[1], Rajn Goel[2], and Duminda Wijesekera[3]

[1] Federal Railroad Administration, U.S. Department of Transportation, Washington, DC, USA
mark.hartong@dot.gov
[2] Department of Information Systems and Decision Sciences,
Howard University, Washington, DC, USA
rgoel@howard.edu
[3] Department of Computer Science, George Mason University, Fairfax, VA USA
dwijesek@gmu.edu

Abstract. Transportation systems are an often overlooked critical infrastructure component. These systems comprise a widely diverse elements whose operation impact all aspects of society today. This chapter introduces the key transportation sectors and illustrates the impacts that can result if their operation is disrupted. Two elements that are common to systems used in all sectors, and that are vulnerable to cyber attack, are discussed. Positive Train Control (PTC), used in the rail sector to prevent or mitigate the consequences of accidents and that makes extensive use of these elements, is discussed in detail as representative of the security issues.

1 Introduction

Transportation systems are ubiquitous to todays modern society. At any given time these systems can be found in operation moving both people and goods around the world. Without transportation systems, life as we know it in the 21st century, would cease to exist. Virtually all raw materials and the finished products used in our daily lives must be moved from one point to another. Modern production processes, typified by just in time deliveries, allow for more efficient use of resources, at the cost of an increased dependence on the proper functioning of the transportation system to deliver the required materials at the proper time. Failure of the transportation system to make deliveries can badly disrupt, or even halt the production of goods. Transportation systems not only allow for the geographical concentration of people from rural to urban areas, but also travel between geographically disperses locations as well. Both support the ability of individuals or populations to specialize, furthering economic development as well as development of the arts and sciences. The financial impact of transportation systems operations to an economy is immense. In the United States alone, transportation services account for over 10% of the U.S. Gross Domestic Product [1].

Because of the potential adverse impacts on a national economy in the event of the disruption or destruction of transportation systems, transportation systems are elements of the critical infrastructure. More specifically:

---

* The views and opinions expressed herein are that of the authors and do not necessarily state or reflect those of the United States Government, the Department of Transportation, or the Federal Railroad Administration, and shall not be used for advertising or product endorsement.

J. Lopez et al. (Eds.): Critical Information Infrastructure Protection, LNCS 7130, pp. 330–355, 2012.

Physical distribution systems critical to supporting the national security and economic well being of nation, including the national airspace systems, airlines, aircraft, and airports; roads and highways, trucking and personal vehicles, ports, waterways and the vessels operating thereon; mass transit, both rail and bus; pipelines, including natural gas, petroleum, and other hazardous materials; freight and long haul passenger rail; and delivery services [2].

This chapter begins by introducing the major transportation modalities and some of the socio-economic impacts resulting from their disruption. Subsequent sections address two common technologies in use by all modalities, and the vulnerabilities of these technologies to cyber attack. Finally a detailed case study of Positive Train Control, a wireless command and control system for railroad use that is being deployed in the United States, and its associated cyber security challenges, is presented to illustrate the detailed cyber security challenges associated with modern information and communication control systems being deployed in all transportation modalities.

2 Transportation Modalities

Various modes of transportation exist, and form the organizational basis for Departments or Ministries of Transportation around the world. While the details of these organizations may vary, they generally provide government oversight of aviation, rail & transit, maritime, highway/motor carrier, and pipeline operation. These modes form the basis for discussion.

2.1 Aviation

The aviation sector provides air transportation of passengers, cargo, and mail. Beside the obvious major elements such as landing strips and airplanes, this sector also includes other critical elements such as air traffic control centers, en-route and terminal flight aids (e.g. radio navigation beacons), and aviation fuel depots. All of these must work together synergistically to support commercial and general aviation.

Globally, the over 250 regularly scheduled commercial aviation carriers had annual revenues in excess of $448 billion, moved over 2,062 million passengers and 33.5 million tons of freight [3]. In the United States alone the aviation transportation sector employs over 561,000 people operating out of over 19,000 air fields with a combination of 8,200 commercial and 224,000 general aviation aircraft [4]. Globally over 5.5 million people are directly employed in the aviation sector, with another 10 million employees in the associated supply chain, with the equivalent Gross Domestic Product of $1.1 trillion. In 2007, 35% of manufactured goods(or $3.5 trillion) was transported by air [5].

The aftermath of the terrorist attack on the morning of September 11, 2001 in New York City is illustrative of the impact that a major disruption in the aviation system can have. As a consequence of the attacks, the U.S. Federal Aviation Administration activated air defense plans and declared an air defense emergency [6]. As part of the response to the emergency all non military air traffic across the entire United States was prohibited to operate. Over 4,000 domestic flights that were en-route were diverted to the nearest airport and grounded. U.S. airspace was closed to all incoming international flights. Transport Canada took similar measures, closing Canadian airspace to all traffic except military, police, and humanitarian flights. This resulted in the grounding of another 1,500 flights.

International traffic already airborne and in bound to the United States and Canada was diverted. Traffic that had exceeded the half-way point to destinations in the U.S. and Canada was ordered to land at the first Canadian airport, while all other traffic was refused entry and was directed to divert to points outside the U.S. or Canada. Of the over 500 international flights that are normally inbound to North America on any given day, less than half were allowed entry into Canadian airspace. All other inbound flights were refused entry and were forced to either return to their origin or diverted.

Normal flight operations were resumed on 13 September 2001. In addition to the inconvenience to the traveling public (almost 45,000 international passengers alone were impacted by the suspension of flight operations) there were significant financial costs. In the three-day period after the attack, the U.S. Federal Reserve Bank was injecting over $100 billion per day in liquidity to stabilize the financial markets. An additional $15 billion ($5 billion in direct grants, $10 billion in loan guarantees) were required to support continued airline operations. Insurance losses exceeded $40 billion. The Gross City product of New York City decreased by over $27 billion dollars. The cost of debris removal and direct aid to business affected exceeded $11 billion, and nearly 130,000 people were displaced from their jobs [7]. To place these costs in context, the entire American Reinvestment and Recovery Act of 2009 to mitigate the impact of to the U.S. economy from the global financial meltdown in the fall of 2008 was $787 billion [8].

2.2   Rail/Transit

Rail/Transit operations can be divided into two separate categories: freight and passenger operations. Operations in this sector are characterized by a high levels of economic and territorial control with most rail companies operating as monopolies or oligopolies. In North America freight service predominates. The seven largest railroads in the United States carry over 1.77 trillion ton-miles of freight with revenues exceeding $52 billion [9]. The National Passenger Rail Corporation (AMTRAK) intercity passenger service accounts for some 5.3 billion passenger miles [10] while U.S. commuter and intra-city passenger operations over 19 billion passenger miles [11]. In contrast, in the European Union, freight accounts for approximately 237 billion ton miles while commuter/ intracity passenger operations exceed 120 billion passenger miles [12], and intercity passenger service accounts for an additional 271 billion passenger miles [13]. Critical elements in the freight infrastructure include the locomotives and their associated consists (either passenger or freight), dispatch centers used to issue movement authorities, track, bridges, and tunnels over which trains operate, wayside equipment that relays movement authorities to the train, and marshalng yards where trains are made up, broke down, and serviced.

The consequences of significant freight disruptions can have severe economic impacts. An example of such a disruption occurred in the Texas service area of the Union Pacific (UP) railroad in 1998. Rail congestion brought on by dispatching issues associated with the UP acquisition of the Southern Pacific railroad resulted in virtual gridlock into and out of the State of Texas on the UP. The ensuring gridlock resulted in direct costs of almost $1.1 billion dollars, and an additional $643 billion in additional costs to consumers [14] in 1998 dollars. That these costs were not larger can only be attributed to the U.S. Surface Transportation Board ordering UP traffic onto competitors railroad lines that were not gridlocked.

While there is no public evidence about any cyber attacks against the rail sector, the RAND Corporation identified 181 attacks on trains and rail related targets worldwide, with over 400 deaths, between 1998 and 2003 . Excluding the casualties associated with the 9/11 attacks, rail has experienced roughly 3 times as many incidents, with 13 times as many deaths [15] as attacks on aviation related targets. The consequences of a successful rail attack could be far worse. Projected casualties from a worst-case scenario of the release of one 90 ton car of chlorine in the downtown Washington DC exceed 100,000 [16]. Until recently over 8,500 such cars moved by rail only blocks away from the U.S. Capital.

2.3   Maritime

Maritime traffic is the oldest of the transportation modes. The earliest archeological evidence of marine commerce dates from the later Bronze Age [17]. Discovered in 1982, cargo recovered from this shipwreck was much as it is today- a mix of raw materials and finished goods. Today it is estimated that 80 percent of all world trade, or about 5.7 billion tons is moved by water [18]. This involves a massive infrastructure suspectable to attack, including 93 thousand merchant vessels with 1.25 million seamen bound for eight thousand ports [19].

The piracy threat to shipping through the South China Sea in the Southeast Asia region alone has cost the world economy a staggering $25 billion per year [20]. The cost of prevention further would further increase the adverse economic impact. The Organization for Economic Co-operation and Development (OECD), for example, has stated that new security measures to counter the threat of terrorist attacks will require an initial investment by ship operators of at least U.S. $1.3 billion and will increase annual operating costs by U.S.$730 million [21].

The links between terrorism and piracy have been extensively examined [22]. While maritime terrorist attacks or threats–that is, politically or ideologically motivated attacks against ships–have been statistically scarce, their potential impact is extremely large. Major disruptions of maritime traffic may result in increased transports costs, reverse globalization and bring to an end the comparative advantage of low cost remote production locations such as China. In tariff-equivalent terms, an explosion in global transport costs would offset all the trade liberalization efforts of the last three decades. Not only does this suggest a major slowdown in the growth of world trade, but also a fundamental realignment in trade patterns [23].

2.4   Highway/Motor Carrier

Highway/Motor carrier transportation is the most ubiquitous of the transportation modalities. Its component elements consist of passenger (bus/automobile) vehicles, freight vehicles, and the supporting highway infrastructure. Most industrialized nations depend on a combination of passenger and freight vehicles operating over an extensive highway infrastructure to move the majority of commodities.

The United States operates the largest fleet of vehicles, as well as the largest highway infrastructure in the world. The vehicle fleet consists of over 254 million cars, 9 million trucks, 7 million motorcycles, and 834 thousand buses traveling over 3 trillion vehicle miles [1] across a 4 million mile road network. The truck fleet moves over 1.2 trillion ton-miles of freight, making it second only to rail in terms of the volume of freight by ton-mile.

The U.S. economy is totally dependent on this infrastructure- 75% of U.S. communities depend solely on trucking for the movement of commodities. While the diversity, dispersion, and redundancy inherent in this mode renders it relatively immune to cyber attacks and precludes a complete shutdown of the sector. the same size and diversity offers a high number of potential targets. For example their are approximately 582,000 bridges over 20 feet in length and 54 tunnels over 1,500 feet [24]- that, if attacked in sufficiently large numbers, can cause serious economic disruptions. This sector constitute a particular challenge to the security community because they are not only a very distributed and independent set of potential targets but the elements of the system can also be used as weapons to attack other assets that are accessible by highway infrastructure. Examples of this include the truck bomb attacks on the Murrah Federal Building in Oklahoma City in April 1995 and the February 1993 bombing of the World Trade Center in New York City.

Table 1. U.S. Fuel Consumption-2006 by Transport Mode [1]

Mode	Fuel Consumption- Million of Gallons
Aviation	15,279
Rail	4,098
Marine	8,446
Highway/Motor Carrier	174,086

Highway/motor carrier transportation however is very vulnerable to disruption in fuel supplies, more so than other transportation modes, as seen in Table 1, Highway/Motor Carriers use over 174 million gallons of fuel, more than 6 times the fuel consumption of aviation, rail, and marine combined.

Disruption of refinery capacity in the United States in 2005 after Hurricane Katrina and Rita, illustrates the vulnerability and economic impact of this sector that arise as a result of its dependence on petroleum products. The Gulf coast of the United States supplies 43% of U.S. refinery capacity, after Hurricane Rita, that capacity was reduced by half. One week prior to Katrina the spot price of wholesale gasoline in the Gulf was $75 per barrel, and the spot diesel price was $76 per barrel. After Katrina, wholesale U.S. gasoline prices spiked to nearly $125 per barrel (almost $3 per gallon) and more than $125 per barrel after Rita. Wholesale U.S. Gulf diesel prices, which increased only slightly after Katrina, surged passed gasoline prices in the week after Rita, spiking to more than $135 per barrel (more than $3.20 per gallon). After Katrina U.S. gasoline stocks fell by more than 1.7 million barrels to 32.6 million barrels. Stocks continued to decline for five weeks until mid-October as refinery disruptions from Hurricane Rita exacerbated the drawdown. Diesel stocks dropped by about 4.4 million barrles per day, causing the spot diesel premium prices to spike to 48 cents [25]. The long term effects of this massive disruption in fuel supplies, and the associated higher energy prices, were significant increases in transportation costs, petroleum based products and utility bills (with a corresponding decrease in disposable income).

2.5   Pipeline

Often the least noticed transportation modalities are pipelines, where most people are unaware that this vast network even exists. This is due to the strong safety record of pipelines and the fact that most of them are located underground. Unlike the other, more visible modalities that involve the transportation of passengers, pipelines are used strictly for the transportation of liquids and other gasses under pressure. Materials moved include natural gas, liquid petroleum (crude oil and refined products made from crude oil, such as gasoline, home heating oil, diesel fuel, aviation gasoline, jet fuels, and kerosene), liquefied ethylene, propane, butane, and other petrochemical feedstocks

Pipelines are easily accessible and present the perfect soft target that can result in economic damage and losses if attacked [26]. Since pipelines supply fuel for vehicles, power plants, aircraft, heating, military bases and other uses, serious disruption of a pipeline network poses additional downstream risks. Oil and gas pipelines have been a favored target of terrorists outside the United States [27]. In Colombia, for example, rebels have bombed Occidental Petroleums Caño Limón pipeline some 950 times since 1986, shutting it for months at a time and costing Colombia's government some $2.5 billion in lost revenues. One of these attacks in 1998 caused a fire that killed or injured over 100 people. In the last 2 years, oil and gas pipelines have also been attacked in Nigeria, Pakistan, Sudan, Myanmar and Iraq. In Saudi Arabia, a planned pipeline attack by al-Qaeda sympathizers at the country's main oil terminal was thwarted in 2002. Although it was unclear whether the planners had the capability to fully execute the Saudi attack, had they been successful, they could have disrupted the movement of over 6% of the worlds daily oil consumption.

2.6   Inter-modal Operations

Inter-modal operations are a direct response to manufactures need for improvement in the logistic chain. By improving the delivery time of raw materials components, and finished products both manufacturers and vendors have been able to reduce the amount of inventory that must be held to support their operations to compensate for disruptions and delays in the logistics pipeline [28]. Intermodal operations require geographical grouping's of independent companies and bodies which are dealing with freight transport (for example, freight forwarders, shippers, transport operators, customs) and with accompanying services (for example, storage, maintenance and repair) operating a shared terminal [29] integrating one or more different transportation modalities. While intermodal operation combinations may include air-motor carrier, air-rail, rail-motor carrier, or marine-rail, maritime-motor carrier, air maimed, the most significant are maritime-rail and maritime motor carrier. Marine container transportation is vital to both the North American and global economies. Over 50 million TEU[1] moved through North American ports in 2008 alone [30]. Disruptions in traffic flows have severe economic consequences. A two-week labor strike at U.S. West Coast ports in 2002 stranded more than 200 ships and 300,000 containers [31] because other ports did not have the capacity to accommodate redirected shipments. The strike required presidential intervention as the delays cost the U.S. economy $1 billion a day [32].

3   Critical Cyber Components of Transportation Systems

Transportation systems are vulnerable to vandalism and terrorist attacks. The infrastructure components of these facilities may be damaged with explosives or by other mechanical means. However this requires physical access to the component to disrupt or destroy the asset. Alternatively, the computer control systems for the transportation assets may be cyber-attacked, allowing disruption or destruction of the transportation asset without the need for physical access by the attacker. A cyber attack can use functionality and characteristics of the transportation system itself to either induce the operator to undertake inappropriate actions, or cause system behaviors, that result in system disruptions without the need for the attacker to expose themselves to direct discovery and capture. Such attacks can cause failures in areas that may never have been construed as vulnerable as practical issues. It is important to note that while cyber and other attacks could have serious impacts on transportation systems operations, with potentially significant losses of life at point locations, the size and geographical dispersion of the transportation system will most likely involve inconvenience and economic losses. This presumes of course, that transportation SCADA systems are designed to support graceful degradation of the system operations.

Specific transportation system cyber vulnerabilities are extremely implementation dependent; consequently a complete vulnerability analysis must be done in the context of the system implementation. However most implementations share two comment functionalities that are susceptible to attack- wireless communications and satellite based positioning.

3.1   Wireless Communications

All transportation modalities may make use of one, or more, parts of the radio frequency spectrum as illustrated in Table 2. When wireless communications are used, they can be classified as fixed communications systems where communications are between stationary end-points, and mobile communications systems where communications are between end points where at least one of them is in motion. Both fixed and mobile systems can be implemented using point-to-point, point-to-multipoint, or multipoint-to-multipoint architectures. Compared to wireline systems, wireless systems offer greater

---

[1] TEU = Twenty-Foot Equivalent Unit, a standard linear measurement used in quantifying container traffic flows. One twenty-foot long container equals one TEU.

flexibility, and are usually deployed in less time and with less cost than wireline alternatives whether by public or private service providers. Most any application found in the wireline domain, can be supported in the wireless domain.

Table 2. U.S. Transportation Related Frequencies [33]

Frequency Range	Use
37,460-37.860 MHz	Power/Water/Pipeline
43.700-44.660 MHz	Transportation-bus/truck
108.000-118.000 MHz	Aero-navigation
118.00-136.000 MHz	Aero-communications
156.025-157.425 MHz	Maritime (Ship)
159.495-160.200 MHz	Transportation-bus/truck
160-215-161.610 MHz	Railroad
161.625-161.760 MHz	Maritime (Coast)
161.500-162.025 MHz	Maritime (Coast)
216.000-218.000 MHz	Maritime (Coast)
219-220 MHz	Maritime- Ship
220-221 MHz	Private Land Mobile (Rail-Base)
221-222 MHz	Private Land Mobile (Rail-Mobile)
420-450 MHz	Radiolocation
452.625-452.950 MHz	Transportation- Truck/Rail
457.050-457.500 MHz	Industry/Transport
457.525-457.600 MHz	Maritime Shipboard
475.625-457.950 MHz	Transportation-Truck/Rail
460.650-460.875 MHz	Business-Airport Use
465.650-465.875 MHz	Business-Airport Use
467.750-467.825 MHz	Maritime-Shipboard
896.000-901 MHz	Business/Industry Mobile (Rail)
935-940 MHz	Business/Industry- Base (Rail)
960-1215 MHz	Aeronautical Navigation

Wireless communications have limitations which increase their vulnerability to cyber attack, not the least of which is that the radio spectrum is a limited natural resource. Frequency spectrum use is tightly managed by the International Telecommunication Union (ITU)[2] and the various member governments., As a consequence there is significant competition for the limited bandwidth that is available. The majority of the spectrum is licensed, and its use restricted to specific frequencies for specific functions. This simplifies the task of the attacker, making it easier to interfere with legitimate users.

While each government makes available one or more frequencies that allow unlicensed operations (for example in the United States this includes spectrum in the 900 MHz, 2.4GHz, 5.2GHz, 5.8GHz, 24GHz, 60 GHz, and the 80-90 GHz bands) access

---

[2] The ITU is a specialized agency of the United Nations (UN) headquartered in Geneva, Switzerland and is responsible for international frequency allocations, worldwide telecommunications standards and telecommunication development activities.

is on a first come/first serve basis in unlicensed bands. Users of the unlicensed bands must be willing to accept interference from other users. While interference is limited to some extent by technical means such as limitations on transmission power for the use of spread spectrum transmissions limitations, there is no spectrum coordinator to resolve usage issues, as is the case with licensed bands.

Although individual transportation systems make use of various different segments of the frequency spectrum using different transmission protocols there is one set of frequencies commonly used by all transportation modalities that use the same communications protocol- the 1575.42 MHz Global Positioning System (GPS) L1 and 1227.60 MHz GPS L2 signals. These signals are used not only for location and navigation information, but also timing references for the communications system. .

3.2   GPS

The GPS was first developed by the United States military and became available for civilian use following the August 1983 destruction of Korean Airlines Flight KAL-007 near Sakhalin Island, Russia. The system, more fully described in reference [34], consists of a constellation of government provided satellites in low earth orbit, their associated ground control/ monitoring stations, and user owned receivers. In addition to GPS other world-wide satellite position systems with similar functionality are in operation or under development. These include Galileo by the European Union, COMPASS by the Peoples Republic of China and GLONASS by the Russian Federation. All of these share common cyber vulnerabilities. While specifically addressing GPS, the vulnerability discussion of reference [35] is applicable to all satellite positioning systems.

For aviation, GPS is used in as the primary means of oceanic, en-route, and terminal navigation as well as approach navigation and control of aircraft. It forms the basis of a number of advanced navigation and control systems planned or under construction. In the United Sates these new systems are intended to replace existing radio based 2 dimensional (bearing and range) non precision instrument approaches with GPS based 3 dimensional (bearing, range, and altitude) high precision instrument approaches, reduce aircraft separation requirements, allow more direct aircraft routing, provide positioning information where it infeasible to install radar surveillance, and to support airport surface operations. Similar efforts are also underway by other International Civil Aviation Organization (ICAO) members.

The International Marine Organization (IMO) requires the use of GPS in the marine environment by the requirement for vessels to carry Automatic Identification Systems (AIS). AIS systems, which integrate GPS receivers with VHF transceivers, provide automated position, velocity, time, course information, and ship identity information to Vessel Traffic Services and other AIS equipped ships. AIS requirements applies to all ships 300 gross tons and above on international voyages, cargo ships greater 500 gross tons and above not on international voyage, and all passenger vessels regardless of size. GPS is also used in the more traditional safety critical roles of vessel position navigation in ocean, costal, harbor and inland waters, search and rescue, and aids to navigation positioning.

Examples of safety critical surface transportation application of GPS in the rail/transit, and highway/motor carrier sectors can be found in PTC in the case of the former, and

Intelligent Transportation Systems (ITS) in the case of the later. Both use GPS as a source of location and speed information for collision avoidance and control as well as emergency alarm and responses. GPS may also support the interaction between ITS and PTC where GPS position information from the rail system is fed to the ITS and used to prevent collisions between trains and surface vehicles.

The use of GPS for safety critical functionality in pipelines operations deals less with the direct operations of the pipeline, but more with supporting activities. As is the case with air and marine communications, GPS is used extensively with pipeline operations as the primary source of precision timing for status and control communications.

Although the U.S. Department of Defense has done extensive testing on the deliberate disruption of Satellite Navigation services, public information regarding the results of those tests is minimal. As a result the full extent of the threat, and its potential impact on all transportation sectors is not fully known. Using results obtained from studies of unintentional disruptions of satellite navigation service, one could extrapolate the impact of deliberate disruptions. For example testing at the U.S. National Satellite Test Bed has demonstrated that even minor changes in the ionosphere caused by solar flares could cause GPS receivers to loose track of satellites in all line of sight directions, resulting in significantly degraded position information for extended period of time [36]. From this at least one conclusion can be drawn- satellite navigation systems cannot serve as the sole source of location information or precision timing for safety critical systems for transportation operations [37].

4   Positive Train Control(PTC)- A Detailed Case Study in Cyber Vulnerability

PTC systems are not unique to the United States, nor are they restricted strictly to the general rail environment. In the U.S. alone, major transit agencies such as the San Francisco Bay Area Rapid Transit (BART), New York City Transit (NYCT), Metropolitan Atlanta Rapid Transit Authority (METRA) and Washington Metropolitan Transit Authority (METRO) have implemented, or are in the process of implementing PTC systems. Other non general rail, driverless CBTC systems can be found in people movers at or near major airports such as Tampa, Orlando, Atlanta, Washington (Dulles), Jacksonville, Las Vegas, San Francisco, Pittsburgh, Huston, Dallas/Ft Worth, and Detroit.

PTC systems are complex Supervisory Control and Data Acquistion (SCADA) systems made up of widely distributed physical, but closely coupled, functional subsystems that have four basic functions, specifically [38]:

- Preventing train-to-train collisions, referred to as positive train separation.
- Enforcing speed restrictions, including civil engineering restrictions and temporary slow orders.
- Protecting roadway workers and their equipment operating under specific authorities.
- Preventing movement of trains through switches misaligned for safe movement.

Successful operation of a PTC system requires a well orchestrated set of interactions. Understanding the basic PTC architecture, PTC functional requirements, and modes of operations assists in understanding PTC system vulnerabilities. All such PTC systems are derivations of a single basic functional architecture, with specific enhancements and modifications to both functions and modes of operations to support the unique requirements and operational needs of the individual railroad purchasing the system.

The basic functional architecture, illustrated in Figure 1, consists of four major functional subsystems: wayside, mobile, communications, and dispatch/control. The wayside subsystem consists of elements such as highway grade crossing signals, switches and interlocks or maintenance of way workers. The mobile subsystem consists of locomotives or other on rail equipment, with their onboard computer and location systems. The dispatch/control unit is the central office that runs the railroad. The communication subsystem links the three previous systems together. Each major functional subsystem consists of a collection of physical components implemented using various databases, data communications systems, and information processing equipment.

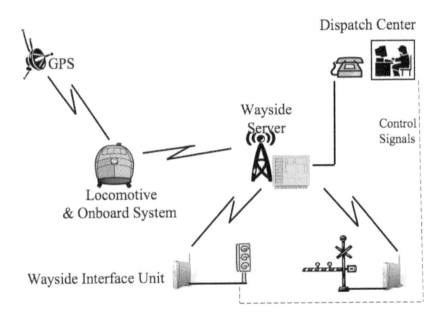

Fig. 1. PTC Architecture

PTC systems can be classified by the extent that they are used to augment the existing method of railroad operations. This classification scheme also provides an example of the flexibility for both regulators and regulated entities with respect to enforcement and compliance issues. Full PTC systems completely change, or replace, the existing method of operations. Overlay PTC systems act strictly as a backup to the existing method of operations; which remains unchanged.

4.1   Modes of Operation

The PTC mode of operations can be further refined in terms of which subsystem is responsible for executing the majority of the operations required for the execution of PTC functionality. In mobile-based modes of operation, a control unit component in the mobile subsystem is responsible for the majority of the effort required to implement the various PTC functions. The wayside subsystem and dispatch/control subsystem communicate required control data to the mobile subsystem control unit. The mobile subsystem control unit analyzes the received data, interprets it into actions for each subsystem and transmits the appropriate directives. The wayside subsystem components, the dispatch/control subsystem, or other components of the mobile subsystem then translates these directives into specific commands appropriate to the underlying hardware implementation that executes them.

In dispatch/control-based modes of operation, a control unit in the dispatch/control subsystem is responsible for most of the logical effort required to implement the various PTC functions. The wayside subsystem and mobile subsystem communicate required control data to the dispatch/control unit. The dispatch/control unit takes and receives data, analyzes it, interprets it into actions for each sub-system, and transmits the appropriate directives. The wayside subsystem components, the mobile unit subsystem components, or other components in the dispatch/control subsystem then translate these functional directives into specific commands appropriate to the underlying hardware.

A similar chain of relationships occurs in wayside based modes of operation- a control unit in the wayside subsystem is responsible for the majority of the logical effort required to implement the PTC functions. Mobile and office/dispatch subsystems communicate data to the wayside control unit. They or other components in the wayside subsystem receive functional directives for the underlying hardware in return. In all three of the preceding modes of operation, the mobile office/dispatch, and wayside subsystems are self-monitoring and can act independently when failures and defects are detected. This assures fail-safe operation even when communications is lost.

4.2   Rationale for PTC

PTC offers significant enhancements in safety by ensuring positive train separation, enforcing speed restrictions, and improving roadway worker protection. In the United States a series of high profile events, all of which were preventable had PTC been installed, were the driving factor behind the Congressional mandate in the Rail Safety Improvement Act of 2008 [38].

The first of these accidents was a collision between a Union Pacific freight train and a BNSF Railway freight train [39]. This June 2004 accident outside of Macadona, Texas caused a breach of chorine tank car. Although the puncture was relatively small and did not result in a catastrophic failure of the tank, approximately 9,400 gallons, about 60 percent of the tank's load, were released. The immediate release resulted in 3 deaths. Of significant concern was the leading edge of the cloud of chlorine gas reached the outskirts of the city of San Antonio. At the time, San Antonio had a population of 2,031,445 (based on the 2008 U.S. Census estimate), making it the 28th-largest metropolitan area in the U.S.

A second, much more significant accident was the 2005 collision of two Norfolk Southern freight trains in Graniteville, South Carolina [40]. This train collision, the result of a mispositioned switch from a mainline to an occupied siding, resulted in 9 deaths and 250 hospitalizations. It also required the evacuation of more than 4,500 citizens, the entire population of Graniteville, for over two weeks while remediation efforts were undertaken. Despite the cleanup, equipment damaged due to chlorine corrosion forced the Avondale Mills' to close its Graniteville manufacturing facility throwing more than 4,000 workers across four states out of work.

The third, and most recent accident was the September 12th, 2008 collision in Chatsworth, CA [41]. In that accident a UP freight train collided with a Metrolink commuter train head on at a combined speed of 82 miles per hour. The resulting collision killed 25 people and injured over another 135 more, 46 of them critically. While the NTSB investigation not complete, all indications were that the lack of a PTC system allowed the Metrolink engineer, who had lost situational awareness, to run a red signal that would have held the commuter train and allowed the freight train to pass.

While these accidents were not the result of cyber attacks against PTC systems, they clearly indicate the potential consequences were a successful cyber attack against a PTC system to occur. Deliberate misuse against a PTC system by a hostile third party would negate the protection offered by a PTC system, and allow the collision with the same results as previously identified. Given the increased number of wireless, GPS based PTC systems currently being deployed in the United States, the risk potential vulnerabilities to cyber attack in have further increased the risk of adverse consequences

4.3   Potential Targets-Current U.S. System Implementations

Today in the U.S. there are 11 PTC systems either deployed or in development on over 3000 route miles on 8 railroads across 21 states. Recent statutory requirements [38] will increase this to almost 80,000 miles by 2015- or roughly one half of the entire U.S. railroad route structure. The systems that are either operational or being deployed for revenue service are the:

- Advanced Civil Speed Enforcement System (ACSES),
- Incremental Train Control System (ITCS),
- Electronic Train Management System (ETMS) Version 1,Version 2, and METRA Configuration,
- Communications Based Train Management System (CBTM),
- Vital Train Management System (VTMS),
- Optimized Train Control (OTC),
- Collision Avoidance System (CAS),and
- Train Sentinel (TS).

The remaining system, the North American Joint Positive Train Control (NAJPTC) System is not currently being deployed in revenue service

4.3.1   ACSES and ITCS

Developed for the U.S. National Passenger Rail Corporation (Amtrak), ACSES is installed and fully operation on 240 route miles of the North East Corridor (NEC) between Boston, MA and Washington, DC. It supports Amtrak's ACELA, currently the fastest passenger service in the U.S., to speeds up to 150 miles per hour. ACSES is a track embedded transponder-based system that supplements the exiting NEC cab signal/automatic train control system. Amtrak also operates the ITCS system to support high-speed passenger operations Niles, MI and Kalamazoo, MI. Operating on 74 route miles, ITCS currently supports speeds up to 95 miles per hour. It is unique from other PTC system implementations in that it includes advanced high-speed highway-rail grade crossing warning system starts using radio communication rather than track circuits. Depending on the reports received from the Highway Grade Crossing Warning (HGCW) system, the ITCS onboard imposes and enforces appropriate speed restrictions. Upon completion of the verification and validation of the software, maximum authorized speeds will be raised to 110 miles per hour.

4.3.2   ETMS

BNSF Railways has undertaken an extensive PTC development and deployment effort to support their freight operations. ETMS Version 1 for low-density train operations has received full approval from the Federal Railroad Administration, and BNSF has stated deployment on 35 of their subdivisions. BNSF also has an enhanced version of ETMS, ETMS Version 2, to support high-density train operations under active test on their Fort Worth and Red Rock Subdivisions in TX. A related configuration of ETMS Versions 1 and 2 is under development for the Commuter Rail Division of the Chicago Regional Transportation Authority (METRA). Created in response to a series of fatal accidents resulting from train over speeding or exceeding, the METRA implementation of ETMS is intended to support passenger commuter, as opposed to freight, operations. This system is under deployment on the Joliet and Beverly Subdivisions in Chicago, IL.

4.3.3   CBTM, VTMS and OTC

Unlike the METRA and BNSF variants of ETMS, which are non-vital overlays, CSXT, UP and NS are developing full (or vital) system variants of ETMS. CSX Transportation is preparing to field test the latest version of CBTM on approximately 200 route miles of their Aberdeen and Andrews SC Subdivisions. Early versions were installed on their Blue Ridge and Spartanburg SC lines. Current CSX efforts are focused on harmonization of CBTM with the BNSF Railways ETMS Version 1 and 2, the Union Pacific (UP) Railroad Vital Train Management System (VTMS), and the Norfolk Southern (NS) Optimized Train Control (OTC) to interoperate freight train.

The UP VTMS has begun test operations on 15 different UP subdivisions in Washington State in the U.S. Pacific Northwest and the Powder River Basin of WY. The NS OTC, which integrates their new NS Computer Aided Dispatch (CAD) System with PTC and other specialized business functionalities, is under test on the NS Charlestown to Columbia SC Subdivisions.

CBTM, VTMS, and OTC, are all developed by the same manufacturer, and share a common software code base with ETMS. They differ from ETMS primiarily in their specific hardware configurations.

4.3.4   CAS

The Alaska Railroad is developing CAS for all 531 miles of their system. Also designed to be a full PTC system, it is built to implement the same PTC functional architecture as other PTC systems using completely different hardware and software. CAS enforces movement authority, speed restrictions, and on-track equipment protection in a combination of Direct Traffic Control (DTC) and signaled territory. All of the wayside and office components have been installed and tested, and onboard system test operations are in progress on the to Portage and Whittier Subdivisions outside of Anchorage, Alaska.

4.3.5   TS

The Ohio Central Railroad System (OCRS) version of a PTC system is the TS. TS is currently in use on various railroads in South and Central America. The OCRS version of TS is based on the TS installation currently operating in mixed passenger and high-speed freight service on the Panama Canal Railroad Balboa and Panama City in the Republic of Panama. The OCRS has completed installation of their office subsystem, and is conducting integrated office, wayside, and onboard subsystem between Columbus, and Newark, OH.

4.3.6   NAJPTC

The NAJPTC, a joint effort of the Federal Railroad Administration, the Association of American Railroads (AAR), and the Illinois Department of Transportation to develop an industry open standard high-speed passenger and freight service, was removed from service due to technical issues associated with communications bandwidth. The system was relocated to the U.S. Department of Transportation (DOT) Technology Transportation Center (TTC) Test facility in Pueblo, CO, for study and resolution of the communications issues associated with the standard in a controlled environment.

4.3.7   Related Work

Finally, although no field-testing or deployment work has occurred, the Port Authority of New York and New Jersey (PATH) has begun design work on entirely separate and independent version from the CSXT Communications Based Train Management (CBTM) System. The PATH CBTM will provide PTC functionality to the Trans-Hudson River Commuter Rail Line running underground between New Jersey and New York City.

4.4   Information Flows

Representative information flows in PTC systems can be illustrated using ETMS [42,43,44] and ITCS [45,46,47]

4.4.1 ETMS

ETMS consists of 4 segments- Onboard, Wayside, Communications, and Office (Computer Aided Dispatch System- CADS- and ETMS Server). ETMS provides for warning and enforcement of speed restrictions (permanent and temporary), work zone boundaries, and route integrity of monitored switches, absolute signals, and track (rail) integrity. During system operation, train crews are notified of potential violations when they are within a sufficient warning distance that allows them to take corrective action. If the crew fails to take corrective action, ETMS applies a full service brake application to stop the train. The method of operations does not change, however, and crews are responsible for complying with BNSF Railways operating rules at all times.

The major components of the ETMS Onboard segment consist of the engineers color display, a brake interface, a radio, a differential GPS system and using a train management computer. The train crew obtains information by a series of complex graphics on the display of the track configuration and geometry, switch position, signal indication, authority limits, train direction and makeup, current speeds, max speed, distance to enforcement, time to enforcement, geographical location and text messages. These are augmented by the use of selective color highlighting and audible alarms. The text messages either describe enforcement action in progress, or advise of a condition or required action. In addition, all applicable active warrants and bulletins can be recalled from the onboard database.

The primary means of determining position is via differential GPS information received by the Onboard segment. The onboard train management computer continuously compares its GPS position with the stored position of speed restriction zones, work zones, and monitored switches and signal from the track data base in non volatile memory. As the train management computer determines that the locomotive position is approaching the position of speed restriction and work zones, the train management computer system automatically calculates and activates the brake interface as required. The braking enforcement curves are updated dynamically based on reported changes.

The Wayside segment consists of a set of interface units that act as a communications front end for switch position, signal indications, and broken rail indications. The onboard system monitors the indication transmitted by the wayside interface units in the trains forward direction of movement. The wayside interface unit provides the latest state of monitored devices, and the onboard system will accept changes in the indication (with the corresponding changes in required enforcement activity) up to a set distance before reaching the monitored device, after which point a change is ignored.

The Communications segment consists of a wireless 802.11b broadband network to transfer track database information and event logs at selected access points along the track, and an extended line of sight communications (ELOS) network for other data exchange. There is direct exchange of data over the Communications segment between the Wayside and the onboard system, as well as between the Office and Onboard system.

The Office segment consists of the Computer Aided Dispatch System (CADS) and an ETMS server for providing train authorities, track data, consist data, and bulletins. Static information, such as track data is stored in the ETMS server portion of the ETMS Office System, while dynamic information, such as authorities are stored in the CADS portion of the ETMS Office System.

4.4.2 ITCS

The ITCS system also consists of the same 4 basic segments: Communications, On-board, Wayside and Office. The system provides for high-speed operations through wireless grade crossing activation and verification, warning and enforcement of speed restrictions (permanent and temporary), work zone boundaries, and route integrity of monitored switches and absolute signal integrity. The system design is such that a system failure results in a guaranteed enforcement. It is integrated with the existing Traffic Control System (TCS) where it obtains its signal indications.

The Communications segment consists of a radio network that allows communications between the Wayside segment components (which like ETMS consists of Wayside Server and Wayside Interface Units associated with each instrumented switch, crossing, and signal) and between the Wayside segment components and the Onboard segment. Also associated with the Communications segment are direct dial telephone lines from the office segment to the Wayside segement components. These lines allow for the gathering of health and management information about the servers as well as posting of temporary speed orders.

The major components of the Onboard segment are an engineers display, differential GPS, an on board computer and brake control interface and a track database, The engineers display is a simple LED display that indicates current speed limit, the actual speed, distance to the next enforcement target in the database, and time remaining to penalty enforcement augmented with audible alarms. An LCD is also provided to display simple text messages on software version and the locomotive type defining the braking enforcement curve.

Similarly to ETMS, the ITCS primary means of determining a train position is via differential GPS to the onboard computer. The ITCS onboard computer also continuously compares the received GPS position with the stored position of switches, signal, and crossings and permanent speed restrictions in a non-volatile track database. The ITCS onboard computer also receives updates from the wayside servers of temporary speed order locations, interlock positions, and signal indications.

Using the received updates and its known position, the ITCS onboard computer automatically calculates warning and enforcement actions and activates the brake interface as required. The braking enforcement curves are not updated automatically- once a particular curve for a particular locomotive type is selected, the selection remains in force until another curve for a different locomotive type is manually selected.

The Wayside segment consists of individual interface units linked to a concentrating server. The individual wayside servers, which aggregate geographically similar wayside interface unit status and control information for communication to the Onboard System. The wayside server stores all work zones, temporary speed restriction, received switch positions, and received highway-grade crossing status indicators.

The Onboard segment can actively control highway-grade crossings via the Wayside segment. If the wayside segment reports a crossing is active, the onboard system signals the Wayside segment to arm the crossing and lower the gate based on the expected arrival time of the train. The Wayside server signals the Wayside Interface Unit, which in turn orders the crossing to lower the gate. Once the crossing indicates the gate is down, it reports through the Wayside Interface Unit and the Wayside server to the onboard system. The Wayside segment monitors the crossing to ensure the crossing continues to report that it is in the down position. The Onboard system continuously evaluates the reported status from Wayside segment. In the event that a fault develops braking is automatically applied by the onboard system.

The Office segment is used to input temporary speed orders for transmission to the various wayside servers, and to display collected health and management data from the wayside servers.

4.5 Cyber Threats

In order to effectively address rail security issues, the security threat and consequences of successful exploitation of security vulnerabilities is required. Understanding the role and risks associated with PTC, and appropriate mitigations, requires an understanding of the entire threat environment as well as the vulnerabilities associated with the communication subsystem. Successful exploitation of non-communication vulnerabilities can aggravate the adverse consequences of communications vulnerabilities, just as successful exploitation of communications vulnerabilities can aggravate the consequences of non-communications vulnerabilities.

Although the communications links between the various PTC subsystems may consist of both wired and wireless links, it is the wireless component of the links that offers the greatest susceptibility to attack relative to the wired component of the links. This is due to the ease of access that an intruder has to the wireless link with respect to the hardwired links. This is, of course, not to say that successful attacks could not be made on PTC system through a hardwired communications links, only that the wireless links offers a significantly easier target to exploit.

Recent research has examined security and possible problems in the rail infrastructure and surveyed systems in use [48,49,50,51]. Completion of recent regulatory initiatives, coupled with accelerated industry efforts in the deployment of PTC systems, have increased the level of risk that the public may potentially be exposed to as a result of the greater use of wireless technology. The most significant source of risk in wireless networks is that the underlying communications medium, the airwave, is open to intruders.

Changes in malicious hacker activity have shifted from conventional fixed wired systems to wireless networks. These networks have included not only traditional telecommunications systems, but also industrial control systems. Studies by the National Research Council and the National Security Telecommunications Advisory Committee [52] show that hacker activity includes the ability to break into wireless networks resulting in the degradation or disruption of system availability. A recent Government Accountability Office study [53] has indicated that successful attacks against control systems have occurred. While these studies were unable to reach a conclusion about the degree of threat or risk, they uniformly emphasize the ability of hackers to cause serious damage. The resources available to potential intruders are significant [54]. Intelligence is already widely available on the Internet that enables intruders to penetrate any sort of traditional computer network and wireless systems. Detailed vulnerability information is publicly discussed on newsgroups.

Tutorials are available that describe how to write automated programs that exploit wireless systems vulnerabilities. Large numbers of automated software tools have been written that enable launching these types of attacks. Publicly available Web sites whose sole purpose is to distribute this data have been established, often ensuring wide spread distribution of the information before public access can be terminated.

The Information Assurance Technical Framework Forum (IATFF), an organization sponsored by the National Security Agency (NSA) to support technical interchanges among U.S. industry, U.S. academic institutions, and U.S. government agencies on the topic of information assurance, has defined five general classes of information assurance attacks- passive, active, close-in, insider, and distribution as specified in Table 3 [55]. These same classes of atacks, traditionaly thought of in terms of attacks against information proccessing systems, are equaliy applicable to SCADA systems [56]. This is especilly true as SCADA systems have evolved from exotic hardware and software implementations of the 1970s to today's systems that include standard PCs and operating systems, TCP/IP communications and Internet access.

The danger of a passive attack is a result of the surreptitious way information is gathered. It is the easiest type of attack to execute, and the hardest to defend against. Since the attacker is not actively transmitting or disturbing the transmitted signal of the signal owner, the signal owner (defender) has no means of knowing that their transmission has been intercepted. This kind of attack is particularly easy for two reasons: 1) frequently confidentiality features of wireless technology are not even enabled, and 2) because of the numerous vulnerabilities in the wireless technology security, determined adversaries can compromise the system.

Active attacks that can be launched against a wireless network come from a broad continuum. In its simplest form, active attacks use some mechanism disabling the entire communications channel between the sender and the receiver. With the original sender and receiver unable to recognize transmissions between each other, they cannot exchange information, and are unable to communicate. No detailed knowledge of the message parameters between sender and receiver is required, only a device capable of blocking communications operating over the entire channel.

More sophisticated forms of active attack are the Denial of Service (DOS) or Distributed Denial of Service (DDOS). The DOS and the DDOS differ primarily in the location of the origin of the attacks. The DOS originates from only one location, the DDOS from multiple locations. The specific mechanisms of a DOS and DDOS are very communications protocol and product implementation dependent, since these attacks exploit weaknesses in both the communications protocol and the products implementation of the protocol.

Other active attacks are based on exploitation attempts associated with the sender (identity theft, where an unauthorized user adopts the identity of a valid sender), weakness associated with the receiver (malicious association, where unsuspecting sender is tricked into believing that a communications session has been established with a valid receiver), or weaknesses associated with the communications path (man in the middle, where the attacker emulates the authorized receiver for the sender- the malicious assertion, and emulates the authorized transmitter for the authorized sender- identity theft). These attacks are primarily geared at disrupting integrity in the form of user

Table 3. IATF Attack Class Definitions [55]

Type	Definition
Passive	Traffic analysis, monitoring of unprotected communications, decrypting weakly encrypted traffic, and capture of authentication information. Passive intercept of network operations can give adversaries indications and warnings of impending actions. These attacks can result in disclosure of information or data files to an attacker without the consent or knowledge
Active	Attempts to circumvent or break protection features, introduce malicious code, or steal or modify information. Active attacks can result in the disclosure or dissemination of data files, denial of service, or modification of data.
Close-in	Individuals gaining close physical proximity to networks, systems, or facilities for the purpose of modifying, gathering, or denying access to information. Close physical proximity is achieved through surreptitious entry, open access, or both
Insider	Malicious insiders intentionally eavesdrop, steal or damage information, use information in a fraudulent manner, or deny access to other authorized users. Non-malicious attacks typically result from carelessness, lack of knowledge, or unintentional circumvention of security for benign reasons
Distribution	Malicious modification of hardware or software at the factory or during distribution. These attacks can introduce malicious code into a product, such as a back door to gain unauthorized access to information or a system function at a later date.

authentication (assurance the parties are who they say they are), data origin authentication (assurance the data came from where it said it did), and data integrity (assurance that the data has not been changed).

Close-In, Insider and Distribution Attacks describe the nature of system access, as opposed to the passive or active nature of the attack. Close-in, insider, and distribution attacks make use of some form of either an active or passive attack whose effectiveness is enhanced by the degree of the attackers access to the system. Insider and distribution attackers usually will utilize their specialized knowledge or access to carry out some form of a passive or active attack.

4.6 Attack Mitigation

The basic security mitigations for information and information processing systems attacks in the United States have generally been codified [57]. Specifically these are confidentiality, integrity, and availability. Confidentiality is concerned with ensuring that the data and system are not disclosed to unauthorized individuals, processes, or systems. Integrity ensures that data is preserved in regard to its meaning, completeness, consistency, intended use, and correlation to its representation. Availability assures that there is timely and uninterrupted access to the information and the system.

Closely related to these three are authenticity, accountability, and identification. Authenticity is the ability to verify that a user or process that is attempting to access information or a service is who they claim to be. Accountability enables events to be recreated and traced to entities responsible for their actions. Authenticity and accountability require the ability to identify a particular entity or process uniquely, as well as the authorizations (privileges) that are assigned to that entity. Identification is the specification of a unique identifier to each user or process.

The preferred mitigation methods for passive attacks are access control and confidentiality. Access control mechanisms are used to prevent unauthorized users accessing services and resources for which they have not been granted permission and privileges as specified by a security policy. Confidentiality should prevent the gain of information about from the content of the messages exchanged. Mitigation methods against active attack include access control, availability, accountability, authentication, and integrity. The access control and availability countermeasures must maintain or improve data availability. The system must be able to ensure the availability of both data and services to all components in the system. In the event that a PTC platform cannot handle its computational and communication load, it must provide graceful degradation of services and notify the operator that it can no longer provide the level and quality of service expected to prevent an unintentional denial of service.

Authentication mechanisms provide accountability for user actions. User authentication and data origin authentication differ in that user authentication involves corroboration of the identity of the originator in real time, while data origin authentication involves corroboration of the source of the data (and provides no timeliness guarantees). User authentication methods range from so called time invariant weak authentication methods such as simple passwords to time variant strong cryptographically based authentication methods. In non-hostile environments no or weak user authentication may be acceptable, while in hostile environments strong user authentication is essential to provide authenticity. Data origin authentication provides assurances regarding both integrity and authentication. They rely on the use of digital signatures and can be either symmetrical or asymmetrical digital signature methods.

Ensuring integrity, authentication, and confidentiality, places restraints on availability and they have performance costs. Signing and or encrypting messages in transit may impose unacceptable delays in environments where near real-time response is required. These restrictions must be carefully considered in the development of any mitigation framework. more critically, they require a trust management system to exchange and control the necessary keying material for the system to work.

4.7   Wireless Security Requirements for PTC

As might be expected, since PTC systems suffer from the same vulnerabilities as any other wireless network system, the security requirements are very similar and can be expressed in terms of Confidentiality, Integrity, Availability, Authenticity, Accountability and Identification.. The following sections address each of these six factors as they apply to PTC requirements.

4.7.1   Confidentiality Requirements

There is most likely no requirement for confidentiality for PTC functions. The information that would be exchanged between the various elements would either already be available through other means such as published time tables and direct observation of wayside indications, or quickly inferred. Trains, as single degree of freedom systems, are highly constrained as to locations that they may actually be. Consequently with a limited set of routes, known terminal departures times, and easily measured speeds, estimated positions and times of attack could be determined equally well without knowing confidential position data from the locomotive. Second, aerial and commercial satellite reconnaissance are available to track the location of any consist. Finally the geographical positions of rail choke points where rail consists would be susceptible to attack can be easily identified.

4.7.2   Integrity

Unlike confidentiality, communications data integrity (meaning, completeness, consistency, intended use, and correlation to its representation) is essential for all aspects of safe PTC operations. One of the fundamental issues associated with loss of integrity, especially in malicious situation, is that the loss of integrity may not be recognized until it is to late. The impacts of loss of integrity are easily to visualize. This may be something as simple as failure to receive the correct speed to things as complex as total corruption of track databases that would allow trains to undertake unauthorized movements and inappropriate train routing

4.7.3   Availability

The unavailability of communications with respect to safety may be considered primarily throughput issue. Simply putting the train into an immediate safe state- stopped with the brake set can mitigate loss of communications. There are, however security implications. The ability of a third party to force a fail stop, at a time and place of their choosing, potentially raises the vulnerability of the train; its crew, and its cargo to hostile activity. This vulnerability can be arranged to occur at a time, place, and location where, if exploited, it can cause the maximum amount of damage

4.7.4   Authenticity, Accountability and Identification

Authenticity of PTC communications is a mandatory. The importance of each element of a PTC system to be able to positively verify with whom it is establishing communications as well as exchanging data and commands is obvious. Transmission of information to the incorrect recipient at the wrong time could result in an accident. It is therefore critical that the sender and receiver be able to correctly identify each other.

5   Summary and Conclusions

When deployed, PTC systems operate with multiple components communicating at the same time, forming a network of systems. Wireless security therefore must not only be considered from a device aspect, but at the network level too. The network level effort must identify sensitive network resources, provide for, and manage the access control mechanisms. Further, the network must prevent intentional or unintentional sabotage and misuse of PTC devices and network resources. Development of the network management and the security systems to protect, monitor and report on the system without adversely impacting overall system performance requires significant financial and technical effort

The imposition of security requirements may have implementation impacts on other requirements. A requirement for confidentiality and integrity, for example, places restraints on availability and may have unacceptable performance costs. The exact impact of individual security requirements on each other is dependent on the specific implementation, Safety and security are two distinct terms. In the context of PTC systems, both words can be used to denote a combination of administrative, technical and managerial features for two different purposes that can occasionally coincide but may also clash.

Although the specific transportation environment in which information and communications systems are deployed, as well the specifics of that deployment differ based on transportation modes under consideration, their use of common technologies creates very similar, if not identical, interactions between their various components. Cybersecurity issues that were identified and discussed in the context of PTC systems are equally of concern in other modes. Just as PTC systems mist strike a balance between safety and security, so too must elements of all other transportation modes. Reaching an appropriate balance between these two equally important, elements, especially in the new threat environment of the 21st century, will be one of the greatest challenges facing transportation planners and engineers.

References

1. Bureau of Transportation Statistics, National Transportation Statistics 2007, U. Department of Transportation, Washington, DC (May 2008)
2. Presidents Commission on Critical Infrastructure Protection, Critical Foundations: Protecting Americas Infrastructure,U.S. Government Printing Office, Washington DC (October 2007)
3. International Airline Transportation Association (IATA) Economics Department. World Air Transport Statistics 52nd Edition, IATA Montreal, Canada (May 2008)

4. U.S. Census Bureau. The 2009 Statistical Abstract, U.S. Government Printing Office, Washington, DC (May 2009)
5. Cooper, A.: Aviation: The Real World Wide Web. Oxford Economics, Oxford, UK (June 2009)
6. AFR60-24, AR 95-21, OPNAVINST 3772.30C, Security Control of Air Traffic and Air Navigation Aids (SCATANA), U.S. Department of Defense, Washington, DC, June 25 (1976)
7. Makinen, G., et al.: The Economic Effects of 9/11: A Retrospective Assessment. Congressional Research Service, U.S. Library of Congress (September 2002)
8. Public Law 111-5 The American Recovery and Reinvestment Act of 2009, U.S. Government Printing Office, Washington, DC (February 2009)
9. Policy and Economics Department, Association of American Railroads. Railroad Facts, 2008 Edition, Association of American Railroads, Washington, DC (November 2008)
10. U.S. Department of Transportation Research and Innovative Technology Administration, Bureau of Transportation Statistics. National Transportation Statistics, `http://www.bts.gov/publications/national_transportation_statistics/` (accessed August 17, 2009)
11. American Passenger Transportation Association (APTA) 2009 Public Transportation Fact Book, APTA, Washington, DC (April 2009)
12. European Rail Research Advisory (ERAC) Council, Suburban and Regional Railways Landscape in Europe, ERRAC (October 2006)
13. Community of European Railway and Infrastructure Companies (CER), Towards a Sustainable Rail Network,-Annual Report 2008, CER, Belgium, My (2009)
14. Weinstein, B., Clower, T.: The Impact of the Union Pacific Service Disruptions on the Texas and National Economies: An Unfinished Story Railroad Commission of Texas (February 1998)
15. Riley, J.: Terrorism and Rail Security, Testimony Presented to the Senate Commerce, Science, and Transportation Committee, The Rand Corporation, March 23 (2004), `http://www.rand.org/pubs/testimonies/CT224/index.html` (accessed August 17, 2009)
16. National Capital Planning Commission (NCPC), Rail Realignment Feasibility Study Securing Freight Transportation in the National Capital Region, NCPC, Washington DC (April 2007)
17. Pulak, C.: The Uluburun Shipwreck: An Overview. IJNA 27(3), 188 (1998)
18. United Nations Conference on Trade and Development (UNCTF), Review of Maritime Transport 2008, Report by the UNCTAD Secretariat United Nations, New York and Geneva (January 2008)
19. Rosenberg, D.: The Political Economy of Piracy in the South China Sea, Naval War College Review Summer 2009, U.S. Naval War College (August 2009)
20. Asia Piracy Costs $25 Bin a Year, Says Expert, Reuters News Agency, Singapore (December 11, 2002)
21. Organization for Economic Co-operation and Development, Price of Increased Maritime Security Is Much Lower than Potential Cost of a Major Terror Attack Paris: Directorate for Science, Technology and Industry, July 21 (2003)
22. Murphy, M.N.: Contemporary Piracy and Maritime Terrorism: The Threat to International Security, International Institute for Strategic Studies, London (2007)
23. Rubin, J., Tal, B.: Will Soaring Transport Costs Reverse Globalization?, CIBC World Markets Inc., StrategEcon (May 27, 2008)
24. Assessment Of Highway Mode Security: Corporate Security Review Results, Highway and Motor Carrier Division TSA Transportation Sector Network Management Office, Washington, D.C. (May 2006)

25. Comparing the Impacts of the 2005 and 2008 Hurricanes on U.S. Energy Infrastructure Security and Energy Restoration, Office of Electricity Delivery and Energy Reliability, U.S. Department of Energy Washington, DC (February 2009)

26. Luft, G.: Pipeline Sabotage is Terrorists Weapon of Choice, Institute for Analysis of Global Security (IAGS) Energy Security, 25/III/2005

27. CRS Report for Congress, Pipeline Security: An Overview of Federal Activities and Current Policy Issues, Congressional Research Service Library of Congress (February 5, 2004)

28. Levinson, M.: The Box. How the Shipping Container Made the World Smaller and the World Economy Bigger. Princeton University Press, New Jersey (2006)

29. European Union (EU), the European Conference of Ministers of Transport (ECMT) and the Economic Commission for Europe of the United Nations (UN/ECE), Terminology on Combined Transport, United Nations, New York and Geneva (2001)

30. North American Container Port Traffic- 2008, American Association of Port Authoriites, http://www.aapa-ports.org/ (accessed August 17, 2009)

31. Gooley, T., Cooke, J.A.: Shippers, Carriers Struggle with Port Shutdown's Aftermath. Logistics Management 41(11), 15–16 (2002)

32. Keane, A.: Insecurity over Ports, Traffic, World, 5, UBM Global Trade Publisher, East Windsor, NJ, USA (April 2004)

33. Table of Frequency Allocations Federal Communications System (FCC) Rules and Regulations, 47 C.F.R. 2.106, U.S. Government Printing Office, Washington, DC (February 2009)

34. U.S. Air Force Fact Sheet, Global Positioning System, Space and Missile Systems Center, Los Angles Air Force Base, El Segundo, CA (January 2009)

35. Commission to Address United States Security Space Management Organization, Report to the House & Senate Committee on Armed Services to Address United States Security Space Management Organization Washington, DC (January 2001)

36. Dehel, T., et al.: National Satellite Test Bed (NSTB) Observations on the Effects of Ionospheric Storms on a Prototype Wide Area Augmentation System. In: Proceedings of the 1999 Technical Meeting of the Institute of navigation & 19th Biennial Guidance Test Symposium San Diego, CA USA, January 25-27 (1999)

37. Vulnerability Assessment of the Transportation Infrastructure Relying on the Global position System,- Final Report, John A Volpe Transportation System Center, Boston, MA (August 2001)

38. PL110-432, Rail Safety Improvement Act of 2008, U.S. Government Printing Office, Washington, DC (February 2009)

39. United States National Transportation Safety Board, Collision of Union Pacific Railroad train MHOTU-25 with BNSF Railway Company Train MEAP-TUL-126-D with Subsequent Derailment and Hazardous Materials Release, Macdona TX, June 28, 2004, NTSB /RAR-06/03 (July 2006)

40. United States National Transportation Safety Board, Report of Railroad Accident: Collision of Norfolk Southern Freight Train 192 with Standing Norfolk Southern Local Train P22 With Subsequent Hazardous Materials Release. Graniteville, South Carolina, NTSB/RAR-05/04, January 6 (2005)

41. United States National Transportation Safety Board, Collision of Southern California Regional Rail Authority (Metrolink) Passenger Train No. 111 and Union Pacific Railroad Freight Train No. LOF65-12 Chatsworth, California September 12, 2008 DCA08MR009 Public Hearing, Washington, D.C, March 3-4 (2009)

42. Docket FRA-2003-15432, Burlington Northern Waiver Petition, U.S. Department of Transportation Document Management System, http://regulations.gov/ (accessed August 17, 2009)

43. Lederer, R.: Electronic Train Management System. BNSF Railways Presentation at National Transportation Safety Board 2005 Symposium on Positive Train Control, Ashburn, VA (2005), `http://www.ntsb.gov/events/sympptc/presentations/14Lederer.pdf`(accessed August 17, 2009)

44. Haag, R.: Electronic Train Management Systems WABTEC Railway Electronics Presentation at National Transportation Safety Board, Symposium on Positive Train Control, Ashburn, VA (2005), `http://www.ntsb.gov/events/sympptc/presentations/16Haag.pdf` (accessed August 17, 2009)

45. Docket FRA 2002-11533,Waiver for Petition of Compliance, U.S. Department of Transportation Document Management System, //regulations.gov/ (accessed August 17, 2009)

46. Kollmar, R.: Michigan Positive Train Control Project Incremental Train Control System. National Passenger Rail Corporation (AMTRAK) Presentation at National Transportation Safety Board 2005 Symposium on Positive Train Control, Ashburn, VA, `http://www.ntsb.gov/events/sympptc/presentations/07Kollmar.pdf` (accessed August 17, 2009)

47. Baker, J.: ITCS Incremental Train Control System. In: GE Global Signaling Presentation at National Transportation Safety Board 2005 Symposium on Positive Train Control, Ashburn, VA (2005), `http://www.ntsb.gov/events/sympptc/presentations/11Baker.pdf` (accessed August 17, 2009)

48. Cyber Security of Freight Information Systems, Transportation Research Board of the National Academy of Sciences, Washington, DC (2003)

49. Chittester, C., Haines, Y.: Risks of Terrorism to Information Technology and to Critical Interdependent Infrastructure. Journal of Homeland Security and Emergency Management 1(4) (2004)

50. Carlson, A., Frincke, D., Laude, M.: Railway Security Issues: A Survey of Developing Railway Technology. In: Proceedings of the International Conference on Computer, Communications, & Control Technology, International Institute of Informatics and Systemics (2003)

51. Craven, P.: A Brief Look at Railroad Communication Vulnerabilities. In: Proceedings 2004 IEEE Intelligent Transportation Systems Conference, Washington, D.C (2004)

52. The Presidents National Security Telecommunications Advisory Committee Wireless Task Force Report Wireless Security U.S. Government Printing Office (January 2003)

53. United States General Accounting Office, GAO Testimony Before the Subcommittee on Technology Information Policy, Intergovernmental Relations and the Census, House Committee on Government Reform, Critical Infrastructure Protection Challenges and Efforts to Secure Control Systems, Tuesday (March 30, 2004)

54. Diversification Of Cyber Threats, Institute For Security Technology Studies At Dartmouth College, Investigative Research For Infrastructure Assurance Group (May 2002)

55. Information Assurance Technical Framework (IATF), Release 3.1, Information Assurance Solutions, U.S. National Security Agency Fort Meade, MD (September 2002)

56. Common Cyber Security Vulnerabilities Observed in DHS Industrial Control Systems Assessments, U.S. Department of Homeland Security National Cyber Security Divisions Control Systems Security Program (CSSP) (July 2009)

57. Federal Information Security Management Act of 2002 (Public Law 107-347), U.S. Government Printing Office, Washington, DC (December 2002)

Author Index